Georges Perrot, Charles Chipiez, Walter Armstrong

A History of Art in Ancient Egypt

Volume 2

Georges Perrot, Charles Chipiez, Walter Armstrong

A History of Art in Ancient Egypt
Volume 2

ISBN/EAN: 9783337230432

Printed in Europe, USA, Canada, Australia, Japan

Cover: Foto ©Thomas Meinert / pixelio.de

More available books at **www.hansebooks.com**

OF

Art in Ancient Egypt

FROM THE FRENCH
OF
GEORGES PERROT,
PROFESSOR IN THE FACULTY OF LETTERS, PARIS; MEMBER OF THE INSTITUTE
AND
CHARLES CHIPIEZ.

ILLUSTRATED WITH FIVE HUNDRED AND NINETY-EIGHT ENGRAVINGS IN THE TEXT,
AND FOURTEEN STEEL AND COLOURED PLATES.

IN TWO VOLUMES.—VOL. II.

TRANSLATED AND EDITED BY
WALTER ARMSTRONG, B.A., Oxon.,
AUTHOR OF "ALFRED STEVENS," ETC.

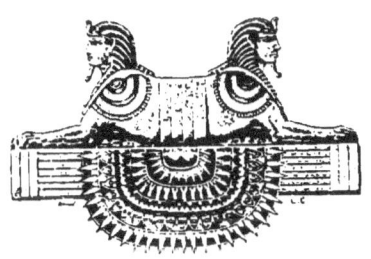

London: CHAPMAN AND HALL, Limited.
New York: A. C. ARMSTRONG AND SON.
1883.

London:
R. CLAY, SONS, AND TAYLOR,
BREAD STREET HILL.

CONTENTS.

CHAPTER I.

CIVIL AND MILITARY ARCHITECTURE.

                                        PAGE

§ 1. The Graphic Processes employed by the Egyptians in their representations of Buildings 1–8
§ 2. The Palace 8–26
§ 3. The Egyptian House . . . . 26—38
§ 4. Military Architecture . . . . 38—50

CHAPTER II.

METHODS OF CONSTRUCTION, THE ORDERS, SECONDARY FORMS.

§ 1. An Analysis of Architectural Forms necessary . . . . 51—52
§ 2. Materials . . . . 52—55
§ 3. Construction . . . . 55—76
§ 4. The Arch . . . . 77—84
§ 5. The Pier and Column.--The Egyptian Orders . . . . 85—133
       Their Origin . . . . 85—91
       General Types of Supports . . . . 91—133
§ 6. The Ordonnance of Egyptian Colonnades . . . . 133—147
§ 7. Monumental Details . . . . 147—155
§ 8. Doors and Windows . . . . 156—162
       Doors . . . . 156—161
       Windows 162
§ 9. The Illumination of the Temples . . . . 162—169
§ 10. The Obelisks . . . . 169—176
§ 11. The Profession of Architect 176–179

CHAPTER III.

SCULPTURE.

		PAGE
§ 1.	The Origin of Statue-making	180—184
§ 2.	Sculpture under the Ancient Empire	184—225
§ 3.	Sculpture under the First Theban Empire	226—238
§ 4.	Sculpture under the Second Theban Empire	239—265
§ 5.	The Art of the Saite Period	265—274
§ 6.	The Principal Themes of Egyptian Sculpture	275—284
§ 7.	The Technique of the Bas-reliefs	284—288
§ 8.	Gems	288—291
§ 9.	The Principal Conventions in Egyptian Sculpture	291—326
§ 10.	The General Characteristics of the Egyptian Style	326—330

CHAPTER IV.

PAINTING.

§ 1.	Technical Processes	331—341
§ 2.	The Figure	341—351
§ 3.	Caricature	351—355
§ 4.	Ornament	355—363

CHAPTER V.

THE INDUSTRIAL ARTS.

§ 1.	Definition and Characteristics of Industrial Art	364—367
§ 2.	Glass and Pottery	367—377
§ 3.	Metal-work and Jewelry	377—390
§ 4.	Woodwork	390—398
§ 5.	The Commerce of Egypt	399—400

CHAPTER VI.

THE GENERAL CHARACTERISTICS OF EGYPTIAN ART, AND THE PLACE OF EGYPT IN ART HISTORY . . . . 401—408

APPENDIX . . . . 409—416

INDEX . . . . 417—434

LIST OF ILLUSTRATIONS.

COLOURED PLATES.

Thebes, the Pavilion of Medinet-Abou, restored . . . . *To face page*	24
Portico in the temple of Medinet-Abou, restored . . . . . . ,,	144
Rahotep and Nefert, Boulak Museum . . . . ,,	186
The *Scribe*, Louvre . . . . ,,	192
The Queen Taia, Boulak Museum . . . . ,,	240
Funerary offerings. fragment of a painting upon plaster, Louvre ,,	334
Tomb of Ptah-hotep, fragment of Western Wall . . . . . . ,,	356
Tomb of Ptah-hotep, ceiling and upper part of Western Wall . ,,	360

FIG.		PAGE
1.	House	3
2.	The adoration of the solar disk by Amenophis IV.	6
3.	Egyptian plan of a villa	7
4.	Part of the plan of a house and its offices	9
5.	Partial restoration of a palace at Tell-el-Amarna	17
6.	Ground plan of the "Royal Pavilion"	19
7.	Plan of the first floor of the "Royal Pavilion"	19
8.	Longitudinal section of the pavilion	19
9.	Transverse section of the pavilion	20
10.	Brackets in the courtyard of the Royal Pavilion	23
11.	Plan of a part of the city at Tell-el-Amarna	29
12.	Bird's-eye view of a villa	31
13.	Model of an Egyptian house	34
14—17.	Plans of houses	34
18.	Piece of furniture in the form of a house	35
19.	House from a Theban wall painting	35
20.	House with a tower	35
21.	Battlemented house	36
22.	Decorated porch	36
23.	House with inscription	36

viii   LIST OF ILLUSTRATIONS.

FIG.		PAGE
24.	House, storehouse, and garden	36
25.	Brewing	37
26.	Granaries	37
27.	Granaries	38
28.	Military post at Abydos	42
29.	Military post	42
30.	Bird's-eye view of the fortress of Semneh	43
31.	A besieged fort	46
32.	Siege of a fortress	47
33.	Brick stamped with the royal ovals	54
34.	The Sarcophagus of Mycerinus	57
35.	Door of a tomb at Sakkarah	60
36.	Stele from the fourth dynasty	61
37.	Stele from the fourth dynasty	62
38.	Flattened form of lotus-leaf ornament, seen in front and in section	63
39.	Lotus-leaf ornament in its elongated form	63
40.	Wooden pavilion	64
41.	Horizontal section, in perspective, of the first pylon at Karnak	67
42.	Workmen polishing a monolithic column	69
43.	Transport of a colossus	73
44.	Arch in the necropolis of Abydos	78
45.	Arch in El-Assassif	79
46.	Arch in El-Assassif	80
47.	Vaults in the Ramesseum	81
48.	Vault in the Ramesseum	81
49.	Elliptical vault	82
50.	Foundations with inverted segmental arches	82
51.	Transverse section of a corridor at Dayr-el-Bahari	83
52.	Section in perspective through the same corridor	83
53.	Vaulted chapel at Abydos	84
54.	Bas-relief from the fifth dynasty	86
55.	Detail of capital	86
56.	Bas-relief from the fifth dynasty	87
57.	Details of columns in Fig. 56	87
58.	Pavilion from Sakkarah	87
59.	Details of columns in Fig. 58	87
60.	Bas-relief from the fifth dynasty	88
61.	Details of the columns	88
62—65.	Columns from bas-reliefs	89
66.	Quadrangular pier	92
67.	Tapering quadrangular pier	92
68.	Pier with capital	92
69.	Hathoric pier	92
70.	Osiride pillar	93
71.	Ornamented pier	94
72.	Octagonal pillar	96

LIST OF ILLUSTRATIONS.   ix

FIG.		PAGE
73.	Sixteen-sided pillar	96
74.	Polygonal column with a flat vertical band	98
75.	Polygonal pier with mask of Hathor	98
76.	Column from Beni-Hassan	99
77.	Column at Luxor	101
78.	Column at Medinet-Abou	101
79.	Column at Medinet-Abou	102
80.	Column from the Great Hall at Karnak	103
81.	Column from the Hypostyle Hall of the Ramesseum	103
82.	Column of Soleb	104
83.	Column of Thothmes at Karnak	104
84.	Corner pier from the temple at Elephantiné	106
85.	Pier with capital	107
86.	Osiride pier	109
87.	Hathoric pier from Eilithya	111
88.	Hathoric pier from a tomb	111
89.	Column at Kalabché	112
90.	Column of Thothmes III.	113
91.	Base of a column	115
92.	Bell-shaped capital	117
93.	Capital at Sesebi	119
94.	Capital from the temple of Nectanebo, at Philæ	119
95.	Capital from the work of Thothmes, at Karnak	120
96.	Arrangement of architraves upon a capital	120
97.	The Nymphæa Nelumbo	123
98.	Papyrus plant	127
99.	Small chamber at Karnak	134
100.	Apartment in the temple at Luxor	134
101.	Hall of the temple at Abydos	134
102.	Plan of part of the Hypostyle Hall at Karnak	134
103.	Tomb at Sakkarah	135
104.	Hall in the inner portion of the Great Temple at Karnak	135
105.	Portico of the first court at Medinet-Abou	135
106.	Portico of the first court at Luxor	135
107.	The portico of the pronaos, Luxor	136
108.	Part plan of the temple at Elephantiné	136
109.	Luxor, plan of the second court	136
110.	Portico in the Temple of Khons	137
111.	Luxor, portico of the first court	137
112.	Part of the portico of the first court, Luxor	138
113.	Portico in front of the façade of the temple of Gournah	138
114.	Part of the Hypostyle Hall in the Great Temple at Karnak	138
115.	Second Hypostyle Hall in the temple of Abydos	139
116.	Hall in the speos of Gherf-Hossein	139
117.	Medinet-Abou : first court	139
118.	Medinet-Abou ; second court	139

VOL. II.   *b*

LIST OF ILLUSTRATIONS.

FIG.		PAGE
119.	Portico of the Temple of Khons	140
120.	Portico of first court at Luxor	140
121.	Anta, Luxor	141
122.	Anta, Gournah	141
123.	Anta, Medinet-Abou	141
124.	Anta in the Great Hall of Karnak	141
125.	Antæ, Temple of Khons	142
126.	Anta and base of pylon, Temple of Khons	142
127.	Antæ, Medinet-Abou	143
128.	Antæ, Medinet-Abou	143
129.	Anta and column at Medinet-Abou	145
130.	Column in the court of the Bubastides	146
131.	Stereobate	148
132.	Stereobate with double plinth	148
133.	Pluteus in the intercolumniations of the portico in the second court of the Ramesseum	150
134.	Doorway	151
135.	Cornice of the Ramesseum	152
136.	Cornice of a wooden pavilion	152
137.	Pedestal of a Sphinx	153
138.	Cornice under the portico	153
139.	Fragment of a sarcophagus	154
140.	Fragment of decoration from a royal tomb at Thebes	154
141.	Plan of doorway, Temple of Elephantiné	157
142.	Plan of doorway, Temple of Khons	157
143.	Plan of doorway in the pylon, Temple of Khons	157
144, 145.	The pylon and propylon of the hieroglyphs	157
146.	Gateway to the court-yard of the small Temple at Medinet-Abou	158
147.	A propylon with its masts	158
148.	A propylon	159
149.	Gateway in the inclosing wall of a Temple	159
150.	Doorway of the Temple of Khons	160
151.	Doorway of the Temple of Gournah	160
152.	Doorway of the Temple of Seti	161
153, 154.	Windows in the Royal Pavilion at Medinet-Abou	162
155.	Attic of the Great Hall at Karnak	163
156.	*Claustra* of the Hypostyle Hall, Karnak	165
157.	*Claustra* in the Hypostyle Hall of the Temple of Khons	166
158.	Method of lighting in one of the inner halls of Karnak	167
159.	Auxiliary light-holes in the Hypostyle Hall at Karnak	167
160.	Method of lighting one of the rooms in the Temple of Khons	167
161.	Light openings in a lateral aisle of the Hypostyle Hall in the Ramesseum	168
162.	The Temple of Amada	168
163.	*Claustra*	168
164.	Window of a house in the form of *claustra*	169
165.	Window closed by a mat	169

LIST OF ILLUSTRATIONS.   xi

FIG.		PAGE
166.	Funerary obelisk	171
167.	The obelisk of Ousourtesen	173
168.	The obelisk in the Place de la Concorde	173
169.	The obelisk of Beggig	175
170.	Upper part of the obelisk at Beggig	175
171.	Limestone statue of the architect Nefer	177
172.	Sepa and Nesa	186
173.	Ra-hotep	188
174—176.	Wooden panels from the tomb of Hosi	191, 193, 195
177.	Limestone head	196
178.	Wooden statue	198
179.	Bronze statuette	199
180.	Bronze statuette	201
181.	Ra-nefer	204
182.	Statue in the Boulak Museum	205
183.	Statue of Ti	205
184.	Wooden statue	206
185.	Statue in limestone	206
186.	Limestone group	207
187.	Wooden statuette	208
188.	Nefer-hotep and Tenteta	208
189.	Limestone statue	209
190.	Limestone statue	209
191.	Limestone statue	210
192.	Limestone statue	210
193.	Woman kneading dough	211
194.	Woman making bread	212
195.	Bread maker	213
196, 197.	Details of head-dresses	213
198, 199.	Nem-hotep	214
200.	Funerary bas-relief	215
201.	Bas-relief from the tomb of Ti	217
202.	Bas-relief from the tomb of Ti	218
203.	Sepulchral bas-relief	219
204.	Bas-relief from the tomb of Ra-ka-pou	219
205.	Statue of Chephren	222
206.	Wooden statue	227
207.	Sebek-hotep III.	229
208.	Sphinx in black granite	231
209.	Head and shoulders of a Tanite Sphinx in black granite	233
210.	Group from Tanis	234
211.	Side view of the same group	235
212.	Upper part of a royal statue	236
213.	Fragmentary statuette of a king	237
214.	Thothmes III.	241
215.	Thothmes III.	243

List of Illustrations.

FIG.		PAGE
216.	Statuette of Amenophis IV	245
217.	Funeral Dance	251
218.	Bas-relief from the tomb of Chamhati	253
219.	Portrait of Rameses II. while a child	255
220.	Statue of Rameses II.	256
221.	Prisoners of war	257
222.	Statue of Rameses II. in the Turin Museum	259
223.	Head of Menephtah	260
224.	Seti II.	261
225.	The Goddess Kadesh	263
226.	Statue of Ameneritis	264
227.	Bronze Sphinx	267
228.	Statue of Nekht-har-heb	268
229.	Statue of Horus	269
230, 231.	Bas-relief from Memphis	270, 271
232.	Horus enthroned	273
233.	Roman head	274
234.	Wooden statuette	279
235.	Bronze cat	280
236.	Lion	281
237.	Bronze lion	282
238.	Sphinx with human hands	283
239.	Quadruped with the head of a bird	284
240.	Portrait of Rameses II.	286
241.	Intaglio upon sardonyx, obverse	289
242.	Reverse of the same intaglio	289
243.	Intaglio upon jasper	290
244.	Reverse of the same intaglio	290
245.	Seal of Armais	290
246.	Bas-relief from Sakkarah	295
247.	The Queen waiting on Amenophis IV.	296
248.	Bas-relief from the eighteenth dynasty	297
249.	Horus as a child	299
250.	Bas-relief from the tomb of Ti	306
251.	Bas-relief at Thebes	307
252.	From a painting at Thebes	308
253.	Painting at Thebes	309
254.	Painting at Thebes	310
255.	Painting at Thebes	311
256.	Bronze statuette	312
257.	Spoon for perfumes	313
258.	Design transferred by squaring	320
259.	Design transferred by squaring	321
260.	Head of a Cynocephalus	323
261.	Head of a Lion	323
262.	Head of a Lioness	323

LIST OF ILLUSTRATIONS. xiii

FIG.	PAGE
263. Outline for a portrait of Amenophis III	333
264. Portrait of Queen Taia	339
265. Painting at Beni-Hassan	341
266. Painting at Beni-Hassan	342
267. Painting at Beni-Hassan	342
268. Painting at Beni-Hassan	343
269. Painting at Thebes	343
270. Painting at Thebes	344
271. Harpist	345
272. European prisoner	347
273. Head of the same prisoner	347
274. Ethiopian prisoner	348
275. Head of the same prisoner	348
276. Winged figure	349
277. Winged figure	350
278. Battle of the Cats and Rats	352
279. The soles of a pair of sandals	354
280, 281. The God Bes	354
282. Vultures on a ceiling	356
283, 284. Details from the tomb of Ptah-hotep	357
285. Carpet hung across a pavilion	358
286. Specimens of ceiling decorations	359
287. Painting on a mummy case	361
288. Winged globe	361
289, 290. Tables for offerings	363
291. Pitcher of red earth	368
292. Red earthenware	369
293. Gray earthenware	370
294. The God Bes	370
295. Pendant for necklace	371
296, 297. Enamelled earthenware	371
298. Enamelled faience	372
299. Doorway in the Stepped Pyramid at Sakkarah	372
300—302. Enamelled plaque from the Stepped Pyramid	373
303—305. Enamelled earthenware plaques	374
306, 307. Glass statuettes	376
308. Mirror-handle	379
309. Bronze hair-pin	379
310. Bronze dagger	379
311. Pectoral	381
312, 313. Golden Hawks	382
314. Ægis	383
315. Necklace	385
316. Osiris, Isis, and Horus	387
317, 318. Rings	387
319, 320. Ear-rings	387

FIG.		PAGE
321.	Ivory Plaque	388
322.	Ivory Castanet	389
323.	Fragment of an Ivory Castanet	391
324.	Workman splitting a piece of wood	392
325.	Joiner making a bed	392
326.	Coffer for sepulchral statuettes	393
327, 328.	Chairs	394
329—331.	Perfume spoons	395, 396
332–334.	Walking-stick handles	397
335.	Wooden pin or peg	398
336.	Hathoric capital	398

A HISTORY

OF

ART IN ANCIENT EGYPT.

A HISTORY OF
ART IN ANCIENT EGYPT

CHAPTER I.

CIVIL AND MILITARY ARCHITECTURE.

§ 1.—*The Graphic Processes employed by the Egyptians in their representations of Buildings.*

WE have seen that sepulchral and religious architecture are represented in Egypt by numerous and well preserved monuments. It is not so in the case of civil and military architecture. Of these, time has spared but very few remains and all that the ancient historians tell us on the subject amounts to very little. Our best aids in the endeavour to fill up this lacuna are the pictures and bas-reliefs of the tombs, in which store-houses, granaries, houses and villas of the Pharaonic period are often figured.

It is not always easy, however, to trace the actual conformation and arrangement of those buildings through the conventionalities employed by the artists, and we must therefore begin by attempting to understand the ideas with which the Egyptians made the representations in question. Their idea was to show all at a single glance; to combine in one view matters which could only be seen in reality from many successive points, such as all the façades of a building, with its external aspect and internal arrangements. This notion may be compared to that which recommends itself to a young child when, in drawing a profile, he insists upon giving it two ears, because when he looks at a front face he sees two ears standing out beyond either cheek.

In these days when we wish to represent an architectural building exhaustively, we do it in geometrical fashion, giving *plans, elevations,* and *sections.* To get a plan we make a horizontal section at any determined height, which gives us the thickness of the walls and the area of the spaces which they inclose. An elevation shows us one of the faces of the building in all its details, while the transverse or longitudinal section allows us to lay the whole of the structural arrangements open to the spectator. Plan, elevation, and section, are three different things by the comparison of which a just idea of the whole building and of the connection of its various parts may be formed.

The Egyptians seem to have had a dim perception of these three separate processes, but they failed to distinguish clearly between them, and in their paintings they employed them in the most *naïve* fashion, combining all three into one figure without any clear indication of the points of junction.

Let us take as an example a representation of a house from a Theban tomb (Fig. 1), and attempt to discover what the artist meant to show us. In the left-hand part of the picture there is no difficulty. In the lower stage we see the external door by which the inclosure surrounding the house is entered; in the two upper divisions there are the trees and climbing plants of the garden. It is when we turn to the house, which occupies two-thirds of the field, that our embarrassments begin. The following explanation is perhaps the best—that, with an artistic license which is not rare in such works, the painter has shown us all the four sides of the building at once. He has spread them out, one after the other, on the wall which he had to decorate. This process may be compared to our method of flattening upon a plane surface the figures which surround a Greek vase, but in modern works of archæology it is customary to give a sketch of the real form beside the flat projection. No such help is given by the Egyptian painter and we are forced to conjecture the shapes of his buildings as best we can. In this case he was attempting to represent an oblong building. The door by which the procession defiling across the garden is about to enter, is in one of the narrow sides. It is inclosed by the two high shafts between which a woman seems to be awaiting on the threshold

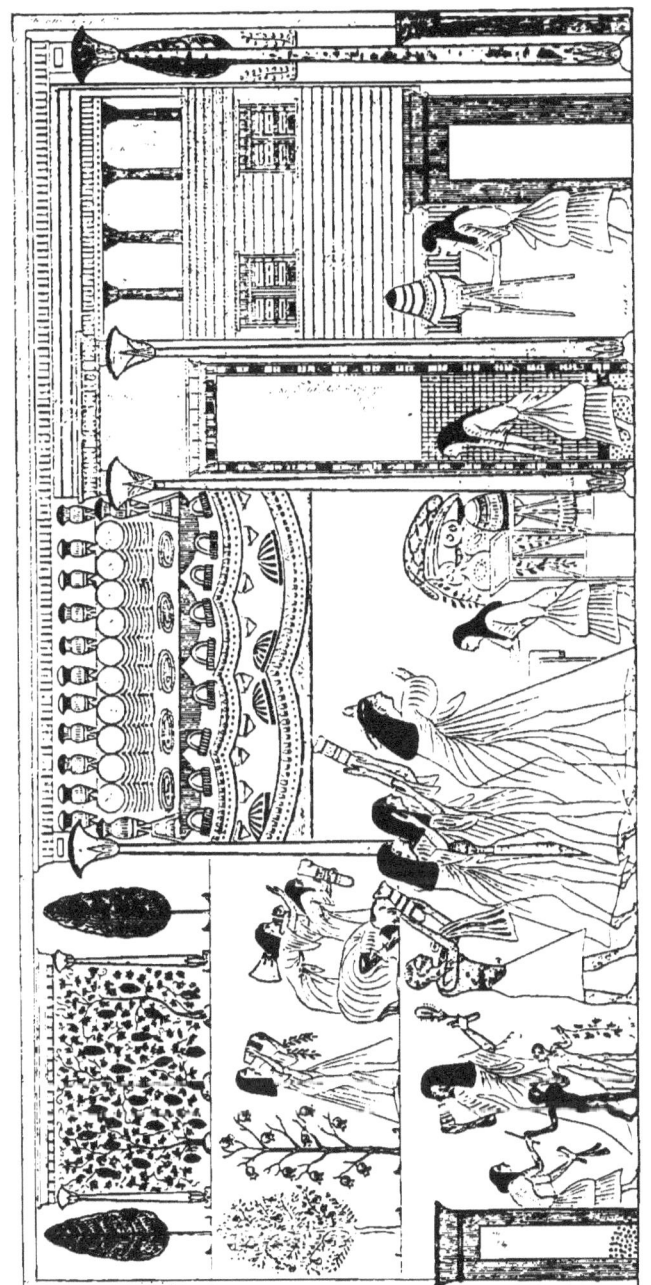

Fig. 1.—House; from Champollion, pl. 174.

the arrival of the guests. On the right we have one of the lateral faces; it is pierced at one angle by a low door, above which are two windows and above them again an open story or terrace with slender columns supporting the roof. Still further to the right, at the extremity of the picture, the second narrow façade is slightly indicated by its angle column and a portal, which appears to be sketched in profile. Want of space alone seems to have prevented the artist from giving as much detail to this portion of his work as to the rest. The left wing, that which is contiguous to the garden, remains to be considered. Those who agree with our interpretation of the artist's aims, will look upon this as the second lateral façade. It presents some difficulty, however, because it shows none of the plain walls which inclose the rest of the building and exclude the eye of the spectator; its walls are left out and leave the interior of the house completely open.

It may be said that this part of the picture represents an awning or veranda in front of the house. But, in that case, how are we to explain the objects which are arranged at the top of it—jars, loaves of bread, and other house-keeping necessaries? It cannot be a veranda with a granary on the top of it. Such a store-room would have to be carefully closed if its contents were to be safe-guarded from the effects of heat, light, and insects. It would therefore be necessary to suppose that the Egyptian painter made use of an artistic license not unknown in our own days, and suppressed the wall of the store-room in order to display the wealth of the establishment. By this means he has given us a longitudinal section of the building very near the external wall. There is no trace of an open story above. The latter seems to have existed only on that side of the house which was in shade during the day and exposed after nightfall to the refreshing breezes from the north.

This picture presents us, then, with a peculiar kind of elevation; an elevation which, by projection, shows three sides of the house and hints at a fourth. Representations which are still more conventionalized than this are to be found in many places. The most curious of these are to be found in the ruins of the capital of Amenophis IV., near the village of Tell-el-Amarna. It was in that city that the heretical prince in question inaugurated the worship of the solar disc, which was represented as darting rays terminating in an open hand (see Fig. 2). Among these ruins we find, upon the sculptured walls of subterranean chambers, representations of royal and princely villas, where elegant pavilions are surrounded by vast offices and dependencies, by gardens and pieces of ornamental water, the whole being inclosed by a crenellated wall. These representations were called by Prisse *plans cavaliers*, a vague term which hardly gives a fair idea of the process, which deserves to be analysed and explained.

They are, as a fact, plans, but plans made upon a very different principle from those of our day. Certain elements, such as walls, are indicated by simple lines varying in thickness, just as they

FIG. 2.—The adoration of the solar disk by Amenophis IV.; from Prisse.

might be in a modern plan, giving such a result as would be obtained by a horizontal section. But this is the exception. The houses, the trees, and everything with any considerable height, are shown in projection, as they might appear to the eye of a bird flying over them if they had been overthrown by some considerate earthquake, which had laid them flat without doing them any other injury. As a rule all objects so treated are projected in one and the same direction, but here and there exceptions to this are found. In a country villa figured upon one of the tombs at Thebes (Fig. 3), one row of trees, that upon the right, is projected at right angles to all the others. The reason for this change in the artist's system is easily seen. Unless he had placed his trees in the fashion shown in the cut, he would not have been able to give a true idea of their number and of the shade which they were calculated to afford.

The process which we have just described is the dominant process in Egyptian figuration. Here and there, as in Fig. 1, it is combined with the vertical section. This combination is conspicuous in the plan found at Tell-el-Amarna, from which we have restored the larger of the two villas which we illustrate farther on. In this plan, as in the case of the Theban house figured on page 3, the artist has been careful to show that

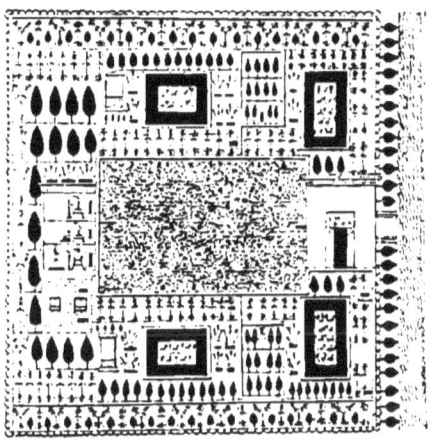

FIG. 3.—Egyptian plan of a villa; from Wilkinson, vol. i. p. 377.

there was no want of provision in the house; the wall of the store-room is omitted, and the interior, with its rows of amphoræ, is thrown open to our inspection.

No scale is given in any of these plans, so that we are unable to determine either the extent of ground occupied by the buildings and their annexes, or their absolute height. But spaces and heights seem to have been kept in just proportion. The Egyptian draughtsman was prepared for the execution of such a task by education and the traditions of his art, and his eye seems to have been trustworthy.

Accustomed as we are to accuracy and exactitude in such matters, these Egyptian plans disconcert us at first by their mixture of conscience and carelessness, artlessness and skill, by their simultaneous employment of methods which are contradictory in principle. In the end, however, we arrive at a complete understanding with the Egyptian draughtsman, and we are enabled to transcribe into our own language that which he has painfully written with the limited means at his command. In the two restorations of an Egyptian house which we have attempted, there is no arrangement of any importance that is not to be found in the original plan.

§ 2. *The Palace.*

Their tombs and temples give us a great idea of the taste and wealth of the Egyptian monarchs. We are tempted to believe that their palaces, by their extent and the luxury of their decoration, must have been worthy of the tombs which they prepared for their own occupation, and the temples which they erected in honour of the gods to whom, as they believed, they owed their glory and prosperity. The imagination places the great sovereigns who constructed the pyramids, the rock tombs of Thebes, the temples of Luxor and Karnak, in splendid palaces constructed of the finest materials which their country afforded.

Impelled by this idea, the earlier visitors to Egypt saw palaces everywhere. They called everything which was imposing in size a palace, except the pyramids and the subterranean excavations. The authors of the *Description de l'Égypte* thought that Karnak and Luxor, Medinet-Abou, and Gournah, were royal dwellings. Such titles as the Palace of Menephtah, applied to the temple of Seti, at Gournah, have been handed down to our day, and are to be found in works of quite recent date, such as Fergusson's *History of Architecture*.[1]

Since the time of Champollion, a more attentive study of the existing remains, and especially of the inscriptions which they bear, has dissipated that error; egyptologists are now in accord as to the religious character of the great Theban buildings on either bank of the river. But while admitting this, there are some archæologists who have not been able to clear their minds

---

[1] FERGUSSON (in vol. i. p. 118, of his *History of Architecture in all Countries*, etc.) proposes that Karnak should be called a *Palace-Temple*, or *Temple-Palace*.

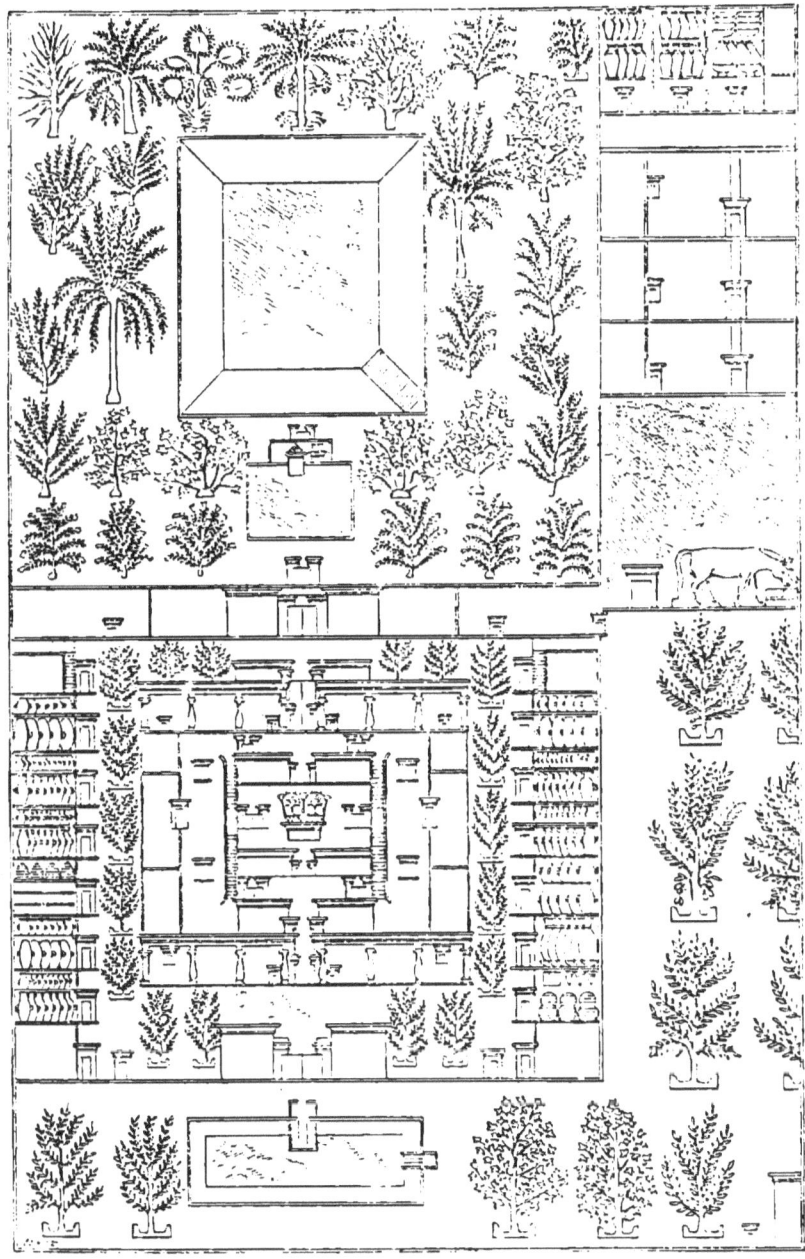

FIG. 4.—Part of the plan of a house and its offices, figured in a tomb at Tell-el-Amarna; from Prisse.

entirely of an idea which was so long dominant. They contend that the royal habitation must have been an annexe to the temple, and both at Karnak and Luxor they seek to find it in those ill-preserved chambers which may be traced behind the sanctuaries. There the king must have had his dwelling, and his life must have been passed in the courts and hypostyle halls.[1]

Among all the inscriptions which have been discovered in the chambers in question there is not one which supports such an hypothesis. Neither in the remains of Egyptian literature, nor in the works of the Greek historians, is there a passage to be found which tends to show that the king lived in the temple or its dependencies, or that his palace was within the sacred inclosure at all.

There is another argument which is, perhaps, even more conclusive than that from the silence of the texts. How can we believe that the kings of such a pleasure-loving and light-hearted race as the ancient Egyptians took up their residence in quarters so dark and so rigidly inclosed. Their dispositions cannot have differed very greatly from those of their subjects, and no phrase is more often repeated in the texts than this : *to live a happy day.* The palace must have been a pleasant dwelling, a place of repose ; and nothing could be better fitted for such a purpose than the light and spacious edifices which lay outside the city, in the midst of large and shady gardens, upon the banks of the Nile itself, or of one of those canals which carried its waters to the borders of the desert. From their high balconies, galleries, or covered terraces, the eye could roam freely over the neighbouring plantations, over the course of the river and the fields which it irrigated, and out to the mountains which shut in the horizon. The windows were large, and movable blinds, which may be distinguished in some of the paintings, allowed the chambers to be either thrown open to the breeze or darkened from the noonday sun, as occasion arose. That shelter which is so grateful in all hot climates was also to be found outside, in the broad shadows cast by the sycamores and planes which grew around artificial basins garnished with the brilliant flowers of the lotus, in the shadows of the spring foliage hanging upon the trellised fruit-trees, or in the open kiosques which were reared here and there upon the banks of the lakes. There, behind the shelter of walls and hedges, and among his

[1] DU BARRY DE MERVAL, *Études sur l'Architecture Égyptienne* (1875), p. 271.

wives and children, the king could taste some of the joys of domesticity. In such a retreat a Thothmes or a Rameses could abandon himself to the simple joy of living, and might forget for a time both the fatigues of yesterday and the cares of to-morrow; as the modern Egyptians would say, he could enjoy his *kief*.

In such architecture as this, in which everything was designed to serve the pleasures of the moment, there was no necessity for stone. The solidity and durability of limestone, sandstone, and granite, were required in the tomb, the eternal dwelling, or for the temples, the homes of the gods. But the palace was no more than a pleasure marquee, it required no material more durable than wood or brick. Painters and sculptors were charged to cover its walls with lively colours and smiling images; it was their business to decorate the stucco of the walls, the planks of acacia, and the slender columns of cedar and palmwood with the most brilliant hues on their palettes and with gold. The ornamentation was as lavish as in the tombs, although in the latter case it had a much better chance of duration. The palaces of the Egyptian sovereigns were worthy of their wealth and power, but the comparative slightness of their materials led to their early disappearance, and no trace of them is left upon the soil of Egypt.

During the whole period of which we have any record, the East has changed but little, in spite of the apparent diversity between the successive races, empires, and religions which have prevailed in it. We know how vast an array of servants and followers Oriental royalty or grandeeship involves. The *konak* of the most insignificant bey or pacha shelters a whole army of servants, each one of whom does as little work as possible. The domestics of the Sultan at Constantinople, or of the Shah at Teheran, are to be counted by thousands. No one knows the exact number of eunuchs, cooks, grooms, and sweepers, of *atechdjis*, *cafedjis*, and *tchiboukdjis*, which their seraglios contain. Such a domestic establishment implies an extraordinary provision of lodgings of some sort, as well as an extensive accumulation of stores. Great storehouses were required where the more or less voluntary gifts of the people, the tributes in kind of conquered nations, and the crops produced by the huge estates attached to the Crown, could be warehoused. In the vast inclosures whose arrangements are preserved for us by the paintings at Tell-el-Amarna there was room for all these offices and granaries. They were built round courtyards which were arranged in long succession on all four sides of the principal building in which the sovereign and his family dwelt. When, in the course of a long reign, the family of the king became very numerous (Rameses II. had a hundred and seventy children, fifty-nine of whom were sons), and it became necessary to provide accommodation for them in the royal dwelling, it was easy to encroach upon the surrounding country, and to extend both buildings and gardens at will.

Although the great inclosure at Karnak was spacious enough for its purpose, the families of the Pharaohs would hardly have had elbow room in it. They would soon have felt the restraint of the high and impassable barriers insupportable, and the space within them too narrow for their pursuits. The palaces of the East have always required wider and more flexible limits than these. If we examine their general aspect we shall find it the same from the banks of the Ganges to those of the Bosphorus. The climate, the harem, and the extreme subdivision of labour, gave, and still gives, a multiplex and diffuse character to royal and princely dwellings; memories of Susa and Persepolis, of Babylon and Nineveh, agree in this with the actual condition of the old palaces at Agra, Delhi, and Constantinople. They were not composed, like the modern palaces of the West, of a single homogeneous edifice which can be embraced at a glance; they in no way resembled the Tuileries or Versailles.[1] They consisted of many structures of unequal importance, built at different times and by different princes; their pavilions were separated by gardens and courts; they formed a kind of royal village or town, surrounded and guarded by a high wall. In that part of the interior nearest the entrance there were richly-decorated halls, in which the sovereign condescended to sit enthroned at stated times, to receive the homage of his subjects and of foreign ambassadors. Around these chambers, which were open to a certain number of privileged individuals, swarmed a whole population of officers, soldiers, and servants of all kinds. This part of the palace was

[1] The contrast between the palaces of the East and Versailles is hardly so strong as M. Perrot seems to suggest. The curious assemblage of buildings of different ages and styles which forms the eastern *façade* of the dwelling of Louis XIV. does not greatly differ in essentials from the confused piles of Delhi or the old Seraglio.—ED.

a repetition on a far larger scale of the *sélamlik* of an Oriental dwelling. The *harem* lay farther on, behind gates which were jealously guarded. In it the king passed his time when he was not occupied with war, with the chase, or with the affairs of state. Between the buildings there was space and air enough to allow of the king's remaining for months, or years if he chose, within the boundary walls of his palace; he could review his troops in the vast courtyards; he could ride, drive, or walk on foot in the shady gardens; he could bathe in the artificial lakes and bath-houses. Sometimes even hunting-grounds were included within the outer walls.

These facilities and easy pleasures have always been a dangerous temptation for Oriental princes. A long list might be formed of those dynasties which, after beginning by a display of singular energy and resource, were at last enfeebled and overwhelmed in the pleasures of the palace. By those pleasures they became so completely enervated that at last a time came when the long descended heir of a line of conquerors was hurled from his throne by the slightest shock. The tragic history of Sardanapalus, which has inspired so many poets and historians, is a case in point. Modern criticism has attacked it ruthlessly; names, dates, and facts have all been placed in doubt; but even if the falsehood of every detail could be demonstrated, it would yet retain that superior kind of truth which springs from its general applicability— a truth in which the real value of the legend consists. Almost all the royal dynasties of the East ended in a Sardanapalus, for he was nothing more than the victim of the sedentary and luxurious existence passed in an Oriental palace.

If we knew more about the internal history of Egypt, we should doubtless find that such phenomena were not singular in that country. The Rammesides must have owed their fall and disappearance to it. The Egyptian palace cannot have differed very greatly from the type we have described, all the characteristic features of which are to be recognised in those edifices which have hitherto been called villas.[1] There was the same

---

[1] NESTOR L'HÔTE a fine connoisseur, who often divined facts which were not finally demonstrated until after his visit to Egypt - also received this impression from his examination of the remains at Tell-el-Amarna: " Details no less interesting make us acquainted with the general arrangement . . . . of the king's palaces, the porticos and propylæa by which they were approached, the inner chambers, the

amplitude of lateral development. We have not space to give a restoration of the most important of the "villas" figured at Tell-el-Amarna in its entirety; but we give enough (Fig. 4) to suggest the great assemblage of buildings, which, when complete, must have covered a vast space of ground (Fig. 5). By its variety, by its alternation of courts and gardens with buildings surrounded here by stone colonnades, there by lighter wooden verandahs, this palace evidently belongs to the same family as other Oriental palaces of later times. Within its wide *enciente* the sovereign could enjoy all the pleasures of the open country while living either in his capital or in its immediate neighbourhood ; he could satisfy all his wishes and desires without moving from the spot.

We have chosen for restoration that part of the royal dwelling which corresponds to what is called, in the East, the sélamlik, and in the West, the reception-rooms. A structure stands before the entrance the purpose of which cannot readily be decided. It might be a reservoir for the use of the palace inmates, or it might be a guard-house ; the question must be left open. Behind this structure there is a door between two towers with inclined walls, forming a kind of pylon. There is a narrower doorway near each angle. All three of these entrances open upon a vast rectangular court, which is inclosed laterally by two rows of chambers and at the back by a repetition of the front wall and three doorways already described. This courtyard incloses a smaller one, which is prefaced by a deep colonnaded portico, and incloses an open hall raised considerably above the level of the two courts. The steps by which this hall is reached are clearly shown upon the plan. In the middle of it there is a small structure, which may be one of those tribune-like altars which are represented upon some of the bas-reliefs. Nestor L'Hôte gives a sketch of one of these reliefs. It shows a man standing upon a dais with a pile of offerings before him. The same writer describes some existing remains of a similar structure at Karnak : it is a quadrilateral block, to which access was obtained by an inclined plane.[1]

store-houses and offices, the courts, gardens, and artificial lakes ; everything, in fact, which went to make up the royal dwelling-place." *Lettres écrites d'Égypte* (in 1838-9 ; 8vo, 1840) : pp. 64-65.

[1] *Lettres écrites d'Égypte*, p. 62. In some other plans from Tell-el-Amarna, given by Prisse, several of these altars are given upon a larger scale, showing the offerings with which they are heaped. One of them has a flight of steps leading up to it.

Perhaps the king accomplished some of the religious ceremonies which were among his duties at this point. In order to arrive at the altar from without, three successive gates and boundary walls had to be passed, so that the safety of the sovereign was well guarded.

Upon the Egyptian plan, which forms a basis for these remarks, there is, on the right of the nest of buildings just described, another of more simple arrangement but of still larger extent. There is no apparent communication between the two; they are, indeed, separated by a grove of trees. In front of this second assemblage of buildings there is the same rectangular structure of doubtful purpose, and the same quasi-pylon that we find before the first. Behind the pylon there is a court surrounded on three sides by a double row of apartments, some of which communicate directly with the court, others through an intervening portico. Doubtless, this court was the harem in which the king lived with his wives and children. Ranged round courts in its rear are storehouses, stables, cattle-stables, and other offices, with gardens again beyond them. The finest garden lies immediately behind the block of buildings first described, and is shown in our restoration (Fig. 5). Here and there rise light pavilions, whose wooden structure may be divined from the details given by the draughtsman. Colonnades, under which the crowds of servants and underlings could find shelter at night, pervade the whole building. The domestic offices are partly shown in our figure. As to the reception halls (the part of the building which would now be called the *divan*), we find nothing that can be identified with them in any of the plans which we have inspected. But it must be remembered that the representations in question are greatly mutilated, and that hitherto they have only been reproduced and published in fragmentary fashion.

We have now sketched the Egyptian palace as it must have been according to all historic probability, and according to the graphic representations left to us by the people themselves. Those of our readers who have followed our arguments attentively, will readily understand that we altogether refuse to see the remains of a palace, properly speaking, in the ruin which has been so often drawn and photographed as the *Royal Pavilion of Medinet-Abou*, or the Pavilion of Rameses III.[1] It would be difficult

---

[1] In this we are supported by the opinions of MARIETTE (*Itinéraire*, p. 213) and EBERS (*L'Égypte, du Caire à Philæ*, p. 317).

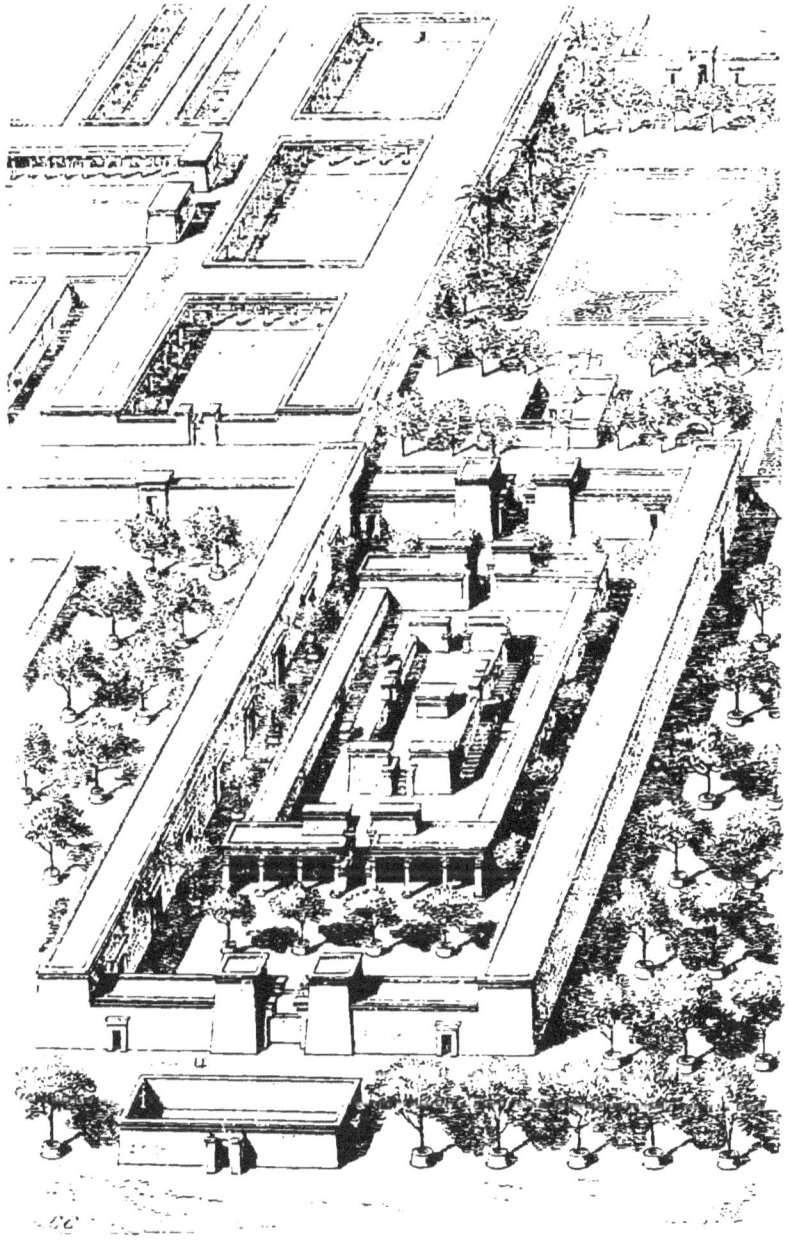

FIG. 5.—Partial restoration of a palace at Tell-el-Amarna ; by Charles Chipiez.

to convey by words alone a true idea of this elegant and singular building. We therefore give two plans (Figs. 6 and 7), a longitudinal and a transverse section (Figs. 8 and 9), and

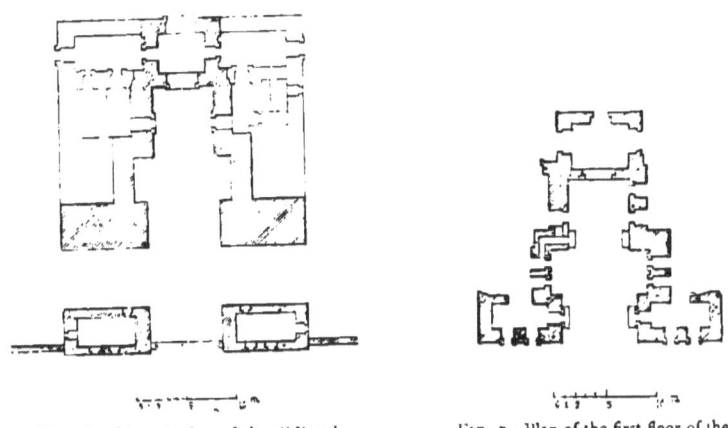

FIG. 6.—Ground plan of the "Royal Pavilion"; from Lepsius.

FIG. 7—Plan of the first floor of the "Royal Pavilion"; from Lepsius.

a restoration in perspective (Plate VII.). To those coming from the plain the first thing encountered was a pair of lodges for guards, with battlements round their summits like the pavilion itself

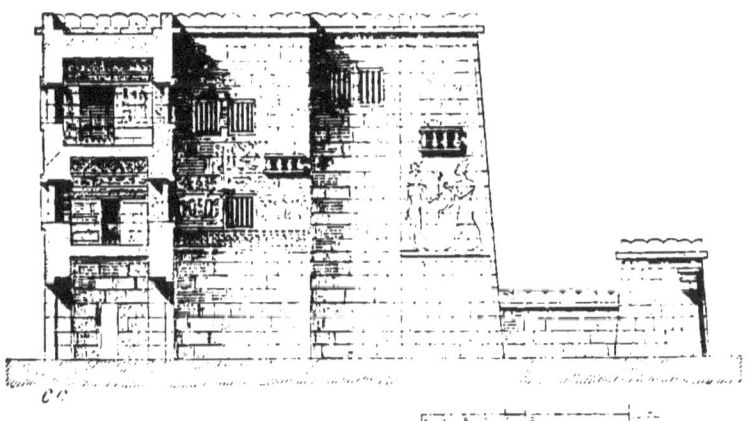

FIG. 8.—Longitudinal section of the pavilion; restored.

and its surrounding walls. The barrier which is shown in our plate between the two lodges is restored from a painting at Thebes, but the two half piers which support its extremities are still in existence. The pavilion itself consists of a main block with two lofty wings standing out perpendicularly to its front. The walls of these wings are inclined, and there is a passage through the centre of the block. There are three stories in all, which communicate with one another by a staircase. This pavilion is entirely covered with bas-reliefs and hieroglyphic texts. The best way to solve the problem which it offers is to accept the teaching of history, and of all that we know concerning the persistent characteristics of royal life in the East. Even in our own day there are few eastern potentates who do not think it necessary to lay down, on the day after their accession, the foundations of a new palace. The Syrian Emir Beschir did so at Beit-el-din in the Lebanon, and Djezzar-Pacha another at St. Jean d'Acre; so too, in Egypt, Mehemet Ali and his successors built palaces at Choubra and other places in the neighbourhood of Cairo and Alexandria. At Constantinople recent Sultans have spent upon building the last resources of their empire. In these matters the East is the home of change. The son seldom inhabits the dwelling of his father. The Pharaohs and the kings of Nineveh and Babylon must have been touched to some extent with the same mania and eager to enjoy the results of their labour at the earliest moment.

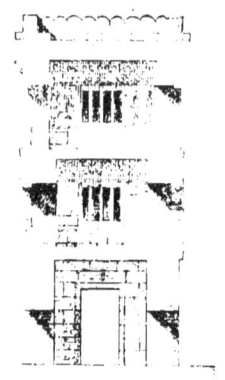

FIG. 9.—Transverse section of the pavilion; restored.

The sovereigns of Egypt must have chosen the sites for their palaces within the zone covered by the annual inundations. In any part of Egypt forced labour would rapidly build up the artificial banks necessary to raise the intended buildings above the reach of the highest floods, while in such a situation trees and shrubs would grow almost as fast as the palace walls. In a few years the royal dwelling would be complete, and with its completion would find itself surrounded by smiling parterres and shadowy groves.

When the whole of the fertile plain was at their disposal, why should they have chosen a site where no vegetation could be reared without the help of the *sakyeh* and the *shadouf*? Why should they, of their own free will, have built their dwellings close to those cliffs in the Libyan chain which give off at night the heat they have absorbed from the sun during the day? The buildings of Medinet-Abou are immediately at the foot of the hill *Gournet-el-Mourraï*, which detaches itself from the chain near the southern extremity of the Theban necropolis, and thrusts itself forward, like a cape into the sea, towards the outer limits of the cultivated ground.

We should not have looked for a palace in such a situation. We may add that the site of the pavilion is not large enough to accommodate the household of a king. It is closely circumscribed by the temple of Thothmes and its propylæa on the right, and by that of Rameses at the back, so that its dimensions would have seemed even more insignificant than they are in comparison with those gigantic fabrics. The greatest width of the pavilion is not more than about 80 feet and its greatest depth than 72, and the small court which almost cuts the building into two parts (see Fig. 6) occupies a good third of the surface inclosed by these measurements. Taken altogether, the three stories could not have contained more than about ten chambers, some of which were rather closets than anything more ambitious. In spite of the comparative simplicity of modern domestic arrangements a middle-class family of our day would be cramped in such a dwelling. How then could a Pharaoh, with the swarm of idlers who surrounded him, attempt to take up his residence in it?

What, then, are we to call the little edifice which stands in front of the temple of Rameses II.? Is it a temple raised by the conqueror in his own honour? If we examine the bas-reliefs which decorate it both within and without, we shall see that it thoroughly deserves the name of *Pavillon Royal* which the French savants gave to it. The personality of Rameses fills it from roof to basement. In the interior we find him at home, in his harem, among his wives and children. Here one of his daughters brings him flowers of which he tastes the scent; there we see him playing draughts with another daughter, or receiving fruit from the hands of a third, whose chin he playfully caresses. Upon the external walls there are battle scenes. Aided by his father, Amen, Rameses overthrows his enemies. With wonderful technical precision the sculptor has given to each figure its distinguishing costume, weapons, and features. The triumph of the king is complete; none of his adversaries can stand before him.

May we not seek the explanation which the arrangements of the building fail to suggest, in this perpetual recurrence of the royal image, figured in all the public and private occupations in which the life of the monarch was passed? The way in which it pervades the whole structure ought to be enough to convince us that the pavilion, like the adjoining temple, is nothing but a monument to his prowess. It is an ingenious and brilliant addition to the public part of the tomb, to the cenotaph. In other buildings of the same kind the temple, with its courts and pylons, is everything; but here, as if to distinguish his cenotaph from those of his predecessors and to impress posterity with a higher notion of his power and magnificence, Rameses has chosen to add a building which groups happily with it and serves as a kind of vestibule. It is difficult to say whence he borrowed the form of this unique edifice. Perhaps from one of the numerous pavilions which went to make up a pharaonic palace. Such, however, was not the opinion of Mariette, who discusses the question more than once. His final opinion was as follows: "The general architectural lines of this pavilion of Rameses, especially when seen from some distance, agree with those of the triumphal towers (*migdol*) which are represented in the bas-reliefs of Karnak, Luxor, the Ramesseum, and Medinet-Abou. These towers were erected on the frontiers of the country by the Egyptian monarchs, where they served both as defensive works and as memorials of the national victories. The royal pavilion of Medinet-Abou was, therefore, a work of military rather than of civil architecture."[1] The warrior-king *par excellence* could not have preserved his memory green in the minds of his subjects by any more characteristic monument.[2]

But whether it is to be considered a palace or a fortress, this is the proper place to study the details of this curious edifice. It forms, indeed, part of an assemblage of funerary buildings, and its situation is immediately in front of a temple, facts which might suggest that its arrangements ought to have been discussed in an earlier chapter. But these arrangements are in fact imitated from those of the ordinary dwellings of the living. Its economy is not that of either tomb or temple. The superposition of one story upon another is found in neither of those classes of buildings

[1] *Itinéraire*, p. 213.
[2] See the curious extracts from the *Papyrus Anastasi III.*, given by Maspero, *Histoire Ancienne*, pp. 267-269.

but it is found both in military and domestic architecture. So, too, with the mode of lighting the various apartments. The darkness of the tomb is complete, the illumination of the temple is far from brilliant, in its more sacred parts it is almost as dark as the tomb. Prayers could be said to Osiris without inconvenience by the scanty daylight which found its way through the narrow doorway of the sepulchral chapel, but the active pleasures of life required a broader day. We find, therefore, that the pavilion was lighted by windows, real windows, and some of them very large. Nothing is more rare, in the buildings which have come down to us from

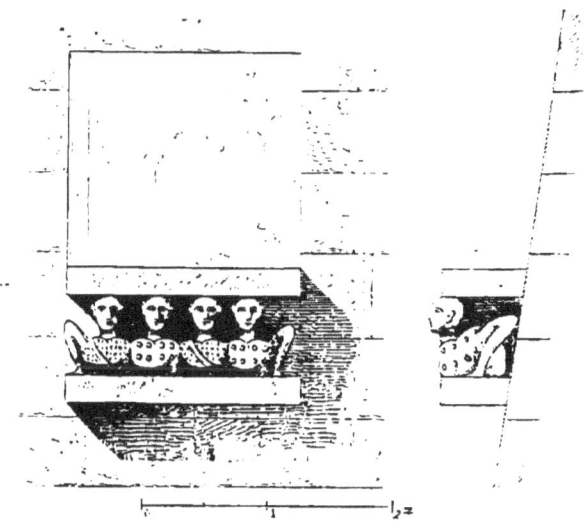

FIG. 10.—Brackets in the courtyard of the Royal Pavilion.

the pharaonic epochs, than such windows: but then most of those buildings are either tombs or temples. Civil architecture in Egypt had to fulfil pretty much the same requirements as in other countries. It was, therefore, obliged to employ the means which have been found necessary in every other country and at every other period.

The employment of the window is not the only structural peculiarity in the pavilion of Medinet-Abou: upon the walls which surround the small court, and between the first and second stories, there are carved stone brackets or consoles, supporting flat slabs of stone. It has sometimes been asserted that these brackets formed supports for masts upon which a velarium was stretched across the court. But neither in engravings nor in photographs have we been able to discover the slightest trace of the holes which would be necessary for the insertion of such masts.

But, leaving their purpose on one side, we must call attention to the curious sculptures which are interposed between the upper and lower slabs of these brackets. They are in the shape of grotesque busts, resting upon the lower slab and supporting the upper one with their heads. In the wall above a kind of framed tablet is inserted.[1] In these figures, which are now very much worn and corroded by exposure, we have a repetition of those prisoners of war which occur frequently upon the neighbouring bas-reliefs in similar uncomfortable positions. Such a motive is entirely in place in a building which, by the general features of its architecture, seems a combination of fortress and triumphal arch.

It is difficult to admit that such a building as this was never utilized. We may well believe that it was never built for permanent occupation, but we must not therefore conclude that chambers so well lighted and so richly decorated were without their proper and well-defined uses. The floors of the first and second stories have disappeared, but that they once existed is proved by the staircase, part of which is still in place. The floors were of wood; the stairs of stone. The general economy of the building shows that it was intended that every room, from the ground-floor to the topmost story, should be used when occasion arose. It is possible that they were employed as reception rooms for the princes and vassal chiefs who came together several times a year for the celebration of funerary rites. In chambers richly decorated like these, and, doubtless, richly furnished also, people of rank could meet together and await at their ease their turn to take part in the ceremonies.[2]

Although the pavilion of Medinet-Abou may, then, have no right to the name of palace, the foregoing observations have justified their position in this chapter by helping us to understand

---

[1] A careful examination of these tablets has yet to be made; at present we are without any information as to their probable uses. The authors of the *Description* thought it likely that they were meant to receive metal trophies of some kind. They might have been covered with a painted decoration, or they might have been intended to be cut into barred windows and left unfinished. In the photographs the stone of which they are made seems to be different in grain from the rest of the walls.

[2] EBERS, *L'Égypte, du Caire à Philœ*, pp. 317-318.

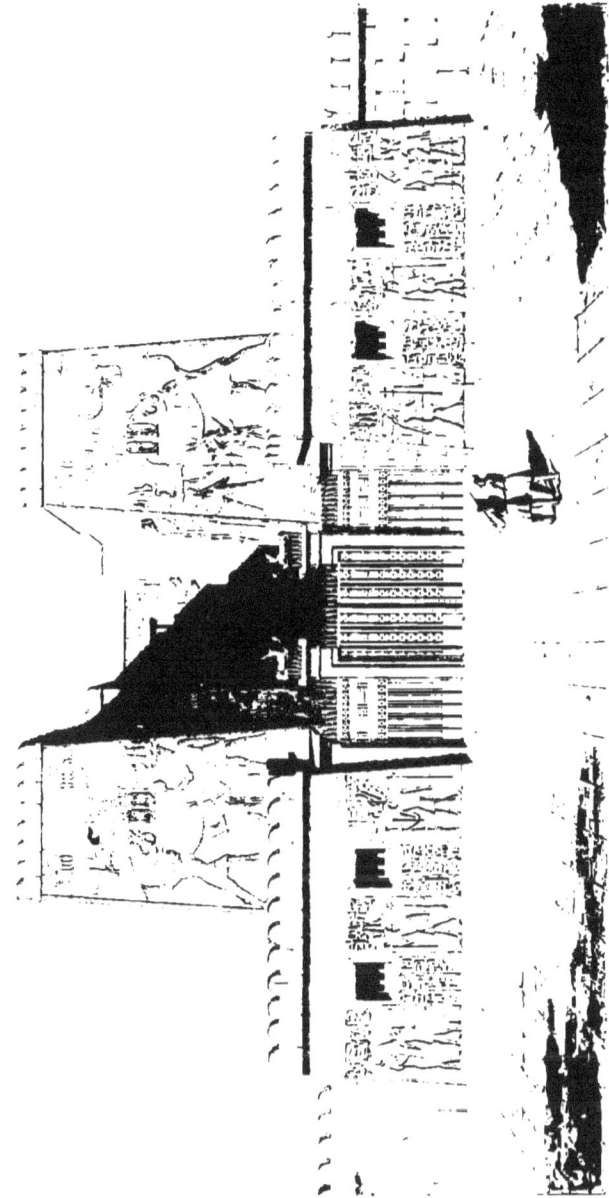

some of the conditions imposed upon the Egyptian architect when he had to meet civil wants. Some of our readers may have expected to find, in this chapter, a description of a more famous monument, of that *Labyrinth* of which Herodotus, Diodorus, and Strabo wrote in such enthusiastic terms.[1]

But we are by no means sure that the ruins in the Fayoum are those of the Labyrinth. These ruins, which were first discovered and described by Jomard and Caristie,[2] and afterwards in greater detail by Lepsius,[3] are upon the western slope of the Libyan chain, about four miles and a half east-by-south from Medinet-el-Fayoum, at a point which must have been on the borders of Lake Mœris, if the position of that lake as defined by Linant de Bellefonds be accepted.[4] Mariette did not admit that the ruins in question were those of the vast building which was counted among the seven wonders of the world. "I know," he once said to us, "where the Labyrinth is: it is under the crops of the Fayoum. I shall dig it up some day if Heaven gives me a long enough life."

However this may be, the ruins are at present in such a state of confusion that every traveller who visits the place comes away disappointed. "If," says Ebers, "we climb the pyramid of powdery grey bricks—once however coated with polished granite —which, as Strabo tells us, stood at one extremity of the Labyrinth, we shall see that the immense palace in which the chiefs of the Egyptian nomes assembled at certain dates to meet the king was shaped like a horse shoe. But that is all that can be seen. The middle of the building and the whole of the left wing are entirely destroyed, while the confused mass of ruined halls and chambers on the right—which the natives of El-Howara think to be the bazaar of some vanished city—are composed of wretched blocks of dry grey mud. The granite walls of a few chambers and the fragments of a few inscribed columns form the only remains of any importance. From these we learn that the structure dates from the reign of Amenemhat III., of the twelfth dynasty."[5]

The plan and description of the building discovered by Lepsius

---

[1] HERODOTUS, ii. 148; DIODORUS SICULUS, i. 64; STRABO, xvii. 37.
[2] *Description de l'Égypte*, vol. iv. p. 478.
[3] *Denkmæler*, vol. i. plates 46-48. *Briefe aus Ægypten*, pp. 65-74.
[4] See a remarkable paper on this question contributed by Mr. F. Cope Whitehouse to the *Revue Archéologique* for June, 1882.—ED.   [5] EBERS, *Ægypten*, p. 174.

hardly correspond with the account of Strabo and with what we learn from other antique sources as to the magnificence of the Labyrinth and the vast bulk of the materials of which it was composed. We shall, therefore, reproduce neither the plan of Lepsius nor the text of the Greek geographer. The latter gives no measurements either of height or length, and under such circumstances any attempt to restore the building, from an architectural point of view would be futile.

§ 3.—*The Egyptian House.*

THE palace in Egypt was but a house larger and richer in its decorations than the others. The observations which we have made upon it may be applied to the dwelling-places of private individuals, who enjoyed, in proportion to their resources, the same comforts and conveniences as the sovereign or the hereditary princes of the nomes. The house was a palace in small, its arrangements and construction were inspired by the same wants, by the same national habits, by the same climatic and other natural conditions.

Diodorus and Josephus tell us that the population of Egypt proper, from Alexandria to Philæ, was 7,000,000 at the time of the Roman Empire, and there is reason to believe that it was still larger at the time of the nation's greatest prosperity under the princes of the eighteenth and nineteenth dynasties.[1] A large proportion of the Egyptian people lived in small towns and open villages, besides which there were a few very large towns. That Sais, Memphis, and Thebes were great cities we know from the words of the ancient historians, from the vast spaces covered by their ruins, and from the extent of their cemeteries.

Neither the Greek nor the Egyptian texts give us any information as to the appearance of an Egyptian town, the way in which its buildings were arranged, or their average size and height. The Greek travellers do not seem to have been sufficiently impressed by anything of the kind to think it worthy of record. The sites of these ancient cities have hardly ever been examined from this point of view, and perhaps little would be discovered if such an examination were to take place. In every

[1] DIODORUS, i. 31, 6.—JOSEPHUS (*The Jewish War*, ii. 16, 4) speaks of a population of seven millions and a half, exclusive of the inhabitants of Alexandria.

country the ordinary dwelling-house is constructed of small materials, and the day arrives, sooner or later, when it succumbs to the action of the weather.

It is only under exceptional circumstances that the private house leaves ruins behind it from which much can be learnt. Pompeii, under its shroud of ashes and fine dust, is a case in point. Sometimes, also, when the house has entirely disappeared, interesting facts may be gleaned as to its extent and arrangement. Instances of this are to be seen at Athens, where, upon several of the hills which were formerly included within its walls, may be traced the foundations of private dwellings cut in the living rock. Neither of these favourable conditions existed in the valley of the Nile.

The sands of the deserts would, no doubt, have guarded the houses of Memphis and Thebes as effectually as the cinders of Vesuvius did those of the little Roman town, if they had had but the same chance. We know how thoroughly they protected the dwellings of the dead upon the plateau of Gizeh, but the homes of the living were built close to the river and not upon the borders of the desert, and we can neither hope to find dead cities under the Egyptian sands, nor such indications of their domestic architecture as those which may sometimes be gleaned in mountainous countries.

Their situation upon the banks of the river, or not far from it, made it necessary for Egyptian cities to be placed upon artificial mounds or embankments, which should raise them above the inundation. Those modern villages which are not built upon the slopes of the mountain, are protected in the same fashion.

The tradition has survived of the great works undertaken during the period of national prosperity in order to provide this elevated bed for the chief cities of the country. According to Herodotus and Diodorus, Sesostris and Sabaco, that is to say the great Theban princes and the Ethiopian conquerors, were both occupied with this work of raising the level of the towns.[1] Some idea of the way in which these works were carried out has been gained by excavations upon the sites of a few cities. When a new district was to be added to a city the ground was prepared by building with crude brick a number of long and thick walls parallel to one another; then cross walls at right angles with the first, chessboard fashion. The square pits thus constructed were

[1] HERODOTUS. ii. 137 ; DIODORUS. i. 57.

filled with earth, broken stone, or anything else within reach. The foundations of the future city or district were laid upon the mass thus obtained, and profited by the operation both in health and amenity. The cities of Memphis and Thebes both seem to have been built in this manner.[1]

As a rule this is all that we learn by excavating on these ancient sites. The materials of the houses themselves have either fallen into dust, or, in a country which has been thickly populated since long before the commencement of history, have been used over and over again in other works. The inevitable destruction has been rendered more rapid and complete by the fellah's habit of opening up any mounds which he has reason to believe ancient, for the sake of the fertilizing properties they possess.

The only point in the Nile valley where the arrangements of an ancient city are still to be traced is upon the site of the new capital of Amenophis IV., built by him when he deserted Thebes and its god Amen.[2] This city, which owed its existence to royal caprice, seems to have been very soon abandoned. We do not even know the name it bore during its short prosperity, and since its fall the site has never been occupied by a population sufficiently great to necessitate the destruction of its remains. The soil is still covered by the ruins of its buildings. These are always of brick. The plans of a few houses have been roughly ascertained, and the direction of the streets can now be laid down with some accuracy. There is a street parallel to the river, and nearly 100 feet wide; from this, narrower streets branch off at right angles, some of them being hardly broad enough to allow of two chariots passing each other between the houses. The most important quarter of the city was that to the north, in the neighbourhood of the vast quadrangular inclosure which contained the temple of the

---

[1] ÉDOUARD MARIETTE, *Traité pratique et raisonné de la Construction en Égypte*, p. 139.
[2] The first elements for the *Restoration of an Egyptian House* which Mariette exhibited in the Universal Exhibition of 1878, were furnished, however, by some remains at Abydos. These consisted of the bases, to the height of about four feet, of the walls of a house. The general plan and arrangement of rooms was founded upon the indications thus obtained; the remainder of the restoration was founded upon bas-reliefs and paintings. The whole was reproduced in the *Gazette des Beaux-Arts* of November 1st, 1878, to which M. A. RHONÉ (*L'Égypte Antique*) contributed an analysis of the elements made use of by Mariette in his attempt to reconstruct an Egyptian dwelling.

Solar Disc. In this part of the city the ruins of large houses with spacious courts are to be found. There is, moreover, on the western side of the main street a building which Prisse calls the palace, in which a forest of brick piers, set closely together, may, perhaps, have been constructed in order to raise the higher floors above the damp soil. This question cannot, however, be decided in the present state of our information. The southern quarter of the city was inhabited by the poor. It contains only small houses, crowded together, of which nothing but the outer walls and a few heaps of rubbish remain.

In the case of Thebes we cannot point out, even to this slight extent, the arrangement of the city. We cannot tell where the palaces of the king and the dwellings of the great were

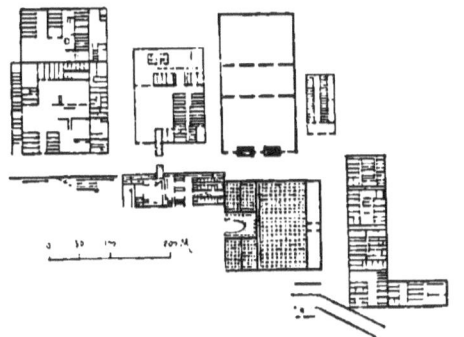

FIG. 11.—Plan of a part of the city at Tell-el-Amarna ; from Prisse.

situated. All that we know is that the city properly speaking, the Diospolis of the Greeks, so called on account of the great temple of Amen which formed its centre, was on the right bank of the river ; that its houses were massed round those two great sacred inclosures which we now call Karnak and Luxor; that it was intersected by wide streets, those which united Karnak and Luxor to each other and to the river being bordered with sphinxes. These great streets were the δρόμοι of the Greek writers; others they called βασιλική ῥύμη, king's street.[1] The blocks of houses which bordered these great causeways were intersected by narrow lanes.[2] The quarter on the left bank of the river was a sort of

[1] See Brugsch-Bey's topographical sketch of a part of ancient Thebes in the *Revue archéologique* of M. E. REVILLOUT, 1880 (plates 12 and 13).

[2] See, in the *Revue archéologique*, the *Données géographiques et topographiques*

suburb inhabited chiefly by priests, embalmers, and others practising those lugubrious branches of industry which are connected with the burial of the dead.[1] The whole of this western city was known in the time of the Ptolemies and the Romans as the *Memnonia*.[2]

We shall not attempt to discuss the few hints given by the Greek writers as to the extent of Thebes. Even if they were less vague and contradictory than they are, they would tell us little as to the density of the population.[3] Diodorus says that there were once houses of four and five stories high at Thebes, but he did not see them himself, and it is to the time of the fabulous monarch Busiris that he attributes them.[4] In painted representations we never find a house of more than three stories, and they are very rare. As a rule we find a ground-floor, one floor above that, and a covered flat roof on the top.[5]

It does not seem likely that, even in the important streets, the houses of the rich made much architectural show on the outside. Thebes and Memphis probably resembled those modern Oriental towns in which the streets are bordered with massive structures in which hardly any openings beside the doors are to be seen. The houses figured in the bas-reliefs are often surrounded by a crenellated wall, and stand in the middle of a court or garden.[6]

sur Thèbes extraites par MM. Brugsch et Revillout des Contrats démotiques et des Pièces corrélatives, p. 177.

[1] E. REVILLOUT, *Tarichentes et Choachytes* (in the *Zeitschrift für Ægyptische Sprache und Alterthumskunde*, 1879 and 1880).

[2] In the Egyptian language, buildings like the Ramesseum and Medinet-Abou were called Mennou, or buildings designed to preserve some name from oblivion. This word the Greeks turned into μεμνόνια, because they thought that the term mennou was identical with the Homeric hero Memnon, to whom they also attributed the two famous colossi in the plain of Thebes. EBERS, *Ægypten*, p. 280.

[3] DIODORUS (i. 45, 4) talks of a circumference of 140 stades (28,315 yards), without telling us whether his measurement applies to the whole of Thebes, or only to the city on the right bank. STRABO (xvii. 46) says that "an idea of the size of the ancient city may be formed from the fact that its existing monuments cover a space which is not less than 80 stades (16,180 yards) in length (τὸ μῆκος)." This latter statement indicates a circumference much greater than that given by Diodorus. DIODORUS (i. 50, 4) gives to Memphis a circumference of 150 stades (30,337 yards, or 17¼ miles). [4] DIODORUS, i. 45, 5.

[5] In a tale translated by M. MASPERO (*Études Égyptiennes*, 1879, p. 10), a princess is shut up in a house of which the windows are 70 cubits (about 105 feet) above the ground. She is to be given to him who is bold and skilful enough to scale her windows. Such a height must therefore have seemed quite fabulous to the Egyptians, as did that of the tower which is so common in our popular fairy stories.

[6] In M. MASPERO's translated *Roman de Satni* (*Annuaire de l'Association pour*

FIG. 12.—Bird's-eye view of a villa, restored by Ch. Chipiez.

When a man was at all easy in his circumstances he chose for his dwelling a house in which all elegance and artistic elaboration was reserved for himself—a bare wall was turned to the noise of the street. Houses constructed upon such a principle covered, of course, a proportionally large space of ground. The walls of Babylon inclosed fields, gardens, and vineyards ;[1] and it is probable that much of the land embraced by those of Thebes was occupied in similar fashion by those inclosures round the dwellings of the rich, which might be compared to an Anglo-Indian "compound."

The house, of which a restoration appears on page 31 (Fig. 12), a restoration which is based upon the plan found by Rosellini in a Theban tomb (Fig. 3), is generally considered to have been a country villa belonging to the king. We do not concur in that opinion, however. It appears to us quite possible that in the fashionable quarters—if we may use such a phrase—of Memphis and Thebes, the houses of the great may have shewn such combinations of architecture and garden as this. There are trees and creeping plants in front of the house shown in Fig. 1 also. Both are inclosed within a wall pierced by one large door.

Even the houses of the poor seem generally to have had their courtyards, at the back of which a structure was raised consisting of a single story surmounted by a flat roof, to which access was given by an external staircase. This arrangement, which is to be seen in a small model of a house which belongs to the Egyptian collection in the Louvre (Fig. 13), does not differ from that which is still in force in the villages of Egypt.[2]

In the larger houses the chambers were distributed around two or three sides of a court. The building, which has been alluded to as the Palace at Tell-el-Amarna, with many others in the same city (Figs. 14, 15, 16), affords an example of their arrangement. Sometimes, as in another and neighbouring house, the chambers opened upon a long corridor. The offices were upon the ground floor, while the family inhabited the stories above it. The flat top of the house had a parapet round it, and sometimes a light outer

l'Encouragement des Études grecques, 1878), the house in Bubastis inhabited by the daughter of a priest of high rank is thus described : "Satni proceeded towards the west of the town until he came to a very high house. It had a wall round it ; a garden on the north side ; a flight of steps before the door."

[1] QUINTUS CURTIUS, v. 1. 127.
[2] WILKINSON, *The Manners and Customs of the Ancient Egyptians*, vol. i. p. 377.

roof supported by slender columns of brilliantly painted wood. This open story is well shown in Fig. 1 and in a box for holding funerary statuettes, which is in the Louvre. It is reproduced in Fig. 18. Upon that part of the roof which was not covered a kind of screen of planks was fixed, which served to

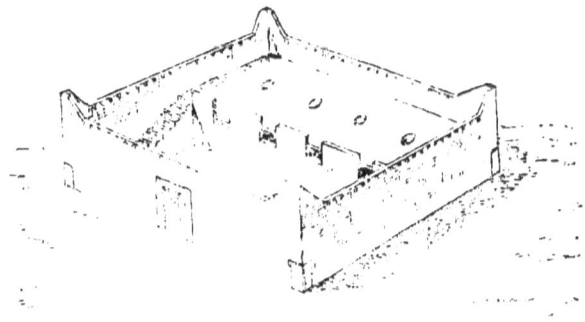

Fig. 13.—Model of an Egyptian house; Louvre.

establish a current of air, and to ventilate the house (Fig. 19). Sometimes one part of a house was higher than the rest, forming a kind of tower (Fig. 20). Finally, some houses were crowned with a parapet finishing at the top in a row of rounded battlements

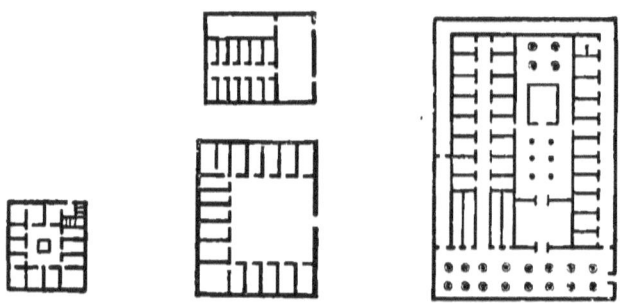

Figs. 14—17.—Plans of houses; from Wilkinson, vol. i. p. 345.

(Fig. 21). In very large houses the entrance to the courtyard was ornamented with a porch supported by two pillars, with lotus flower capitals, to which banners were tied upon *fête* days (Fig. 22). Sometimes the name of the proprietor, sometimes a hospitable sentiment, was inscribed upon the lintel (Fig. 23).

"Egyptian houses were built of crude bricks made of loam mixed with chopped straw. These bricks were usually a foot long and six inches wide. The ceilings of the larger rooms were of indigenous or foreign wood; the smaller rooms were often vaulted.

FIG. 18.—Piece of furniture in the form of a house; Louvre.

"Doors and windows opened generally in the middle. They opened inwards, and were fastened by means of bolts and latches. Some of them had wooden locks like those which are still in use

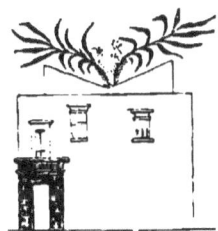 

FIG. 19.—House from a Theban wall painting; from Wilkinson, i. p. 361.

FIG. 20.—House with a tower, from a painting; Wilkinson, i. p. 361.

in Egypt. Most of the inner doors were closed merely by hangings of some light material. For the decoration we must turn to the pictures in the rock-cut tombs. The walls of the houses were coated with stucco, and painted with religious and domestic scenes. The galleries and columns of the porch were coloured in imitation of stone or granite. The ceilings were covered with what we call arabesques and interlacing ornaments of all kinds, while the floors were strewn with mats woven of many-coloured reeds."[1]

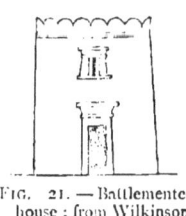 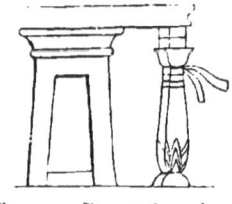 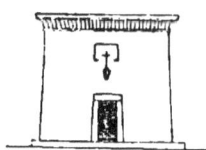

FIG. 21.—Battlemented house; from Wilkinson, i. p. 362. FIG. 22.—Decorated porch; from Wilkinson, i. p. 346. FIG. 23.—House with inscription; from Wilkinson, i. 32.

We shall describe the tasteful and convenient furniture which these rooms contained in our chapter upon the industrial arts.

The flat roof seems to have been universal in Egypt. It added to the accommodation of the house, it afforded a pleasant rendezvous for the family in the evening, where they could enjoy the view and

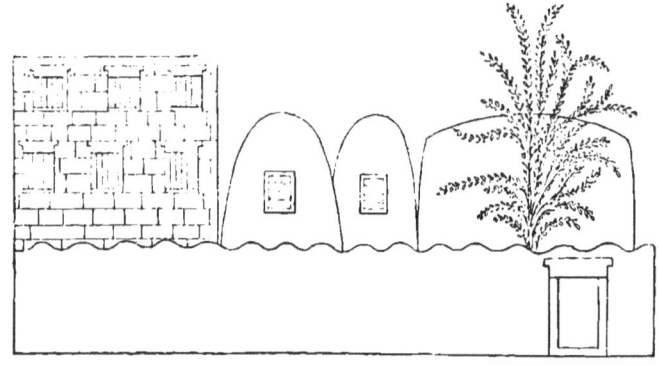

FIG. 24.—House, storehouse, and garden ; from Prisse, p. 218.

the fresh breezes which spring up at sunset. At certain seasons they must have slept there.[2] On the other hand the granaries,

[1] We have borrowed this short description from a Review of M. GAILHABAUD'S *Monuments anciens et modernes, Style Égyptien. Maisons.* Those who require further details may consult Chapter V. of Sir GARDNER WILKINSON'S *Manners and Customs of the Ancient Egyptians.*

[2] HERODOTUS (ii. 95) says that they did so in the marshy parts of Lower Egypt.

barns, and storehouses were almost always dome-shaped (Fig. 24). Those which had flat roofs seem to have been very few indeed. This we see in a painting which seems to represent the process of brewing. The Egyptians were great beer drinkers (Fig. 25).

FIG. 25.—Brewing, Beni-Hassan; from Champollion, pl. 39S.

These brick vaults must have been very thick, and they were well fitted to preserve that equable and comparatively low temperature which is required for the keeping of provisions. The bas-reliefs often show long rows of storehouses one after the other. Their number was no doubt intended to give an idea of their proprietor's

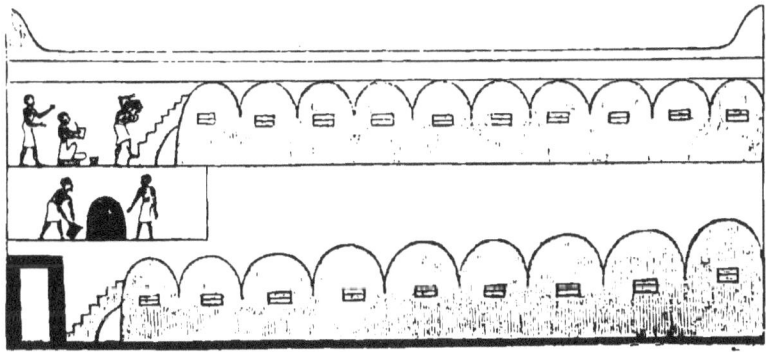

FIG. 26.—Granaries, Beni-Hassan; from Wilkinson.

wealth. Some of them seem to have had their only opening half-way up their sides and to have been reached by an external incline or flight of steps (Fig. 26). A sketch made by M. Bourgoin in a tomb at Sakkarah shows us another form of granary. It (Fig. 27) is shaped like a stone bottle, it has a door at the ground level and a little window higher up.[1]

The Egyptians had country houses as well as those in town, but the structural arrangements were the same in both. The dwelling of the peasant did not differ very greatly from that of the town-bred artisan, while the villas of the wealthy were only distinguished from their houses in the richer quarters of Thebes and

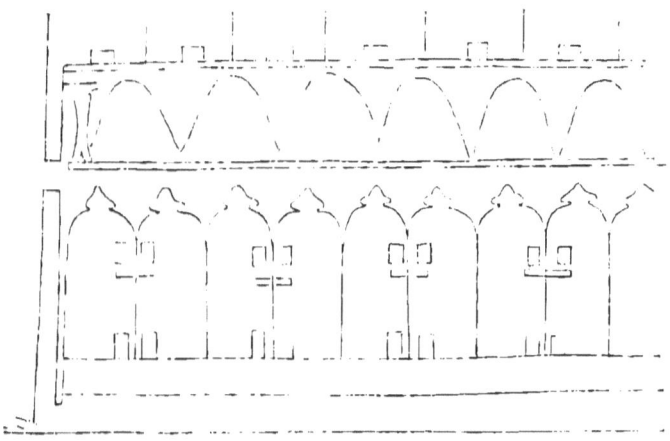

FIG. 27.—Granaries ; Sakkarah.

Memphis by their more abundant provision of shady groves, parks, and artificial lakes. Their paintings prove conclusively that the Egyptians had carried horticulture to a very high pitch ; they even put their more precious trees in pots like those in which we place orange-trees.[2]

§ 4. *Military Architecture.*

The Ancient Egyptians have left us very few works of military architecture, and yet, under their great Theban princes, more than one fortress must have been built outside their own country to preserve their supremacy over neighbouring peoples. In the later periods of the empire fortresses were erected in the Delta

[1] It is difficult to say what the artist meant by the little oblong mark under these windows. Perhaps it represents an outside balcony by which the window could be reached either for the purposes of inspection or in order to add to the store within.

[2] These trees must have been planted in large terra-cotta pots, such as are still used in many places for the same purpose.

and in the upper gorges of the Nile, but, unfortunately such works were always carried out in brick and generally in crude brick. The Egyptian architect had at hand in great abundance the finest materials in the world, except marble, and yet they were used by him exclusively for the tomb and the temple. When it was a question of providing an indestructible dwelling for the dead, and so of perpetuating the efficacy of the funeral prayers and offerings, "eternal stone" was not spared; but when less important purposes had to be fulfilled they were content with clay. Baking bricks was a more rapid process than quarrying and dressing stone, and if the house or fortress in which they were used had comparatively slight durability, it was easy enough to replace it with another.

The crude bricks, dried simply in the sun, became disintegrated with time and fell into powder; the kiln dried bricks were carried off from the ruins of one building to be used in another. The few piers or fragments of wall which remain are confused and shapeless. A few blocks of stone, sometimes even a single chip of marble, is enough to enable us to tell the history of a building which has been long destroyed. Such a chip may be the only surviving fragment of the edifice to which it belonged, but it preserves the impression of the chisel which fashioned it, that is of the taste and individuality of the artist who held the chisel. We have nothing of the kind in the case of a brick. Bricks were almost always covered with a coat of stucco, so that nothing was required of them beyond that they should be of the right size and of a certain hardness. It is only by their inscriptions, when they have them, that the dates of these bricks can be determined; when they are without them they tell us nothing at all about the past. Sometimes a brick structure presents, from a distance, an imposing appearance, and the traveller approaches it thinking that he will soon draw all its secrets from it. But after carefully studying and measuring it he is forced to confess that he has failed. It has no trace of decoration, and it is the decoration of an ancient building which tells us its age, its character, and its purpose. Stone, even when greatly broken, allows mouldings to be traced, but bricks preserve nothing; they are as wanting in individual expression as the pebbles which go to make a shingly beech.

Even if it had come down to us in a less fragmentary condition, the military architecture of Egypt would have been far less interesting than that of Greece. The latter country is mountainous;

the soil is cut up by valleys and rocky hills ; the Greek towns, or, at least, their citadels, occupied the summits of rocky heights which varied greatly in profile and altitude. Hence the military architecture of the country showed great diversity in its combinations. In Egypt the configuration of the soil was not of a nature to provoke any efforts of invention or adaptation. All the cities were in the plain. Fortified posts were distinguished from one another only by the greater or less extent, height, and thickness of their walls. We shall, however, have to call attention to the remains of a few defensive works which, like those established to guard the defiles of the cataracts, were built upon sites different enough from those ordinarily presented by the Nile valley. In these cases we shall find that the Egyptian constructors knew how to adapt their military buildings to the special requirements of the ground.

Egyptian cities seem always to have been surrounded by a fortified *enceinte ;* in some cases the remains of such fortifications have been found, in others history tells us that they existed. At Thebes, for instance, no traces have, so far as we know, been discovered of any wall. Homer's epithet of *hundred-gated* (ἑκατόμπυλος) may be put on one side as evidence, because the Greek poet did not know Egypt. He described the great metropolis of the Empire of the South as he imagined it to be. The Homeric epithet is capable also of another explanation, an explanation which did not escape Diodorus,[1] it may have referred, not to the gates of the city, but to the pylons of the temples, and should in that case be translated as " *Thebes of the hundred pylons* " instead of hundred gates. We have better evidence as to the existence of fortifications about the town in the descriptions left to us by the ancient historians of the siege of Ptolemy Physcon : the city could not have resisted for several years if it had been an open town. It was the same with Memphis. On more than one occasion, during the Pharaonic period as well as after the Persian conquest, it played the part of a fortress of the first class. It was the key of middle Egypt. It even had a kind of citadel which included almost a third of the city and was called the *white wall* (λευκὸν τεῖχος).[2] This name was

---
[1] DIODORUS, i. 45, 6.
[2] THUCYDIDES, i. 104. Cf. HERODOTUS, iii. 94, and DIODORUS, xi. 74. After the Persian conquest it was occupied by the army corps left to ensure the submission of the country.

given, as the scholiast to Thucydides informs us, "because its walls were of white stone, while those of the city itself were of red brick." The exactness of this statement may be doubted. The Egyptians made their defensive walls of a thickness which could only be attained in brick. It seems likely therefore that these walls consisted of a brick core covered with white stone. An examination of the remains of Heliopolis suggested to the authors of the *Description de l'Égypte* that the walls of that city also were cased with dressed stone. They found, even upon the highest part of the walls, pieces of limestone for which they could account in no other way.

Nowhere else is there anything to be discovered beyond the remains of brick walls, which have always been laid out in the form of a parallelogram.[1] These walls are sometimes between sixty and seventy feet thick.[2] In some cases their position is only to be traced by a gentle swelling in the soil; at Saïs, however, they seem to have preserved a height of fifty-seven feet in some parts.[3] No signs of towers or bastions are ever found. At Heliopolis there were gates at certain distances with stone jambs covered with inscriptions.[4] The best preserved of all these *enceintes* is that of the ancient city of Nekheb, the Eilithyia of the Greeks, in the valley of El-Kab. The rectangle is 595 yards long by 516 wide; the walls are 36 feet thick.[5] About a quarter of the whole *enceinte* has been destroyed for the purposes of agriculture; the part which remains contains four large gates, which are not placed in the middle of the faces upon which they open. In all the paintings representing sieges these walls are shown with round-topped battlements, which were easily constructed in brick.

The only fort, properly speaking, which has been discovered in Egypt, appears to be the ruin known as *Chonnet-es-Zezib* at Abydos.[6] This is a rectangular court inclosed by a double wall,

---

[1] Plate 55 of the first volume of Lepsius's *Denkmæler* contains traces of the *enceintes* of Saïs, Heliopolis, and Tanis. See also the *Description de l'Égypte, Ant.,* Ch. 21, 23, 24.

[2] At Heliopolis they were 64 feet thick (*Description*), at Saïs 48 feet (*ibid.*) while at Tanis they were only 19 feet.

[3] ISAMBERT, *Itinéraire de l'Égypte*.   [4] MAXIME DU CAMP, *Le Nil*. p. 64.

[5] LEPSIUS, *Denkmæler*, vol. ii. pl. 100.—EBERS, (*Ægypten,*) makes the *enceinte* of Nekheb a square.

[6] MARIETTE, *Abydos, Description des Fouilles,* vol. ii. pp. 46-49, and plate 68.

and it still exists in a fair state of preservation, to the west of the northern necropolis (Fig. 28). After examining many possible hypotheses, Mariette came to the conclusion that this was a military post intended to watch over the safety of the necropolis, and to keep an eye upon the caravans arriving from the desert. Robber tribes might otherwise be tempted to make use of any moment of confusion for the pillage of the temple. There were

FIG. 28.—Military post at Abydos; perspective from the plans, etc., of Mariette.

curious arrangements for the purpose of guarding against a *coup-de-main*. Within the outer wall, which is provided with small gateways, there is a covered way extending round the whole fort, and commanded by the inner wall. Before the inner court could be reached, an enemy had to traverse a narrow and crooked passage in the thickness of the wall, which was well calculated to secure the necessary time for a moment of preparation in case of surprise (Fig. 29).

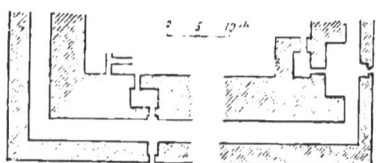

FIG. 29.—Military post. Plan of the entrances; from Mariette.

The most curious relic of the military engineering of the Egyptians is to be found in Nubia. Thirty-seven miles southward of the cataracts of Wadi-Halfah the Nile has worn a channel through a long chain of granite hills which run across the valley from east to west. On each side of the river-bed these hills rise to some height and across its torrent there are a few detached rocks, which once formed a natural dam, but between which

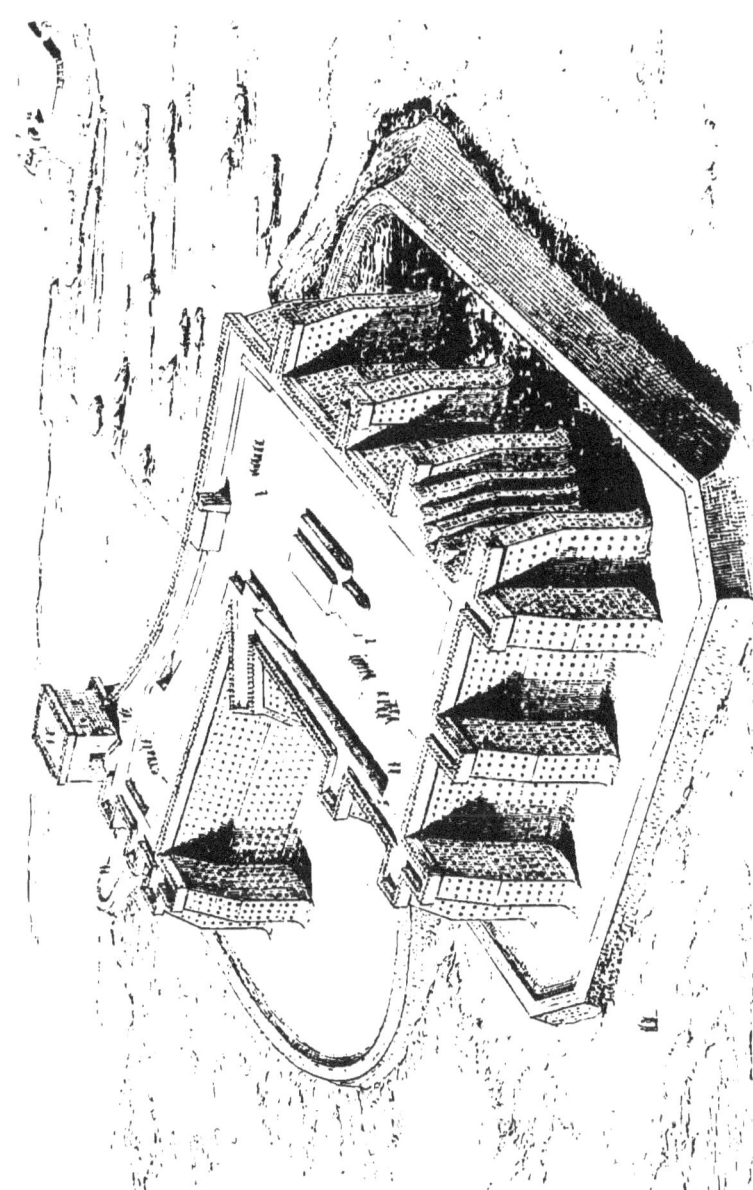

FIG. 30.—Bird's-eye view of the fortress of Scunneh; restored by Charles Chipiez.

the water now rushes impetuously. Navigation is only possible among these rapids during the inundation. This point in the river's course was therefore well fitted to be the gate of Egypt and to be fortified against the incursions of the southern tribes. During the first Theban Empire, the Pharaohs of the twelfth dynasty drew the national frontier at this point, and resolved to establish themselves there in force. The Third Ousourtesen seems to have built the two fortresses of which substantial remains exist even now. Each fortress contained a temple and numerous houses. Lepsius gives the name of *Kummeh* to that on the right bank and reserves the name *Semneh*, which has usually been applied to the whole group, to the building on the left bank only.

For our restoration (Fig. 30) we have had to depend very little upon conjecture.[1] The only flight of fancy in which we have indulged is seen in the extra height which we have given to the tower at the north-eastern angle of the building It seemed to us probable that at some point upon such a lofty terrace there would be a belvedere or watch-tower to facilitate the proper surveillance of the country round about. For the rest we have merely re-established the upper part of the works and restored its depth to the ditch, which had been filled in by the falling of the parapets. The line of walls and bastions can be easily followed except at one point upon the southern face, where a wide breach exists. The destruction of this part of the wall alone and the clearing of the ground upon which it stood, suggests that it was broken down by man rather than by time. It is probable that the fortress was taken by some Ethiopian conqueror, by Sabaco or Tahraka, and that he took care to render its fortifications useless in a way that could not be easily repaired.

Our view of the fort shows it as it must have appeared from a hill in the Libyan Chain, to the south-west. The engineer lavished all his skill on rendering the castle impregnable from

---

[1] We have been able to make use, for this reconstruction, of two plans which only differ in details, and otherwise mutually corroborate each other. One is given by LEPSIUS, Plate 111, vol. ii. of his *Denkmæler*; the plans of the two fortresses are in the middle of his map of the valley where they occur. In plate 112 we have a pictorial view of the ruins and the ground about them. In the *Bulletin archéologique de l'Athenæum Français* (1855, pp. 80-84, and plate 5). M. VOGÜÉ also published a plan of the two forts, accompanied by a section and a description giving valuable details, details which Lepsius, in his *Briefe aus Ægypten*, passed over in silence.

the side of the desert. An attack upon the flank facing the stream was impossible; on that side the walls rested upon precipitous rocks rising sheer from the rapids of the Nile.

The trace of the walls was a polygon not unlike a capital L. The principal arm was perpendicular to the course of the river. Its flat summit (see Fig. 30) was about 250 feet by 190 feet. The interior was reached by a narrow passage in the thickness of the masonry, the entrance to which was reached by an inclined plane. The entrance is not visible in our illustration but the incline which leads to it is shown. The walls on the three sides which looked landwards were from fifty to eighty feet high, according to the ground. They increased in thickness from twenty-six

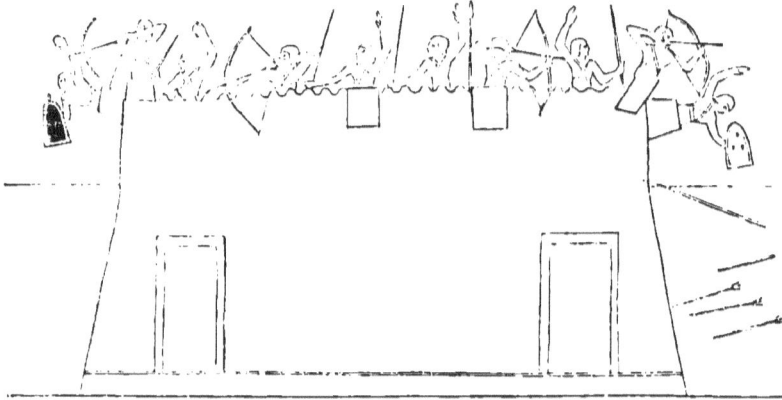

FIG. 31.—A besieged fort, Beni-Hassan; from Champollion, pl. 379.

feet at the base to about twelve or thirteen at the summit. Externally their upper parts fell backwards in such fashion that no ladder, however high, would have availed to reach the parapet. We find a similar arrangement in the walls of a fortress represented at Beni-Hassan (Fig. 31).[1]

The walls of Semneh were strengthened, both structurally and from a military point of view, by salient buttresses or small bastions on all the sides except that which faced the river. These buttresses were either twelve or thirteen in number and from six to eight feet wide at the top. In the re-entering angle

[1] In this case the inclination is, however, in the lower half of the wall; a device which would be far less efficient in defeating an escalade than that at Semneh. - ED.

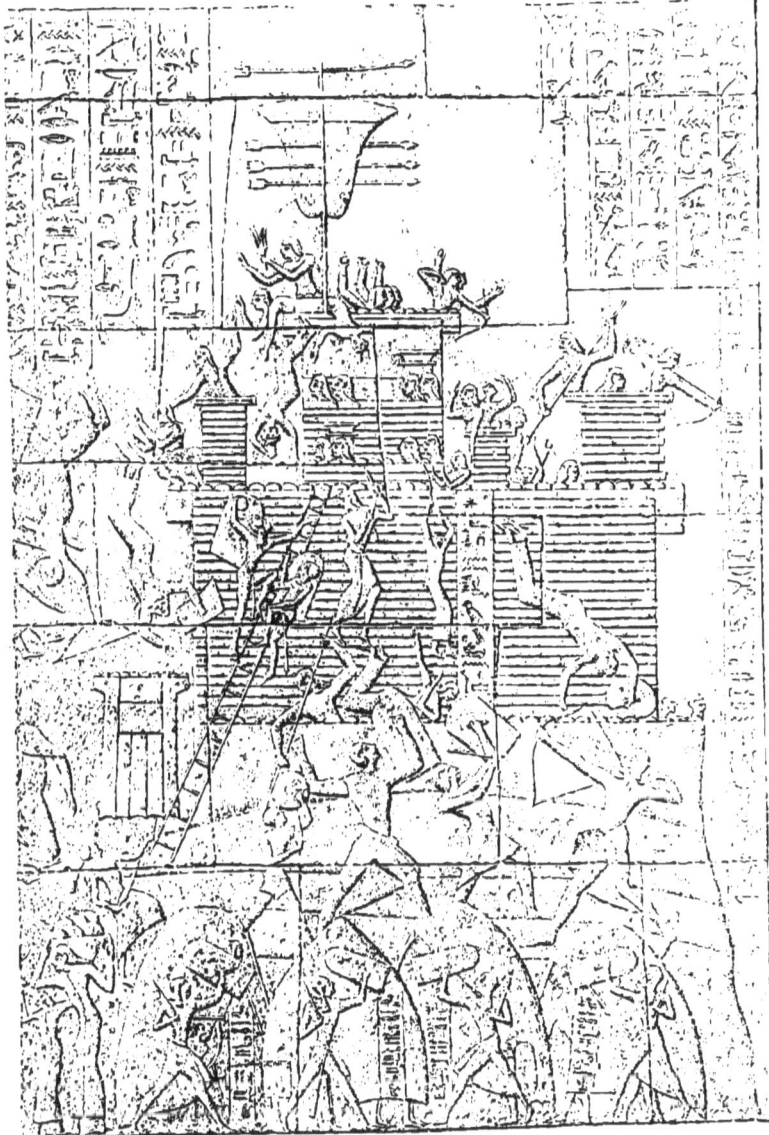

FIG. 32.—Siege of a fortress; from the Ramesseum, Thebes.

which faces north-west there is a long diagonal buttress, by the use of which the engineer or architect at once economized material and protected a weak part of his structure in a most efficient manner. The salient angles of the *enceinte* were protected by double towers, very well disposed so as to command the ditch. A symmetrical regularity is not to be found here any more than in the funerary and religious structures of Egypt. The curtain wall between two of the towers on the southern face is broken up into small buttresses of various degrees of salience, instead of being planned on a straight line like the rest.

When the fortress was prepared for defence the parapets may have been furnished with wooden structures acting as machicolations, whence the besieged could cast javelins and stones and shoot arrows at an enemy attempting to scale or batter the walls. A bas-relief at Thebes which represents the siege of a fortress seems to indicate that the parapets were crowned by wooden erections of some kind (Fig. 32).[1]

The walls were surrounded by a ditch, which was from 95 to 125 feet wide. We cannot now tell what its depth may have been, but it appears to have been paved. The counterscarp and certain parts of the scarp were faced with stone, carefully polished, and fixed so as to augment the difficulty of approach. Moreover, the crown of the glacis and the wide glacis itself were also reveted with stone. All this formed a first line of defence, which had to be destroyed before the assailants could reach the place itself with their machines. The external line of the ditch does not follow all the irregularities of the *enceinte*, its trace is the same as that of the curtain wall, exclusive of the towers or buttresses. The clear width from the face of the latter is about sixty-four feet. Neither ditch nor glacis exist on the eastern face, where the rapids of the Nile render them unnecessary.

We must not forget to draw attention to the curious way in which the body of the fort is constructed. It is composed of crude bricks transfixed horizontally, and at rather narrow intervals, by pieces of wood. The situation of these beams may be easily recognized as they have decayed and left channels in the brickwork. That the holes with which the walls are pierced at regular distances (see Fig. 30) were thus caused, is beyond doubt, especially

[1] Both the plate in the *Description de l'Égypte* (*Ant.* vol. ii. pl. 31), and that in LEPSIUS (part iii. pl. 166), suggest this interpretation.

since a few fragments of wood which the centuries have spared have been found. These fragments have been recognized as having come from the *doum* palm, which is very common in Upper Egypt, and commoner still in Nubia.

We need not dwell upon the other fortress—that on the right bank. It may be seen in the distance in our restoration of Semneh. Being built upon rocks which were on all sides difficult of access, it did not require any very elaborate works. It was composed of an *enceinte* inclosing an irregular square about 190 feet each way. It had but a few salient buttresses; there were only two on the north east, towards the mountains, and one, a very bold one, on the south-west, commanding the river. There was no room for a wide ditch. But at a distance of thirteen feet from the walls there was a glacis similar to that at Semneh. It had the same casing of polished stone, but on account of the irregularities of the rock, the height of its crown varied considerably, and its slope was very steep, almost vertical. The trace of the counterscarp followed that of the *enceinte*, including the buttresses. Moreover, at its northern and southern angles it followed a line which roughly resembled the bastions of a modern fortification. Its structure was similar to that of Semneh.

Lepsius does not hesitate to ascribe both these forts to Ousourtesen III., whose name appears upon all the neighbouring rocks, and who, with the deities of the south, was worshipped at Semneh.[1] They would thus date back, according to the chronology which is now generally adopted, to the twenty-seventh or twenty-eighth century B.C. In any case they cannot be later than the time of Thothmes III., who, in the course of the seventeenth century B.C. restored the temples which they inclose, and covered their walls with his effigies and royal cartouches. Even if we admit that these two castles are not older than the last-named epoch, we shall still have to give to Egypt the credit of possessing the oldest examples of military architecture, as well as the oldest temples and the oldest tombs.

[1] LEPSIUS, *Briefe aus Ægypten*, p. 259.—See also MASPERO, *Histoire Ancienne*, pp. 111-113.

CHAPTER II.

METHODS OF CONSTRUCTION, THE ORDERS, SECONDARY FORMS.

§ 1. *An Analysis of Architectural Forms necessary.*

WE have now described the tomb, the temple, and the house in ancient Egypt. We have attempted to define the character of their architecture, and to show how its forms were determined by the religious beliefs, social condition, and manners of the nation, as well as by the climate of the country. We have therefore passed in review the most important architectural creations of a people who were the first to display a real taste and feeling for art.

In order to give a complete idea of Egyptian art, and of the resources at its disposal, we must now take these buildings to pieces and show the elements of which they were composed. The rich variety of supports, the numerous " orders " of pillar and column, the methods employed for decoration and illumination, must each be studied separately. We have commenced by looking at them from a synthetic point of view, but we must finish by a methodical analysis. From such an analysis alone can we obtain the necessary materials for an exhaustive comparison between the art of Egypt and that of the nations which succeeded her upon the stage of history. An examination of the Egyptian remains carries the historian back to a more remote date than can be attained in the case of any other country, and yet he is far from reaching the first springs of Egyptian civilization. Notwithstanding their prodigious antiquity, the most ancient of the monuments that have survived carry us back into the bosom of a society which had long emerged from primitive barbarism. The centuries which saw the building of the Pyramids and the mastabas of the Memphite necropolis had behind them a long and well-filled past. Although we possess no relic from that past, we can divine its character to some extent from the impression which it made upon the taste and fancy of latter ages. Certain effects of which the artists of Memphis were very fond can only be explained by habits contracted during a long course of centuries. In the forms and motives employed by Egyptian architects we shall find more than one example of these survivals from a previous stage of development, such as forms appropriate to wood or metal employed in stone, and childish methods of construction perpetuated without other apparent cause.

§ 2. *Materials.*

In our explanation of the general character of Egyptian architecture we have already enumerated the principal materials of which it disposed, and pointed out the modifications arising from the choice of one or another of those materials. We should not here return to the subject but for a misconception which has gained a wide acceptance.

People have seen a few granite obelisks standing in two or three of the European capitals, and they have too often jumped to the conclusion that the Egyptians built almost exclusively in granite. The fact is that there is but one building in Egypt the body of which is of granite, and that is the ancient temple at Gizeh which is called the *Temple of the Sphinx* (Figs. 202 and 203, vol. i.). Even there the roof and the casing of the walls was of alabaster. Granite was employed, as a rule, only where a very choice and expensive material was required. It was brought into play when certain parts of a building had to be endowed with more nobility and beauty than the rest. Thus there are, in the great temple at Karnak, a few small rooms, called *The Granite Chambers* (Fig. 215, H, vol. i.), in which the material in question has alone been employed. Elsewhere in the same building it was only used incidentally. In the pyramid of Cheops the lining of the Grand Gallery is of granite.[1] In many of the Theban temples it was employed for the bases of columns, thresholds, jambs, and lintels of doors. It was also used for isolated objects, such as

[1] It is of Mokattam limestone (see vol. i., p. 223). M. Perrot probably meant to refer to the two upper "chambers," both of which are lined with granite.—ED.

tabernacles, monolithic statues, obelisks, and sarcophagi. The enormous quantity of granite which Egypt drew, from first to last, from the quarries at Syene, was mostly for the sculptor. The dressed materials of the architect came chiefly from the limestone and sandstone quarries. Sometimes we find a building entirely constructed of one or the other, sometimes they are employed side by side. "The great temple at Abydos is built partly of limestone, very fine in the grain and admirably adapted for sculpture, and partly of sandstone. The sandstone has been used for columns, architraves, and the frames of doors, and limestone for the rest."[1]

Bricks were employed to a vast extent by the Egyptians. They made them of Nile mud mixed with chopped straw, a combination which is mentioned in the Biblical account of the hardships inflicted upon the Israelites. "And Pharaoh commanded the same day the taskmasters of the people and their officers, saying, Ye shall no more give the people straw to make brick as heretofore: let them go and gather straw for themselves. And the tale of the bricks which they did make heretofore ye shall lay upon them; ye shall not diminish aught thereof, for they be idle."[2]

This manufacture was remarkable for its extreme rapidity—an excellent brick earth was to be found at almost any point in the Nile valley. An unpractised labourer can easily make a thousand bricks a day; after a week's practice he can make twelve hundred, and, if paid "by the piece" as many as eighteen hundred a day.[3] Sometimes drying in the sun was thought sufficient; the result was a crude brick which was endowed with no little power of resistance and endurance in such a climate as that of Egypt. When baked bricks were required the operation was a little complicated as they each had to pass through the kiln. Egyptian bricks were usually very large. Those of a pyramid in the neighbourhood of Memphis average 15 inches long by 7 wide

---

[1] MARIETTE, *Voyage dans la Haute-Égypte*. vol. i. p. 59.
[2] *Exodus* v. 6-8.
[3] MARIETTE, *Traité pratique et raisonné de la Construction en Égypte*. p. 59. All these operations are shown upon the walls of a tomb at Abd-el-Gournah (LEPSIUS, *Denkmæler*, p. 111, pl. 40). Labourers are seen drawing water from a basin, digging the earth, carrying it in large jars, mixing it with the water, pressing the clay into the moulds, finally building walls which are being tested with a plumb-line by an overseer or foreman (see also Fig. 16).

and 4¾ inches thick.[1] After the commencement of the Theban epoch they were often stamped with the royal oval—as the Roman bricks had the names of the consuls impressed upon them—and thus they have preserved the dates at which the buildings of which they form part were erected (Fig. 33).[2]

We see, then, that the Egyptians had no lack of excellent building materials of a lapidary kind. On the other hand, they were very poorly provided with good timber. Before the conquest of Syria they must have been almost entirely confined to their indigenous woods. The best of these were the *Acacia nilotica*, or gum acacia, and the *Acacia lebbak*, but neither of these trees furnished beams of any size. Sycamore wood was too soft; its root alone being hard enough for use.[3] And yet in default of better wood it was sometimes employed. The same may be said of the date palm, whose trunk furnished posts and rafters, and, at times, very poor flooring planks. During the hey-day of Theban supremacy, the timber for such buildings as the pavilion at Medinet-Abou must have been brought from Syria at great cost. The Theban princes, like those of Nineveh in later times, no doubt caused the Phœnicians, who were their vassals, to thin the cedar forests of Lebanon for their benefit. In structures of less importance carpenters and joiners had to do as best they could with the timber furnished by their own country. The difficulty which they experienced in procuring good planks explains to some extent the care which they lavished upon their woodwork. They contrived, by an elaborate system of "parquetting," of combining upright and horizontal strips with ornamental members, to avoid the waste of even the smallest piece of material. In some ways this work resembles the ceilings, doorways, and panels of a

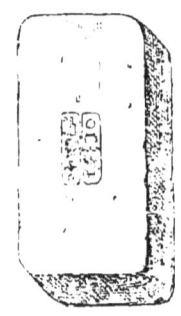

FIG. 33.—Brick stamped with the royal ovals; from Prisse.

---

[1] PRISSE, *Histoire de l'Art Égyptien*, letter-press, p. 179.
[2] LEPSIUS (*Denkmæler*, part iii. plates 7, 25A, 26, 39) has reproduced a certain number of these stamped bricks.
[3] We do not here refer to the kind of maple which is often erroneously called a sycamore with us, but to a tree of quite a different family and appearance, the *Ficus Sycomorus* of Linnæus.

modern Arab house, of the *moucharabichs* of Cairo. The principle is the same in both cases, although the decorative lines are somewhat different; similar necessities have suggested the employment of similar processes.[1]

§ 3. *Construction.*

In spite of the bad quality of Egyptian timber the earliest efforts at construction made by the ancestors of the people were made in wood. Their dwellings cannot have been very unlike those which the traveller even yet encounters in Nubia. These are cabins with walls formed of palm branches interlaced and plastered over with clay and straw. Their roofs are branches or planks from the same tree laid horizontally across. In Lower Egypt, upon the borders of Lake Menzaleh, the huts of the people are formed of long and thick faggots of reeds. Wherever wood was abundant and the rain less to be feared than the heat of the sun, the first dwelling was a hut of branches. The manufacture of bricks required a good deal more patience, calculation, and effort, than to plant a few boughs in the soil and weave them together.

We do not mean to pretend that earth, either in the form of bricks or pisé, did not very soon come into use when men began to form shelters for themselves, but it seems certain that wooden construction was developed before any other. It was the first to aim at ornament, and to show anything which could be called a style. This is proved by the fact that the most ancient works in stone have no appropriate character of their own; they owe such decorative qualities as they possess to their docile imitation of works in the less durable material.

We may take the sarcophagus of Mycerinus as an example of this. That sarcophagus had a short but adventurous career after its discovery by Colonel Howard Vyse in 1837. It was then empty, but in a state of perfect preservation, with the exception of the lid, which was broken, but could be easily restored. The precious relic was removed from the pyramid and embarked, together with the wooden coffin of the king, on board a merchant ship at Alexandria. On her voyage to England the ship was

[1] ED. MARIETTE, *Traité Pratique*, etc., p. 95.

wrecked off Carthagena, and the sarcophagus lost. The coffin floated and was saved. Happily the sarcophagus had been accurately drawn, and we are enabled to give a perspective view of it compiled from Perring's elevations (Fig. 34).

From its appearance no one would guess that this sarcophagus was of basalt. The whole of its forms were appropriate to wooden construction alone. Each of its longer sides was divided into three compartments by four groups of minute pilasters, slight in salience, and crowned by a kind of entablature formed of four transverse members which were unequal in length and relief. The lower parts of the three compartments consist of a kind of false door with very complicated jambs. Above this there are deeply cut hollows with cross bars, suggesting windows, and still higher a number of fillets run along the whole length of the sarcophagus. The little pilasters are separated by narrow panels, which terminate in an ornament which could readily be cut in wood by the chisel, viz., in that double lotus-leaf which is so universally present in the more ancient tombs.

The ends of the sarcophagus were similar to the sides, except that they had only one compartment. The corners and the upper edge, exclusive of the lid, are carved into a cylindrical moulding which resembles the rounded and tied angles of a wooden case. The upper member of the whole, a bold cornice, is the only element which it is not easy to refer to the traditions of wooden construction.[1]

The first idea suggested by the design of this sarcophagus is that of a large wooden coffer. When we come to look at it a little more closely, however, the imitations of doors and windows and other details incline us to believe that its maker was thinking of reproducing the accustomed aspect of a wooden house. In that case we should have in it a reduction of a building belonging to the closed category of *assembled* constructions. It is by the

---

[1] In his *Histoire de l'Habitation*, VIOLLET-LE-DUC has sought to find the origin of this cornice in an outward curve imparted to the upper extremity of the reeds of which primitive dwellings were made, and maintained by the weight of the roof. He published a drawing in justification of his hypothesis. There are, however, many objections to it. It requires us to admit the general use of the reed as the material for primitive dwellings. Branches which were ever so little rigid and firm could not have been so bent, and yet they are often found in the huts to which we refer. It may even be doubted whether the reeds employed would bear such a curvature as that of the Egyptian cornice without breaking.

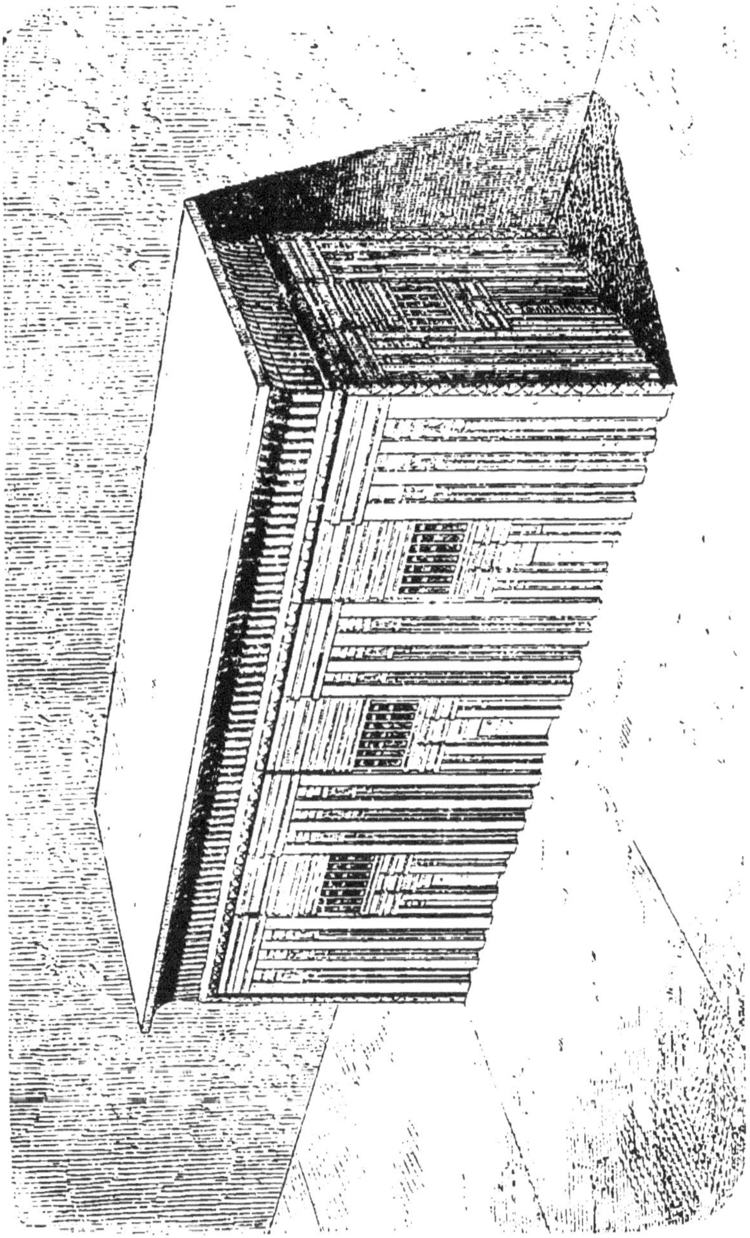

FIG. 34.—The Sarcophagus of Mycerinus. Drawn in perspective from Perring's elevations.

VOL. II.

study of imitative works of this kind and by comparing with one another the forms originally conceived by carpenters and joiners, and afterwards employed in stone architecture, that, in our chapter upon the general principles of Egyptian construction, we were enabled to attempt a restoration which may be taken as a type of the early wooden architecture (Fig. 83, vol. i.).

The foregoing observations may be applied with equal justice to the sarcophagus of Khoo-foo-Ankh figured on pp. 183, 184, vol. i. It is of the same period, and displays the same arrangement of panels and fillets, the same lotus-leaf ornament, and the same imitation of a barred window. There is no cornice or gorge at the top, but the upper part of the flat sides is decorated with the perpendicular grooves which are found in the hollow of the cornice elsewhere. In wood this ornament, which was well adapted to add richness to the cornice by the shadows which it cast, could easily be made with a gouge; so that even if the gorge itself was not borrowed from wooden construction its ornamentation may well have originated in that way.

If still further proofs be required of the imitative character of this early stone architecture, we shall find them in the door of a tomb (Fig. 35). Nothing can be clearer than the way in which the lintel obtained its peculiar character. It is formed of a thick slab engaged at each end in the upright beams of stone which form the jambs. This slab appears beyond the jambs, and ends in a deep groove, which divides them from the walls. Underneath the lintel, and well within the shadow which it casts, there is another and more curious slab; it is, in shape, a thick cylinder, corresponding in length to the width of the door. In the deep groove already mentioned the ends of the spindles or trunnions upon which it is supported are suggested. They are not, indeed, in their right places: they are too near the face of the building. The workman would have had to make the groove very deep in order to show them in their proper places, and he was therefore content to hint at them with sufficient clearness to enable those who saw them to understand what they meant.

We have none of the wooden models under our eyes which were familiar to the stonemason who carved these doors, but yet we can easily see the origin of the forms we have just described. The cylinder was a circular beam of acacia or palm, upon which a mat or strip of cloth of some kind was nailed. By means of coils in the groove at the side the cylinder could be made to revolve, and the curtain would thus be easily drawn up and down. These curious forms are thus at once accounted for if we refer them to the wooden structures which were once plentiful but have now disappeared. Nothing could be more difficult than to find an explanation of them in forms appropriate to stone or granite. Of what use could such a cylinder be if carried out in either of those

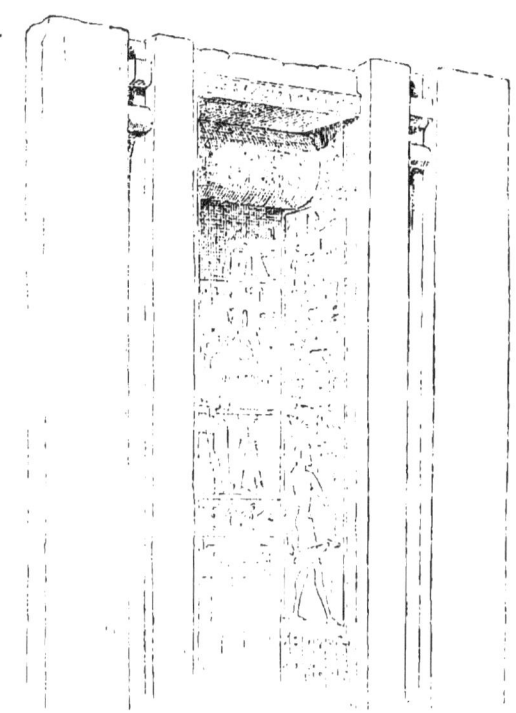

FIG. 35.—Door of a tomb at Sakkarah ; drawn by Bourgoin.

materials? It could not revolve, and the deep lateral grooves, which have such an obvious use in a wooden building, would be purposeless.

We find these features repeated in a rectangular stele from the fourth dynasty, which we reproduce on page 61. In Fig. 37 we give some of its details upon a larger scale. The upper part of this stele displays two motives which will be recognised at the first glance as borrowed from carpentry. The first of these is the row of hexagonal studs, which forms a kind of frieze above the pilasters. In the wooden original they must have been formed of six small pieces of wood fixed around a hexagonal centre. Oriental cabinetmakers to this day ornament ceilings and wainscots in the same fashion. Something like them is certain to have

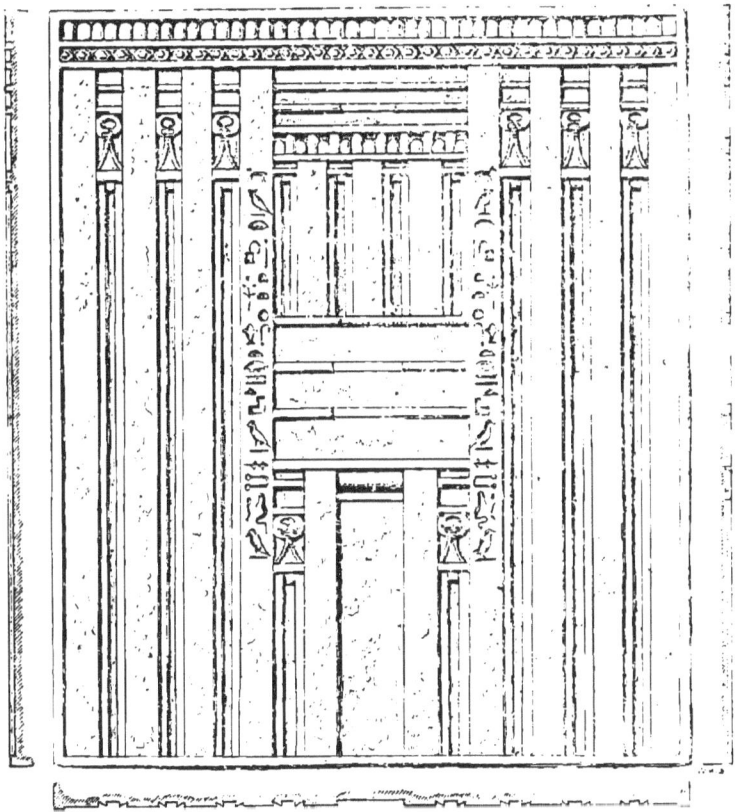

FIG. 36.—Stele from the 4th dynasty; drawn by Bourgoin.

existed in that *okel*, whose delicately ornamented walls were so greatly admired by the visitors to the Exhibition of 1867. The same may be said of the row of billets which forms the upper member of the frieze, to which something of an ovoid form has been given by rounding their upper extremities. The same source of inspiration is betrayed by other details of this monument, which has been treated by time with extraordinary tenderness.

Tombs have been found at Gizeh and Sakkarah, which are referred to the second and third dynasties. The king Persen, whose name occurs in some of the inscriptions upon these tombs, belongs to that remote period. In many of these tombs the ceiling is carved to represent trunks of palm-trees; even the roughnesses of the bark being reproduced. Most of the sepulchres in which these details have been noticed are subterranean, but they are also to be discovered in a chamber in the tomb of Ti. It is probable that if more mastabas had come down to us

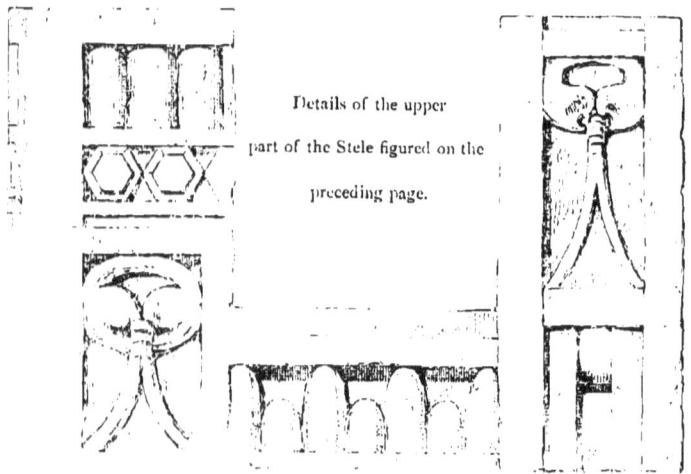

Fig. 37.—Stele from the 4th dynasty; drawn by Bourgoin.

with their roofs intact we should find many instances of this kind of decoration.[1]

Our Figures 38 and 39 are taken from another tomb, and show varieties of that ornament which is universally employed as a finial to the panels we have mentioned. In its most careful form it consists of two petals united by a band, which allows the deep slit characteristic of the leaves of all aquatic plants to be clearly visible.

[1] This imitation of wooden roofs was noticed by the *savants* of the *Institut d'Égypte*. They drew a rock-cut tomb in which the ceiling is carved to look like the trunks of palm trees (*Description, Antiquités*, vol. v. pl. 6, figs. 3, 4, and 5). See also BAEDEKER, part i. p. 360.

CONSTRUCTION. 63

This motive seems to have had peculiar value in the eyes of the Egyptians. It is also found in the tombs at Thebes, and its persistence may, perhaps, be accounted for by the association of the lotus with ideas of a new birth and resurrection.[1] Under the Rameses and their successors it was, with the exception of the vertical and horizontal grooves (Fig. 201, vol. i.), the only reminiscence of wooden construction preserved by stone architecture. In the doors of the rock-cut tombs at Thebes no trace of the circular beam, nor of any other characteristic of the joiner-inspired stone-carving of early times, is to be found. The

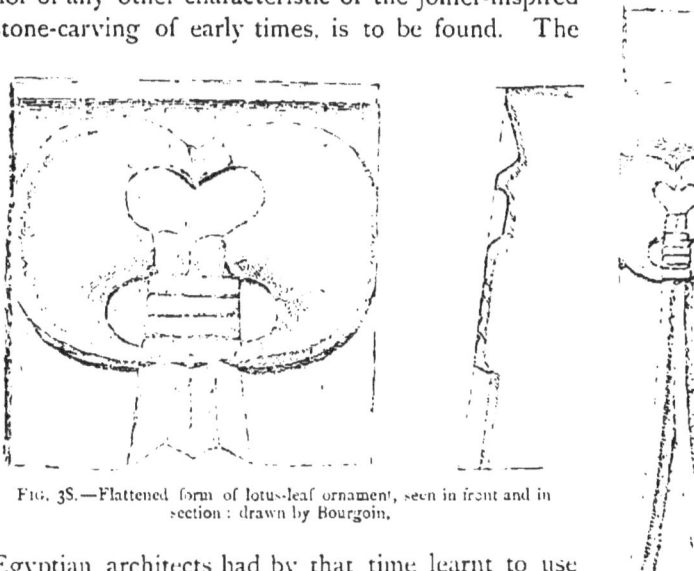

FIG. 38.—Flattened form of lotus-leaf ornament, seen in front and in section: drawn by Bourgoin.

FIG. 39.—Lotus-leaf ornament in its elongated form: drawn by Bourgoin.

Egyptian architects had by that time learnt to use stone and granite in a fashion suggested by their own capabilities. We see, however, by the representations preserved for us by the bas-reliefs, that wooden construction maintained the character which belonged to it during the first days of the Ancient Empire (Fig. 40).

We know from the pyramids, from the temple of the sphinx, and from some of the mastabas, that the Egyptian workmen were thoroughly efficient in the cutting and dressing of stone, even in the time of the first monarchs. However far we go back in the history of Egypt we find no trace of any method of construction

[1] PIERRET, *Dictionnaire d'Archéologie Égyptienne.*

corresponding to that which is called Cyclopean in the case of the Greeks. We find no walls built like those of Tiryns, with huge and shapeless masses of rock, the interstices being filled in with small stones. We do not even find polygonal masonry—by which we mean walls formed of stone dressed with the chisel, but with irregular joints, and with stones of very different size and shape placed in juxtaposition with one another. In the ancient citadels of Greece and Italy this kind of construction is to be found in every variety, but in Egypt the stones are always arranged into horizontal courses. Here and there the vertical joints are not quite vertical, and sometimes we find stones which rise higher, or sink lower, than the course to which they belong, tying it to the one above it or below it. Such accidents as these do not, however, affect the general rule, which was to keep each course self-contained and parallel with the soil. All these varieties in Egyptian masonry may be seen in a horizontal section of the first pylon at Karnak (Fig. 41). This pylon is in such a ruined state that by means of photographs taken from different sides we can form a very exact idea of its internal composition.[1]

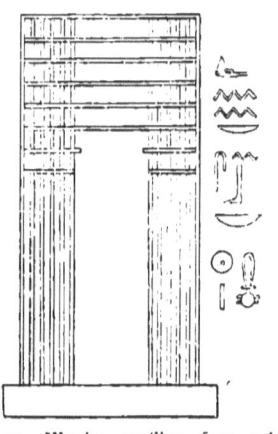

Fig. 40.—Wooden pavilion, from a bas-relief at Luxor (Champollion, pl. 339).

Great care in execution, and great size in the units of construction, are only to be found in comparatively few of the Egyptian monuments. We have already remarked upon the painstaking skill with which the granite or limestone casing of the chambers and passages in the Gizeh pyramids was fixed. Certain buildings of the Theban period, such as the vaulted chapels in the Great Temple at Abydos, and the courts of Medinet-Abou, are notable for excellence of a similar kind. Everything, however, must in this respect give way to the Grand Gallery in the pyramid of Cheops.

The Egypt of the early Pharaohs set more than one good

[1] This pylon dates from the Ptolemies, but if there was anything that did not change in Egypt, it was their processes of construction.

example which later generations failed to follow. The extraordinary number of buildings which the great Theban princes carried on at one and the same time, from the depths of Nubia to the shores of the Mediterranean, made their subjects more easily satisfied in the matter of architectural thoroughness. The habit of covering every plain surface with a brilliant polychromatic decoration contributed to the same result. The workmen were always hurried. There were hardly hands enough for all the undertakings on foot at once. How, then, could they be expected to lavish minute care upon joints which were destined to be hidden behind a coat of stucco? We never encounter in Egyptian buildings any of those graceful varieties of masonry which have been adopted from time to time by all those artistic nations that have left their stonework bare. None of the various kinds of rustication, none of the alternation of square with oblong blocks none of that undeviating regularity in the height of the courses and in the direction of the joints which by itself is enough to give beauty to a building, is to be found in the work of Egyptian masons.[1]

It was for similar motives that the Egyptians did not, as a rule, care to use very large stones. Their obelisks and colossal statues prove that they knew how to quarry and raise blocks of enormous size, but they never made those efforts except when they had good reason to do so. They did not care to exhaust themselves with dragging huge stones up on to their buildings, where they would ever after be lost to sight under the stucco. In the most carefully built Theban edifices the average size of the stones hardly exceeds that of the materials which are used by our modern architects. A single course was from 30 to 38 inches high, and the length of the blocks varied between 5 feet and rather more than 8. In the great pylon of Karnak the lintel over the doorway is a stone beam more than 25 feet long. In the hypostyle hall the architraves of the central aisle

[1] This has been well shown by Champollion à propos of one of the Nubian buildings constructed by the Theban kings. He speaks thus of the *hemispeos* of Wadi-Esseboua: "This is the worst piece of work extant from the reign of Rameses the Great. The stones are ill-cut; their intervals are masked by a layer of cement over which the sculptured decoration, which is poorly executed, is continued. . . . Most of this decoration is now incomprehensible because the cement upon which a great part of it was carried out, has fallen down and left many and large gaps in the scenes and inscriptions."—*Lettres d'Égypte et de Nubie*, 121.

are at least 29 feet long.¹ It is said that some attain a length of nearly 32 feet.

The Egyptian architect was therefore quite ready to use monoliths of exceptional size for the covering of voids when they were necessary, but he did not wantonly create that necessity, as those of other nations have often done. Most of the travellers who visit Egypt expect to find huge monolithic shafts rearing their lofty heads on every side, and their surprise is great when they are told that the huge columns of the hypostyle halls are not cut from single blocks. Their first illusion is fostered by the large number of monolithic granite columns which are found at Erment at Antinoé, at Cairo, in most of the modern Egyptian mosques. When they arrive at Thebes they discover their error. At Karnak and at Luxor, at Medinet-Abou and in the Ramesseum, the columns are made up of drums placed one upon another. In many cases even these drums are not monolithic, but consist of several different stones. Under the Roman domination the Egyptians deliberately chose to make their columns of single stones, and most of those which are of exceptional size date from that late epoch. We know but one case to which these remarks do not apply; we mean that of the monolithic supports in the chambers of the labyrinth which were mentioned by Strabo, and discovered, as some believe, by Lepsius.² We are told by that traveller that they were of granite, but he only saw them when broken. Strabo says that the chambers were roofed in with slabs of such a size that they amazed every one who saw them, and added much to the effect which that famous structure was otherwise calculated to produce. Prisse describes and figures a column of red granite which he ascribes to Amenophis III., and which, according to him, was brought from Memphis to Cairo. Without the base which, as given in his drawing, must be a restoration, it is 13 feet 8½ inches high, including the capital.³ It belongs to the same kind of pillar as those observed by Lepsius in the Fayoum. In a painting in one of the Gournah tombs, three workmen are shown polishing a column exactly similar to that figured by Prisse, with the single exception that its proportions are more slender (Fig. 42). Monolithic columns of red granite have been discovered to the

---

¹ *Description de l'Égypte, Antiquités*, vol. ii. p. 437.
² STRABO, xvii. 37.— LEPSIUS, *Briefe aus Ægypten*, p. 74.
³ PRISSE, *Histoire de l'Art Égyptien*, text, p. 364.

FIG. 41.—Horizontal section, in perspective, of the first pylon at Karnak ; by Charles Chipiez.

west of the present city of Alexandria which are nearly 22 feet high. Their capitals are imitated from truncated lotus-buds, like that in Fig. 42.

It would seem, then, that monolithic columns were in fashion during the early centuries of the second Theban empire, but that, in later times, the general custom was to build up columns, sometimes for their whole height, of moderately sized, and sometimes of very small stones (Fig. 17).[1]

To all that concerns the quality of the building similar remarks may be applied. We have mentioned a few examples of careful and scientific construction, but, as a rule, Egyptian buildings were put together in a fashion that was careless in the extreme.[2] The foundations were neither wide enough nor deep enough. It is not

FIG. 42.—Workmen polishing a monolithic column; Champollion, pl. 161.

until we come to the remains of the Ptolemaic period, such as the temples at Edfou and Denderah, that we discover foundations sinking 16 or 18 feet into the ground. The Pharaonic temples were laid upon the surface rather than solidly rooted in the soil. Mariette attributes the destruction which has overtaken the temples at Karnak less to the violence of man or to earthquakes than to inherent faults of construction, and to the want

---

[1] The columns at Luxor are constructed in courses. The joints of the stone are worked carefully for only about a third of their whole diameter. Their centres are slightly hollowed out and filled in with a mortar of pounded brick which has become friable. (*Description de l'Égypte, Antiquités*, vol. ii. p. 384.)

[2] See p. 29, vol. i. (Note 1) and p. 170. The engineers who edited the *Description* make similar remarks with regard to Karnak. (*Antiquités*, vol. ii. pp. 414 and 500.)

of foresight shown by their architects in not placing them at a sufficient elevation above the inundations. For many centuries the waters of the Nile have reached the walls of the temples by infiltration, and have gradually eaten away the sandstone of which they are composed. "Similar causes produce similar effects, and the time may be easily foreseen when the superb hypostyle hall will yield to the attacks of its enemy, and its columns, already eaten through for three quarters of their thickness, will fall as those of the western court have fallen." [1]

At the time when Karnak was built there were in the country buildings which were from ten to fifteen centuries old, to which the architects of the time might have turned for information upon doubtful points. In them the gradual rising of the valley level must have been clearly shown. This want of foresight need cause us, however, no great surprise; but it is otherwise with the carelessness of the architects in arranging their plans, and in failing to compel the workmen to follow those plans when made. "Except in a few rare instances," says Mariette, "the Egyptian workman was far from deserving the reputation he has gained for precision and care in the execution of his task. Only those who have personally measured the tombs and temples of Egypt know how often, for instance, the opposite walls of a single chamber are unequal in height." [2]

The custom of building as fast as possible and trusting to the painted decoration for the concealment of all defects, explains the method most usually taken to keep the materials together. The system of using large dressed stones made the employment of mortar unnecessary. The Greeks, who used the same method and obtained from it such supreme effects, put no mortar between their stones. Sometimes they were held together by tenons of metal or wood, but the builder depended for cohesion chiefly upon the way in which his materials were dressed and fixed. The two surfaces were so intimately allied that the points of junction were almost invisible. The Egyptians were in like manner able to depend upon the *vis inertiæ* of their materials for the stability of their walls, and their climate was far better fitted even than that of Greece for the employment of those wooden or metal

---

[1] MARIETTE, *Itinéraire*, p. 179. The pavement of the great temple is now about six feet below the general level of the surrounding plain.
[2] MARIETTE, *Les Tombes de l'Ancien Empire*, p. 10.

tenons which would prevent any slipping or settlement in the interior of the masonry. The dangers attending such methods of fixing would thus be reduced to a minimum. "In consequence of a dislocation in the walls caused by the insufficiency of the foundations, it is possible, at several points of the temple walls at Abydos, to introduce the arm between the stones and feel the sycamore dovetails still in place and in an extraordinary state of preservation. A few of these dovetails have been extracted, and, although walled in for eternity so far as the intentions of the Egyptians were concerned, they bear the royal ovals of Seti I., the founder of the temple, the hieroglyphs being very finely engraved."[1]

We see, then, that in many buildings the Egyptians employed methods which demanded no little patience, skill, and attention from the workman, but as a rule they preferred to work in a more expeditious and less careful fashion. They used a cement made of sand and lime; traces of it are everywhere found, both in the ruins of Thebes and in the pyramids, between the blocks of limestone and sandstone.[2] Still more did bricks require the use of mortar, which in their case was often little more than mud.

Among the processes made use of for the construction of the great temple at Thebes there was one which bore marks of the same tendency. Mariette tells us that traces exist in the front of the great temple of a huge inclined plane made of large crude bricks. This incline was used for the construction of the pylon. The great stones were dragged up its slopes, and as the pylon grew, so did the mass of crude brick. When the work was finished the bricks were cleared away, but the internal face of the pylon still bears traces of their position against it. This work was carried out, according to Mariette, under the Ptolemies,[3] but the primitive method of raising the stones must have come down from times much more remote.[4]

---

[1] MARIETTE, *Abydos*, vol. i. p. 8.—*Catalogue général des Monuments d'Abydos*, p. 585. Similar tenons were found by the members of the *Institut d'Égypte* in the walls of the great hall at Karnak (*Description de l'Égypte, Antiquités*, vol. ii. p. 442. —See also *Plates*, vol. ii. pl. 57, figs. 1 and 2). We took this illustration for our guide in compiling our diagram of Egyptian bonding in Fig. 69.

[2] *Description de l'Égypte. Ant.*, vol. v. p. 153. JOMARD, *Recueil d'Observations et de Mémoires sur l'Égypte Ancienne et Moderne*, vol. iv. p. 41.

[3] MARIETTE, *Karnak*, p. 18.

[4] This is clearly indicated by DIODORUS (i. 63, 66): τὴν κατασκευὴν διὰ χωμάτων γενέσθαι.

The first travellers who visited Egypt in modern times were struck with the colossal size of some buildings and of a few monoliths, and jumped to the conclusion that the Egyptians were peculiarly skilled in mechanics and engineering. They declared, and it has been often repeated, that this people possessed secrets which were afterwards lost; that many an Archimedes flourished among them who excelled his Syracusan successor. All this was a pure illusion. Their only machines seem to have been levers and perhaps a kind of elementary crane.[1] The whole secret of the Egyptians consisted in their unlimited command of individual labour, and in the unflinching way in which they made use of it. Multitudes were employed upon a single building, and kept to their work by the rod of the overseer until it was finished. The great monoliths were placed upon rafts at the foot of the mountains in which they were quarried, and floated during the inundation by river and canal to a point as near as possible to their destined sites. They were then placed upon sledges to which hundreds of men were harnessed, and dragged over a well-oiled wooden causeway to their allotted places. Fig. 43, which is taken from a hypogeum of the twelfth dynasty, gives an excellent idea of the way in which these masses of granite were transported. In this picture we see one hundred and seventy-two men arranged in pairs and, to use a military term, in four columns, dragging the sledge of a huge seated colossus by four ropes.[2] This colossus must have been about twenty-six feet high, if the pictured proportions between the statue and its convoy may be taken as approaching the truth. Upon the pedestal stands a man, who pours water upon the planks so that they shall not catch fire from the friction of so great a mass.[3] The engineer, who presides over the whole operation, stands upright upon the knees of the statue and "marks time" with his hands. At the side of the statue walk men carrying instruments of various kinds, overseers armed with rattans, and relays of men to take the place of those who may fall out of the ranks from

---

[1] WILKINSON, *Manners and Customs*, etc., vol. ii. p. 309. In speaking of the pyramids Herodotus mentions what seems to have been a kind of crane, but he gives us no information as to its principle or arrangement (ii. 125).

[2] The painting in question dates from the reign of Ousourtesen II. and was found at El-Bercheh, a short distance above the ruins of Antinoë.

[3] The position of this man and the general probabilities of the case suggest perhaps, that his jar contains oil rather than water.—ED.

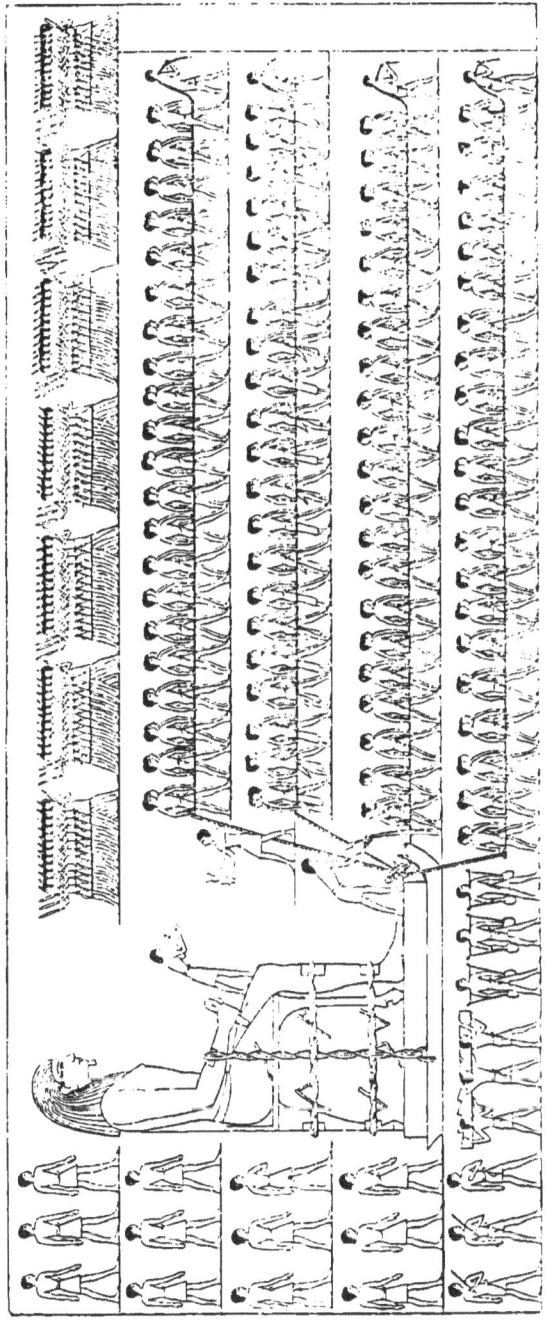

Fig. 43.—Transport of a colossus (Wilkinson, vol. ii., p. 305).

fatigue. In the upper part we see a numerous troop of Egyptians carrying palm branches, who seem to be leading the procession.

From the first centuries of the monarchy blocks of granite of unusual size were thus transferred from place to place. We learn this from the epitaph of a high official named Una, who lived in the time of the sixth dynasty.[1] He recounts the services which he had rendered in bringing to Memphis the blocks of granite and alabaster required for the royal undertakings. Mention is made of buildings which had been constructed for the reception of monoliths. The largest of those buildings was 60 cubits (about 102 feet) long by 30 cubits wide. A little farther on we are told that one monolith required 3,000 men for its transport.

Thanks to their successful wars the great Theban princes had far wider resources at their command than their predecessors. Their architects could count upon the labour not only of the fellahs of the *corvée*, but also upon thousands of foreign prisoners. It was not astonishing, therefore, that the enterprises of the ancient empire were thrown into the shade. Neither were the Sait monarchs behind those of Thebes. According to Herodotus the monolithic chapel which Amasis brought from the Elephantiné quarries was 39 feet high by nearly 23 feet wide and 13 feet deep, outside measurement.[2] Taking the hollow inside into consideration such a stone must have weighed about 48 tons. Two thousand boatmen were occupied for three years in transporting this chapel from Elephantiné into the Delta. Another town in the same region must have had a still larger monolithic chapel, if we are to believe the Greek historian's account of it. It was square, and each of its sides measured 40 cubits (nearly 70 feet).[3]

How did they set about erecting their obelisks? Upon this point we have no information whatever, either from inscriptions or from figured monuments. They may have used an inclined plane, to the summit of which the obelisk was drawn by the force

---

[1] BRUGSCH, *Histoire d'Égypte*, vol. i. pp. 74 *et seq.*
[2] We agree with Wilkinson in taking for the height that which Herodotus calls the length. In all monuments of the kind the height is the largest measurement. Herodotus's phrase is easily explained. The monolith appears to have been lying in front of the temple into which they had failed to introduce it. (κεῖται παρὰ τὴν ἔσοδον, he says). Its height had thus become its length.
[3] HERODOTUS, ii. 155.

of innumerable arms, and then lowered by the gradual removal of the part supporting its lower end. It is certain that the process was often a slow and laborious one. We know from an inscription that the obelisk which now stands before the church of San Giovanni Laterano in Rome was more than thirty-five years in the hands of the workmen charged with its erection in the southern quarter of Thebes.[1] Sometimes, however, much more rapid progress was made. According to the inscription on the base of the obelisk of Hatasu at Karnak, the time consumed upon it, from the commencement of work in the quarry to its final erection at Thebes, *was only seven months*.[2]

Whatever may have been their methods we may be sure that there was nothing complicated or particularly learned in them. The erection of the obelisks, like that of the colossal statues, must have been an affair merely of time and of the number of arms employed.

"One day," says Maxime du Camp, "I was sitting upon one of the architraves supported by the columns of the great hall at Karnak, and, glancing over the forest of stone which surrounded me, I involuntarily cried out: 'But how did they do all this?'"

"My dragoman, Joseph, who is a great philosopher, overheard my exclamation, and began to laugh. He touched my arm, and pointing to a palm tree whose tall stem rose in the distance, he said: 'That is what they did it all with; a hundred thousand palm-branches broken over the backs of people whose shoulders are never covered, will create palaces and temples enough. Ah yes, sir, that was a bad time for the date trees; their branches were cut a good deal faster than they grew!' And he laughed softly to himself as he caressed his beard."

"Perhaps he was right."[3]

---

[1] The text in question is quoted in the notes contributed by Dr. BIRCH to the last edition of WILKINSON (vol. ii. p. 308, note 2). PLINY's remarks upon the obelisks are intersprinkled with fabulous stories and contain no useful information (H. N., xxxvi. 14).

[2] PIERRET, *Dictionnaire d'Archéologie Égyptienne*. (The dates upon which this assertion depends have been disputed. M. CHABAS reads the inscription "from the first of Muchir in the year 16, to the last of Mesore in 17," making nineteen months in all, a period which is not quite so impossible as that ordinarily quoted.—ED.)

[3] MAXIME DU CAMP, *Le Nil*. pp. 261 and 262.

§ 4. *The Arch.*

We have already said that among the Egyptians the arch was only of secondary importance; that it was only used in accessory parts of their buildings. We are compelled to return to the subject, however, because a wrong idea has generally been adopted which, as in the case of the monoliths, we must combat evidence in hand. The extreme antiquity of the arch in Egypt is seldom suspected.

It was an article of faith with the architects of the last century that the arch was discovered by the Etruscans. The engineers of the French expedition did not hesitate to declare every arch which they found in Egypt to be no older in date than the Roman occupation. But since the texts have been interpreted it has been proved that there is more than one arch in Egypt which was constructed not only as early as the Ptolemies, but even under the Pharaohs. Wilkinson mentions brick arches and vaults bearing the names of Amenophis I., and Thothmes III. at Thebes, and judging from the paintings at Beni-Hassan, he is inclined to believe that they understood the principle as early as the twelfth dynasty.[1]

Wilkinson was quite right in supposing these eighteenth dynasty vaults to be from the first constructed by Egyptian architects. The scarcity of good timber must soon have set them to discover some method of covering a void which should be more convenient than flat ceilings, and as the supply always follows the demand, they must have been thus led towards the inevitable discovery. The latest editor of Wilkinson, Dr. Birch, affirms more than once that the arch has been recently discovered among the remains from the Ancient Empire, and in the *Itinéraire* of Mariette we find:[2] "It is by no means rare to find in the necropolis of Abydos, among the tombs of the thirteenth and even of the sixth dynasty, vaults which are not only pointed in section as a whole, but which are made up of bricks in the form of *voussoirs*." Being anxious that no uncertainty upon such a

---

[1] WILKINSON, *Manners and Customs*, etc., vol. i. pp. 357-358; vol. ii. pp. 262, 298-299.
[2] P. 148.

subject should remain, we asked Mariette for more information during the last winter but one that he spent in Egypt. We received the following answer, dated 29th January, 1880: "I have just consulted my journal of the Abydos excavations. I there find an entry relating to a tomb of the sixth dynasty with the accompanying drawing (Fig. 44): *a* is in limestone, and there can be no doubt that in it we have a keystone in the form of a true voussoir; *b, b,* are also of stone. The rest is made up of crude bricks, rectangular in shape, and kept in place by pebbles imbedded in the cement.

"Obviously, we have here the principle of the arch. Speaking generally, I believe that the Egyptians were acquainted with that principle from the earliest times. They did not make an extensive use of the arch because they knew that it carried within it the seeds of its own death. *Une maille rongée emporte tout l'ouvrage,* and a bad stone in a vault may ruin a whole building. The Egyptians preferred their indestructible stone beams. I often ask myself how much would have been left to us of their tombs and temples if they had used the arch instead."[1]

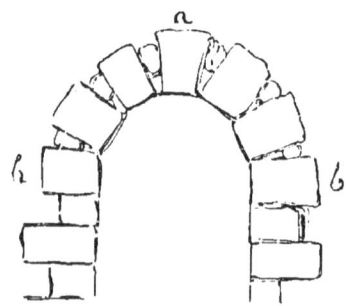

FIG. 44.—Arch in the necropolis of Abydos; communicated by Mariette.

Mariette adds that the Serapeum contains the oldest known example of a vault of dressed stone, and as it dates from the time of Darius the son of Hystaspes, we suppose that the fine limestone arch at Sakkarah, bearing the cartouch of Psemethek I., which is figured at the head of Sir Gardner Wilkinson's tenth chapter, no longer exists.

It was in their brick buildings that the Egyptians chiefly employed arches. Such structures were looked upon as less sacred, less monumental than those in which stone was used, and a process might therefore be admitted which would be excluded from the latter. We shall here give several examples of the Egyptian arch and its principal varieties, and it will not surprise our readers to find that they are all taken from the New Empire. The remains from earlier periods consist almost entirely

[1] "An arch never sleeps" says the Arab proverb.

of tombs, while those left to us by the eighteenth dynasty and its successors are of vast dimensions, such as the great Theban temples, and have annexes comprising buildings erected for a vast variety of purposes.

Groined vaults were unknown to the Egyptians, but almost every variety of arch and of plain vault is to be found in the country.

The semicircular arch is more frequently met with than any other. That which exists in an old tomb at Abydos has been already figured (Fig. 44), we shall give two more examples, dating from the Saït epoch. The illustration below (Fig. 45), represents the gate in the encircling wall of one of the tombs in the valley of El-Assassif, at Thebes. The wall diminishes gradually in thickness from sixteen feet eight inches at the bottom to nine

FIG. 45.—Arch in El-Assassif, present condition ; from Lepsius.

feet nine inches at the top, both faces being equally inclined. This latter feature is a rare one in Egypt, the slope being as a rule confined to the external face. In order to show it clearly we have interrupted the wall vertically in our illustration, isolating the part in which the arch occurs (Fig. 46), and restoring the summit. The arch itself is formed of nine courses of brick.

The sarcophagus in " Campbell's Tomb " is protected by a plain cylindrical vault of four courses (see Fig. 200. vol. i.), which covers a polygonal vault formed of three large slabs. Both vaults are pierced by a narrow opening, which may, perhaps, have been intended to allow the scents and sounds of the world above to reach the occupant of the sarcophagus. Its arrangement is so careful that it must have had some important purpose to fulfil.

In the group of ruins which surrounds the back parts of the Ramesseum (see p. 379. vol. i.) there are vaults of various kinds. A few verge slightly towards the pointed form (see Fig. 47), others are elliptic (Fig. 48). The latter are composed of four courses, and their inner surfaces show a curious arrangement of the bricks; their vertical joints are not parallel to either axis of the vault. The ends of the courses are slightly set off from its face (see Fig. 48).

FIG. 46.—Arch in El-Assassif, restored from the plans and elevations of Lepsius.[1]

A tomb near the *Valley of the Queens*, at Thebes, has a strongly marked elliptical vault (Fig. 49).[2]

Finally, the inverted segmental arch is not unknown. It is found employed in a fashion which, as described by Prisse, made a great impression upon Viollet-le-Duc. "The foundations of certain boundary walls," says the former, "are built of baked bricks to a height of one-and-a-half metres (about four feet ten

---

[1] *Denkmæler*, part i. pl. 94.
[2] RAMÉE, *Histoire générale de l'Architecture*, vol. i. p. 262.

inches) above the ground. The bricks are thirty-one centimetres (about twelve-and-a-quarter inches) long, and the courses are arranged in a long succession of inverted segmental arches."[1]

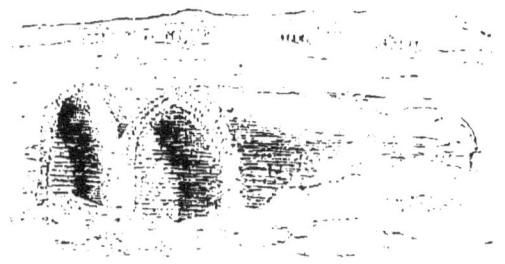

FIG. 47.—Vaults in the Ramesseum.

Our figure has been compiled from the plans and elevations of Prisse with a view to making the arrangement easily understood

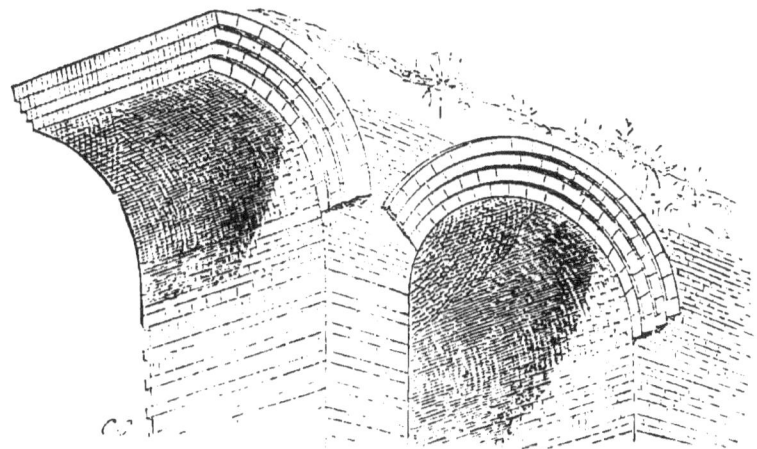

FIG. 48.—Vault in the Ramesseum; compiled from the data of Lepsius.

(Fig. 50); it represents the lower part of one of the walls in question. According to M. Viollet-le-Duc, the Egyptian architects

[1] PRISSE, *Histoire de l'Art Égyptien.* p. 174.—MARIETTE (*Voyage dans la Haute-Égypte,* vol. ii. pp. 59-60) was struck by a similar arrangement. "Murray's Guide," he says, "tells us, in speaking of Dayr-el-Medineh, that the walls which inclose the courts of this temple present a striking peculiarity of construction. Their bricks are laid in concave-convex courses which rise and fall alternately over the whole length of the walls." This curious arrangement deserved to be noticed, but Dayr-el-Medinêh

had recourse to this contrivance in order to guard against the effects of earthquakes. He shows clearly that a wall built in such a fashion would offer a much more solid resistance to their attacks

FIG. 49.— Elliptical vault; Thebes.

than one with foundations composed of horizontal courses.[1] If we are to take it as established that the vault or arch was among the primitive methods of Egyptian construction, we have no reason to believe that *off-set* arches were older, in Egypt at least, than true arches. We have described this form of arch elsewhere, and explained the contrivance by which the superficial appearance of a vault was obtained.[2] The process could obviously

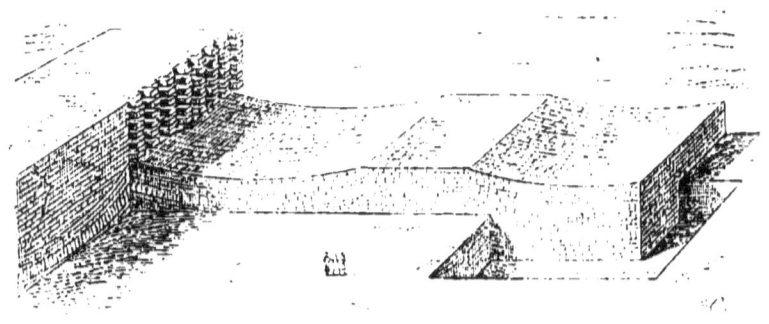

FIG. 50.—Foundations with inverted segmental arches; compiled from Prisse.

only be carried out in stone. We shall here content ourselves with giving two examples of its employment.

The first dates from the eighteenth dynasty, and occurs in the temple of Dayr-el-Bahari.[3] Our Fig. 51 gives a transverse

is not the only place where it is to be found. The bounding wall of the temple of Osiris at Abydos affords another instance of it. It should also be noticed that the problem offered to us by such a mode of building is complicated by the fact that, in the quay at Esneh and in some parts of the temple of Philæ, it is combined with the use of very large sandstone blocks."

[1] VIOLLET-LE-DUC, *Histoire de l'Habitation humaine*, pp. 85-88. Alberti and other Renaissance architects recommended this method of construction for building upon a soft surface. (*L'Architettura di Leon Batista Alberti, tradotta in lingua fiorentina da Cosimo Bartoli.* Venice, 1565, 4to, p. 70.)

[2] See p. 110, Vol. I., and Figs. 74, 75, 76. [3] See p. 111, Vol. I., *et seq.*

section of a passage leading to one of the chambers cut in
the rock. Fig. 52 offers a view in perspective of the same passage and of the
discharging chamber which really bears
the thrust of the weight above.

The second example of this construction comes from a famous work of the
nineteenth dynasty, the temple of Seti I.
at Abydos. Our figure (53) shows one
of the curious row of chapels in which
the originality of that building consists.[1]
This quasi-vault, for which Mariette finds
a reason in the funerary character of the
building, has been obtained by cutting into three huge sandstone

FIG. 51.—Transverse section of a corridor at Dayr-el-Bahari; from Lepsius, i. pl. 87.

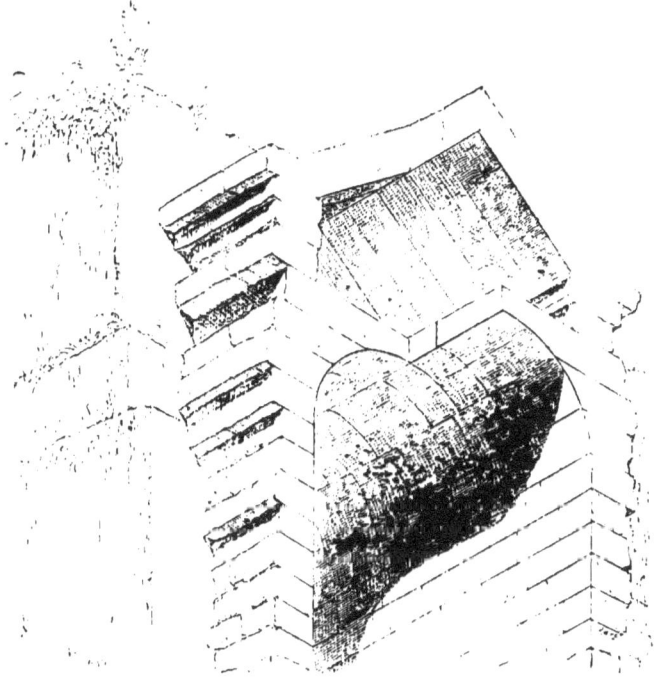

FIG. 52.—Section in perspective through the same corridor; composed from the elevation of Lepsius.

---

[1] See also pp. 385-392, Vol. I. and Fig. 224.—Our perspective has been compiled from the *Description de l'Égypte*, from Mariette's work and from photographs.

slabs in each horizontal course. The stone forming the crown of the vault is especially large.

Brick vaults and arches must have been far more numerous in Egypt than might be supposed from the few examples that remain. They must have suggested the use of off-set vaults in the case of stone, which, it must not be forgotten, would seem to the Egyptians to offer all the advantages of a vault without its drawbacks. In other countries the stages of progression were different, and the true arch came very late into use; but in Egypt it certainly seems to have preceded the off-set arch. In the valley of

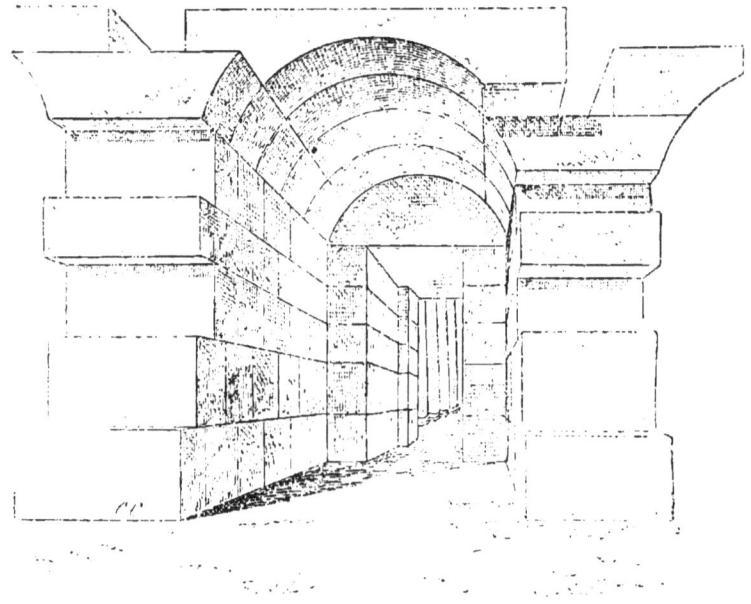

FIG. 53.—Vaulted chapel at Abydos.

the Nile the latter is an imitative form. The form of elliptic arch which we find in certain funerary chambers at Abydos seems to show this. When the architect of a tomb or temple wished to substitute a concave surface for a flat ceiling he made use of this hollowed-out vault. He thus saved himself from any anxiety as to the stability of his structure, he avoided the necessity of introducing what would seem to him a cause of eventual destruction, while he gave variety of line and, perhaps, additional symbolic meaning to his work.

§ 5 *The Pier and Column.—The Egyptian Orders.*

THEIR ORIGIN.

After the wall and the covering which the wall supports, we must study in some detail the pier, and the column which is the perfected form of the pier. Thanks to these latter elements of construction the architect is able to cover large spaces without impeding circulation, to exactly apportion the strength and number of his points of support to the weight to be carried and to the other conditions of the problem. By the form of their bases and capitals, by the proportions of their shafts, by the ornament laid upon them in colour or chiselled in their substance, he is enabled to give an artistic richness and variety which are practically infinite. Their arrangements and the proportions of their spacing are also of the greatest importance in the production of effect.

In attempting to define a style of architecture and its individual expression, there is no part to which so much attention should be paid as the column. It should be examined, in the first place, as an isolated individual, with a stature and physiognomy proper to itself. Then in its social state, if we may use such a phrase ; in the various groups which go to make porticos, hypostyle halls, and colonnades. We shall begin, therefore, by examining what may be called the Egyptian orders, and afterwards we shall describe the principal combinations in which they were employed by the Theban architects.

Our readers must remember the distinction, to which we called attention in the early part of our task, between two systems co-existing at one and the same time in Egypt : wooden architecture and that in which stone was the chief material used.[1] Under the Ancient Empire the only kind of detached support which appears to have been known in stone architecture, was the quadrangular pier, examples of which we find in the Temple of the Sphinx (Fig. 204, vol. i.). It was not so, however, in wooden construction. We find in the bas-reliefs belonging to that early epoch numerous representations of wooden columns, which, though all possessing the same slender proportions, were surmounted by capitals of

[1] See Chapter II. vol. i.

various designs. In these capitals occur the first suggestions of the forms which were afterwards developed with success in stone architecture.

The type of capital which occurs most frequently in the buildings of the New Empire is certainly that which has been compared to a truncated lotus-bud;[1] we may call it the *lotiform* capital, and a bas-relief has come down to us from the fifth dynasty, in which two columns are shown crowned by capitals of this type, differing only from later stone examples in their more elongated forms (Figs. 54 and 55).

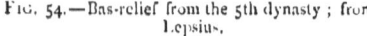

FIG. 54.—Bas-relief from the 5th dynasty; from Lepsius.

FIG. 55. Detail of capital; from the same bas-relief.

After the type of capital just mentioned, that which occurs most frequently at Karnak and elsewhere is the *campaniform* type, in which the general outline resembles that of an inverted bell. It has been referred to the imitation of the lotus-flower when in full bloom. However that may be, it is the fact that in a bas-relief of the fifth dynasty we find a capital presenting the outline, in full detail, of a lotus-flower which has just opened its petals (Figs. 56 and 57).

Rarer and later types than these are also foreshadowed in the early bas-reliefs. We shall hereafter have to speak of a campaniform capital in which the bell is not inverted, in the part

[1] These slender columns with lotiform capitals are figured in considerable number in the tomb of Ti. MARIETTE, *Voyage dans la Haute-Égypte*, vol. i. pl. 10.

constructed by Thothmes of the great temple at Karnak. Its prototype may certainly be recognized in a figured pavilion at Sakkarah, dating from the sixth dynasty. We reproduce it from a squeeze sent to us by M. Bourgoin (Figs. 58 and 59).

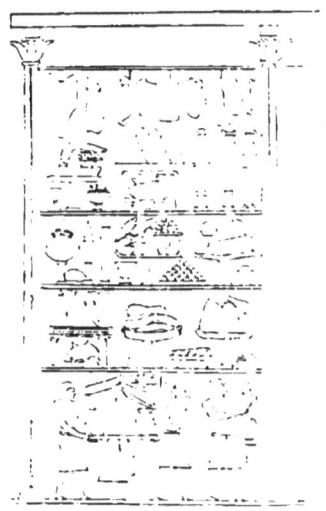

FIG. 56.—Bas-relief from the 5th dynasty: from Lepsius.

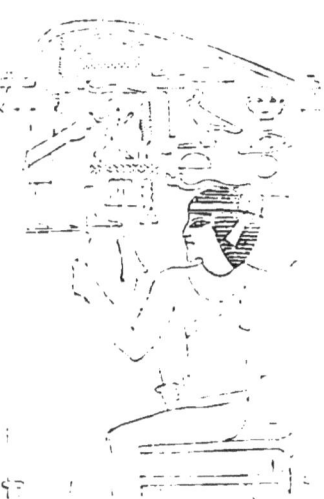

FIG. 58. - Pavilion from Sakkarah, 6th dynasty.

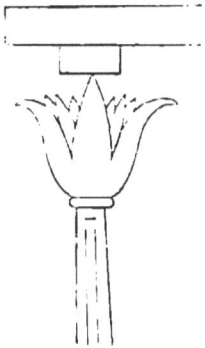

FIG. 57.—Details of columns in Fig. 56.

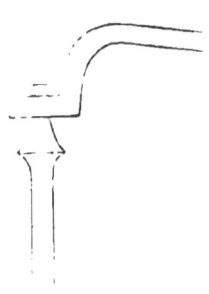

FIG. 59.—Details of column in Fig. 58.

During the Ptolemaic period, the Egyptian architects made frequent use of the form of capital which is now called *hathoric*. in which a masque of Hathor, the cow-headed goddess. is the ruling principle. This capital is to be seen, in a rudimentary condition, in a pavilion dating from the fifth dynasty (Figs. 60 and 61). It there occurs, as will be seen by referring to our illustrations, as the roughly blocked-out head of a cow.

In connection with the last two bas-reliefs, we must call attention to the fact that the structures from which they were imitated must have been erected in some kind of metal. Their forms are inconsistent with the use of any other material. The way in which the capital is connected with the member to which it acts as support, in Fig. 59, and the open-work of the architrave in Fig. 61, are especially suggestive. In the latter bas-relief the figures introduced are evidently behind a grille, and the whole structure is expressive of metal-work.

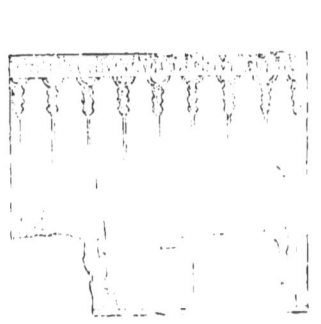

FIG. 60.—Bas-relief from the 5th dynasty; from Lepsius.

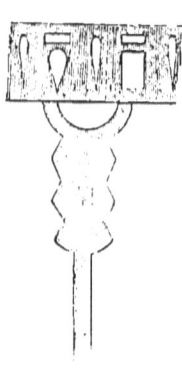

FIG. 61.—Details of the columns.

We suspect that the pavilion shown in Fig. 56 was also of metal, which seems to have played an important part in all that light form of architecture with which we make acquaintance in the sepulchral decorations. This is very clearly seen in the examples of painted columns, which we borrow from Prisse (Figs. 62—65). They present forms which could only have been compassed by the use of some metal like bronze. If the use of metal be admitted, we have no difficulty in accounting for the playful and slender grace found in some of these columns, and the ample tufted capitals of others. The natural tendency in painted decorations of this kind to exaggerate the characteristics of their models must not, however, be overlooked. Not being compelled to apportion the strength of supports to the weight which they have to carry, it is always inclined to elongate forms. The decorations at Pompeii are a striking instance of this. Pompeian painters gave impossible proportions to their columns, which evidently existed

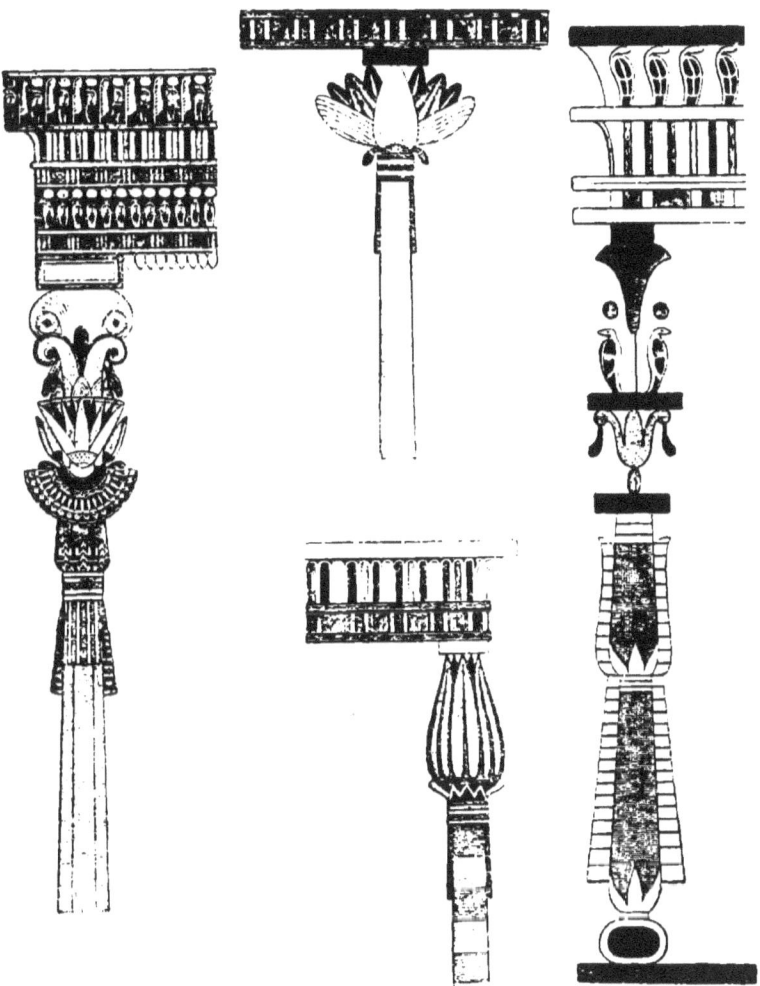

FIGS. 62—65.—Columns from bas-reliefs (Prisse).

no where but in their own fancies. We admit that the Egyptian decorators did something of the same kind, that they exaggerated proportions and accumulated motives on a single capital, which were not to be found co-existing in reality. But, with these reserves, we think it more than probable that the columns shown in their paintings have preserved the general aspect of the supports employed in those curiously elegant pavilions to which they belonged. The forms in Fig. 62 are explained, on the one hand, by the imitation of vegetable forms, on the other by the behaviour of a metal plate under the hand of the workman. The curve which was afterwards, under the name of a *volute*, to play such an important part in Greek architecture, was thus naturally obtained.

It will thus be seen that during the Ancient Empire the lighter forms of architecture were far in advance of that which made use of stone. It possessed a richness and variety of its own, which were rendered possible by the comparative ease with which wood and metal could be manipulated, an ease which gradually led the artist onwards to the invention of forms conspicuous for their playful originality and their singular diversity.

As for the quadrangular pier, with which the stone architecture of the Ancient Empire was contented, we are assured that it had its origin in the rock-cut tombs. In the oldest works of the kind in Egypt, the funerary grottos of Memphis, "these piers (we are told) owe their existence to the natural desire to cause the light from without to penetrate to a second or even to a third chamber. In order to obtain this result, openings were made in the front wall on each side of the door, and the parts of the rock which were left for support became for that reason objects of care, and finally took the form of piers. The rock over these piers was the prototype of the architrave." [1]

It may be so. But, on the other hand, the pier of dressed stone may have had a still more simple origin. It may have resulted from the obvious requirements of construction. As soon as wooden buildings began to be supplemented by work in stone, it became necessary to find supports strong enough for the weight of stone roofs. Nothing could be more natural than to take a

---

[1] EBERS, *Ægypten*, vol. ii., p. 186. All this passage of Ebers is, however, nothing more than an epitome of a paper by LEPSIUS, entitled: *Ueber einige Ægyptische Kunstformen und ihre Entwickelung* (in the *Transactions of the Berlin Academy*, 1871, 4to). This paper contains many just observations and ingenious notions; but, to our mind, it is over systematized, and its theories cannot all be accepted.

block of stone as it came from the quarry, and to set it up on end. In course of time its faces would be dressed and its section accommodated to a square, for the love of symmetry is innate in man. The pier may also be seen foreshadowed in the squared beams of that closed form of wooden architecture which has been already noticed.

We see, then, that the earliest Egyptian art of which we have any remains comprised the principal elements of which later architects made use. But it is among the ruins of the great monuments constructed during the Theban supremacy that we must attempt to form an exhaustive list of their architectural forms, and to show how the genius of the race, obeying that mysterious law which governs all organic development, arrived at the complete realization of the ideal towards which it had been advancing through so many centuries. At Thebes alone can the architectural genius of the Egyptians be judged.

GENERAL TYPES OF SUPPORTS.

In the following pages all the principal varieties of Egyptian pier and column are passed in review. We believe that no type of any importance has been omitted. The illustrations are all drawn to one scale of about ten feet to the inch. The difference in the size of the reproductions is therefore a guide to the relative proportions of the originals, and an idea can be easily formed of their comparative importance in the buildings in which they occur.

The quadrangular pier is the simplest form of support, and, as might be expected, it is also the most ancient. In the example which we have taken from a tomb in the necropolis of Sakkarah, a tomb dating from the Ancient Empire, it has already a base (Fig. 66), an addition which is not to be found in the Temple of the Sphinx (Fig. 204, vol. i.). Elsewhere it tapers to the top; an instance of this, dating from a much later period, is found in the speos of Phré, at Ipsamboul (Fig. 67). In all these cases the architrave rests directly upon the shaft, an arrangement which gives the pier an archaic character in spite of its base.

A very different appearance was obtained when, in the time of Rameses, the pier was provided with a more ample base, and covered with hieroglyphs and figures. It received a capital at the same time, and became worthy of playing its part in a richly-decorated building like the great temple at Karnak, from which our Fig. 68 is taken. The same may be said of the hathoric pier. The example shown in Fig. 69 is taken from the speos of

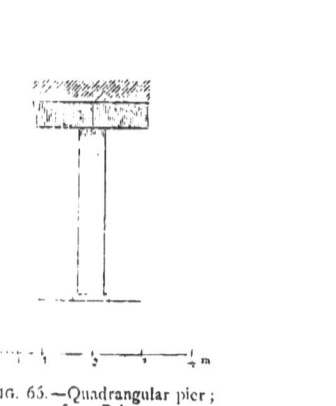
Fig. 66.—Quadrangular pier; from Prisse.

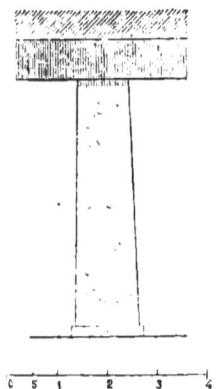
Fig. 67.—Tapering quadrangular pier; from Gailhabaud.

Hathor at Ipsamboul. The lower part of the shaft is covered with inscriptions above which appears a mask of Hathor.

Fig. 68.—Pier with capital; from Prisse.

Fig. 69.—Hathoric pier; from Gailhabaud.

The form of pier called *osiride* is still more elaborate and decorative. These piers consist of two parts; a quadrangular shaft covered with inscriptions, and a colossal statue of the king who was the constructor of the building in which they are found, endowed with the head-dress and other attributes of Osiris. The motive was a favourite one with the princes of the nineteenth dynasty, and it is continuously repeated both in the great temples of the left bank at Thebes and in the rock-cut temples of Nubia. Our illustration is taken from an osiride pier in the second court of Medinet-Abou. The word *caryatid* cannot strictly be applied

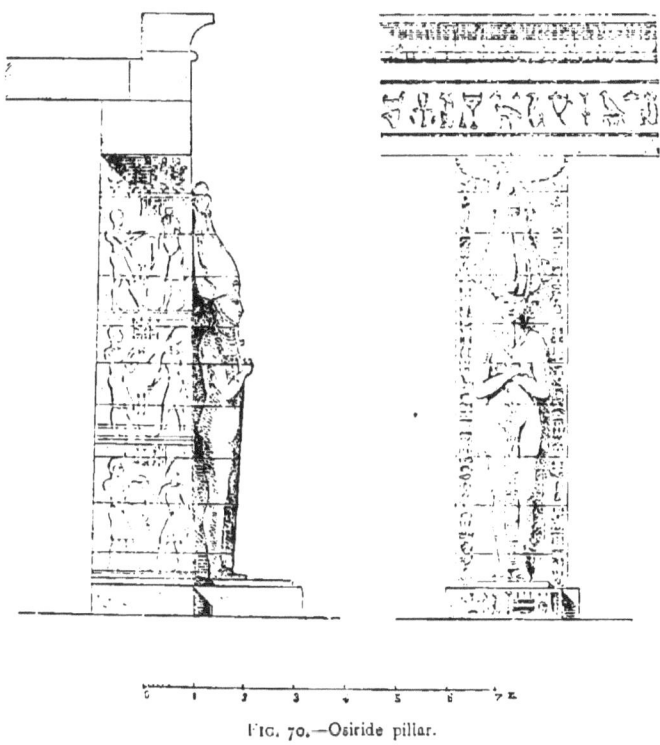

FIG. 70.—Osiride pillar.

to these piers, because the statues do not help to support the mass above, they are merely affixed to the pier which actually performs that office.

The Ethiopian architects borrowed the motive of these osiride pillars. They introduced into colonnaded buildings, copied from those of the Rameses, some colossal figures in which the Typhon of the Greeks has sometimes been recognized. They probably represent the god Set. They, too, are only applied to the supports. There is but one instance in the whole of Egyptian architecture of the human figure being frankly employed as a support, namely, in the case of those brackets or balconies which overhang the courts of the Royal Pavilion at Medinet-Abou (Fig. 10). But even here the support is more apparent than real, for the slabs between which the figures are crouched are upheld by the wall at their backs. In this there is nothing that can be compared to the work done by the dignified virgins of the Erectheum or the muscular giants of Agrigentum, in upholding the massive architraves confided to their strength.

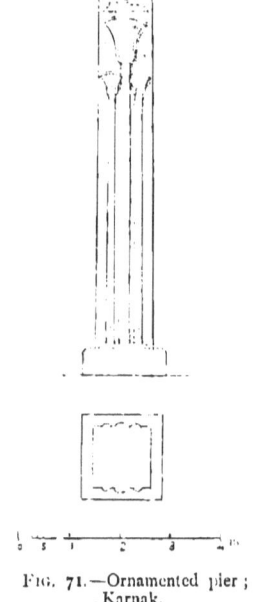

FIG. 71.—Ornamented pier; Karnak.

A last and curious variety of pier is found in the granite chambers of the Great Temple at Karnak. Upon two of their faces are carved groups of three tall stems surmounted by flowers. Upon one face these flowers are shaped like inverted bells (see Fig. 71), on the other they resemble the curling petals of the lily. Flower and stem are painted with colours which make them stand out from the red of the polished granite. These piers are two in number, and the faces which are without the decoration described are covered with finely executed sculptures in intaglio.[1]

These piers are 29 feet high. "Their height, as well as their situation, seems to indicate that they never bore any architrave. They were once, however, crowned by some royal symbol; probably by bronze hawks, which may have been ornamented with enamel. There are many representations of such arrangements in the bas-reliefs at Karnak."[2] Supposing this hypothesis to be well founded, these piers had something in common with a stele; had their height been less they might have been called pedestals; had their shape been less uncompromisingly rectangular, they might have been called obelisks.

---

[1] See PRISSE, *Histoire de l'Art Égyptien*, pp. 359, 360.
[2] *Ibid.*

Like the steles they are self-contained and independent of their surroundings.[1]

We see, then, that as time went on the Egyptian architects have transformed the old, plain, rectangular pier—by giving it capital and base, by adorning it with painted and sculptured decorations—until it became fit to take its place in the most ornate architectural composition. We have yet to follow the same constructive member in a further series of modifications which ended by making it indistinguishable from the column proper.

In order thoroughly to understand all these intermediary types we must return to the rock-cut tombs, in which the ceilings were upheld by piers left standing when the excavation was made. The desire to get as much light as possible past these piers led to their angles being struck off in the first instance, and thus a quadrangular pier became an octagonal prism (Fig. 72), and was connected with the soil by a large, flat, disk-shaped base.

By repeating the same process and cutting off the eight angles of this prism, a sixteen-sided shaft was obtained, examples of which are to be found at Beni-Hassan in the same tomb as the octagonal column (Fig. 73).

"The practical difficulty of cutting these sixteen faces with precision and of equalizing the angles at which they met each other, added to the natural desire to make the division into sixteen planes clearly visible, and to give more animation to the play of light and shade, inspired the Egyptian architects with the happy notion of transforming the obtuse angles into salient ridges by hollowing out the spaces between them."[2] The highest part, however, of these pillars remained quadrangular, thus preserving a reminiscence of the original type, and supplying a connecting

---

[1] At Dayr-el-Bahari there are some pillars of the same shape but engaged in the wall. They support groups—carved in stone and painted—comprising a hawk, a vulture, cynocephali, and so on. They are in the passage which leads to the north-western *speos*. Their total height, inclusive of the animals which surmount them, is nearly 18 feet, of which the groups make up nearly a third. The lower part is ornamented by mouldings in the shape of panels. These pilasters should be more carefully studied and reproduced if they still exist; the sketches from which we have described them were made some fifteen years ago. In that monument of Egyptian sculpture which is, perhaps, the oldest of all, namely, the bas-relief engraved by Seneferu upon the rocks of Wadi-Maghara, a hawk crowned with the *pschent* stands before the conqueror upon a quadrangular pier which has panels marked upon it in the same fashion as at Dayr-el-Bahari.

[2] EBERS, *Ægypten*, vol. ii., p. 184.

link between the shaft and the architrave which almost exactly corresponds to the Greek *abacus*. This quadrangular member was advantageous in two ways; it prevented any incoherence between the diameter of the shaft and the depth of the architrave, and it supplied an unchanging element to the composition.[1] The persistence of this square abacus helps to call our attention to the continual changes undergone by the shaft which it surmounts. The slight inclination of the sides gives to the latter the effect of a cone, and the contrast between its almost circular top and the

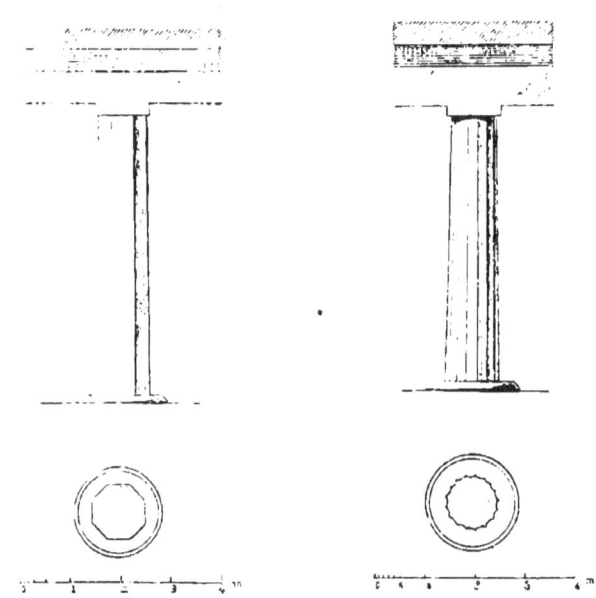

FIG. 72.—Octagonal pillar; Beni-Hassan.   FIG. 73.—Sixteen-sided pillar; fluted.

right-angles of the abacus helps us to remember that the square pier was its immediate progenitor.

The conical form of the pillars at Beni-Hassan, their want of a well-marked base, their sixteen flutes, the square abacus interposed between their shafts and the architrave, made, when taken together, a great impression upon the mind of Champollion. He thought that in them he had found a first sketch for the oldest of the Greek orders, and that the type brought to perfection by the builders of Corinth and Pæstum had its origin in the tombs of

[1] CHIPIEZ, *Histoire critique des Origines et de la Formation des Ordres Grecques*, p. 44.

Beni-Hassan; he accordingly proposed to call their columns *proto-doric*.

Here we shall not attempt to discuss Champollion's theory. It would be impossible to do so with advantage without having previously studied the doric column itself, and pointed out how little these resemblances amount to. The doric column had no base; the diminution of its diameter was much more rapid; its capital, which comprised an echinus as well as an abacus, was very different in importance from the little tablet which we find at Beni-Hassan. The general proportions of the Greek and Egyptian orders are, however, almost identical; the shafts are fluted in each instance, and they both have the same air of simplicity and imposing gravity.

But it is futile to insist upon any such comparison. The polygonal column had long been disused when the Greeks first penetrated into the Nile valley and had an opportunity of imitating the works of the Egyptians. It was in use in the time of the Middle Empire, during the eleventh and twelfth dynasties. The earlier princes of the Second Theban Empire introduced it into their stone buildings, but there are no examples which we can affirm to be later than the eighteenth dynasty. The Rameses and their successors preferred forms less bold and severe; their columns were true columns with swelling entasis and rich and varied capitals. It is no doubt true that towards the seventh century the Greeks could find the polygonal column which we have described in many an ancient monument. But those early visitors were not archæologists. Astonished and dazzled by the pompous buildings of a Psemethek or an Amasis, they were not likely to waste their attention upon an abandoned and obsolete type. Their admiration would be reserved for the great edifices of the nineteenth and later dynasties, for such creations as Medinet-Abou, the Ramesseum, and the Great Hall at Karnak; creations which had their equals in those cities of the Delta which were visited by Herodotus and Hecatæus. If Greek art had borrowed from the Egypt of that day it would have transferred to its own home not the simple lines of the porticos at Beni-Hassan, but something ornate and complex, like the order of the small temple of Nectanebo at Philæ.

These few words had to be given, in passing, to an hypothesis which has found much favour since the days of Champollion, but we hasten to resume our methodical analysis of the Egyptian orders, and to class them by the varieties of their proportions and by the ever-increasing complication of their ornaments.

At Beni-Hassan and elsewhere we find pillars with two or four flat vertical bands dividing their flutes into as many groups. These bands are covered with incised inscriptions. Sometimes, as at Kalabché (Fig. 74), there are four flat bands inclosing five flutes between each pair. Such an arrangement accentuates the difference between these so-called proto-doric pillars and the Greek doric column. They take away from the proper character of the pillar, the inscribed tablet becomes the most important member of the composition, and the shaft to which it is attached

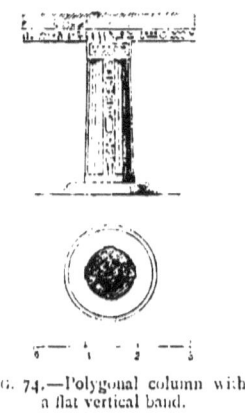

FIG. 74.—Polygonal column with a flat vertical band.

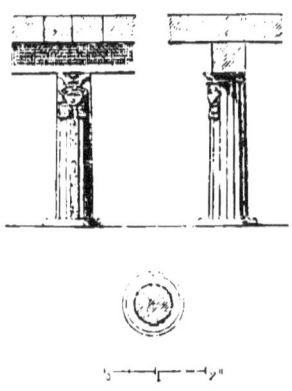

FIG. 75.—Polygonal pier with mask of Hathor; from Lepsius.

seems to have been made for its display. In the Greek order, on the other hand, we always find the structural requirements brought into absolute harmony with those of the æsthetic sentiment; every line of every detail is necessary both to builder and artist.

A later variety of this type is found in a pillar in which the vertical band is interrupted to make room for a mask of Hathor, which is placed immediately below the abacus (Fig. 75). We find it in a temple situated eastwards of El-Kab, dating, according to Lepsius, from the eighteenth dynasty.

After the eleventh dynasty we find monolithic rock-cut supports at Beni-Hassan, which, although side by side with true polygonal piers, are columns in the strictest sense of the word; that is to say,

THE EGYPTIAN ORDERS.   99

their vertical section offers curvilinear forms, and they are provided with capitals. Singularly enough, they are so far from being a development from the pier that they do not even distantly resemble it. They may fairly be compared, however, with a type of column which we have already noticed in speaking of the ephemeral wooden or metal architecture whose forms have been preserved for us in the bas-reliefs of the Ancient Empire (see Fig. 54).[1]

The shaft is formed of four bold vertical ribs, cruciform in plan, and bound together at the top by narrow fillets. The re-entering angles between the ribs are deep. The horizontal section of the capital is similar to that of the shaft, from which it seems to burst;

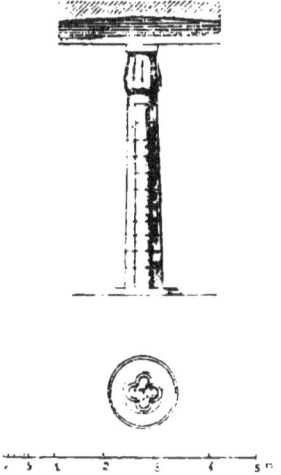

FIG. 76.—Column from Beni-Hassan; from Lepsius.

it then gradually tapers to the top, where it meets the usual quadrangular abacus (Fig. 76).

If four stems of lotus, each ending in an unopened bud, be tied together immediately beneath the point where the stem joins the bud, something bearing a rude resemblance to this column will be formed, and to the imitation of such a faggot its origin has often

[1] MARIETTE has shown this clearly in his *Voyage dans la Haute-Égypte* (p. 52). "This light column or shaft was not abandoned, it reappeared in stone . . . . it reappeared to give birth to the great faggot-shaped column which rivalled the pier in size, solidity, and weight. This column, with its capital in the shape of a lotus-bud or flower, is seen in its full development at Karnak, at Luxor, and in the first temple of the New Empire."

been attributed. The fillets which surround the shaft at its summit represent the cord wound several times round the stalks, the reeds which fill up the upper parts of the hollows between the ribs are meant for the ends of the knots.

Not far from the remains of the labyrinth some columns formed upon a similar principle have been discovered. Their shafts are composed of eight vertical ribs, which are triangular on plan like stalks of papyrus. The lower part of the shaft has a bold swell. It springs from a corona of leaves and tapers as it rises. The stalks are tied at the top with from three to five bands, the ends hanging down between the ribs. The buds which form the capital are also surrounded with leaves at their base.

The number of its parts and their complicated arrangement, the leaves painted upon it and its general proportions, show that this column was the product of an art much more advanced than that of Beni-Hassan. Between the first and second Theban empires the form of the column underwent a development similar to that which we have already described in the case of the pier. Its surface became less incoherently irregular; its horizontal section betrayed a constantly increasing tendency towards a circular form. Moreover, like the edifices of which it formed a part, as it increased in size it turned its back upon its monolithic origin and became a carefully constructed succession of horizontal courses.

Thus we arrive, under the New Empire, at a column of which we find several varieties in the buildings at Thebes. Its proportions are various, and so are the methods in which it is capped and decorated. The variant which preserves most resemblance to the column from Beni-Hassan is found at Luxor (Fig. 77). It is faggot-shaped like its prototype, but the natural origin of its forms is much less clearly marked. The capital recalls a bunch of lotus-buds in a very slight degree, the stems are not frankly detached one from another and the ligatures are repeated in unmeaning fashion. We feel that with the passage of time the original combination has lost its early significance.

The change becomes still more striking when we turn to another column from the New Empire, from Medinet-Abou (Fig. 78). The lotiform type may still be recognised, but the shaft is no longer faggot-shaped, except in a rudimentary fashion and over a very small part of its surface. There is a ligature just below the

[1] Ebers, *L'Égypte*, p. 185.

capital, but the latter is encircled by a smooth band and is decorated with the uræus; the bottom of the slightly tapering shaft springs from an encircling band of painted leaves.

Side by side with the type which we have just described we find another to which the hollow outward curve of the capital has given the name of *campaniform*. Nothing like it is to be found at Beni-Hassan, and no example, in stone, is extant from an earlier

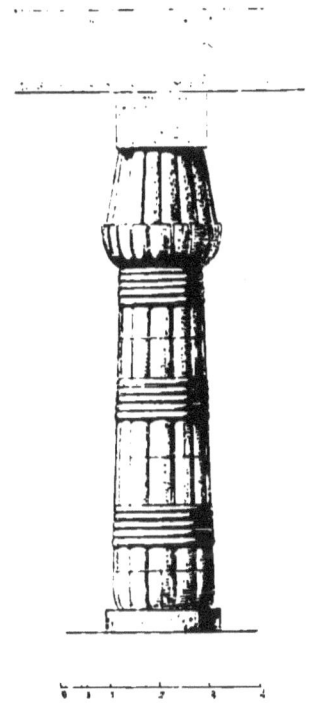

FIG. 77.—Column at Luxor; *Description*, vol. iii., pl. 8.

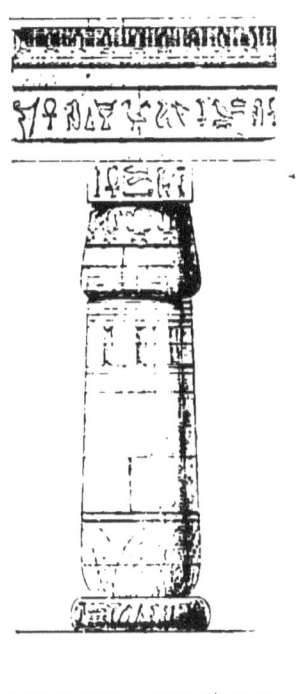

FIG. 78.—Column at Medinet-Abou; *Description*, vol. ii., pl. 4.

time than that of the Second Theban Empire.[1] The base is small. The flutes or separate stems have disappeared. The shaft is either smooth or decorated with bas-reliefs and inscriptions. The ligatures under the capital are still introduced. The springing

[1] We shall call attention, however, to a hypogeum at Gizeh, which is numbered 81 in Lepsius's map of that tomb-field. As at Beni-Hassan the chamber is preceded by a portico. In Lepsius's drawing (vol. i. pl. 27. fig. 1), the columns of this portico are campaniform.

of the capital is decorated with leaves and flowers painted in brilliant colours. A cubic abacus or die of stone stands upon the circular surface of the capital and transmits the resisting power of the column to the architrave.

The proportions and general appearance of the shaft vary greatly. In the first court at Medinet-Abou it is short and stumpy, and the capital alone has received a few ornaments in relief.

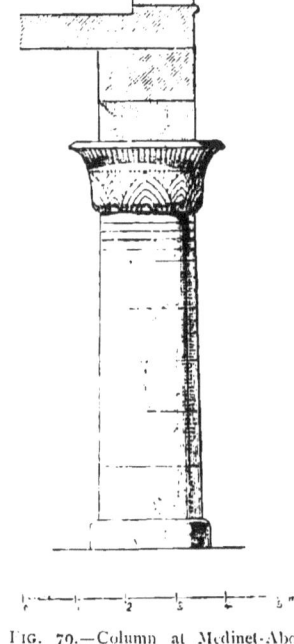

FIG. 79.—Column at Medinet-Abou ; *Description*, vol. ii., pl. 6.

In the Great Hall at Karnak, on the other hand, it is taller, more graceful in form and richer in decoration than in any other Egyptian building (Fig. 80). To give an idea of the colossal dimensions of these columns we need only repeat the often-made assertion that a hundred men can sit upon the upper surface of their capitals, which measure no less than 70 feet in circumference.

The shafts of both these columns diminish gradually from base to summit. The diminution is so slight that it is hardly perceptible by the eye. In the hypostyle hall of the Ramesseum (Fig. 81), on the other hand, it tapers rapidly. The columns in the central aisle come, by their proportions, midway between the thick-set type of Medinet-Abou and the lofty shafts of Karnak. Their lower parts have the bulbous form which we have already noticed in speaking of the lotiform type of column. The painted and sculptured ornament, although not so rich as that of Karnak, covers about one half of the whole surface.

We may cite, as showing interesting variations upon the campaniform type, the column of Soleb, dating from the eighteenth dynasty (Fig. 82), and that of Thothmes, from Karnak (Fig. 83). The capital of the former seems to have been suggested by a bunch of palm leaves arranged about a central

THE EGYPTIAN ORDERS.

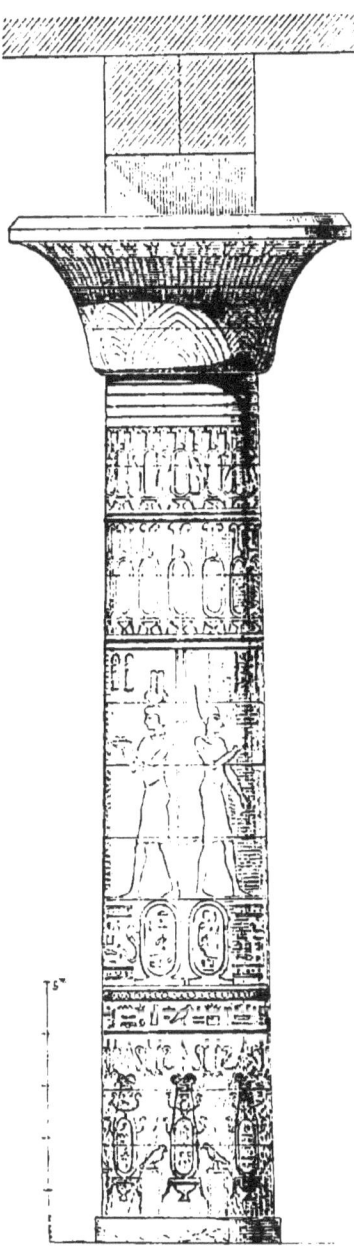

FIG. 80.—Column from the Great Hall at Karnak; *Description*, iii. 30.

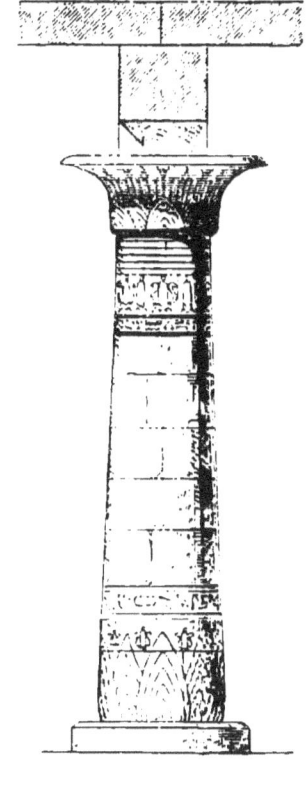

FIG. 81.—Column from the Hypostyle Hall of the Ramesseum; from Horeau.

post. In curving outwards the extremity of each leaf forms a lobe, which is shown in the plan (Fig. 82). The architect here made free use of the forms occurring in nature, but in the

Ptolemaic temples we find the palm tree copied in a far more literal fashion. There are capitals at Esneh composed of palm branches grouped in stages about the central shaft and copied leaf for leaf. Sometimes, as at Philæ, we even find date clusters mingled with the leaves.

The other capital to which we have alluded as occurring in the work of Thothmes at Karnak, is shaped like a suspended bell. The upper part of the shaft swells slightly so as to coincide with the outer rim of the bell; it is encircled with fillets below which is cut a vertical band of hieroglyphs. The capital is decorated with leaves growing downwards and on the whole it may be taken as showing the companiform type reversed.

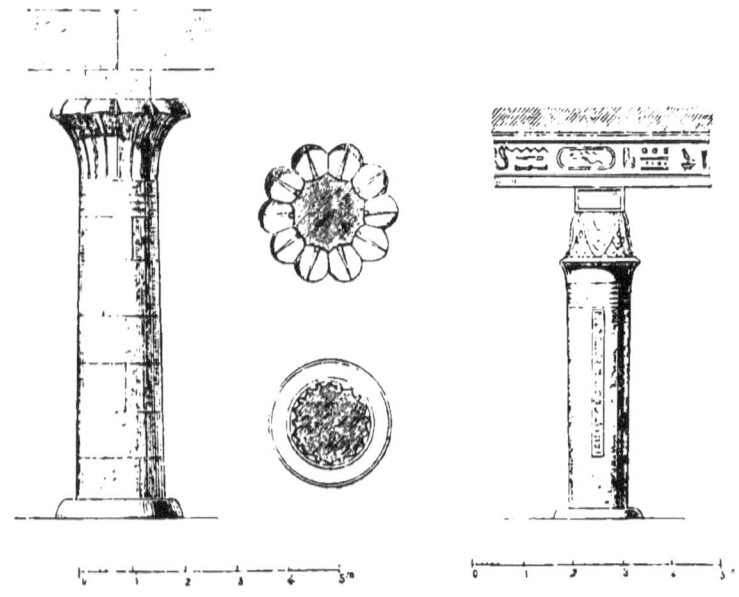

Fig. 82.—Column of Soleb; from Lepsius, part i., pl. 117.

Fig. 83.—Column of Thothmes at Karnak; from Lepsius, part i., pl. 81.

In this comparison between the different forms which were successively given to the Egyptian column, we might, if we had chosen, have included other varieties; and yet we do not think we have omitted any that are of importance. We have figured them to one scale so that their relative proportions can be at once grasped, and we have now to analyse the methods in which they were allied with their supports and superstructures. For that purpose we shall have to reproduce several of the piers and columns already mentioned and figured, on a larger scale and in perspective instead of elevation. We count upon these reproductions to show the individual characteristics of the Egyptian orders and the origin of their peculiar physiognomy.

When the architects of the New Empire made use of the square pier without giving it either capital or base, they covered it with bas-reliefs and inscriptions. Thus adorned it could be used without incongruity in rich and elaborate compositions. The truth of this statement may be seen from the adjoining reproduction of an angle from the peristyle of the Elephantine temple (Fig. 84).[1]

The firm and simple lines of the pier contrast well with the modest projection of the stylobate and the bolder profile of the cornice, and help, with the double base, to give dignity and solidity to the encircling portico.

When the pier is honoured with a capital, that capital does not in the least resemble those of the column proper. Being, in its essence, a vertical section of wall, it is treated as such, and given for crown a capital composed exactly in the same fashion as the cornice which crowns every Egyptian wall. Between this quasi-capital and the architrave a low abacus is introduced (Fig. 85).

The figure on page 109, represents one of the seven osiride piers in the first court of the temple at Medinet-Abou. The pier at the back of the statue is slightly wider than the base upon which the latter stands. At each side of the Pharaoh one of his children stands sculptured in very high relief, almost in the round. Without in any way compromising the dignity of the colossus the sculptor has bent his head slightly backwards so as to obtain a natural support for his lofty and complicated head-dress. Thanks to this artifice the head-dress in question is securely allied to the massive pier behind it without the intervention of any unsightly thicknesses of stone, and the expression of the whole glypto-architectural group is rendered more forcible and more suggestive of that strength in repose which is the characteristic of Egyptian architecture.[2]

[1] See also p. 396, Vol. I., and Fig. 230.

[2] There is no pier at Medinet-Abou in so perfect a condition as that figured by us. In order to complete our restoration, for so it is, we had the use of drawings which had been made long ago and of excellent photographs, and by combining one figure with another we obtained all the details necessary.

106　A HISTORY OF ART IN ANCIENT EGYPT.

FIG. 84.—Corner pier from the temple at Elephantine; from the elevation in the *Description*, i. 36.

The next illustration (Fig. 87) shows the upper part of a polygonal column with a hathoric capital of the oldest and most simple form. In later ages, during the Saït dynasties, the mask of the goddess was repeated upon the four sides of the column, and sometimes superimposed upon a bell-shaped capital. In this instance, where there is but one mask, the vertical band of hieroglyphs below it serves to show that the face where it occurs is the principal one.

This capital is one of the most singular achievements of Egyptian art. Why, out of all the multitude of Egyptian gods and goddesses, was Hathor alone selected for such a distinction? What is the meaning of the small naos or shrine upon her head? The explanation is still uncertain. Perhaps it is to be found in the simple fact that the word Hathor means the dwelling of Horus. This capital is found in the tombs as well as in the temples. We reproduce (Fig. 88) a hathoric pier from the tomb of a certain Nefer-Hotep who lived under the eighteenth dynasty; it is now in the museum at Boulak. The anterior face displays the mask of Hathor over the symbol *tet*, which has been interpreted to mean-*steadfastness* or *stability*.[1] A rich collar hangs down upon her breast.

FIG. 85.—Pier with capital, Karnak; from the elevation of Prisse.

On a column in the speos of Kalabché we find the band of hieroglyphs repeated upon four faces (Fig. 89). The flutes of this column are unusually numerous and closely spaced, and it therefore approaches the true cylindrical form. The abacus, however, which overhangs the shaft at every point, still serves to recall the monolithic pier and the tablet which was reserved at its summit when its angles were first struck off in order to give freer passage to the light.

The faggot-shaped column (Fig. 90) is not to be explained by any theory of development from the pier. We have reproduced its upper and lower extremities, together with the entablature and flat roof which it supports. The extreme

[1] See PIERRET, *Dictionnaire d'Archéologie Égyptienne*.

nakedness of the base given by the Egyptians to their columns is a curious feature. Shaft and capital may be carved into various shapes and adorned with the most brilliant colours, but the base is always perfectly bare and simple. Between one column and another there is no difference in this respect except in size. The only attempt at ornamentation ever found is a narrow band of hieroglyphs engraved, as at the Ramesseum, round its circumference (Fig. 91). On the other hand, the lower part of the shaft is always richly decorated. The principal element in this decoration is the circlet of leaves which are found both in the faggot-shaped columns and in those whose shafts are smooth. In the latter, however, the ornament is carried farther than in the former. Slender shoots are introduced between the larger leaves, which mount up the shaft and burst into leaf at the top. Above these, again, come the royal ovals, surmounted by the solar disk between two uræus serpents.

In the upper part of the column of Thothmes (Fig. 90), the pendants which fill the re-entering angles and the four rings at the top of the shaft, the pointed leaves and other ornaments of the capital, are rendered conspicuous by being painted in colours, yellow and blue, which will be found reproduced in Prisse's plate. We should have liked to give one of these columns with all its coloured decorations, but we hesitated to do so because we were not satisfied with the accuracy as to tone and tint of those coloured plates which had been introduced into previous works. And we wished to give no coloured reproductions except those made expressly from the monuments themselves, as in the case of the tomb from the Ancient Empire whose painted decorations are produced in plates xiii. and xiv.

It will be observed that in this case the abacus does not extend beyond the architrave, as it does in the Doric order of the Greeks.

We have given a column from the central aisle of the Great Hall at Karnak, as affording a good type of the bell-shaped capital (Fig. 80). We also give an example, with slight variations, from the Ramesseum (Fig. 92). It comes from the principal order in the hypostyle hall, and shows Egyptian architecture perhaps at its best. The profile of the capital combines grace with firmness of outline in the most happy manner. By dint of closely examining and comparing many reproductions we have succeeded, as we believe, in giving a more exact rendering

FIG. 86.—Osiride pier; Medinet-Abou

of its curves than any of our predecessors. Leaves and flowers are most happily arranged, and are painted also with an exquisite finish not to be found elsewhere. The decoration as a whole is of extraordinary richness. The royal ovals, with the disk of the sun and the uræus, encircle the shaft; vultures with outspread

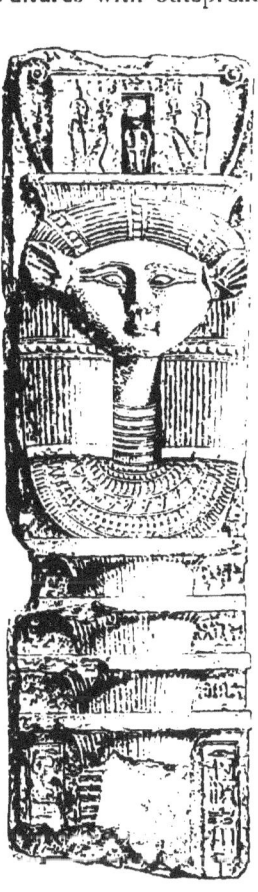

FIG. 87.—Hathoric pier from Eilithya. Lepsius, part i., pl. 100.

FIG. 88.—Hathoric pier from a tomb. Boulak.

wings cover the ceiling, and the architrave is carved on its visible sides, with long rows of hieroglyphs.[1]

[1] The slabs of which the roof is formed are grooved on their upper surfaces at their lines of junction (see Fig. 92), a curious feature which recurs in other Egyptian buildings, but has never been satisfactorily explained.

Of the derived and secondary forms of the campaniform capital there are but two upon which we need here insist. The first is that which is exemplified by the columns of a temple built by Seti I. at Sesebi, in Nubia (Fig. 93). It is very like the one at Soleb already figured (Fig. 82). The motive is the same, but the Sesebi example shows it in a more advanced stage of development. Its forms are fuller and more expressive, and the palm branches from which the idea is derived are more frankly incorporated in the design. It is not an exact copy from nature, as at Esneh, but a good use has been made of the fundamental vegetable forms.

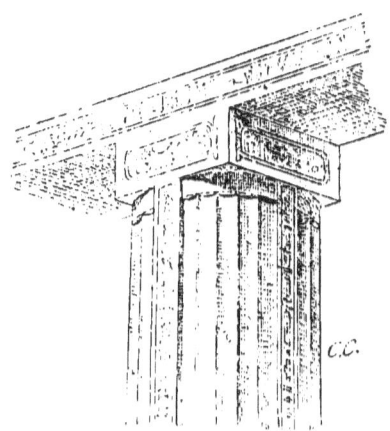

Fig. 89.—Column at Kalabché; from the elevation of Prisse.

The other variation upon the same theme is a much later one; it is to be found in the temple built by Nectanebo on the island of Philæ (Fig. 94). The simplicity of the Sesebi and Soleb capitals has vanished; the whole composition is imbued with the love for complex form which distinguished the Sait epoch. The swelling base of the column seems to spring from a bouquet of triangular leaves. The anterior face of the column is ornamented with a band of hieroglyphs; its upper part is encircled by five smooth rings, above which, again, it is fluted. According to Prisse, who alone gives particulars as to this little building, some of the capitals have no ornament beyond their finely-chiselled palm-leaves; others have half-opened lotus-flowers between each pair of leaves. Finally, the square die or abacus which supports the architrave

Fig. 90.—Column of Thothmes III.; from the Ambulatory of Thothmes, at Karnak. From Prisse's elevation.

is much higher and more important than in the columns hitherto described, and it bears a mask of Hathor surmounted by a naos upon each of its four sides. This unusual height of abacus, the superposition of the hathoric capital upon the bell-shaped one, and the repetition of the mask of Hathor upon all four sides, are the premonitory signs of the Ptolemaic style.

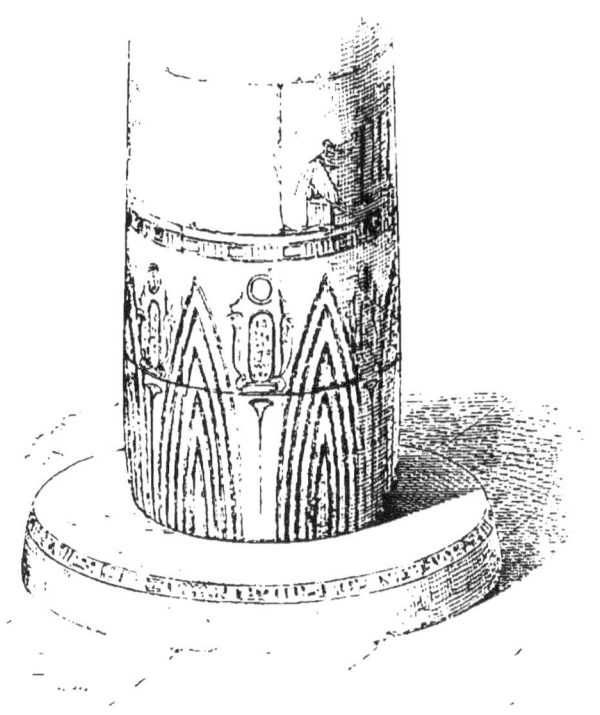

FIG. 91.—Base of a column; from the great hall of the Ramesseum, central avenue.

The capital from the Ambulatory of Thothmes, at Thebes, presents a type both rare and original (Fig. 95). Between our illustration and that of Lepsius there is a difference which is not without importance.[1] According to the German *savants*, the abacus is inscribed within the upper circumference of the bell; but if we may believe a sketch made by an architect upon the spot, the truth is that the upper circumference of the capital is

[1] LEPSIUS, *Denkmæler*, part i. pl. 81.

contained within the four sides of the abacus, which it touches at their centres The four angles of the abacus, therefore, stand out well beyond the upper part of the capital, uniting it properly to the architrave, and giving a satisfactory appearance of solidity to the whole.

This peculiar form of capital has generally been referred to the individual caprice of some architect, anxious, above all things, to invent something new.[1] But the same form is to be found in the architectural shapes preserved by the paintings of the ancient empire (Fig. 59) which seems fatal to this explanation. It is probable that if we possessed all the work of the Egyptian architects we should find that the type was by no means confined to Karnak. It was, however, far less beautiful in its lines than the ordinary shape, and though ancient enough, never became popular.

The Egyptians were not always content with the paint-brush and chisel for the decoration of their capitals, they occasionally made use of metal also. This has been proved by a discovery made at Luxor in the presence of M. Brugsch, who describes it in these terms: "The work of clearing the temple began with the part constructed by Amenophis III. and gave some very unexpected results. The capitals of the columns were overlaid with copper plates, to which the contour of the stone beneath had been given by the hammer. They had afterwards been painted. Large pieces of these plates were found still hanging to the capitals, while other pieces lay among the surrounding *débris*. Thus a new fact in the history of Egyptian art has been established, namely, that stonework was sometimes covered with metal."[2]

This process was not generally, nor even frequently, employed, as we may judge by the vast number of capitals painted in the most brilliant colours, which remain. If the surface of the stone was to be covered up such care would not have been taken to beautify it. The fact that the process was used at all is, however, curious;

[1] WILKINSON, vol. i. p. 40. In the *Description de l'Égypte* (*Antiquités*, vol. ii. p. 474), we find this shape accounted for by opposition of two lotus-flowers, one above another. Such an explanation could only be offered by one who had a theory to serve.

[2] Extract from a letter of M. Brugsch, published by Hittorf in the *Athenæum Français*, 1854, p. 153.

FIG. 92.—Bell-shaped capital, from the hypostyle hall of the Ramesseum. From the chief order.

it seems to be a survival from the ancient wooden architecture in which metal was commonly used.

The architrave which was employed with all these varieties of capital was sometimes of a kind which deserves to be noticed (Fig. 102). Whenever the dimensions of the column were sufficiently great the stone beams which met upon the die or abacus had oblique joints. The motive of the architect in making use of such a junction is obvious enough; it was calculated to afford

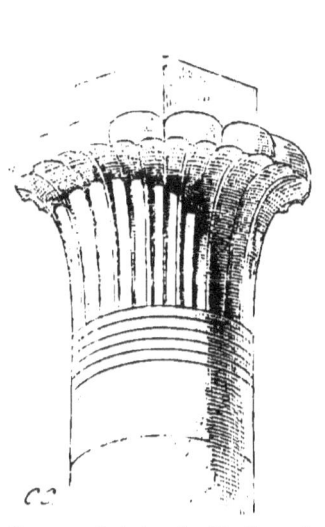

Fig. 93.—Capital at Sesebi. From the elevation of Lepsius, *Denkmäler*, part i., pl. 119.

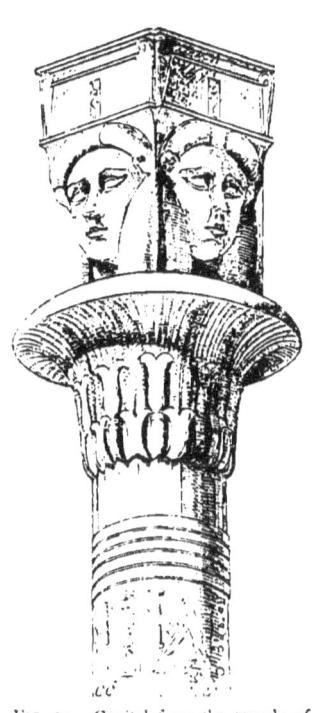

Fig. 94.—Capital from the temple of Nectanebo, at Philæ. From the elevation of Prisse.

greater solidity, and it was the most convenient way in which lateral architraves could be united with those disposed longitudinally. Any other arrangement would have involved a sacrifice of space and would have left a certain part of the abacus doing nothing.

We have now brought our analysis of the principal types of pier and column used by the Egyptians to an end. They suggest, however, certain general reflections to which we must next endeavour to give expression. In spite of the great apparent diversity of their forms, we are enabled to perceive that the Egyptian orders obeyed an unchanging law of development, and that certain characteristic features persistently reappear through all their transformations. We must attempt to define these laws and characteristics, as, otherwise, we shall fail to make the originality of Eyptian art appreciated, we shall be unable to classify its successes, or to mark with accuracy the limits which it failed to pass.

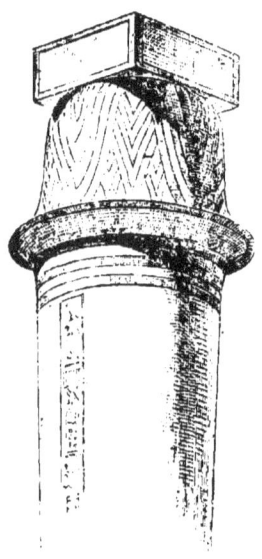

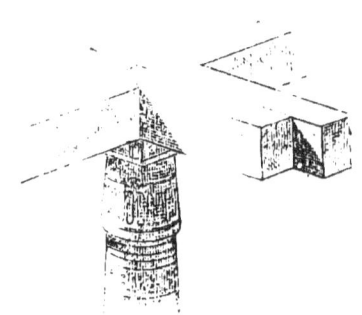

FIG. 95.—Capital from the work of Thothmes at Karnak.

FIG. 96.—Arrangement of architraves upon a capital. From the plans and elevations of Lepsius.

Between the square pier with neither base nor capital of the early Empire and the graceful columns of the Ramesseum there is a difference which marks ages of progress. The general form of the support became gradually more complex and more refined. As occurred elsewhere, it was divided into parts, each of which had its proper duty and its proper name. The base was distinguished from the shaft, and the shaft from the capital. Each of these parts was shaped by the sculptor and clothed in colour by the painter. For long centuries the architect never relaxed his efforts to perfect his art. The simple and sturdy prismatic column gave way to the elaborate forms which exist in the great temples of the Ramessids; the latter in turn lost their power to satisfy and new motives were sought for in the combination of all those which had gone before. In the series of Egyptian types the capital of Nectanebo would therefore occupy a place corresponding to that of the composite capital in the series of Græco-Roman orders.

The general movement of art in Egypt may therefore be compared to that of art in Greece and Italy; and yet there is a difference. From the rise of Greek architecture until its decay, the proportions of its vertical members underwent a continual, *but consistent*, modification of their proportions. Century after century the figure in which their height was expressed proportionately with their bulk, became greater. In the height of the Doric columns of the old temple at Corinth there are fewer diameters than in those of the Parthenon, and in those of the Parthenon there are fewer than in the doric shafts of Rome. This tendency explains the neglect which befel this order about the fourth century before our era. In the sumptuous buildings of Asia Minor and Syria and of the "Lower Period" in Egypt, it was replaced by the graceful and slender outlines of the Ionic order. A similar explanation may be given of the favour in which the Corinthian order was held throughout the Roman world.

Such a development is not to be found in Egypt. The forms of Egyptian architecture did not become less substantial with the passage of the centuries. It is possible that familiarity with light structures of wood and metal had early created a taste for slender supports. The polygonal and faggot-shaped columns of Beni-Hassan are no thicker than those of far later times. A comparison of the columns at Thebes points to the same conclusion. The shortest and most thick-set in its proportions of them all (Fig. 78) is at Medinet-Abou, and is about two centuries later than those of the same order which decorate the second court at Luxor (Fig. 77). Its heaviness is even more apparent when we compare it with the great columns of a different order, at Karnak (Fig. 80), and the Ramesseum (Fig. 81), which precede it by at least a century.

The progress of Egyptian art was, then, less continuous and less regular than that of classic art. It had moments of rest, of exhaustion, even of retrogression. It was not governed by internal logical principles so severe as those of the Greeks.

The manner in which the capital is allied to the shaft below, and the architrave above shows changes of the same kind.

The first duty of the capital is to oppose a firm and individual contour to the monotony of the shaft. The constructor has to determine a point in the length of the latter where it shall cease to be, where its gradual diminution in section, a diminution which could not be prolonged to the architrave without compromising the safety of the building, shall be arrested. The natural office of the capital would seem to be to call attention to this point. The architect, therefore, gives it a diameter greater than that of the shaft at the point where they meet. This salience restores to the column the material which it has lost; it completes it, and determines its proportion, so that it is no longer capable of either increase or diminution.

Again, when the salience is but the preparation for a greater development above, it seems to add to the solidity of the edifice by receiving the architrave on a far larger surface than the shaft could offer. The support seems to enlarge itself, the better to embrace the entablature.

The two requirements which the capital has to fulfil may, then, be thus summarized: in the first place, it has to mark the point where the upward movement of the lines comes to an end; and, secondly, it has to make, or to seem to make, the column better fitted to play its part as a support. Its functions are dual in principle; it has to satisfy the æsthetic desires of the eye, and the constructive requirements of the material. The latter office may be more apparent than real, but, in architecture, what seems to be necessary is so.

The Greek capital, in all its forms, thoroughly fulfils these double conditions, while that of Egypt satisfies them in a very imperfect manner. Let us take the ancient polygonal column as an example. The feeble tablet which crowns its shaft neither opposes itself frankly to the upright lines below it, nor, in the absence of an echinus, is it happily allied with the shaft. It gives, however, a greater appearance of constructive repose to the architrave than the latter would have without it.

In the column which terminates in a lotus-bud the capital is of more importance, but the contrast between it and the shaft is often very slightly marked. At Luxor and Karnak the smooth capital seems to be nothing more than an accident, a gentle swelling in the upper part of the cone; besides which it really plays no part in the construction, as the surface of the abacus above it is no greater than a horizontal section through the highest and most slender part of the shaft.

Of all the Egyptian capitals, that which seems the happiest in conception is the campaniform. This capital, far from being folded back upon itself, throws out a fine and bold curve beyond the shaft. But we are surprised and even distressed to find that the surface thus obtained is not employed for the support of the architrave, which is carried by a comparatively small cubic abacus,

FIG. 97.—The Nymphæa Nelumbo; from the *Description de l'Égypte : Hist. Naturelle*, pl. 61.

which rests upon the centre of the capital. At Karnak and Medinet-Abou this abacus is not so absurdly high as it afterwards became in the Ptolemaic period,[1] but yet its effect is singular rather than pleasant. We feel inclined to wonder why this fine calyx of stone should have been constructed if its borders were to remain idle. It is like a phrase commenced but never finished. Without this fault the composition, of which it forms a part, would be worthy both in proportion and in decoration, of being placed side by side with the most perfect of the Greek columns.

[1] A good idea of this can be gained from the building known as *Pharaoh's Bed*, at Philæ. It is shown on the right of our sketch at p. 431, Vol. I.

The last or, it may be, the first question, which is asked in connection with the form of column employed by any particular race, has to do with its origin. We have preferred to make it the last question, because we thought that the analysis of form which we have attempted to set forth would help us to an answer. There are many difficulties in the matter, but after the facts to which we have called attention, it will not be denied that the forms of wooden construction, which were the first to be developed in Egypt, had a great effect upon work in stone.

Ever since men began to interest themselves in Egyptian art, this has found an important place in their speculations. In the two forms which alternate with one another at Thebes, many have seen faithful transcriptions of two plants which filled a large space in Egyptian civilization by their decorative qualities and the practical services which they rendered; we mean, of course, the lotus and the papyrus.

There were in Egypt many species belonging to the family of the *Nymphæaceæ*, a family which is represented in our northern climates by the yellow and white nenuphars or water-lilies. Besides these Egypt possessed, and still possesses, the white lotus (*Nymphæa lotus* of Linnæus), and the blue lotus (*Nymphæa cærulea* of Savigny); but the true Egyptian lotus, the red lotus (the *Nymphæa nelumbo* of Linnæus, the *Nelumbium speciosum* of Wild) exists no longer in a wild state, either in Egypt or any other known part of Africa (Fig. 97). The accurate descriptions given by the ancient writers have enabled botanists, however, to recognize it among the flora of India. It is at least one third larger than our common water-lily, from which it differs also in the behaviour of its leaves and of the stems which bear the flowers. These do not float on the surface of the water but rise above it to a height of from twelve to fifteen inches.[1] The flower, which stands higher than the leaves, is borne upon a stalk which instead of being soft and pliant like that of the water-lily has the firmness and consistency of wood. It has an agreeable smell like that of anise. In the bas-reliefs the ancient Egyptians are often seen holding it to their nostrils. The fruit, which is shaped like the rose of a watering-pot, contains seeds as large as the stone of an olive.

---

[1] These upstanding flowers and stalks form the distinguishing characteristic of the Nelumbo species.

These seeds, which were eaten either green or dried,[1] were called *Egyptian beans* by the Greek and Latin writers because they were consumed in such vast quantities in the Nile valley.[2] The seeds of the other kinds of nymphæaceæ, which were smaller (Herodotus compares them with those of a poppy), gave, when pounded in a mortar, a flour of which a kind of bread was made. Even the root was not wasted; according to the old historians, it had a sweet and agreeable taste.[3]

The papyrus belongs to the family of *Cyperaceæ*, which is still represented in Egypt by several species, but the famous plant which received the early writings of mankind, the *Papyrus antiquorum* of the botanist, has also practically disappeared from Egypt, where it is only to be found in a few private gardens. The ancients made it an object of special care. It was cultivated in the Sebennitic nome, its roots being grown in shallow water. Strabo gave a sufficiently accurate idea of its appearance when he described it as a "peeled wand surmounted by a plume of feathers."[4] This green plume or bouquet is by no means without elegance (Fig. 98). According to Theophrastus the plant attained to a height of ten cubits, or about sixteen feet.[5] This may, however, be an exaggeration. The finest plants that I could find in the gardens of Alexandria did not reach ten feet. Their stems were as thick as a stout broom-handle and sharply triangular in section.

The reed-brakes which occur so frequently in the paintings consist of different varieties of the papyrus (Fig. 8, Vol. I.). The uses to which the plant could be put were very numerous. The root was used for fuel and other purposes. The lower part of the stalk furnished a sweet and aromatic food substance, which was chewed either raw or boiled, for the sake of the juice.[6] Veils, mats, sandals, &c., were made from the bark; candle and torch wicks

---

[1] HERODOTUS, ii. 92.

[2] For the different species of the lotus and their characteristics see *Description de l'Égypte, Hist. Naturelle*, vol. ii. pp. 303-313 and *Atlas*, plates 60 and 61.—In the *Recueil de Travaux*, etc., vol. i. p. 190, there is a note by M. VICTOR LORET upon the Egyptian names for the lotus.

[3] STRABO, xvii. 1, 15.—DIODORUS, i. 34.

[4] STRABO, xvii. 1, 15.

[5] Strabo only speaks of ten feet, which would agree better with modern experience.

[6] DIODORUS, i. 80.

from the bark; baskets and even boats from the stalk.[1] As for the processes by which the precious fabric which the Greeks called βίβλος was obtained they will be found fully described in the paper of Dureau de-la-Malle *Sur le Papyrus et la Fabrication du Papier*.[2] Our word *paper* is derived from *papyrus*, and forms a slight but everlasting monument to the great services rendered to civilization by the inventive genius of the Egyptians. The importation of the papyrus, which followed the establishment of direct relations between Greece and Egypt in the time of the Sait princes,[3] exercised the greatest influence upon the development of Greek thought. It created prose composition, and with it history, philosophy, and science.

The two plants which we have mentioned were so specially reverenced by the Egyptians that they constituted them severally into the signs by which the two great divisions of the country were indicated in their writings. The *papyrus* was the emblem of the Delta, in whose lazy waters it luxuriated, and the lotus that of the Thebaïd.[4]

Besides this testimony to their importance, the careful descriptions left by the ancient travellers in Egypt, Herodotus and Strabo, also show the estimation in which these two plants were held by the Egyptians; the palm alone could contest their well-earned supremacy. It is easy, then, to understand how the artist and ornamentist were led to make use of their graceful forms. We have already pointed out many instances of such employment, and we are far from underrating its importance, but we have yet to explain the method followed, and the kind and degree of imitation which the Egyptian artist allowed himself.

The lotus especially has been found everywhere by writers upon Egypt.[5] The pointed leaves painted upon the lower parts

[1] PIERRET, *Dictionnaire d'Archéologie Égyptienne*, see *Papyrus*. Upon the different varieties of papyrus, see also WILKINSON, vol. ii. p. 121; pp. 179-189; and EBERS, *Ægypten*, pp. 126, 127.

[2] *Mémoires de l'Académie des Inscriptions*, vol. xix. p. 140, with one plate.

[3] EGGER, *Des Origines de la Prose dans la Littérature Grecque*. (*Mémoires de Littérature Ancienne*, xi.)

[4] MASPERO, *Histoire Ancienne*, p. 8.

[5] *Description de l'Égypte; Hist. Naturelle*, vol. ii. p. 311. *Antiquités*, vol. i. *Description générale de Thèbes*, p. 133: "Who can doubt that they wished to imitate the lotus in its entirety? The shaft of the column is the stem, the capital the flower, and, still more obviously, the lower part of the column seems to us an exact representation of that of the lotus and of plants in general."

of columns have been recognized as imitations of "those scaly

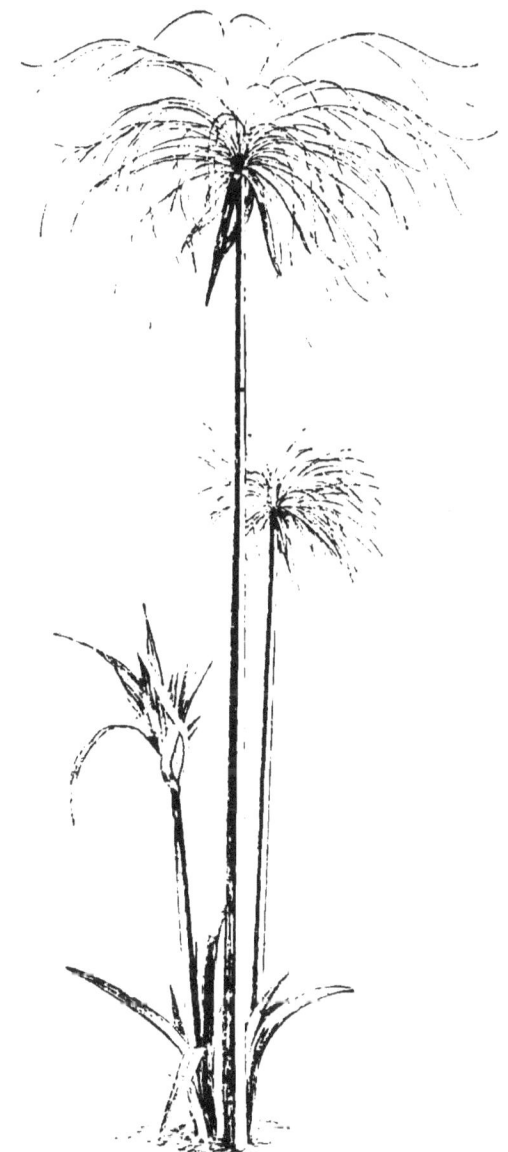

Fig. 98.—Papyrus plant, drawn in the gardens of the Luxembourg, Paris, by M. Saint-Elme Gautier.

leaves which surround the point where the stem of the lotus, the papyrus, and many other aquatic plants, merges in the root." According to this theory the ligneous stem which rises from a depth beneath the water of, perhaps, six feet, and carries the large open flower at its top, was the prototype of the Egyptian column. The bulbous form with which so many shafts are endowed at the base, would be another feature taken directly from nature. The leaves, properly speaking, which spread around the flower, are found about and below the capital, while the capital itself is nothing else, we are told, than the flower, sometimes fully opened, sometimes while yet in the bud. When the shaft is smooth it represents a single stem, when it is grooved, it means a faggot of stems tied together by a cord.

Others make similar claims for the papyrus. They refuse to admit that the whole of the Egyptian orders were founded upon the lotus. Mariette allowed that the capitals which we have called lotiform were copied from that plant, but he contended that the bell-shaped capital was freely copied from the plume of its rival. He proposed that this latter capital should be called *papyriform*, and to my objections, which were founded upon the composition of a head of papyrus, he answered that the Egyptians neglected what may be called internal details, and were contented with rendering the outward contours. In support of his idea, he called attention to the fact that some of the faggot-shaped columns present triangular sections, like that of the papyrus stem.

In spite of this latter fact, Mariette did not convert me to his opinion. The columns in which this triangular section is found are not crowned by an open flower. The profiles of their capitals resemble that of a truncated bud, a form which cannot possibly be obtained from the papyrus, and they seem, therefore, to combine characteristics taken from two different plants. His explanation of the campaniform capital seems still less admissable. It is impossible to allow that in the tuft of slender filaments gracefully yielding to the wind, which is figured on page 127, we have the prototype of those inverted bells of stone, whose uninterrupted contours express so much strength and amplitude. No less difficult is it to discover the first idea of those sturdy shafts which seem so well proportioned to the mighty architraves which they have to support, in the slender stalk of the famous water plant. The hypostyle halls may be compared to palm groves, to forests of pine, of oak, or of beech. In such a comparison there would be nothing surprising, but the papyrus, with its attenuated proportions and yielding frame, would seem to be, of all vegetables, the least likely to have inspired the architects of Karnak and Luxor.

The lotus seems to us to have no more right than the papyrus to be considered the unique origin of the forms which we are considering. All those resemblances, of which so much has been made, sink to very little when they are closely examined. It requires more than good will to recognize the formless *folioles* which cluster round the base of the stalk in those large and well-shaped triangular leaves with parallel ribs, which decorate the bases of Egyptian columns. Moreover, these leaves reappear in other places, such as capitals, in which, if this explanation of their origin is to be accepted, they could have no place. They frequently occur, also, at the foot of a wall. As for the true circular leaf of the lotus, it is not to be found, except, perhaps in a few Ptolemaic capitals. Its stem, concealed almost entirely by the muddy water, is very slender, and is hardly more suggestive than that of the papyrus of a massive stone column. The bulbous form of the lower part of the shaft would be a constant form if it were an imitation of nature, whereas it is, in fact, exceptional. With the capitals, however, it is different. Those which are to be found at Thebes are referred, by common consent, to the lotus-bud. And yet, perhaps, they resemble any other bud as much as that of the lotus. It is, however, when they are fully open, that one flower is easily distinguishable from another by the shape and number of their petals, as well as by the variety of their colours. Like babies in their cradles, unopened buds are strangely alike. But seeing the place occupied by the lotus in the minds of the Egyptians, in their wooden architecture and painted decorations, it is natural enough to believe that it gave them their first hint for the capital in question ; we have, therefore, not hesitated to use the epithet lotiform which has been consecrated to it by custom.

As for the campaniform capital we find it difficult to allow that it represents the open flower of the lotus. From a certain distance it no doubt resembles the general lines of some flowers, but those belong to the family of the *Campanulaceæ* rather than to that of the nymphæaceæ. The profile of this inverted bell, however, does not seem to have been suggested by the wish to imitate any flower whatever, least of all that of the lotus. The capitals at Soleb and Sesebi (Figs. 82 and 93) embody careful imitations of, at least, the general shapes and curves of date-tree branches. Here there is nothing of the kind. There is not the slightest indication of the elongated and crowded petals of the lotus. Both at Karnak and at the Ramesseum, the latter may be easily recognised among the stalks of papyrus and other freely imitated flowers, but *upon* the columns and not in their shapes. Both base and capital were ornamented with leaves and flowers. Their contours have been gently indicated with a pointed instrument and then filled in with brilliant colours, which help to relieve them from their ground. The whole decoration is superficial; it is not embodied in the column and has no effect upon its general form and character.

The following explanation of the resemblances which do undoubtedly exist between certain details of Egyptian architecture and the forms of some of the national plants, is the most probable. The stalks of the lotus and the papyrus are too weak and slender ever to have been used as supports by themselves, but it is quite possible that on *fête* days, they were used to decorate pillars and posts of more substantial construction, being bound round them like the outer sticks of a faggot. This fashion has its modern illustration in the Italian habit of draping the columns of a church with cloth or velvet on special occasions, and in the French custom of draping houses with garlands and white cloth for the procession of the *Fête Dieu*.

The river and the canals of Egypt offered all the elements for such a decoration. The lotus and papyrus stems would be attached to the column which they decorated, at the top and bottom. The leaves at the roots would lie about its base, those round the flower and the flower itself would droop gracefully beneath the architrave, would embrace and enlarge the capital when it existed, or supply its place when there was none. The eyes of a people with so keen a perception of beauty as the Egyptians could not be insensible to the charm of a column thus crowned with the verdure of green leaves, with the splendour of the open flower and with the graceful forms of the still undeveloped bud. It is probable enough that the architect, when he began to feel the necessity for embellishing the bare surface of his column, took this temporary and often-renewed decoration for his model

The first attempt to imitate these natural forms would be made in wood and metal, substances which would lend themselves to the unpractised moulder more readily than stone, but in time the difficulties of the latter material would be overcome. The deep vertical grooves cut in the shaft would afford a rough imitation of the round stems of the lotus and the triangular ones of the papyrus. The circular belts at the top would suggest the cords by which they were tied to the shaft. The leaves and flowers painted upon the lowest part of the shaft and upon the capital, may be compared to permanent chromatic shadows of the bouquets of colour and verdure which had once hidden those members. Finally, the artist found in the swelling sides of the bud and the hollow curves of the corolla those flowing lines which he desired for the proper completion of his column.

This hypothesis seems to leave no point unexplained, and it receives additional probability from a detail which can hardly be satisfactorily accounted for by the advocates of the rival theory. We mean the cube of stone which is interposed as a kind of abacus between the capital and the architrave. If we refer the general lines to those of a plain column bound about with flowering stalks, there is no difficulty. The abacus then represents the rigid column behind the decoration, raising its summit above the drooping heads of lotus and papyrus, and visibly doing its duty as a support. Its effect may not be very happy, but its *raison d'être* is complete. On the other hand its existence is quite inexplicable, if we are to look upon the column as a reproduction in stone, a kind of petrifaction of a single stem. To what, in that case, does this heavy stone die correspond? To those who believe the capital to be the representation of a single flower with its circlet of graceful petals, its presence must seem nothing less than an outrage.

In their light structures only do we find the Egyptians frankly imitating flowers and half-opened buds (Figs. 57, 63, and 64), but even there the imitation is far from literal. The petals in a single "bloom" are often of different colours, some blue, some yellow, others again red or pink, a mixture which is not to be found in nature. The Egyptian decorator thought only of decoration. He used his tints capriciously from the botanist's point of view, but he often reproduced the forms of Egyptian plants with considerable fidelity, especially those splendid lotus-flowers which occupied so large a part in his affections long before the poets of India sang their praise. In fashioning slender shafts which had little weight to support, the artist could give the reins to his fancy, he could mould his metal plates or his precious timber into the semblance of any natural form that pleased his eye, and the types thus created would, of course, be present in the minds of the first architects who attempted to decorate rock-cut tombs or temples and constructed buildings. We affirm again, however, that neither the stone column of the Egyptians, nor that of the Greeks, in its most complete and dignified form, resulted from the servile imitation, nor even from the intelligent interpretation of living nature.

The column was an abstract creation of plastic genius. Its forms were determined by the natural properties of the material employed, by structural necessities, and by a desire for beauty of proportion. Different peoples have had different ideas as to what constitutes this beauty; they have had their secret instincts and individual preferences. The artist, too, who wishes to ornament a column, is sure to borrow motives from any particular form of art or industry in which the race to which he belongs may have earned distinction In some cases, therefore, his work may resemble carved wood, in others chased or beaten metal. He will also be influenced, to some extent, by the features and characteristic forms of the plants and animals peculiar to his country. But wherever a race is endowed with a true instinct for art, its architects will succeed in creating for stone architecture an appropriate style of its own. The exigencies of the material differ from those of metal or wood. Its unbending rigidity places a great gulf between it and the elasticity and perpetual mobility which characterize organic life. The Egyptian architects saw from the first that this difference, or rather contrast, would have to be reckoned with. They understood perfectly well that the shaft which was to support a massive roof of stone must not be a copy of those slender stems of lotus or papyrus which bend before the wind, or float upon the lazy waters of the canals. The phrase *column-plant* or *plant-column*, which has sometimes been used in connection with the columns of Luxor and Karnak, is a contradiction in terms.

But why should we dwell upon these questions of origin? In the history of art, as in that of language, they are nearly always insoluble, especially when we have to do with a race who created all their artistic forms and idioms for themselves. The case is different when we have to do with a nation who came under the influence of an earlier civilization than their own. Then, and then only, can such an inquiry lead to useful results. The word origin is then a synonym for affiliation, and an inquiry is directed towards establishing the method and the period in which the act of birth took place.

In our later volumes we shall have to go into such questions in detail, but in the case of Egypt we are spared that task. All that we mean by civilization had its origin in Egypt, so far, at least, as we can tell. It is the highest point in the stream to which we can mount. Any attempt to determine the genesis of each particular æsthetic motive in a past so distant that a glance into its depths takes away our breath, would be a mere waste of time and ingenuity.

§ 6. *The Ordonnance of Egyptian Colonnades.*

A French writer tells us that uniformity is sure to give birth to weariness sooner or later, and there are many people who would believe, if they thought about it, that his words exactly apply to the art of Egypt. The character which was given to it when its creations first became known to modern Europe clings to it still. Our museums are full of objects dating from the last centuries of the monarchy and even from the Greek and Roman period. A very slight study of Egyptian architecture is sufficient, however, to destroy such a prejudice, in spite of its convenience for those who are lazily disposed. The pier and column were extremely various in their types, as we have seen, and each type was divided into numerous species. The same variety is found in the arrangement, or ordonnance, of the columns, both in the interior and exterior of their buildings. We cannot prove this better than by placing a series of plans of hypostyle halls and porticos before the eye of the reader, accompanied by a few illustrations in perspective which will suffice to show the freedom enjoyed by the Egyptian architect and the number of different arrangements which he could introduce into a single building.

The fullest development of Egyptian columnar architecture is to be found in their interiors.

The simplest arrangement is to be found in the small chambers where the roof is sustained by a single row of columns (Fig. 98). When the apartment was slighty larger it contained two rows, the

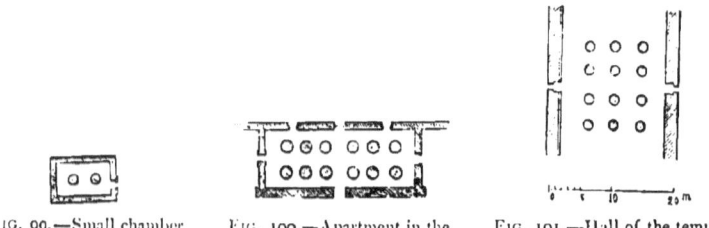

FIG. 99.—Small chamber at Karnak.

FIG. 100.—Apartment in the temple at Luxor.

FIG. 101.—Hall of the temple at Abydos; *Description*, vol. ii. p. 41.

space between the rows being wider than that between the columns and the wall (Fig. 100). Sometimes in still larger halls we find three rows of columns separated from one another by equal spaces in every direction (Fig. 101). Finally in those great chambers which are known as hypostyle halls, the number of columns seems to be practically unlimited. At Karnak there are

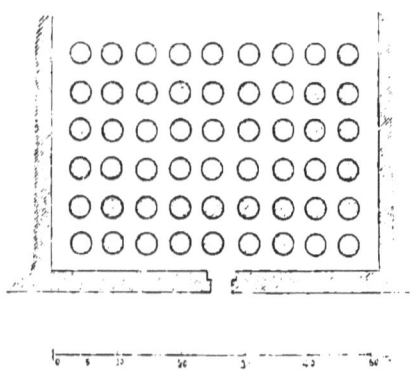

FIG. 102.—Plan of part of the Hypostyle Hall at Karnak.

a hundred and thirty-four (Fig. 102), at the Ramesseum forty-eight, at Medinet-Abou twenty-four.

The full effect of the hypostyle hall is to be seen at Karnak and at the Ramesseum. In those halls the central aisle is higher than the parts adjoining and is distinguished by a different type of column (Plate IV). It is more than probable that this happy arrangement was not confined to Thebes. We should no doubt have encountered it in more than one of the temples of Memphis and the Delta had they been preserved to our time. Its principle was reproduced in the propylæa of the acropolis at Athens, where the Ionic and Doric orders figured side by side.

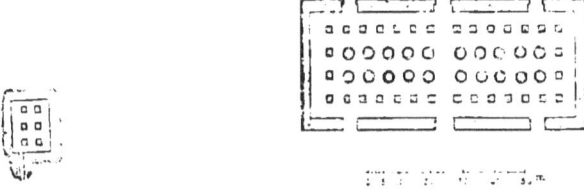

FIG. 103.—Tomb at Sakkarah.

FIG. 104.—Hall in the inner portion of the Great Temple at Karnak.

In the ancient tombs at Sakkarah the quadrangular pier alone was used to support the roof (Fig. 103). In the Theban temples it was combined with the column. In the chamber called the ambulatory of Thothmes (J in Fig. 215, Vol. I.), at Karnak, a row of square piers surrounds an avenue of circular columns which to bear the roof (Fig. 104).

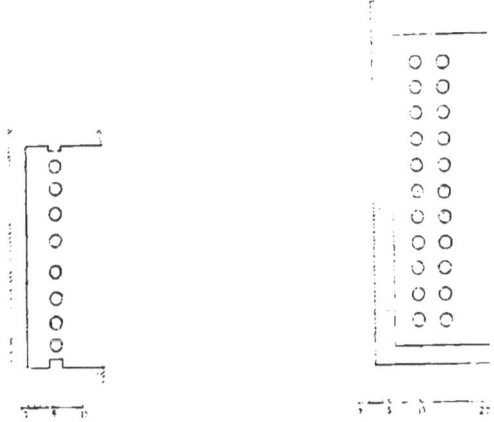

FIG. 105.—Portico of the first court at Medinet-Abou.

FIG. 106.—Portico of the first court at Luxor.

The external porticos are no less remarkable for variety of plan. At Medinet-Abou we find one consisting of only a single row of columns (Fig. 105). At Luxor the columns are doubled upon all four sides of the first court (Fig. 106), and upon two sides of the second; upon one side of the latter, the side nearest to the sanctuary, there are four rows of columns (Fig. 107).

All these are within the external walls of the courts, but the peripteral portico, embracing the temple walls, like those of Greece, is also to be found in a few rare instances (Fig. 108); as,

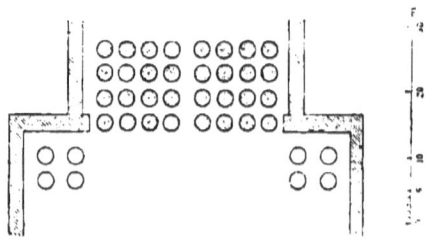

FIG. 107.—The portico of the pronaos, Luxor.

for example, in the small temple at Elephantiné which we have already described.[1]

In the cases where the portico is within the courts, it is sometimes confined to two sides, as at Luxor (Fig. 109); the columns shown at the top of our plan belong to the pronaos and not to

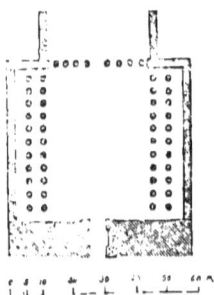

FIG. 108.—Part plan of the temple at Elephantiné.

FIG. 109.—Luxor, plan of the second court.

the court. In the Temple of Khons it surrounds three sides (Fig. 110), while the fine court added to the temple of Luxor by Rameses II. has a double colonnade all round it (Fig. 111).

Both in the interior of the halls and in the external porticos we find an apparently capricious irregularity in spacing the

[1] Chapter iv. pp. 396-400, Vol. I.

columns. Sometimes intercolumniations vary at points where we should expect uniformity, as in the outer court of Luxor (Fig. 112). On two of the faces the columns are farther apart than on the other two. The difference is not easily seen on the ordinary small plans, but it is conspicuous in the large one of the *Description*.[1]

It is easy to understand why the spacing should have been increased in front of a door, an arrangement which exists at Gournah (Fig. 113), and at Luxor (Figs. 109 and 111).

In the hypostyle halls we find columns of different sizes and orders. Six of the great columns which form the central avenue at Karnak cover as much ground, measuring from the first to the sixth, as nine of the smaller pillars. Between supports so

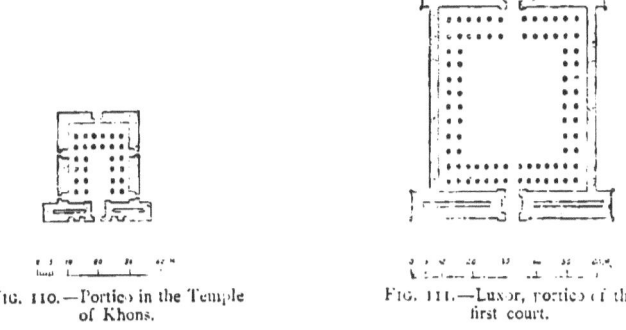

FIG. 110.—Portico in the Temple of Khons.

FIG. 111.—Luxor, portico of the first court.

arranged and proportioned no constant relation could be established (Fig. 114). The transverse lines passing through the centres of each pair of great columns correspond to the centres neither of the smaller shafts nor of the spaces which divide them. The central aisle and the two lateral groves of stone might have been the creations of separate architects, working without communication with one another and without any desire to make their proportions seem the result of one coherent idea.

In the inner hypostyle hall at Abydos the intercolumniations which lead respectively to the seven sanctuaries vary in width (Fig. 115). This variation is not shown by Mariette, from whose work our plan of the temple as a whole was taken, but it is clearly seen in the plan given in the *Description*. These are not the only

[1] *Description de l'Égypte*, plates, vol. iii. pl. 5.

instances in which those early explorers of Egypt excelled their successors in minute accuracy.

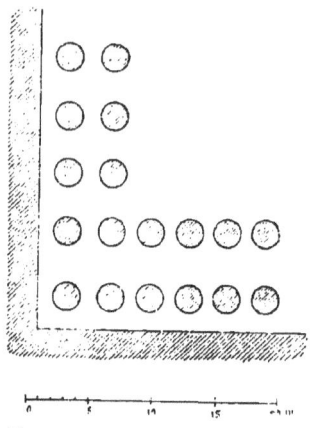

FIG. 112.—Part of the portico of the fir t court, Luxor. From the *Description*, iii. 5.

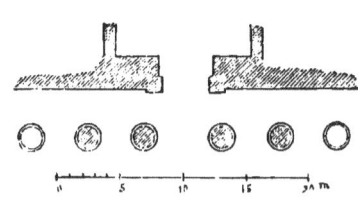

FIG. 113.—Portico in front of the façade of the temple of Gournah. From the *Description*, ii. 41.

Here and there we find the spaces in a single row of columns increasing progressively from the two ends to the centre (Fig. 105).

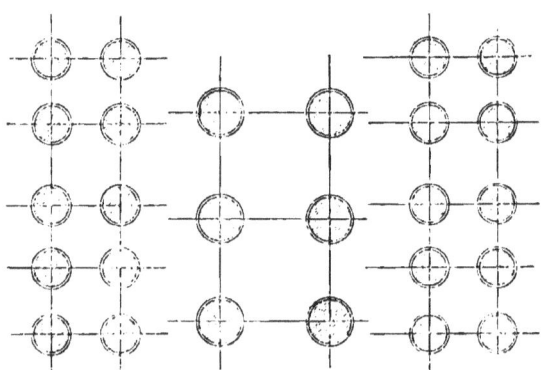

FIG. 114.—Part of the Hypostyle Hall in the Great Temple at Karnak.

The combination of quadrangular with Osiride piers and of the latter with columns proper was also productive of great variety. In the speos of Gherf-Hossein six Osiride piers are inclosed by six of quadrangular section (Fig. 116). In the first court at

THE ORDONNANCE OF EGYPTIAN COLONNADES. 139

Medinet-Abou a row of Osiride piers faces a row of columns (Fig. 117), while in the second court there is a much more complicated arrangement. The lateral walls of the court are

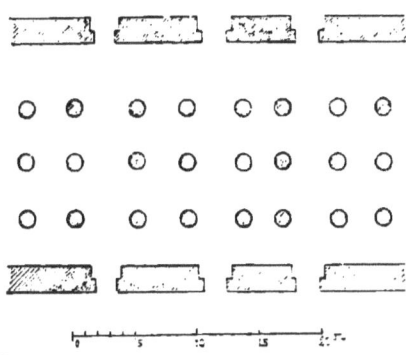

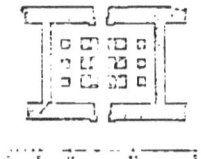

FIG. 115.—Second Hypostyle Hall in the temple of Abydos. *Description*, iv. 36.

FIG. 116.—Hall in the speos of Gherf-Hossein (from Prisse).

prefaced each by a row of columns. The wall next the entrance has a row of Osiride piers before it; while that through which the pronaos is gained has a portico supported by, first, a row of Osiride piers, and, behind them, by a row of columns (Fig. 118).

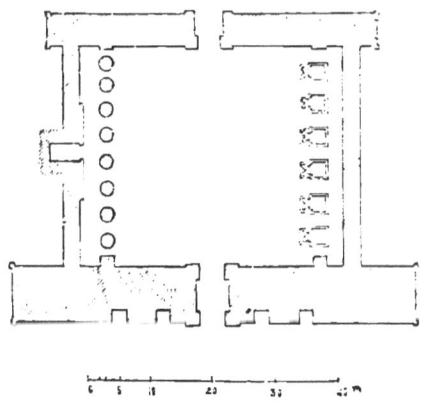

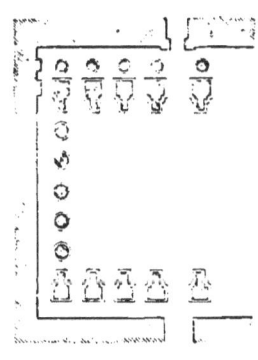

FIG. 117.—Medinet-Abou; first court.

FIG. 118.—Medinet-Abou; second court.

In the temple of Khons the peristyle is continued past the doorway in the pylon (Fig. 119), and the inclosure is reached through one of the intercolumniations.[1] At Luxor, on the other hand, the portico was brought to an abrupt termination against the salient jambs of the doorway (Fig. 120).

The Egyptian architect, like his Greek successor, made frequent use of the *anta*, that is, he gave a salience to the extremities of his walls which strengthened his design and afforded structural

FIG. 119.—Portico of the Temple of Khons, looking towards pronaos.

members, akin to pilasters or quadrangular pillars, which were combined in various ways with columns and piers. Sometimes the anta is nothing but a slight prolongation of a wall beyond the point where it meets another (Fig. 121); sometimes it is the commencement of a returning wall which appears to have been broken off to give place to a row of columns (Fig. 122); a good instance of the latter arrangement is to be found on the façade

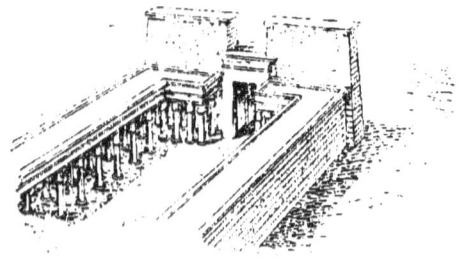

FIG. 120.— Portico of first court at Luxor.

of the temple at Gournah. Sometimes, as at Medinet-Abou, it is a reinforcement to the extremity of a wall, and serves to form a backing for colossal Osiride statues (Fig. 123), sometimes it gives

[1] This is a mistake. By a reference to Fig. 208, Vol. I., or to Fig. 126 in this volume, it will be seen that the peristyle was not continued along the inner face of the pylon.— ED.

accent and strength to an angle, as in the Great Hall at Karnak (Fig. 124). At the Temple of Khons the terminations of the two rows of columns which form the portico are marked by antæ on the inner face of the pylon (Fig. 126), while the wall which

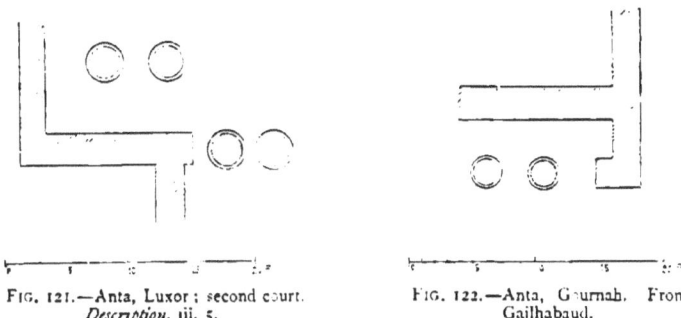

FIG. 121.—Anta, Luxor; second court. *Description*, iii. 5.

FIG. 122.—Anta, Gourmah. From Gailhabaud.

incloses the pronaos is without any projection except the jambs of the door. This arrangement has an obvious *raison d'être*; if the columns were brought close up to the pylon their outlines would not combine happily with its inclined walls. At the other

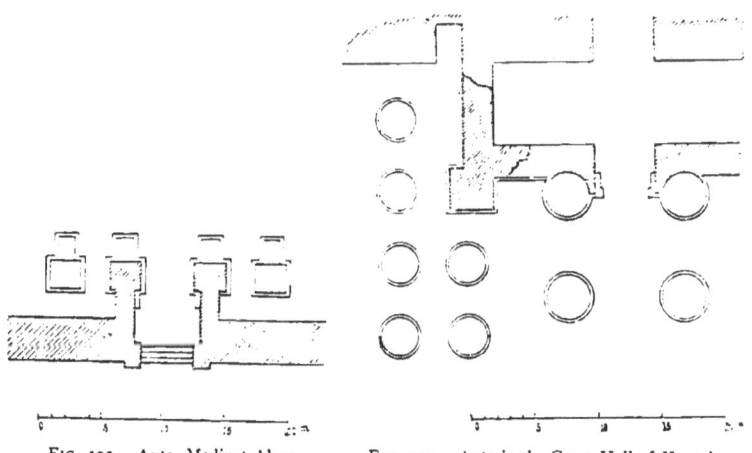

FIG. 123.—Anta, Medinet-Abou.

FIG. 124.—Anta in the Great Hall of Karnak.

extremity of the court, the wall being perpendicular, there was no necessity for such an arrangement.[1] A glance at Fig. 126 will

[1] The arrangement in question is capable of another and, perhaps, more simple explanation. The two rows of columns of which the portico in

make this readily understood. At Medinet-Abou the portico is terminated laterally by two antæ, one corresponding to the row of columns, the other to the row of caryatid piers. In another court of the same temple the antæ on either side vary in depth, at one end of the portico there is a bold pilaster, at the other one which projects very slightly indeed (Fig. 128). This is another instance of the curious want of symmetry and regularity which is one of the most constant characteristics of Egyptian architecture.

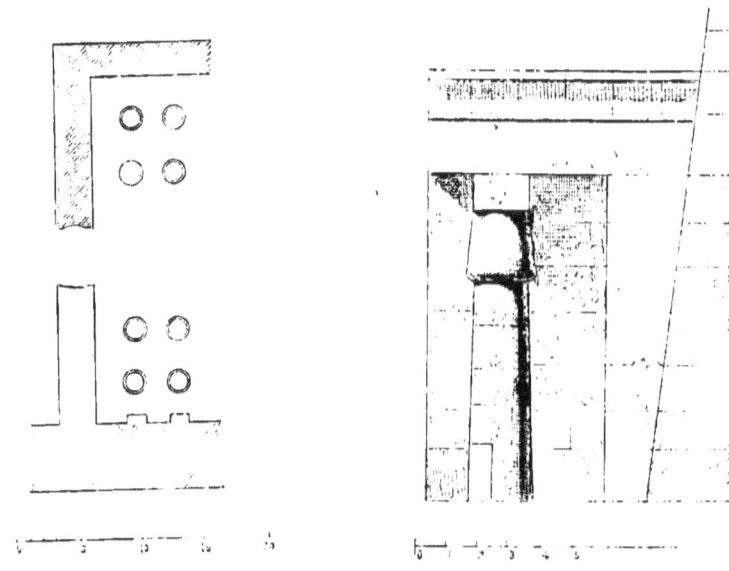

FIG. 125.—Antæ, Temple of Khons. *Description*, iii. 54.

FIG. 126.—Anta and base of pylon, Temple of Khons. *Description*, iii. 55.

The anta is often without a capital, as, for instance, in the temple of Khons (Fig. 126). Elsewhere the architect seems to have wished to bring it into more complete harmony with the magnificence of its surroundings, and accordingly he gives it a capital, as at Medinet-Abou, but a capital totally unlike those

question is composed, run in an unbroken line round the court with the exception of the side which is filled by the pylon. It was natural enough, therefore, that they should each be stopped against an anta, even if there had not been an additional reason in the inclination of the pylon. The ordonnance as a whole may be compared to a long portico, like that in the second court of the temple at Gournah, bent into two right angles.—ED.

THE ORDONNANCE OF EGYPTIAN COLONNADES. 143

proper to the column.[1] It was identical in form with that gorge or cornice which crowns nearly every Egyptian wall. Considering that the anta was really no more than a prolongation or momentary salience of the wall, such an arrangement was judicious in every way (Fig. 129).

The width of the intercolumniations also varied between one court or hall and another, and, at least in the present state of the Egyptian remains, we are unable to discover any rule governing the matter, such as those by which Greek architects were guided. We may affirm generally that the Egyptian constructor, especially in the time of the New Empire and when using columns of large

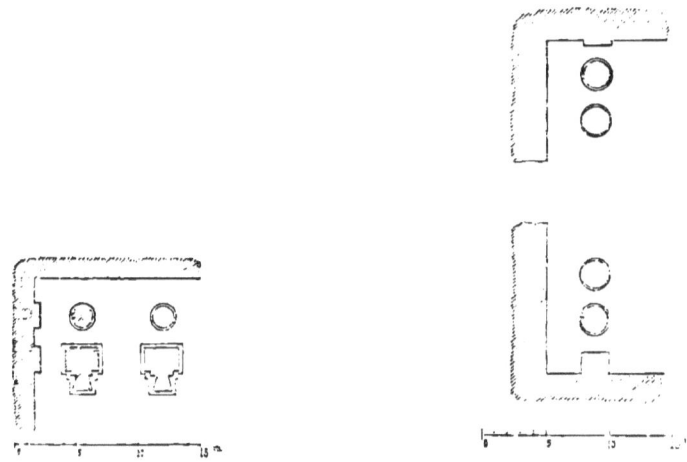

FIG. 127.—Antæ, Medinet-Abou.   FIG. 128.—Antæ, Medinet-Abou.

dimensions, preferred close spacing to wide. His tendency to crowd his columns is to be explained, partly by the great weight of the superstructure which they had to support, partly by the national taste for a massive and close architecture. The spaces between the great columns in the hypostyle hall of Karnak, measured between the points of junction between the bases and the shafts, is slightly less than two diameters. The spaces between the smaller columns on each side are hardly more than one diameter.

A better idea of the original character of these ordonnances may perhaps be gathered from the plate which faces the next page

[1] In this the Greek architects took the same course as those of Egypt.

(Pl. viii) than to any plan to which we could refer the reader. It represents that part of the colonnade, in the second court of the temple at Medinet-Abou, which veils the wall of the pronaos, and it shows how little space the Egyptian architects thought necessary for the purposes of circulation. The spaces between the columns and the wall on the one hand and the osiride piers on the other, are not quite equal to the diameter of the bases of those columns, which have, however, been expressly kept smaller than was usual in Egypt. If they had been as large as some that we could point out, there would have been no room to pass between them and the wall.

Did the Egyptians ever employ isolated columns, not as structural units, but for decorative purposes, for the support of a group or a statue? Are there any examples of pillars like those which the Phœnicians raised before their temples, or the triumphal columns of the Romans, or those reared for commemorative purposes in Paris and other cities of Modern Europe? It is impossible to give a confident answer to this question. The remains of the great colonnade which existed in the first court at Karnak, of which a single column with bell-shaped capital is still upright (Fig. 130), suggest, perhaps, that such monumental pillars were not unknown to the Egyptians. These columns display the ovals of Tahraka, of Psemethek, and of Ptolemy Philopator. The width of the avenue between them, measuring from centre to centre, is so great, about fifty-five feet, that it is difficult to believe that it could ever have been covered with a roof. Even with wood it would have been no easy matter—for the Egyptians—to cover such a void. We have, moreover, good reason to believe that they never used wood and stone together in their temples. A *velarium* has been suggested, but there is nothing either in the Egyptian texts or in their wall paintings to hint at their use of such a covering.

It would have been quite possible to connect the summits of these columns together lengthwise. The architraves would have had less than twenty feet to bridge over. But not the slightest relic of such a structure has been found, and it is difficult to see what good purpose it could have served had it existed.

The authors of the *Description* came to the conclusion that there had been no roof of any kind to the avenue formed by the columns, that they merely formed a kind of monumental approach

to the hypostyle hall.[1] Mariette also discards the idea of architraves, which would have to be unusually long, but he cannot accept the notion that the columns were merely colossal venetian masts bordering the approach to the sanctuary. He supposes the centre of the courtyard to have contained a small hypæthral temple built by Tahraka. This temple figures upon his plan, but neither he himself, by his own confession, nor any one else has ever found the slightest trace of it in reality.[2] In the excavations made by him in 1859, he did not find a vestige even of

FIG. 129.—Anta and column at Medinet-Abou.

the two columns which he inserts upon each of the two short sides of the rectangle. These columns were necessary in order to

[1] *Description. Antiquités.* vol. v. pp. 120, 121. In their *Description Générale de Thèbes* (ch. ix. section 8, § 2), the same writers add: "We are confirmed in our opinion by the discovery on a bas-relief of four lotus stems with their flowers surmounted by hawks and statues, and placed exactly in the same fashion as the columns which we have just described. They are votive columns. We are also confirmed in this opinion by the fact that we find things like them among those amulets which reproduce the various objects in the temples in small." This bas-relief is figured in the third volume of plates of the *Description*, pl. 33, Fig. 1.

[2] MARIETTE, *Karnak*, p. 19, pl. 4. *Voyage dans la Haute-Égypte*, pp. 13, 21, 22.

VOL. II. U

complete a peripteral arrangement, similar to that which exists in the hypæthral temples at Philæ and in Nubia. The closest study of the site has brought to light nothing beyond the twelve columns shown in our plan (Fig. 214, E, Vol. I.).

The most probable explanation is that which we have hinted at above.[1] These great columns were erected to give majesty to the approach to the hypostyle hall, and to border the path followed by the great religious processions as they issued from the hall and made for the great doorway in the pylon. They must always

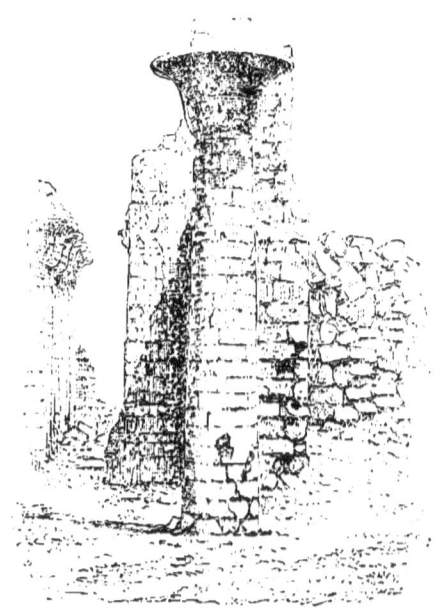

FIG. 130.—Column in the court of the Bubastides, at Karnak.

have been isolated, and it is possible that formerly each carried upon the cubic die which still surmounts the capital, groups of bronze similar to those which, to all appearance, crowned those stele-like piers which we described in speaking of the work of Thothmes in the same temple (page 94). This was also the opinion of Prisse d'Avennes, who studied the monuments of Egypt, both as an artist and as an archæologist, more closely,

[1] This explanation seems to have been accepted by Prof. EBERS; *Ægypten im Bild und Wort*, vol. ii. p. 331.

perhaps, than any one else.¹ It has been objected that the columns would hide each other, and that the symbolic animals perched upon their summits could not have been seen; but this would only be the case with those who looked at them from certain disadvantageous positions—from between the columns, or exactly on their alignment. From the middle of the avenue, or from one side of it, they would be clearly visible, and the vivid colours of their enamels would produce their full effect.

The question might be decided in a very simple fashion. The summit of the column which is still upright might be examined, or the abacus of one of those which have fallen might be discovered; in either case traces of the objects which they supported would be found, supposing our hypothesis to be correct. More than one doubtful question of this kind would long ago have been solved had the Egyptian monuments been studied on the spot by archæologists and artists instead of being left almost entirely to the narrower experience of engineers and egyptologists.

In the absence of evidence to the contrary, we shall, then, look upon it as probable that the Egyptians sometimes raised columns, like other people, not for the support of roofs and architraves, but as gigantic pedestals, as self-contained decorative forms, with independent parts of their own to play. Such a proceeding was doubtless an innovation in Egyptian art—one of those fresh departures which date from the latter years of the Monarchy. Even in Egypt motives grew stale with repetition at last, and she cried out for something new.

§ 7. *Monumental Details.*

We have seen that the proportions, the entasis, the shape, and the decoration of the Egyptian column, were changed more than once and in many ways. The Egyptian artist, by his fertility of resource and continual striving after improvement, showed that he was by no means actuated by that blind respect for tradition which has been too often attributed to him. Besides, the remains which we possess are but a small part of Egyptian architecture. The buildings of Memphis and of the Delta have perished. Had they been preserved we should doubtless have found among them

¹ MAXIME DU CAMP, *Le Nil*, p. 251.

forms and details which do not exist in the ruins of Abydos, of Thebes, or in the Nubian hypogea; we should have been able to describe arrangements and motives which do not occur in the works of the three great Theban dynasties.

On the other hand, the mouldings and other details of the same kind are monotonous in the extreme. Their want of variety is not to be explained, like that of Assyria, by the nature of the materials. Brick, granite, limestone, and sandstone constituted a series of materials in which a varied play of light and shade, such as that which characterized Greek architecture, should have been easy. The real cause of the poverty of Egyptian design in this particular is to be found in their habit of covering nearly

FIG. 131.—Stereobate, Luxor.

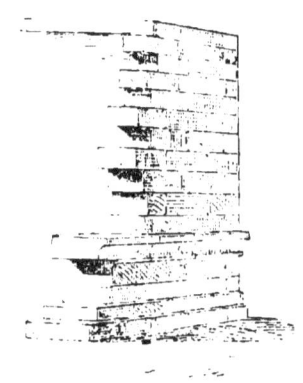

FIG. 132.—Stereobate with double plinth, Luxor.

every surface with a carved and painted decoration. More elaborate or bolder mouldings might have interfered with the succession of row upon row of pictures from the bottom to the top of a wall. The eye was satisfied with the rich polychromatic decoration, and did not require it to be supplemented by architectural ornament.

When the slope of a wall was ornamented with projections in the shape of mouldings it was because the wall was bare. At Luxor, for example, in the external face of the wall which incloses the back of the temple, the lowest course projects beyond the others, forming a step, and a few courses above it there is a hollow moulding similar in section to the cornice at the top; the lower part of the wall is thus formed into a stereobate (Fig. 131). At another point in the circumference of this temple there is a stereobate of a more complicated description. It is terminated above by a cornice-shaped moulding like that just described, but it rests upon two steps instead of one (Fig. 132). By this it appears that the Egyptian architects understood how to add to apparent solidity of their buildings by expanding them at their junction with the ground. This became a true continuous stylobate, carrying piers, in peripteral temples like that at Elephantiné (Fig. 230, Vol. I.). In the latter building its form is identical with that which we have just described.

We have now to describe an arrangement which, though rare in the Pharaonic period, was afterwards common enough. The portico which stretches across the back of the second court in the Ramesseum is closed to about a third of its height by a kind of pluteus (Fig. 133).[1] This barrier formed a sort of tablet, surrounded by a fillet, and crowned by a cornice of the usual type, between each pair of Osiride piers. In the Ptolemaic temples the lower part of the portico was always closed in this fashion. It constitutes the only inclosure in front of the fine hypostyle hall at Denderah.

We have now studied buildings in sufficient number to become familiar with the *Egyptian Gorge*. As early as the Ancient Empire the architects of Egypt had invented this form of cornice, and used it happily upon their massive structures. It is composed of three elements, which are always arranged in the same order. In the first place there is the circular moulding or torus with a carved ribbon twisting about it. This moulding occurs at the edge where two faces meet in most Egyptian buildings. It serves to give firmness and accent to the angles and, when used at the top of the wall, to mark the point where the wall ends and

---

[1] The *Description de l'Égypte* indicates the existence of this pluteus both in the Ramesseum (vol. ii. pl. 29) and at Medinet-Abou (vol. ii. pl. 7, Fig. 2). Photographs do not show a trace of it, but many parts of those buildings had disappeared before the beginning of the present century. There is no reason to suppose that the Ramesseum underwent any modification after the termination of the Theban supremacy. In his restoration of Dayr-el-Bahari, M. Brune has introduced a similar detail, which he would assuredly not have done unless he had found traces of it under the portico. Unfortunately his restoration is on a very small scale. That at Dayr-el-Bahari must have been the earliest example of such an arrangement.

the cornice begins. Above this there is a hollow curve with perpendicular grooves, which, again, is surmounted by a plain fillet which makes a sharp line against the sky. In all this there is a skilful opposition of hollows to flat surfaces, of deep shadow to brilliant and unbroken sunlight, which marks the upward

FIG. 133.—Pluteus in the intercolumniations of the portico in the second court of the Rameseum·

determination of the great masses upon which it is used in the most effective manner.

Although the Egyptian architect repeated this cornice continually, he contrived to give it variety of effect by modifying its proportions, and by introducing different kinds of ornaments. In the pylons, for instance, we often find that the cornice of the doorway was both deeper and of bolder projection than those upon the two masses of the pylon itself (Fig. 134). It was generally ornamented with the winged globe, an emblem which was afterwards appropriated by the nations which became connected with Egypt.

This emblem in its full development was formed of the solar disk supported on each side by the *uræus*, the serpent which meant royalty. The sun was thus designated as the greatest of kings,

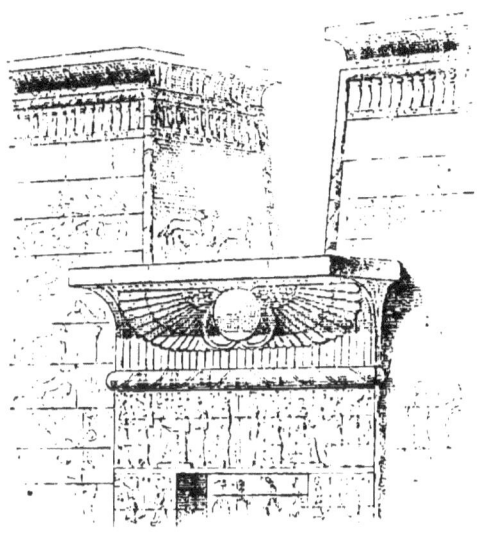

FIG. 134.—Doorway, Luxor. *Description*, iii. 6.

the king who mounted up into space, enlightening and vivifying the upper and lower country at one and the same time. The disk and its supporters were flanked by the two wide stretching wings with rounded, fan-shaped extremities, which symbolized the untiring activity of the sun in making its daily journey from one extremity of the firmament to the other. Egyptologists tell us that the group as a whole signifies the triumph of right over wrong, the victory of Horus over Set. An inscription at Edfou tells us that, after the victory, Thoth ordered that this emblem should be carved over every doorway in Egypt, and, in fact, there are very few lintels without it.[1] It first appears at about the time of the twelfth dynasty, according to Mariette, but its form was at first more simple. There were no *uræi*, and the wings were shorter, and pendent instead of outstretched.[2] Towards the eighteenth dynasty it took the shape in which it is figured in our illustrations, and became thenceforward the Egyptian symbol *par excellence*.

In the more richly decorated buildings, such as the Ramesseum, we sometimes find cartouches introduced between the vertical grooves of the cornice (Fig. 135). In the representations of architecture on the painted walls the upper member of the cornice as usually constituted, is often surmounted by an ornament composed of the uræus and the solar disk, the latter being upon the head of the former (Fig. 136). This addition gives a richer

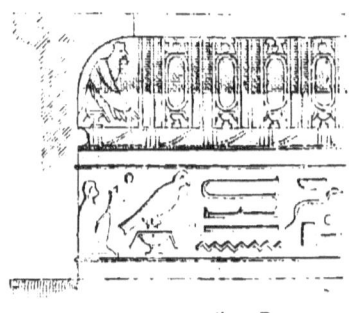

FIG. 135.—Cornice of the Ramesseum. *Description*, ii. 30.

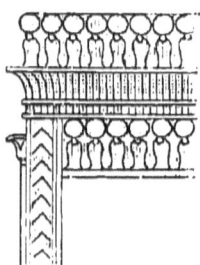

FIG. 136.—Cornice of a wooden pavilion; from Prisse.

and more ample cornice, which the Ptolemaic architects carried out in stone. It is not to be found thus perpetuated in any Pharaonic building, but the same motive occurs at Thebes, below the cornice, and its existence in the bas-reliefs shows that even in early times it was sometimes used. Perhaps it was confined to those light structures in which complicated forms were easily carried out.

This cornice seemed to the Egyptians to be so entirely the proper termination for their rising surfaces, that they placed it at

[1] The history and signification of this symbol were treated by BRUGSCH in a paper entitled: "*Die Sage von der geflügelten Sonnenscheibe nach alt Ägyptischen Quellen dargestellt.*"

[2] In this restricted and comparatively mean form the emblem in question is found at Beni-Hassan. (LEPSIUS, *Denkmæler*, part ii. pl. 123.)

the top of their stylobates (Figs. 131 and 132) and their pedestals (Fig. 137). They also used it within their buildings at the top of the walls behind their colonnades, as, for instance, in the peripteral temple at Elephantiné (Fig. 138).

The number of buildings in which this cornice was not used is very small. The Royal Pavilion at Medinet-Abou is surrounded, at the top, by a line of round-headed battlements; in the Temple of Semneh, built by Thothmes I.,[1] and in the pronaos of the Temple of Amada, the usual form gives place to a square cornice which is quite primitive in its simplicity.

Traces of other mouldings, such as those which we call the *cyma*, and the *cyma reversa*, may be found in Egyptian

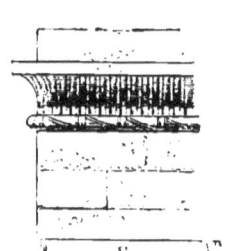

FIG. 137.—Pedestal of a Sphinx at Karnak. *Description*, iii. 29.

FIG. 138.—Cornice under the portico, Elephantiné.

temples, but they occur so rarely that we need not dwell upon them here or figure them.[2]

Besides these mouldings, which were used but very rarely, we need only mention one more detail of the kind, namely, those vertical and horizontal grooves which occur upon the masonry walls and were derived from the structures in wood. They were chiefly used for the ornamentation of the great surfaces afforded by the brick walls (Fig. 261, Vol. I.), but they are also to be found upon stone buildings. We give, as an example, a fragment found at Alexandria, which is supposed to belong to the

---

[1] LEPSIUS, *Denkmæler*, vol. ii. pl. 83, and vol. v. pl. 56.
[2] See CHIPIEZ, *Histoire Critique des Ordres Grecques*, p. 90.

lower part of a sarcophagus. A curious variation of the same ornament exists in one of the royal tombs at Thebes (Fig. 140), in which each panel is separated from its neighbours by the figures of headless men with their hands tied behind their backs. They represent, no doubt, prisoners of war who have been

FIG. 139.—Fragment of a sarcophagus. *Description*, v. 47.

beheaded, and the decorator has wished, by the use of a somewhat barbarous though graceful motive, to suggest the exploits of him for whom the sepulchre was destined.

Not much variety was to be obtained from the use of these grooves, but yet they disguised the nudity of great wall spaces, they prevented monotony from becoming too monotonous, while

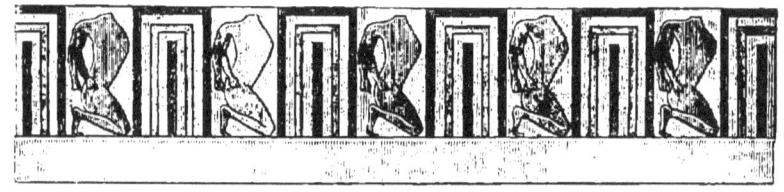

FIG. 140.—Fragment of decoration from a royal tomb at Thebes. *Description*, ii. 86.

they afforded linear combinations which had some power to please the eye. The Assyrians made use of hardly any other mode of breaking up the uniformity of their brick walls.

It has been asserted that the first signs of that egg-moulding which played so great a part in Greek architecture are to be found in Egypt. Nestor L'Hôte thought that he recognised it in the entablature, under the architrave, of some pavilions figured in decorations at Tell-el-Amarna and at Abydos.[1] He was certainly mistaken. The outline of the ornament to which he referred has a distant resemblance to the moulding in question, but the place which it occupies gives it an entirely different character; it seems to be suspended in the air under the entablature. In other painted pavilions the same place is occupied by flowers, bunches of grapes, and fruits resembling dates or acorns, suspended in the same fashion.[2] If such forms must be explained otherwise than by the mere fancy of the ornamentist, we should be inclined to see in them metal weights hung round the edges of the awnings, which supplied the place of a roof in many wooden pavilions.

The same remarks may be applied to those objects, or rather appearances, to which the triglyphs of the Doric order have been referred. It is true that in the figured architecture of the bas-reliefs many of the architraves seem to show vertical incisions arranged in groups of three, each group being separated from the next by a square space which recalls the Greek metope (Figs. 62-64). But sometimes these stripes follow each other at regular intervals, sometimes they are in pairs, and sometimes they are altogether absent, the architrave being either plain or decorated with figures and inscriptions. Where the stripes are present they represent sometimes applied ornaments, sometimes the ends of transverse joists appearing between the beams of the architrave. Similar ornaments surround the paintings in the tombs, and are to be found upon the articles of furniture, such as chairs, which form part of most Egyptian museums. Neither these so-called triglyphs and metopes, which do slightly resemble the details so named of the Doric order, nor the egg moulding, which is a pure delusion, ever received that established form and elemental character which alone gives such things importance. Architecture—stone architecture—made no use of them, and the analogies which some have endeavoured to establish are misleading. The apparent coincidence resulted from the nature of the material and from the limited number of combinations which it allowed.

[1] *Lettres*, pp. 68, 117.
[2] See the plate in PRISSE entitled *Détails de Colonnettes de Bois*.

§ 8. *Doors and Windows.*

So far we have been concerned with the structure and shape of Egyptian buildings; we have now to describe the openings pierced in their substance for the admission of light, for the circulation of their inhabitants and for the entrance of visitors from without. The doors and windows of the Egyptians were peculiar in many ways and deserve to be carefully described.

Doors.

The plans of Egyptian doorways do not always show the same arrangements. The embrasure of which we moderns make use is seldom met with. It occurs in the peripteral temple at Elephantiné, but that is quite an exception (Fig. 141). The doorways of the temples were generally planned as in Fig. 142, and in the passage which traverses the thickness of the pylons, there is in the middle an enlargement forming a kind of chamber into which, no doubt, double doors fell back on either side (Fig. 143).

In their elevations doorways show still greater variety.

Let us consider in the first place those by which access was gained to the *temenos*, or outer inclosure, of the temple. They may be divided into three classes.

First of all comes the pylon proper, with its great doorway flanked on either side by a tower which greatly excedes it in height (Fig. 207, Vol. I.). Champollion has pointed out that even in the Egyptian texts themselves a distinction is made between the *pylon* and that which he calls the *propylon*. The latter consists of a door opening through the centre of a single pyramidoid mass, and instead of forming a façade to the temple itself, it is used for the entrances to the outer inclosure. Figs. 144 and 145 show the different hieroglyphs which represent it.[1]

These propylons, to adopt Champollion's term, seem to have included two different types which are now known to us only through the Ptolemaic buildings and the monumental paintings, as

---

[1] From Champollion, *Grammaire Égyptienne*, p. 53.

the boundary walls of the Pharaonic period have almost entirely disappeared and their gateways with them.

We have illustrated the first type in our restoration, page 339, Vol. I. (Fig. 206). The doorway itself is very high, in which it resembles many propylons of the Greek period which still exist at Karnak and Denderah.[1] The thickness of the whole mass and its double cornice, between which the covered way on the top of the walls could be carried, are features which we also encounter in the propylon of Denderah and in that of the temple at Daybod in

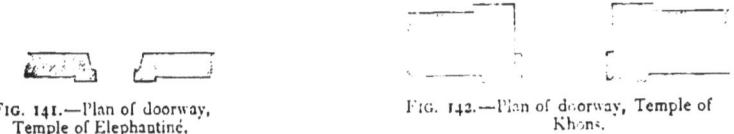

FIG. 141.—Plan of doorway, Temple of Elephantiné.

FIG. 142.—Plan of doorway, Temple of Khons.

Nubia.[2] We have added nothing but the wall, and a gateway, in Egypt, implies a wall; for there is no reason to suppose that the Egyptians had anything analogous to the triumphal arches of the Romans. The temple was a closed building, to which all access was forbidden to the crowd. The doors may well have been numerous, but, if they were to be of any use at all, they must have been connected by a continuous barrier which should force the traffic to pass through them.

FIG. 143.—Plan of doorway in the pylon, Temple of Khons. *Description*, iii. 54.

FIGS. 144, 145.—The pylon and propylon of the hieroglyphs.

In our restorations this doorway rises above the walls on each side and stands out from them, on plan, both within and without. We may fairly conjecture that it was so. The architect would hardly have wasted rich decoration and a well designed cornice upon a mass which was to be almost buried in the erections on each side of it. It must have been conspicuous from a distance, and this double relief would make it so. There are, moreover, a few

[1] EBERS, *Ægypten*, p. 250.
[2] FELIX TEYNARD, *Vues d'Égypte et de Nubie*, pl. 106.

instances in which these secondary entrances have been preserved together with the walls through which they provided openings, and they fully confirm our conjectures. One of these is the gateway to the outer court of the Temple of Thothmes at Medinet-Abou (Fig. 146). This gateway certainly belongs to the Ptolemaic part of the building, but we have no reason to suppose that the architects of the Macedonian period deserted the ancient forms.

The propylons were decorated with masts like the pylons, as we see by a figure in a painting in one of the royal tombs at Thebes, which was reproduced by Champollion[1] (Fig. 147). Judging from the scenes and inscriptions which accompany it, Champollion thought this represented a propylon at the

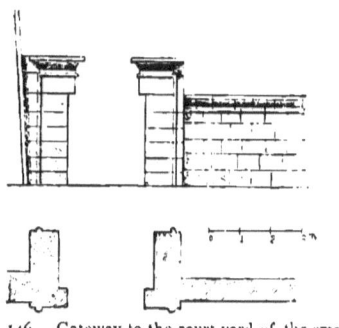
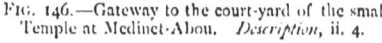

Fig. 146.—Gateway to the court-yard of the small Temple at Medinet-Abou. *Description*, ii. 4.

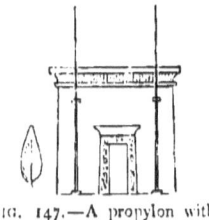

Fig. 147.—A propylon with its masts.

Ramesseum. That the artist should, as usual, have omitted the wall, need not surprise us when we remember how monotonous and free from incident those great brick inclosures must have been.

The second type of propylon differs from the first in having a very much smaller doorway in comparison with its total mass. In the former the door reaches almost to the cornice, in the latter it occupies but a very small part of the front. This is seen in Fig. 147, and, still more conspicuously, in Fig. 148, which was also copied by Champollion from a tomb at Thebes.[2] In one of these examples the walls are nearly vertical, in another they have a considerable slope, but the arrangement is the same and the

---

[1] *Monuments de l'Égypte et de la Nubie. Notices Descriptives*, p. 504.
[2] *Notices Descriptives*, p. 431.

proportions of the openings to the towers themselves do not greatly differ. Our Fig. 149, which was composed by the help of those representations, is meant to give an idea of the general composition of which the door with its carved jambs and architrave, and the tower with its masts and banners, are the elements. The two types only differ from one another in the relative dimensions of their important parts, and the transition between them may have been almost imperceptible. It would seem that in the Ptolemaic epoch the wide and lofty doors were the chief objects of admiration, while under the Pharaohs, the towers through which they were pierced were thought of more importance.

FIG. 148.—A propylon.

If we examine the doorways of the temples themselves we shall there also find great variety in the manner in which they are combined architecturally with the walls in which they occur.

In the Temple of Khons the jambs of the door are one, architecturally, with the wall. The courses are continuous. The

FIG. 149.—Gateway in the inclosing wall of a Temple. Restored by Ch. Chipiez.

lintel alone, being monolithic, has a certain independence (Fig. 150). In the Temple of Gournah, on the other hand, the doorway forms a separate and self-contained composition. The jambs are monoliths as well as the lintel, and the latter, notwithstanding the great additional weight which it has to carry, does not exceed the former in section. At Abydos, on the other hand, the capital part which this stone has to play is indicated by the great size of the sandstone block of which it is composed (Fig. 154).

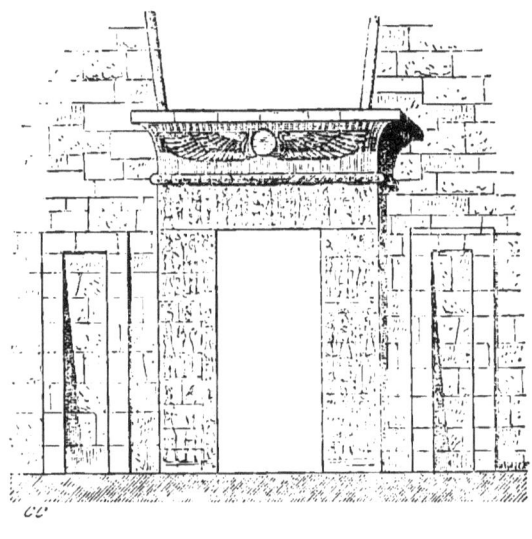

Fig. 150.—Doorway of the Temple of Khons. *Description*, iii. 54.

One of the doorways we have represented, that in Fig. 146, requires to be here mentioned again for a moment. Its lintel is

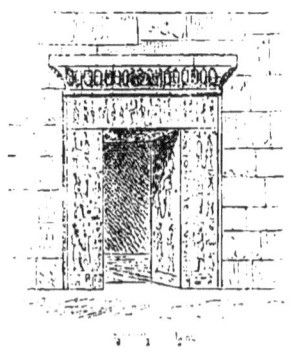

Fig. 151.—Doorway of the Temple of Gournah. *Description*, ii. 42.

discontinuous. The doorway in question dates from the Ptolemaic period, but there is undoubted evidence that the same form was sometimes used in the Pharaonic period for the openings in inclosing walls. There is a representation of such a door in a bas-relief at Karnak, where it is shown in front of a pylon and forms probably an opening in a boundary wall.[1] It was this representation that decided us to give a broken lintel to the

Fig. 152.—Doorway of the Temple of Seti, at Abydos.

doorway opposite to the centre of the royal pavilion at Medinet-Abou (Plate VIII.). This form of entrance may have originated in the desire to give plenty of head-room for the canopy under which the sovereign was carried, as well as for the banners and various standards which we see figured in the triumphal and religious processions of the bas-reliefs (Fig. 172, Vol. I.).

[1] Prisse, *Histoire de l'Art Égyptien*.

WINDOWS.

The royal pavilion at Medinet-Abou is the only building in Egypt which has preserved for us those architectural features which we call windows. They differ one from another, even upon this single building, as much as the doors. One of them (Fig. 153) is enframed like the doorway at Gournah; but the jambs are merely the ends of the courses which make up the

FIGS. 153, 154.—Windows in the Royal Pavilion at Medinet-Abou.

wall, and their salience is very slight. On the other hand a window frame with a very bold relief (Fig. 154) is to be found in the same building. This window is a little work of art in itself. It is surmounted by a cornice, over which again appear various emblems carved in stone, making up one of the most graceful compositions to be found in Egyptian architecture.

§ 9. *The Illumination of the Temples.*

We have described the way in which the Egyptian architects treated doors and windows from an artistic point of view; we have yet to show the method which they adopted for allowing sufficient light to penetrate into their temples, that is, into those

FIG. 155.—Attic of the Great Hall at Karnak. Restored by Ch. Chipiez.

buildings, which, being closely shut against the laity, could not be illuminated from windows in their side walls. Palaces and private houses could have their windows as large and as numerous as they chose, but the temple could only be lighted from the roof, or at least from parts contiguous to the roof.

The hypostyle hall at Karnak, with its lofty walls and close ranges of columns, would have been in almost complete darkness had it been left to depend for light upon its doors alone. But the difference of height between the central aisle and those to the right and left of it, was taken advantage of to introduce the light required for the proper display of its magnificent decorations.

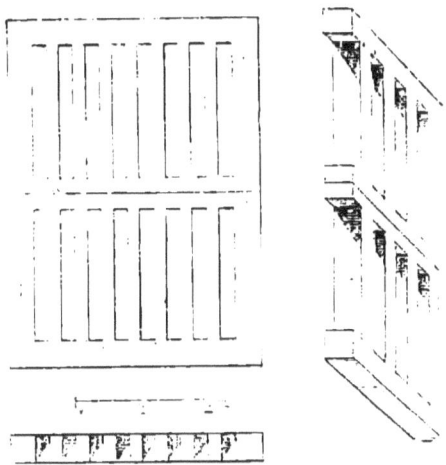

FIG. 156.—*Claustra* of the Hypostyle Hall, Karnak. *Description*, iii. 23.

The wall which filled up the space between the lower and upper sections of roof, forming something almost identical with the clerestory of a Gothic cathedral, was constructed of upright sandstone slabs, about sixteen feet high, which were pierced with numerous perpendicular slits. Stone gratings, or *claustra* as the Romans would have called them, were thus formed, through which the sunlight could stream into the interior. The slits were about ten inches wide and six feet high. The illustration on page 163 shows how the slabs were arranged and explains, moreover, the general disposition of the roof. Fig. 156 gives the *claustra* in detail, in elevation, in plan, and in perspective.

The hypostyle halls are nearly always lighted upon the same principle. The chief differences are found in the sizes of the openings. At the Temple of Khons, where the space to be lighted was not nearly so large, the slabs of the *claustra* were much smaller and the openings narrower (Fig. 157). In one of the inner halls at Karnak a different system has been used. The light penetrates through horizontal openings in the entablature, between the architrave and the cornice, divided one from another by cubes of stone (Fig. 158). In the inside the architrave was

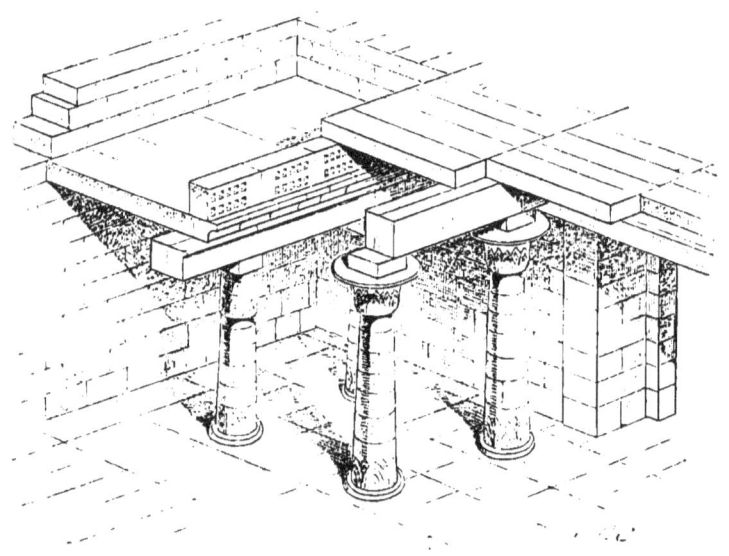

FIG. 157.—*Claustra* in the Hypostyle Hall of the Temple of Khons. Compiled from the elevations in the *Description*, iii. 28.

bevelled on its upper edge, so as to allow the light to penetrate into the interior at a better angle than it would otherwise have done.

The use of these *claustra*, full of variety though they were in the hands of a skilful architect, were not the only methods of lighting their temples to which the Egyptians had recourse. They were helped in their work, or, in the case of very small chambers, replaced, by oblique or vertical openings contrived in the roof itself. These oblique holes are found in the superior angles of the hypostyle hall at Karnak (Fig. 159). After the roof was in place it was seen, no doubt, that the *claustra* did not of themselves give enough light for the huge chamber, and these

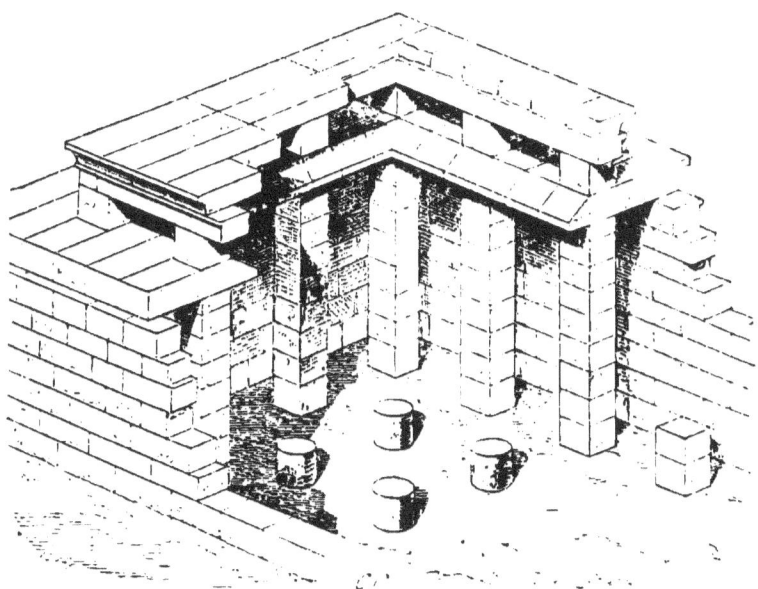

FIG. 158.—Method of lighting in one of the inner halls of Karnak. Compiled from the plans and elevations of the *Description*.

narrow openings were laboriously cut in its ceiling. One of the inner chambers of the Temple of Khons is feebly lighted by vertical holes cut through the slabs of the roof (Fig. 160). Similar

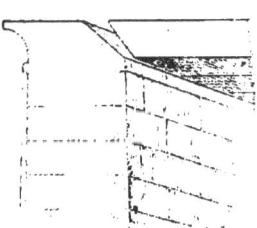

FIG. 159.—Auxiliary light-holes in the Hypostyle Hall at Karnak. *Description*, iii. 26.

FIG. 160.—Method of lighting one of the rooms in the Temple of Khons. *Description*, iii. 55.

openings are to be seen in the lateral aisles of the hypostyle hall in the Ramesseum. The slight upward projection which surrounds the upper extremities of these holes should be noticed (Fig. 161). Finally there are buildings in which these openings are the only sources of illumination. This is notably the case in the Temple of Amada. The upper part of our plan (Fig. 162) represents the roof of that temple and the symmetrically arranged openings with which it is pierced.

FIG. 161.—Light openings in a lateral aisle of the Hypostyle Hall in the Ramesseum. From a photograph.

The Ptolemaic Temple of Edfou is much more generously treated in the matter of light. Its flat roof is pierced by two large rectangular openings resembling the *compluvium* of a Pompeian house, and making it, in a certain sense, hypæthral. No example of such an arrangement has been met with in the Pharaonic

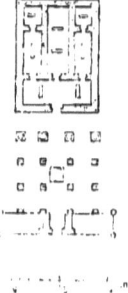

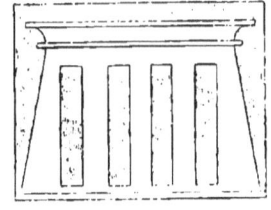

FIG. 162.—The Temple of Amada.   FIG. 163.—*Claustra*, from a painting.

temples. It is possible that its principle was directly borrowed from the Greeks. It is hardly so consistent with the national ideas and traditions as the *claustra*.

Palaces and private houses were, as we have said, better lighted than the temples. The illustrations in the preceding chapter show private houses with their windows. Some of those houses had windows formed of stone *claustra*. The window copied by Champollion[1] from the walls of a small chamber in the Temple of Thothmes at Medinet-Abou (Fig. 163), shows this, as well as an

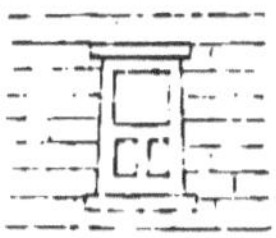

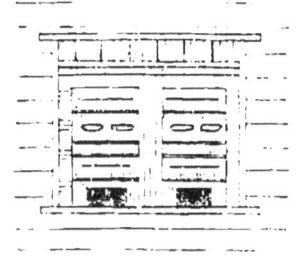

FIG. 164.—Window of a house in the form of *claustra*.

FIG. 165.—Window closed by a mat.

opening in the house illustrated in Fig. 19, which we here reproduce upon a larger scale (Fig. 164). We do the same for a window belonging to the building shown in Fig. 1. It is closed by a mat which was raised, no doubt, by means of a roller and cords (Fig. 165).

§ 10. *The Obelisks.*

We cannot bring our analysis of the forms and motives of Egyptian architecture to an end without mentioning a monumental type which is peculiar to Egypt, that of the *obelisks*. These are granite monoliths[2] of great height, square on plan, dressed on all four faces, and slightly tapering from base to summit. They usually terminate in a small pyramid, whose rapidly sloping sides contrast strongly with the gentle inclination of the main block beneath. This small pyramid is called the pyramidion.

The tall and slender shapes of these monoliths and their pointed summits have led to their being compared, in popular language, with needles and spindles.[3] The first Greeks who

---

[1] *Notices Descriptives.* p. 332, fig. 2.

[2] In front of the sphinxes which stand before the great pylon at Karnak there are two small obelisks of sandstone.

[3] The Italians call them *guglie*, needles, and the Arabs *micellet Faraoun*, Pharaoh's needles. The obelisks now in London and New York respectively, which were taken by the Romans from the ruins of Heliopolis, in order to be erected in front of the Cæsareum at Alexandria, were known as Cleopatra's Needles. Herodotus

visited the country and found a monumental type so unlike anything they had at home, wished to convey a good idea of it to their compatriots; they accordingly made use of the word ὀβελός, a spindle. It is difficult to understand how their descendants came to prefer ὀβελίσκος, a little spindle.[1] A diminutive hardly seems the right kind of word under the circumstances; an augmentative would, perhaps, have been better. But it was this diminutive that the Romans borrowed from the Greeks of Alexandria and transmitted to the modern world.

This is not the place for an inquiry into the meaning of the obelisk. It may symbolize, as we have often been told, the ray of the sun, or it may be an emblem of Amen-Generator.[2] It seems to be well established, that in the time of the New Empire at least, it was used to write the syllable *men*, which signified *firmness* or *stability*.[3]

The usual situation of the obelisks was in front of the first pylon of the temples. There they stood in couples, one upon each side of the entrance. Those instances where they are found, as at Karnak, surrounded by the buildings of the temple, are easily explained. The two obelisks in the caryatid court were erected during the eighteenth dynasty, at a time when those parts of the temple which lie between the obelisks and the outer wall were not yet in existence. The obelisks of Hatasu, when first erected, were in front of the Temple of Amen as it was left by the early sovereigns of the eighteenth dynasty.

But the obelisk was not the exclusive property of the temples. Some little ones of limestone have been found in the mastabas,[4] and Mariette has described those which formerly stood in front of the royal tombs belonging to the eleventh dynasty, in the Theban necropolis. He has published the inscription which covers the four faces of one of these obelisks, a monolith some ten feet nine

only used the expression, ὀβελός. Ἐν τῷ τεμένει ὀβελοὶ ἑστᾶσι μεγάλοι λίθινοι (ii. 172; also ii. 111).

[1] DIODORUS (i. 57, 59), always uses the word ὀβελίσκος. The termination is certainly that of a diminutive. See AD. REGNIER, *Traité de la Formation des Mots dans la Langue Grecque*, p. 207.

[2] DE ROUGÉ, *Étude sur les Monuments de Karnak*.

[3] PIERRET, *Dictionnaire d'Archéologie Égyptienne*.

[4] A small funerary obelisk, about two feet high, is now in the museum of Berlin. It is figured in the *Denkmæler*, part ii. pl. 88. It was found in a Gizeh tomb dating from the fifth dynasty.

inches high.[1] Obelisks seem also to have been employed for the decoration of palaces, as we may conclude from a Theban painting in which one appears before the principal entrance to a villa surrounded with beautiful gardens.[2] Judging by the sizes of people in the same painting, this obelisk must have been about thirteen feet high.

Diodorus speaks of obelisks erected by Sesostris which were 120 cubits, nearly 180 feet, high;[3] and different texts allude to monoliths which were 130, 117, and 114 feet high. We have some difficulty in accepting the first of these figures. The obelisk of Hatasu, at Karnak, which is the tallest known, is 108 feet 10 inches in height.[4] That which is still standing at Matarieh, on the site of the ancient Heliopolis, is only 67 feet 4 inches high. But the fact that it is the oldest of the colossal obelisks of Egypt makes it more interesting than some which surpass it in size (Fig. 167). It bears the name of Ousourtesen I., of the twelfth dynasty. As a rule, the inscriptions cut upon the four sides of those obelisks which are complete are very insignificant. They consist of little but pompous enumerations of the royal titles.[5]

FIG. 166.—Funerary obelisk in the Necropolis of Thebes. From Mariette.[6]

The two obelisks erected by Rameses II. in front of the first pylon at Luxor were slightly unequal in height. One was 83 feet 4 inches, the other 78 feet 5 inches. To hide this difference to some extent they were set upon bases also of unequal height, and the shorter was placed slightly in advance of its companion, *i.e.* slightly nearer to the spectator approaching the temple by the dromos.[7] By these means they hoped to make

---

[1] MARIETTE, *Monuments Divers*, pl. 50. The obelisks illustrated in this chapter are all drawn to the same scale in order to facilitate comparison.

[2] WILKINSON, *Manners and Customs*, etc., p. 396.   [3] DIODORUS, i. 57.

[4] Recent measurement has shown that the height given on page 105, Vol. I., is incorrect.—ED.

[5] In the *Dictionnaire d'Archéologie Égyptienne* of M. PIERRET, a translation of the hieroglyphics upon one side of the Paris obelisk will be found under the word *Obélisque*. The *Athenæum* for October 27, 1877, contains a complete translation of the inscription upon the London obelisk, by DR. BIRCH.—ED.

[6] *Monuments Divers*, pl. 50.

[7] *Description, Antiquités*, vol. ii. pp. 371-373. In our view of Luxor on page 345

the difference between the two less conspicuous. This difference may have been caused by any slight accident, or by the discovery of a flaw in the granite during the operation of cutting it in the quarry. In dealing with huge blocks like these, such *contretemps* must have been frequent.

The smaller of the two obelisks was chosen for transport to Paris in 1836. In its present situation on the Place de la Concorde it is separated from the sculptured base upon which it stood at Luxor. The northern and southern faces of that pedestal were each ornamented with four cynocephali adoring the rising sun; the other two had figures of the god Nile presenting offerings to Amen (Fig. 168).

In order to restore this and other obelisks to the form which they enjoyed in the days of the Pharaohs we should have to give them back their original summits as well as their pedestals. Hittorf has shown that these probably consisted of caps of gilded copper fitted over the pyramidion,[1] in those cases where the latter was not ornamented with carved figures. A curious passage in Abd-al-latif, which has been often cited, proves that the pyramid of Ousourtesen preserved its cap as late as the thirteenth century. "The summit," says the Arab historian, "is covered with a kind of funnel-shaped copper cap, which descends about three cubits from the apex. The weather of so many centuries has made the copper green and rusty, and some of the green has run down the shaft of the obelisk."[2] In the plate attached to his essay, Hittorf gives us a plan and elevation of the pyramidion of the smaller obelisk of Luxor. He shows how its broken and irregular mass implies a metallic covering, a covering whose existence is moreover proved by the groove or rebate, about an inch and a half deep, which runs round the summit of the shaft. His Figs. 3 and 4 show that this groove was carefully polished. His conclusions have failed to find acceptance in some quarters. It has been asserted that the rays of the sun, striking upon such a surface, would be reflected in a dazzling fashion, and that the

we have restored the base of the larger obelisk after that belonging to the one now at Paris. We were without any other means of ascertaining its form.

[1] *Précis sur les Pyramidions de Bronze doré Employés par les Anciens Égyptiens comme couronnement de quelques-uns de leurs Obélisques,* etc. J. J. HITTORF, 8vo, 1836.

[2] ABD-AL-LATIF, *Relation de l'Égypte;* French translation by Silvestre de Sacy, published in 4to. in 1810. p. 181.—ED.

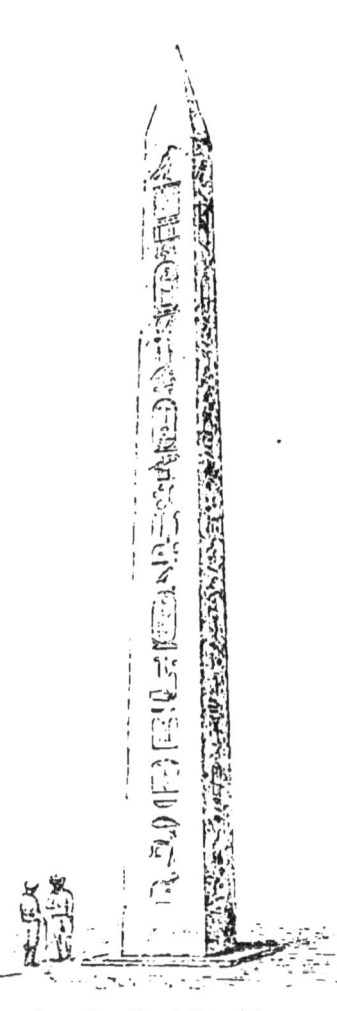

Fig. 167.—The obelisk of Ousourtesen.
Description, v. 26.

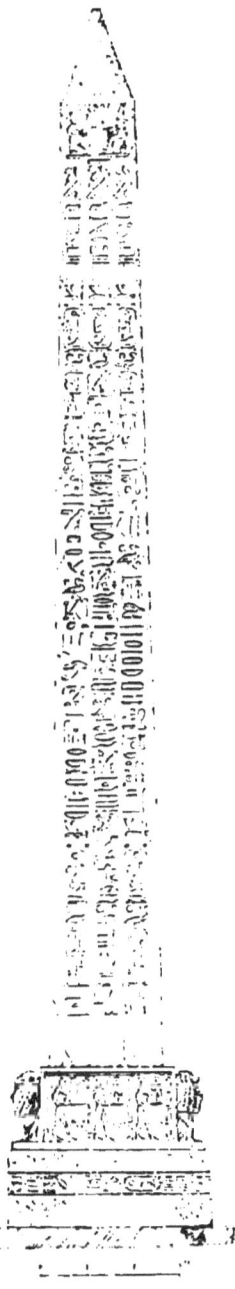

Fig. 168.—The obelisk in the Place de la Concorde, restored to its original base. From Prisse.

general effect would have been unsatisfactory. The Egyptians had no such fear. They made lavish use of gold in the decoration of their buildings. According to the inscription which covers the four sides of the pedestal under the obelisk of Hatasu at Karnak, the pyramidion was covered "with pure gold taken from the chiefs of the nations," which seems to imply either a cap of gilded copper, like that of the obelisk at Heliopolis, or a golden sphere upon the very apex. An object of this latter kind is figured in some of the bas-reliefs at Sakkarah. Besides this there is no doubt that the obelisk in question was gilded from head to foot. " We remark, in the first place, that the beds of the hieroglyphs were carefully polished; secondly, that the four faces of the obelisk itself were left comparatively rough, from which we should conclude that the latter alone received this costly embellishment, the hieroglyphs preserving the natural colour of the granite." [1]

In that transplantation of which the Ptolemies first set the example, the obelisk at Paris was deprived of its original pedestal, as we have seen; it was erected in an open space of such extent that its dimensions seem almost insignificant; it was placed upon a pedestal which, neither in dimensions nor design, has anything Egyptian about it; and finally it was deprived of its metal finial. It can therefore give but little idea of the effect which the obelisks produced while they still remained in the places for which they were designed. The artistic instinct of Théophile Gautier was quite alive to this fact when he penned his fanciful but charming lines on the *Nostalgie d'Obélisque*.

A curious fact has been ascertained in connection with the obelisks of Luxor. Their faces present a slight convexity, the total protuberance at the base being rather more than an inch and three-tenths. It is probable that the same arrangement would be found in other obelisks if they were carefully examined. Its explanation is easy. If the surfaces had been absolute planes they would have been made to appear concave by the sharpness of the corners. It was necessary, therefore, to give them a gentle entasis which should gradually diminish towards the summit, completely disappearing by the time the pyramidion was reached.[2]

[1] MARIETTE, *Itinéraire de la Haute-Égypte*, third edition, p. 142.
[2] *Description, Antiquités*, vol. ii. p. 369. CHARLES BLANC, *Voyage dans la Haute-Égypte*, p. 150.

The obelisk at Beggig, in the Fayoum, offers a singular variant upon the type which we have described. It was formerly a monolith about 43 feet high; it is now overthrown and broken into two pieces. It bears the ovals of Ousourtesen I., and would seem, therefore, to be contemporary with the obelisk at Heliopolis.[1] Its peculiarity consists in its shape. It is a rectangular oblong, instead of a square, on plan. Two of its sides are 6 feet 9 inches wide, and the other two about 4 feet. It has no pyramidion. The summit is rounded from front to back,

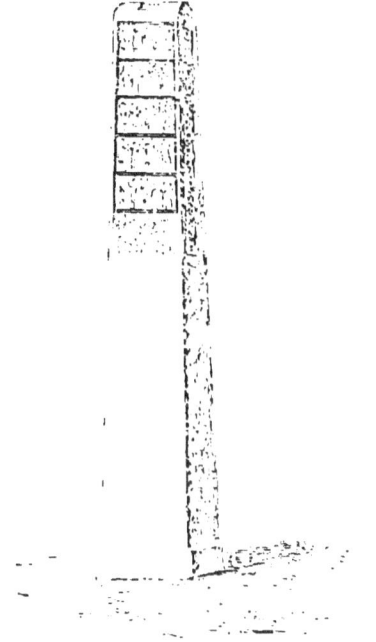

FIG. 169.—The obelisk of Beggig. From the elevation of Lepsius.[2]   FIG. 170.—Upper part of the obelisk at Beggig. From the elevation of Lepsius.

forming a ridge, and the upper part of its principal faces are filled with sculptures in low relief (Fig 170). All this makes it resemble a gigantic stele rather than an obelisk (Fig. 169).

Whatever may have been the origin of this form it never became popular in Egypt. In Nubia alone do we find the type

[1] For an interesting description of the present state and curious situation of this obelisk, see *The Land of Khemi*, by LAURENCE OLIPHANT, pp. 98-100, (Blackwood. 1882).—ED.   [2] *Denkmäler*, part ii. pl. 119.

repeated, and that only in the debased periods of art. On the other hand, the obelisks proper seem to have been made in truly astonishing numbers in the time of the Middle and New Empires. Egypt has supplied Rome, Constantinople, Paris, London, and even New York with these monoliths, and yet she still possesses many at home. Of these several are still standing and in good preservation, others are broken and buried beneath the ruins of the temples which they adorned. At Karnak alone the sites of some ten or twelve have been found. Some of these are still standing, some are lying on the ground, while of others nothing is left but the pedestals. At the beginning of the century the French visitors to the ruins of San, the ancient Tanis, found the fragments of nine different obelisks.[1]

§ 11. *The Profession of Architect.*

It may seem to some of our readers that we have spent too much time and labour on our analysis of Egyptian architecture. Our excuse lies in the fact that architecture was the chief of the arts in Egypt. We know nothing of her painters. The pictures in the Theban tombs often display great taste and skill, but they seem to have been the work of decorators rather than of painters in the higher sense of the word. Sculptors appear, now and then, to have been held in higher consideration. The names of one or two have come down to us, and we are told how dear they were to the kings who employed them.[2] But the only artists who had a high and well defined social position in ancient Egypt, a country where ranks were as distinctly marked as in China, were the architects or engineers, for they deserve either name. Their

[1] *Description, Antiquités*, ch. 23.—M. EDOUARD NAVILLE has recently (June 16, 1882) published in the *Journal de Genève* an account of a visit to these ruins, during which he counted the fragments of no less than fourteen obelisks, some of them of extraordinary size.—ED.

[2] The sculptor who made the two famous colossi of Amenophis III. had the same name as his master, Amenhotep. (BRUGSCH, *History*, 1st edition, vol. i. pp. 425-6). Iritesen, who worked for Menthouthotep II. in the time of the first Theban Empire, was a worker in stone, gold, silver, ivory, and ebony. He held a place, he tells us, at the bottom of the king's heart, and was his joy from morning till night. (MASPERO, *la Stèle C. 14 du Louvre*, in the *Transactions of the Society of Biblical Archæology*, vol. v. part ii. 1877.)

names have been preserved to us in hundreds upon their elaborate tombs and inscribed steles.

We might, then, amuse ourselves by making out a long list of Egyptian builders, a list which would extend over several thousands of years, from Nefer, of Boulak (Fig. 171[1]), who may have built one of the Pyramids, to the days of the Ptolemies or of the Roman emperors. In the glyptothek at Munich there is a beautiful sepulchral statue of Bakenkhonsou, who was chief prophet of Amen and principal architect of Thebes, in the time of Seti I. and Rameses II. From certain phrases in the inscription, Devéria believes that Bakenkhonsou built the temple of Gournah.[2] In his epitaph he boasts of the great offices which he had filled and of the favour which had been shown to him by his sovereign. Every Egyptian museum contains some statue and inscription of the same kind. Brugsch has proved that under the Memphite dynasties the architects to the king were sometimes recruited among the princes of the blood royal, and the texts upon their tombs show that they all, or nearly all, married daughters or grand-daughters of Pharaoh, and that such a marriage was not looked upon as a *mesalliance*.[3]

FIG. 171.—Limestone statue of the architect Nefer, in the Boulak Museum. Drawn by Bourgoin.

Similar evidence is forthcoming in connection with the first Theban Empire, but it was chiefly under the three great dynasties that the post of architect to Pharaoh became one of great responsibility, and carried with it great influence and authority.

---

[1] See *Notice des Principaux Monuments exposés dans le Musée de Boulak*, 1876. No. 458.
[2] DEVÉRIA, *Bakenkhonsou (Revue Archéologique,* new series, vi. p. 101).
[3] BRUGSCH, *History of Egypt* (English edition), vol. i. p. 47. Ti, whose splendid tomb has been so often mentioned, was "First Commissioner of Works" for the whole of Egypt, as well as "Secretary of State" to Pharaoh.

For the building and keeping in repair of the sumptuous monuments then erected a great system of administration must have been devised, and Thebes, like modern London, must have had its "district-surveyors."[1]

So far as we can tell there was a chief architect, or superintendent general of buildings, for the whole kingdom; his title was *Overseer of the buildings of Upper and Lower Egypt*.[2] For how many scribes and draughtsmen must the offices of Bakenkhonsou or of Semnat, the favourite architect of the great regent Hatasu, have found employment?[3]

Who would not like to know the course of study by which the ancient Egyptian builders prepared themselves for the great public enterprises which were always going on in their country? We may admit that the methods employed by their engineers were much more primitive than it has been the fashion to suppose, we may prove that their structures were far from possessing the accuracy of plan that distinguishes ours, but yet we cannot deny that those who transported and raised the obelisks and colossal statues, and those who constructed the hypostyle hall of Karnak, or even the pyramids of Gizeh, must have learnt their trade. How and where they learnt it we do not know. It is probable that they learnt it by practice under a master. Theory cannot have held any great part in their teaching. Their system must have been composed of a collection of processes and receipts which grew in number as the centuries passed away. There is nothing in the texts to show that these receipts were the property of any close corporation, but heredity is sure to have played an important part and to have made them, to some extent, the property of a class. Architects were generally the sons of architects. Brugsch has given us one genealogical table in which the profession descended from father to son for twenty-two generations. By help of the inscriptions he traced the family in question from the

---

[1] We have here ventured to take a slight liberty with M. Perrot's local tints.—ED. PAUL PIERRET ("*Stèle de Suti et de Har, architectes de Thèbes*," in the *Recueil de Travaux*, vol. i. p. 70), says, "This is said by him who has charge of the works of Amen in Southern Ap." Suti-Har says in his turn: "I have the direction of the west, he of the east. We are the directors of the great monuments in Ap, in the centre of Thebes, the city of Amen."

[2] PIERRET, *Dictionnaire d'Archéologie Égyptienne*, p. 59.

[3] See BRUGSCH, *History of Egypt*, 1st edition, vol. i. p. 302.

THE PROFESSION OF ARCHITECT. 179

time of Seti I. to that of Darius the son of Hystaspes. But even then he may not have tracked the stream to its source. The rule and compass may have entered that family long before the time of Seti; their use may also have continued long after the Persian kings had been driven from Egypt.

CHAPTER III.

SCULPTURE.

§ 1. *The Origin of Statue-making.*

THE art of imitating living forms by means of sculpture was no less ancient in Egypt than architecture. We do not mean to say that it already existed in those remote ages when the first ancestors of the Egyptian people built their mud cabins upon the banks of the Nile; but as soon as their dwellings became something more than mere shelters and began to be affected by the desire for beauty, the figures of men and animals took a considerable place in their decoration. The oldest mastabas that have been discovered have bas-reliefs upon their walls and statues in their mummy-pits.

The existence of these statues and their relative perfection show that sculpture had advanced with strides no less rapid than those of the sister art. It may even be said that its progress had been greater than that of architecture. Given the particular kind of expressive beauty which formed the ambition of the Egyptian sculptor, he produced masterpieces as early as the time of the Pyramid builders. We cannot say as much of the architect. The latter showed himself, indeed, a master in the mechanical processes of dressing and fixing stone, but the arrangement of his buildings was simple, we might say elementary, and many centuries had to pass before he had become capable of imagining and creating the sumptuous temples of the New Empire, with those ample porticos and great hypostyle halls which were the culminating achievements of Egyptian architecture.

In order to explain this curious inequality we need not inquire which of the two arts presents the fewest difficulties. It is with nations as with individuals. Some among them succeed with ease in matters which embarrass their neighbours. It is a question of circumstances, of natural qualifications, and of surroundings. Among the Egyptians the progress of sculpture was accelerated by that national belief in a posthumous life for the body which we have described in connection with their funerary architecture. By the existence of this constant and singular belief we may explain both the early maturity of Egyptian sculpture and the great originality of their most ancient style.

We have already described the arrangements which were necessary to enable the inhabitant of the tomb to resist annihilation. Those arrangements were of two kinds, a provision of food and drink, which had to be constantly renewed, either in fact or by the magic multiplication which followed prayer, and a permanent support for the *ka* or double, a support that should fill the place of the living body of which it had been deprived by dissolution. This support was afforded to some extent by the mummy; but the mummy was liable to be destroyed or to perish by the action of time. The Egyptians were led to provide against such a catastrophe by the invention of the funerary statue. In the climate of Egypt, stone, and even wood, had far better chances of duration than the most carefully embalmed body. Statues had the additional advantage that they could be multiplied at will. There was nothing to prevent ten, twenty, any number of them, being placed in a tomb.[1] If but one of these images survived all the accidents of time, the *double* would be saved from that annihilation to which it would otherwise be condemned.

Working under the impulse of such an idea, the sculptor could not fail to do his best to endow his statue with the characteristic features of the original. "It is easy, then, to understand why those Egyptian statues which do not represent gods are always portraits of some individual, executed with all the precision of which the artists were capable. They were not ideal figures to which the desire for beauty of line and expression had much to say, they were stone bodies, bodies which had to reproduce all the individual contours of their flesh-and-blood originals. When the latter was ugly, its reproduction had to be ugly also, and ugly in

---

[1] The *serdabs* of the tomb of Ti contained twenty, only one of which was recovered uninjured. MARIETTE, *Notice du Musée de Boulak*, No. 24.

the same way. If these principles were disregarded the double would be unable to find the support which was necessary to it."[1]

The first Egyptian statue was not so much a work of art as a cast from nature. If photography had been invented in the time of Menes, photographers would have made their fortunes in Egypt. Those sun-portraits, which are supposed to present a perfect resemblance, would have been put in the tomb of a deceased man in hundreds. Wanting such things, they were contented to copy his figure faithfully in stone or wood. His ordinary attitude, his features and costume, were imitated with such scrupulous sincerity that the serdabs were filled with faithful duplicates of himself. To obtain such a likeness the artist cannot have trusted to his memory. His employer must have sat before him, the stone body must have been executed in presence of him whose immortality it had to ensure. In no other way could those effigies have been produced whose iconic character is obvious at first sight, effigies to which a contemporary would have put a name without the slightest hesitation.

This individuality is not, however, equally well preserved in all Egyptian sculpture, a remark which applies to the early dynasties as well as to the later ones, though not in the same degree. In those early ages the beliefs which led the Egyptian to inclose duplicates of his own body in his last resting-place were more powerful over his spirit, and the artist had to exert himself to satisfy the requirements of his employers in the matter of fidelity. Again, those centuries had not to struggle against such an accumulation of precedents and fixed habits, in a word, against so much conventionality as those which came after. There were no formulæ, sanctioned by long custom, to relieve the artist from the necessity for original thought and continual reference to nature; he was compelled to make himself acquainted both with the general features of his race and those of his individual employers. This necessity gave him the best possible training. Portraiture taken up with intelligence and practised with a passionate desire for truth has always been the best school for the formation of masters in the plastic arts.

In those early centuries, then, Egypt produced a few statues which were masterpieces of artistic expression, which were admirable portraits. In all countries, however, great works are

---

[1] MASPERO, in Rayet's *Monuments de l'Art Antique*.

rare. The sepulchral statues were far from being all equal in value to those of the Sheik-el-Beled, of Ra-Hotep from Meidoum, or of the scribe in the Louvre. This intelligent and scientific interpretation of nature was not reached at a bound; Egyptian sculpture had its archaic period as well as that of Greece.

Moreover, even when the art had come to maturity, there was, as in other countries a crowd of mediocre artists whose work was to be obtained at a cost smaller than that of the eminent men whom they surrounded. The leading sculptors were fully employed by the kings and great lords, by ministers and functionaries of high rank: their less able brethren worked for that great class of functionaries of the second order, who composed what may be called the Egyptian middle class. It is probable too, that, although his work was to be hidden in the darkness of the serdab, the artist took more care in reproducing the features of a great personage whose appearance might be known from one end of the Nile valley to the other, than when employed by some comparatively humble individual. Before descending into the tomb, the statue must for a time have been open to inspection, and its creator must have had the chance of receiving those praises which neither poet nor artist has been able to do without, from the days of Memphis to those of Modern Europe.

In most cases, however, he had to reproduce the features and contours of some obscure but honest scribe, some insignificant unit among the thousands who served Cheops or Chephren; and his conscience was more easily satisfied. If we pass in review those limestone figures which are beginning to be comparatively common in our museums, we receive the impression that many among them bear only a general resemblance to their originals: they preserve the Egyptian type of feature, the individual marks of sex and age, the costume, the familiar attitude, and the attributes and accessories required by custom, and that is all. It may even be that, like a certain category of funerary steles among the Greeks of a later age, these inferior works were bought in shops ready carved and painted, and that the mere inscription of a name was supposed to give them that iconic character upon which so much depended. A name indeed is not always found upon these images, but it is always carved upon the tombs in which they were placed, and its appearance there was sufficient to consecrate the statues and all other contents of the sepulchre to the support of the *double* to which it belonged. Whether it was copied from a sitter or bought ready-made, the statue became from the moment of its consecration an auxiliary body for the double. It preserved more of the appearance of life than the corpse saturated with mineral essences and hidden under countless bandages; the half-open smiling lips seemed about to speak, and the eyes, to which the employment of enamel and polished metal give a singular brilliance, seemed instinct with life.

The first statues produced by the Egyptians were sepulchral in character, and in the intentions both of those who made them and of those who gave the commissions, they were portraits, executed with such fidelity that the double should confidingly attach himself to them and not feel that he had been despoiled of his corporeal support. As the power and wealth of the Egyptians grew, their artistic aspirations grew also. They rose by degrees to the conception of an ideal, but even when they are most visibly aiming at grandeur of style the origin of their art may still be divined; in their happiest and most noble creations the persistent effect of their early habits of thought and belief is still to be surely traced.

§ 2. *Sculpture under the Ancient Empire.*

The most ancient monument of sculpture to which we can assign, if not a date, at least a chronological place in the list of Egyptian kings, is a rock-cut monument in the peninsula of Sinai. This is in the Wadi-maghara, and represents Snefrou, the last monarch of the third dynasty, destroying a crouching barbarian with his mace. In spite of its historic importance, we refrain from producing this bas-relief because its dilapidated state takes away its interest from an artistic point of view.[1]

There are, besides, other statues in existence to which egyptologists ascribe a still greater age. The Louvre contains three before which the historian of art must halt for a moment.

Two of these are very much alike, and bear the name of a personage called Sepa, who enjoyed the style and dignity of *prophet and priest of the white bull*. The third is the presentment

All the monuments in the Wadi-maghara are figured in the *Denkmæler* of LEPSIUS (part ii. plates 2, 39, and 61); casts of them have also been made.

of Nesa, who is called a relation of the king, and was, in all probability, the wife of Sepa (Fig. 172). These statues were of soft limestone. Both man and woman have black wigs with squared ends, which descend, in the case of the former, to the shoulders, in that of the latter, to the breasts. Sepa holds a long staff in his left hand, and in his right the sceptre called *pat*, a sign of authority. His only robe is a plain *schenti*, a kind of cotton breeches fastened round his waist by a band. His trunk and legs are bare, and the latter are only half freed from the stone in which they are carved. Nesa is dressed in a long chemise with a triangular opening between the breasts. Upon her arms she has bracelets composed of twelve rings. In each figure the wig, the pupils, eyelids, and eyebrows, are painted black, while there is a green stripe under the eyes. The bracelets are also green.

De Rougé asserted boldly that these were the oldest statues in the world.[1] He believed them to date from the third dynasty, and his successors do not think he exaggerated; they would perhaps give the works in question an even more venerable age.

This impression of great antiquity is not caused by the short inscriptions on the plinths. The well-carved hieroglyphs which compose them are in relief, but this peculiarity is found in monuments of the fourth and fifth dynasties. The physiognomies and general style of the figures are much more significant. They betray an art whose aims and instincts are well developed, although it has not yet mastered its mechanical processes. The sculptor knows thoroughly what he wants, but his hand still lacks assurance and decision. He has set out upon the way which will be trodden with ever-increasing firmness by his successors. He follows nature faithfully. Observe how frankly the breadth of Sepa's shoulders is insisted upon, how clearly the collar-bones and the articulations of the knees are marked. The rounded contours of Nesa's thighs betray the same sincerity. And yet there is a certain timidity and awkwardness in the group which becomes clearly perceptible when we compare it with works in its neighbourhood which date from the fifth dynasty. The workmanship lacks freedom, and the modelling is over-simplified. The arms, which elsewhere are laid upon the knees, or, in the case of the

---

[1] *Notice des Monuments exposés dans la Galerie d'Antiquités Égyptiennes. Salle du Rez-de-chaussé et Palier de l'Escalier*, 1875, p. 26.

woman, passed round the neck of her husband, are too rigid. One is held straight down by the body, the other is bent at a right angle across the stomach. The pose is stiff, the placid features lack expression and will.

The induction to which we have been led by the style of these figures is confirmed by an observation made during recent explorations in the necropolis of Memphis. The patch of green paint under the eyes has, as yet, only been found in statues from

FIG. 172.—Sepa and Nesa, Louvre. Four feet eight inches high.

a certain peculiar class of tombs at Gizeh and Sakkarah. These are chambers cut in the rock, in which the roofs are carved into imitations of timber ceilings of palm wood. Some of the texts which have been found in them contain the name of a king whose chronological place has not yet been satisfactorily determined, but who seems to have been anterior to Snefrou. The figures upon which the adornment in question occurs would appear therefore

to be contemporary with the oldest tombs in the neighbourhood of the pyramids.[1]

Progress was rapid between the end of the third dynasty and that of the fourth. It was during the latter dynasty that the art of the Ancient Empire produced its masterpieces. Mariette attributes the two famous statues found in a tomb near the pyramid of Meidoum to the reign of Snefrou, the predecessor of Cheops. They are exhibited, under glass, in the Boulak Museum (Plate IX).[2]

"One of them represents Ra-hotep, a prince of the blood, who enjoyed the dignity of general of infantry, a very rare title under the Ancient Empire; the other is a woman, Nefert, *the beauty*; her statue also informs us that she was related to the king. We do not know whether she was the wife or sister of Ra-hotep. The interest excited by the extreme beauty of these figures is increased by our certainty of their prodigious antiquity. In the mastaba where they were found everything is frankly archaic, everything is as old as the oldest of the tombs at Sakkarah, and those date from before the fourth dynasty. A neighbouring tomb which, as is proved by the connection between their structures, dates from the same period as that of Ra-hotep, is that of a functionary attached to the person of Snefrou I. We may, therefore, fairly assign the two statues from Meidoum to the last reign of the third dynasty."[3]

Each of these figures, with its chair-shaped seat, is carved from a single block of limestone about four feet high. The man is almost nude; his only dress is a ribbon about his neck, and white breeches like those to which we have already alluded. The woman is robed in the long chemise, open between the breasts, which we have seen upon Nesa. Besides this a wide and richly designed necklace spreads over her chest. Upon her head she has a square-cut black wig, which, however, allows her natural hair to be visible in front. Over the wig she has a low flat cap with a decorated border. The carnations of the man are brownish red, those of the woman light yellow.

[1] The Boulak Museum also contains specimens of these figures. See *Notice*, Nos. 994 and 995.

[2] *Notice des principaux Monuments exposés à Boulak*, No. 973. These figures were discovered in January, 1872. They had a narrow escape of being destroyed by the pickaxes of the superstitious fellaheen. Mariette fortunately arrived just in time to prevent the outrage. *Recueil de Travaux*, vol. i. p. 160.

[3] MARIETTE, *Voyage dans la Haute-Égypte*, p. 47.

These statues betray an art much more advanced than that of Sepa and Nesa. The pose is much easier and more natural, but the right arm of Ra-hotep is stiff and held in a fashion which would soon cause cramp in a living man. The modelling of the body is free and true, though without much knowledge or subtlety. The breasts, arms, and legs of Nefert are skilfully suggested under her robe. But the care of the sculptor has been mainly given to the heads. By means of chisel and paint-brush he has given them an individuality which is not readily forgotten. The arched eyebrows surmount large well-opened eyes; the eyelids seem to be edged with heavy lashes and to stand out well from the eyeball. In the case of the latter the limestone has retained its primitive whiteness, giving a strong contrast with the pupil and iris (Fig. 173). The noses, especially that of Ra-hotep are fine and pointed; the thick but well-drawn lips seem about to speak. Her smooth cheeks and soft dark eyes, eyes which are still common among the women of the East, give Nefert a very attractive look. Her smiling and restful countenance is in strong contrast to that of Ra-hotep, which is full of life and animation not unmingled with a little hardness.

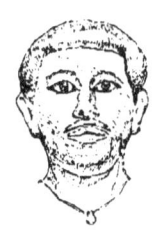

FIG. 173.—Ra-hotep. Drawn by Bourgoin.

The longer we look at these figures the less ready are we to turn away from them. They are portraits, and portraits of marvellous sincerity. If they could be gifted with life to-morrow, if we could encounter Ra-hotep and Nefert working under the sun of Egypt, the man semi-nude, sowing the grain or helping to make an embankment, his companion robed in the long blue chemise of the fellah women and balancing a pitcher upon her head, we should know them at once and salute them by name as old acquaintances. We find none of the marks of inexperience and archaism which are so conspicuous in the statues of Sepa and Nesa. A few later figures may seem to us more delicately modelled and more full of detail, but taking them all in all, we cannot look upon these statues as other than the creations of a mature art, of an art which was already in full command of its resources, and of a sculptor who had a well-marked personal and original style of his own.

We find the same qualities in another group of monuments

ascribed by Mariette to no less remote a period.[1] The same eye for proportion, the same life-like expression, the same frankness and confidence of hand are to be found in those sculptured wooden panels of which the museum at Boulak possesses four fine examples. They were found at Sakkarah in the tomb of a personage called Hosi, where they were enframed in four blind doorways. They are on the average about 3 feet 10 inches high and 1 foot 8 inches wide. The drawings which we reproduce give a good idea of the peculiarities of style and execution by which they are distinguished (Figs. 174-176).[2]

At first sight these carvings are a little embarrassing to the eye accustomed to works in stone. The type of figure presented is less thickset. The body, instead of being muscular, is nervous and wiry. The arms and legs are thin and long. In the head especially do we find unaccustomed features : the nose, instead of being round, is strongly aquiline ; the lips, instead of being thick and fleshy, as in almost all other Egyptian heads, are thin and compressed. The profile is strongly marked and rather severe. The general type is Semitic rather than Egyptian. And yet the inscriptions which surround them prove that the originals were pure Egyptians of the highest class. One of them, he who is represented standing in two different attitudes, is Ra-hesi ; the other, who is sitting before a table of offerings, bears the name of Pekh-hesi. The decipherable part of the inscription tells us that he was a scribe, highly placed, and in great favour with the king.

The tomb in which these panels were found was not built on the usual plan of the mastaba. Mariette alludes to certain peculiarities which are to be found in it, but he does not describe them in detail. The hieroglyphs are grouped in a peculiar fashion ; many of them are of a very uncommon form. The arrangement of the objects borne in the left hand of Ra-hesi is quite unique. Struck by these singularities, Mariette asserts that "the style of these panels is to Egyptian art what the style called archaic is to that of Greece."[3] This assertion seems to us inaccurate. Not

---

[1] "According to all appearance these panels date from before the reign of Cheops." *Notices des principaux Monuments*, etc. Nos. 987-92.

[2] There is a panel of the same kind in the Louvre (*Salle Historique*, No. 1 of Pierret's *Catalogue*), but it is neither so firm, nor in such good preservation as those at Cairo.

[3] MARIETTE, *La Galerie de l'Égypte Ancienne au Trocadéro*, 1878. p. 122.

that we mean to contest the validity of the reasons which Mariette gives for ascribing these panels to an epoch anterior to the great pyramids; but, whatever may be their age, it seems to be impossible, in view of the style in which they are executed, to call them archaic. They show no more archaism than the statues of Meidoum. The Egyptian artist never carved wood with greater decision or with more subtlety and finesse than are to be seen in these panels. As for the differences of execution which have been noticed between these figures and the stone statues of the same epoch, they may easily be explained by the change of material and by the Egyptian love for fidelity of imitation. Wood is not attacked in the same fashion as soft stone. Its constitution does not lend itself to the ample and rounded forms of lapidary sculpture. It demands, especially when a low relief is used, a more delicate and subtle modelling. Again, these were portraits; all the Egyptians were not like one another, especially in that primitive Egypt in which perhaps various races had not yet been blended into a homogeneous population. Among the contemporaries of Cheops, as in our day, there were fat people and thin people. Men who were tall and slender, and men who were short and thickset. Countenances varied both in features and expression.[1] In time art succeeded in evolving from all these diversities a type of Egyptian manhood and beauty. As the ages passed away the influence of that type became more and more despotic. It became almost universal, except in those cases where there was a rigid obligation to reproduce the personal characteristics of an individual with fidelity. But at the end of the third dynasty that consummation was still far off. And we need feel no surprise that the higher we mount in the stream of Egyptian civilization the more particular are the concrete images which it offers to us, and the more striking the variation between one work of art and another.

It must not be supposed, however, that the features which we have mentioned as peculiar in the cases of Ra-hesi and Pekh-hesi are not to be found elsewhere. If we examine the profile of Nefert, still more that of Ra-hotep, we shall find that they also have the

---

[1] Thus we find in a tomb which, according to Lepsius, dates from the fourth dynasty, certain thickset sculptured forms, which contrast strongly with figures taken from mastabas in the same neighbourhood, at Gizeh. The body is short, the legs heavy and massive. LEPSIUS, *Denkmæler*, part ii. pl. 9.

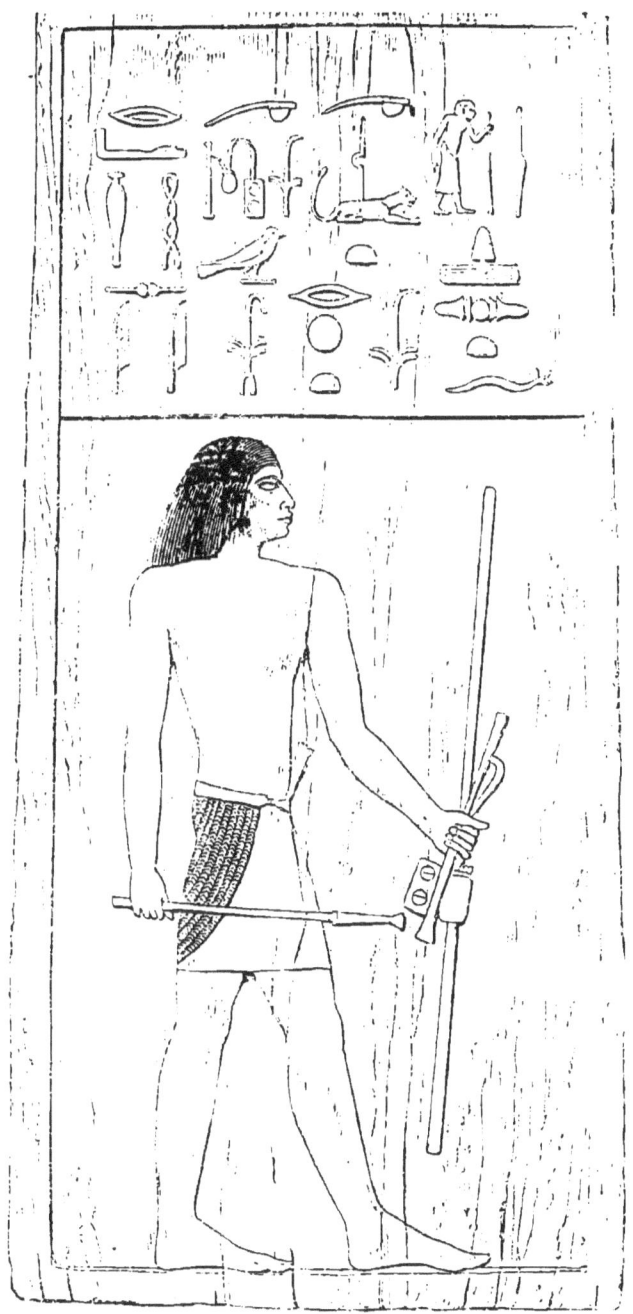

FIG. 174.—Wooden panel from the Tomb of Hosi. Drawn by Bourgoin.

sloping forehead and aquiline nose. The body of Ra-hotep is rounder and fatter than those in the wooden reliefs, but the lines of his countenance have a strong resemblance to those which have excited remark in the figures on the panels.

In the case of a limestone head, covered with red paint, which stands in the *Salle Civile*, in the Louvre, the cranium is no less elongated, the cheekbones are no less large, the cheeks themselves are as hollow, the chin as protuberant, and the whole head as bony and fleshless. We do not know whence it came, but we have no hesitation in agreeing with De Rougé, Mariette, and Maspero, that this head is a masterpiece from one of the early dynasties. It may be put by the side of the Meidoum couple for its vitality and individual expression. The unknown original must have been ugly almost to vulgarity, but it rouses in the spectator the same kind of admiration as a Tuscan bust of the fifteenth century, and a pleasure which is not diminished by the knowledge that the man whose faithful image is under his eyes passed from the world some five or six thousand years ago (Fig. 177).

The little figure which occupies the place of honour in this same saloon (Plate X.), though more famous, is hardly superior to the fragment just described. It was found by Mariette in the tomb of Sekhem-ka, during his excavation of the Serapeum. Other figures of the same kind were found with it, but are hardly equal to it in merit. They are believed to date from the fifth or sixth dynasty.

This scribe is seated, cross-legged, in an attitude still familiar to those who have visited the East. The most superficial visitor to the Levant must have seen, in the audience-hall of the *cadi* or *pacha*, the *kiatib* crouching exactly in the same fashion before the chair or divan, registering sentences with his rapid *kalem*, or writing out despatches. Our scribe is listening; his thin and bony features are vibrating with intelligence; his black eye-balls positively sparkle; his mouth is only closed because respect keeps him silent. His shoulders are high and square, his chest ample, his pectoral muscles very large. People who follow a very sedentary occupation generally put on much fat on the front of their bodies, and this scribe is no exception to the rule. His arms are free of his sides; their position is easy and natural. One hand holds a strip of papyrus upon which he writes with the other, his pen being a reed. The lower parts of the body and the thighs

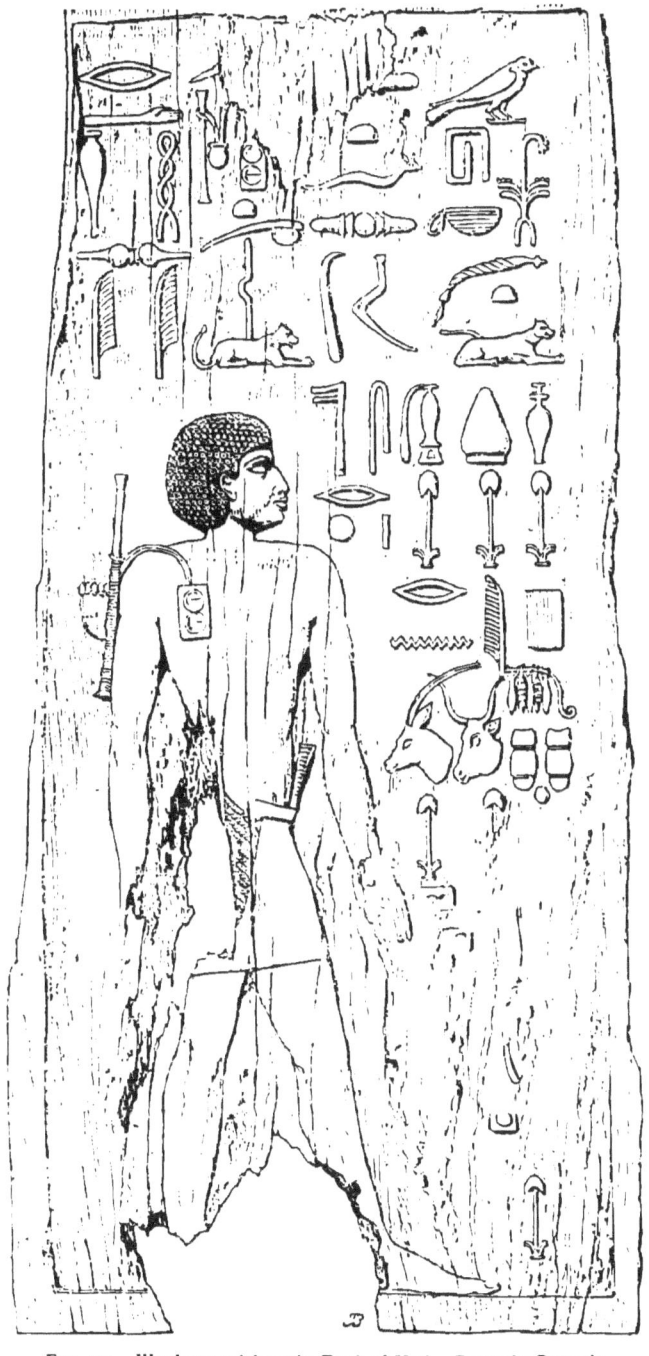

FIG. 175.—Wooden panel from the Tomb of Hosi. Drawn by Bourgoin.

are covered with a pair of drawers, whose white colour contrasts with the brownish red of the carnations. The breadth and truth with which the knee-joints are indicated should be remarked. The only details that have, to a certain extent, been "scamped," are the feet. Trusting to their being half hidden by the folded legs, the sculptor has left them in a very rudimentary condition.

The eyes form the most striking feature in this figure. "They consist of an iris of rock crystal surrounding a metal pupil, and set in an eyeball of opaque white quartz. The whole is framed in continuous eyelids of bronze."[1]

This clever contrivance gives singular vitality and animation to the face. Even the Grecian sculptor never produced anything so vivacious. The latter, indeed began by renouncing all attempts to imitate the depth and brilliancy of the human eye. His point of departure differed entirely from that of his Memphite predecessor; his conception of his art led him, where the Egyptian would have used colour, to be content with the general characteristics of form and with its elevation to the highest pitch of nobility of which it was capable. This is not the place for a comparison of the two systems, but accepting the principles of art which prevailed in early Egypt, we must do justice to those masters who were contemporary with the Pyramids. It must be acknowledged that they produced works which are not to be surpassed in their way by the greatest portraits of modern Europe. In later years the Egyptian sculptor ceased to paint the eyes. Even in the time of the Ancient Empire the Egyptian custom in this particular was the same as the Greek, so far as statues in hard stone were concerned. The great statue of Chephren is an instance. In it the chisel has merely reproduced the contours of the eyelids and the salience of the eyeball. No attempt has been made to imitate the iris or to give brightness to the pupil. In none of the royal statues that have come down to our time do we find any effort to produce this kind of illusion, either by the use of paint or by the insertion of naturally coloured substances.

There is a statue at Boulak which may, perhaps, be preferred even to the scribe of the Louvre. We have already alluded to it as the *Sheik-el-Beled* (Fig. 7, Vol. I.). In its present state (it is without either feet or base) it has no inscription but it is sometimes called Ra-em-ké, because that was the name of the

---

[1] DE ROUGÉ, *Notice sommaire des Monuments Égyptiens*, 1865, p. 68.

FIG. 176.—Wooden panel from the Tomb of Hosi. Drawn by Bourgoin

person in whose tomb it was found. It is of wood, and, with the exception of its lower members, is in marvellous preservation. The eyes are similar to those of the scribe, and seem to be fixed upon the spectator while their owner advances upon him. The type is very different from those we have hitherto been describing. The face is round and flat, and so is the trunk.

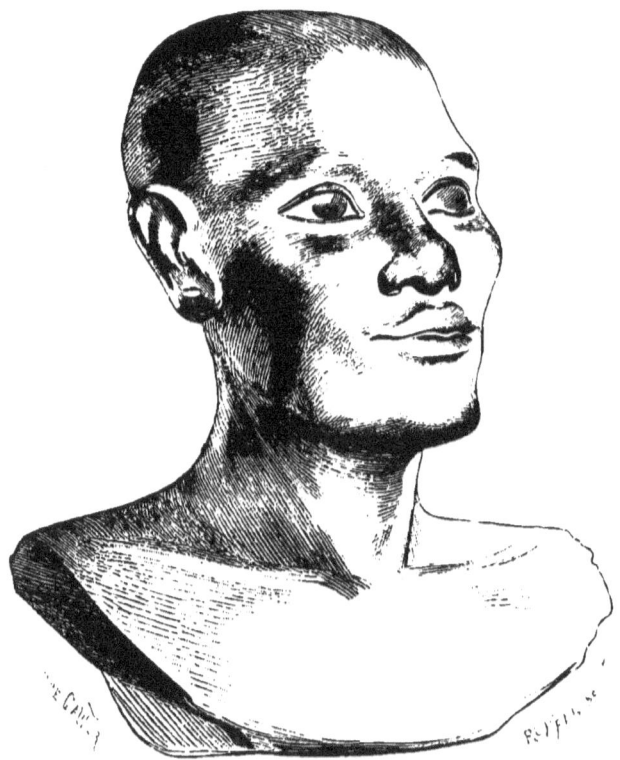

FIG. 177.—Limestone head, in the Louvre. Drawn by Saint-Elme Gautier.

The smiling good humour of the expression and the *embonpoint* of the person indicate a man well nourished and comfortably off, a man content both with himself and his neighbours.[1]

[1] Another wooden statue of equal merit as a work of art was found in the same tomb. It represents a woman, standing. Unfortunately there is nothing left of it but the head and the torso. *Notice des principaux Monuments du Musée de Boulak*, No. 493.

This statue is dressed in a different fashion from those we have hitherto encountered. The sheik has his hips covered with a kind of petticoat gathered into pleats in front. His legs, torso, and arms are bare. The last named are of separate pieces of wood, and one of them, the bent one, is made in two parts. When the statue was first finished the joints were invisible. The whole body was covered with fine linen, like a skin. Upon this linen a thin layer of plaster was spread, by means of which, when wet, refinement could be added to the contours by the modelling stick; the colours of nature were afterwards added by the brush. Such figures as these have therefore come down to us in a condition which resembles their primitive state much less than that of the works in stone. They have, so to speak, lost their epidermis, and with it the colours which served to distinguish the flesh from the drapery.[1]

It would seem that the sculptor in wood often counted upon this final coat of stucco to perfect his modelling. There are in fact wooden statues which seem to have been but roughly blocked out by the chisel. There are three figures in the Louvre in which this character is very conspicuous. The largest of the three is reproduced in our Fig. 178.[2] Acacia and sycamore wood is used for this kind of work.[3]

Finally, in this epoch or perhaps a little later, under the fifth and sixth dynasties, funerary statues were cast in bronze. This notable fact was first proclaimed by M. de Longpérier. We quote the observations which he addressed to the Academy of Inscriptions.[4]

"The fact that bronze was employed in Egypt in very ancient

[1] The *Description de l'Égypte* (*Antiquités*, vol. v. p. 33) gives the details of a mummy-mask in sycamore wood, of fairly good workmanship, which was found at Sakkarah. The eyebrows and edges of the eyelids were outlined with red copper; a fine linen was stretched over the wood; over this there was a thin layer of stucco, upon which the face was painted in green.

[2] The figure in the Louvre is split deeply in several places, one of the fissures being down the middle of the face. This latter our artist has suppressed, so as to give the figure something of its ancient aspect. These fissures are sure to appear in our humid climate. The warm and dry air of Egypt is absolutely necessary for the preservation of such works, which seem doomed to rapid destruction in our European museums.

[3] MASPERO (*Journal Asiatique*, March-April. 1880), *Sur quelques Peintures Funéraires*, p. 137. See also BRUGSCH, *Die Egyptische Gräberwelt*. No. 87.

[4] *Comptes Rendus de l'Académie des Inscriptions*, 1875, p. 345.

times has long been ascertained. The knob from the Sceptre of Papi, a Pharaoh of the sixth dynasty, which exists in the British Museum, is enough to prove this fact. M. Chabas has called our attention to the fact that bronze is mentioned in texts

Fig. 178.—Wooden statue in the Louvre. Three feet eight inches high. Drawn by Saint-Elme Gautier.

which date from a period anterior to the construction of the great Pyramids.[1]

"That the earliest Egyptian bronzes representing the human

[1] Chabas, *Sur l' Usage des Bâtons de Main*, p. 12. (Lyons, 8vo, 1875.)

Fig. 179. — Bronze statuette. Two feet two inches high. Drawn by Saint-Elme Gautier.

figure are much older than was formerly thought, is proved by two statuettes belonging to M. Gustave Posno. One of these is twenty-six inches high, the other nineteen. They merit a short description: "No 1: A man standing; left foot forward, the left hand closed and raised to a level with the breast. This hand, doubtless, held a spear. The right hand which hangs straight down by the thigh formerly clasped, in all probability, the small sceptre which is represented in many bas-reliefs. The loins are girt with the garment called the *schenti*, the band of which supports a dagger. The hair is arranged into regular rows of small square knobs. The eyes and eyebrows, which were inlaid, have disappeared (Fig. 179)."[1]

"No 2: A man standing; his loins girt with the *schenti*, his left foot forward, his right hand raised to the level of his breast, the left hanging by his left thigh. The inlaid eyes and eyebrows have been abstracted. His hair, which is less abundant than that of his companion and allows the contour of his head to be easily seen, is arranged into very small knobs. A vertical inscription on the left side of his chest gives the name of the personage, in or after which appears the ethnic *Schasou*, which seems to indicate an Oriental origin. The Schasous are mentioned in several Egyptian texts and seem to have occupied the country which bordered Egypt on the North-East (Fig. 180)."[2]

"In these two statuettes the muscles of the arms and legs, and the articulation of the knees, are expressed with a care and truth which denote a very remote age. We cannot fail to recognize a phase of art earlier than the Second Empire. But if the first mentioned figure recalls, by its features and the management of the hair, the sculptures in stone of the fifth and sixth dynasties, the second cannot, perhaps, be referred to quite such an early period. In the latter the vertical line of the back and right leg slopes slightly forward, betraying an attempt to express movement; the dorsal line of the first figure is, on the other hand, quite perpendicular.

"Even in the photographs certain details are visible, such as the form of the hair, the features, the rendering of the anatomical contours, which denote a school anterior to that of the eighteenth dynasty.

[1] Catalogue of the Posno Collection, No. 468.
[2] *Ibid.*, No. 524.

Fig. 189.—Bronze statuette. One foot seven inches high. Drawn by Saint-Elme Gautier.

"Egypt, then, was first in the field in bronze casting, as she was in stone and wood carving. One at least of the Posno statuettes carries us so far back in the history of humanity that it is difficult to see where we can look for earlier works of art, especially of so advanced a style. We have already ascertained that the first named of these two figures is far superior, both in style and modelling, to the Asiatic canephorus of Afadj,[1] a work which was dedicated to a goddess by a king, and must therefore be considered a good example of the art of Western Asia."

We agree with M. de Longperier in all but one point, and that one as to which he is careful not to commit himself. According to him the second figure is later than the sixth dynasty and earlier than the eighteenth, so that it would belong to the first Theban Empire. But we do not see why, supposing the Egyptians of the Ancient Empire capable of making the first figure, they should not have made the second. Between the two statuettes there are but slight differences of handling, differences much the same as those to be found in the wooden and stone statues which we have already mentioned. Neither the artists nor their sitters had quite the same capabilities.

The technical skill shown in these bronzes is extraordinary. The most ancient Etruscan and Greek bronzes are solid castings, on the base of which are rough protuberances, sometimes of considerable length, resulting from the fact that the metal was allowed to solidify in the orifice by which it was poured into the mould. Here there is nothing of the kind. No imperfection in the mechanical part of the work is allowed to interfere with its artistic effect. The casting is light, hollow, and in one piece ; the method employed must have been excellent in itself and thoroughly understood.[2] They also understood how to add finish by chasing the metal after its relief from the mould. The small circular ornaments on the chest of the second figure, ornaments which are so delicate in execution that they could not be reproduced in our engraving without giving them too much

---

[1] DE LONGPERIER, *Musée Napoléon III*. pl. 1.
[2] M. Pisani, who mounted the numerous bronzes in M. Posno's collection, assures me that their insides are still filled with the core of sand around which they were cast. The outward details of the casting are repeated inside, showing that the method used was what we call *fonte au carton*.

importance, and the hieroglyphs cut in the same figure, are instances of this.

That so few bronze statuettes have come down to us seems to show that the use of the metal by sculptors was quite exceptional. They used wood far more than bronze, and stone more than wood. Most of the sepulchral statues are cut in soft limestone (see Figs. 6, 49, 88, 89, Vol. I., and Fig. 172, Vol. II.). Sometimes these statues are isolated, sometimes they form family groups, often consisting of father, mother, and children.

Statues of men are the most numerous. Differences between one and another are many and frequent, but they are, on the whole, less striking than the points of resemblance. Here we find a head bare, there enveloped in either a square or rounded wig. The bodies are never completely nude, and the garment which covers their middles is arranged in a variety of ways. Fashions, both for men and women, seem to have changed in Egypt as elsewhere. In the statues ascribed to the last dynasties of the Ancient Empire the national type seems more fixed and accentuated than in earlier works. These funerary statues are the portraits of vigorous and powerful men, with broad shoulders, well-developed pectoral muscles, thin flanks and muscular legs. Ra-nefer, priest of Ptah and Sokar, stands upright, his arms by his sides, and each hand grasping a roll of papyrus (Fig 181).[1] A dagger is passed through the belt of his drawers.

The person represented in Fig. 182 is distinguished from Ra-nefer by the fashion in which he wears his hair and by his costume. His loose skirt is arranged in front so as to form a kind of triangular apron. This peculiar fall of the garment was obtained by the use of starch and an instrument similar to our flat-iron. It is better seen in the statue of Ti, the great personage to whose gorgeous tomb we have so often referred.[2] The Albanians obtain the curious folds of their kilts in the same fashion.[3] Ti wears a periwig of a different kind from that of

[1] A sketch of this statue also appears on page 10, Vol. 1. Fig. 6; but as, according to Mariette, it is one of the best statues in the Boulak Museum, we have thought well to give it a second illustration, which, in spite of its smaller scale, shows the modelling better than the first.

[2] *Notice des principaux Monuments du Musée de Boulak*, No. 24.

[3] Wooden instruments have been found which were used for the pleating of linen stuffs. One of these, which is now in the museum of Florence, is figured in WILKINSON (*Manners and Customs*, vol. i. p. 185). The heavy and symmetrical

Ra-nefer. The Egyptians shaved their heads from motives of cleanliness. The priests were compelled to do so by the rules of their religion, which made purity of person even more imperative upon them than upon the laymen. It was necessary, however, that the head should be thoroughly protected from the sun, hence the wig. The shaved Mohammedans of our day replace the periwig with the turban.

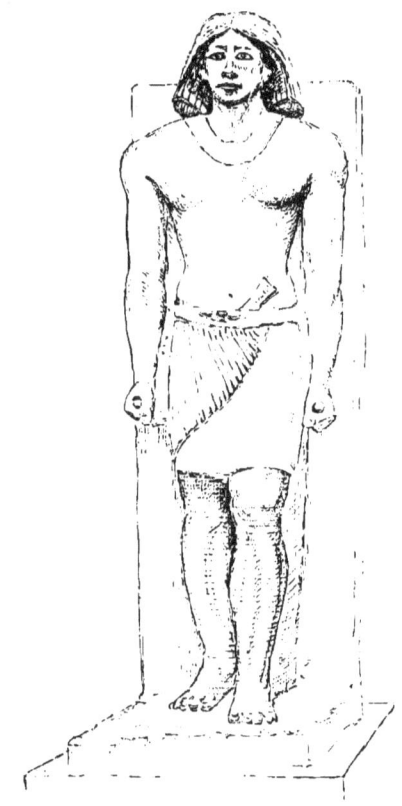

FIG. 181.—Ra-nefer. Boulak. Drawn by Bourgoin.

One wooden statue at Boulak offers a variety of costume which is at present unique among the remains of Egyptian civilization. It is, unfortunately, in very bad preservation. It represents a man, standing, and draped in an ample robe which covers him folds which are thus obtained are found, as we shall see, in the drapery of Greek statues of the archaic period.

from head to foot. His right arm is free; it is held across the body, and meets the left hand, which is thrust through an opening in the robe. The place where this statue was found, the material of which it consists, and the character of the workmanship, all combine to prove that it is a production of the early dynasties (Fig. 184).[1]

Fig. 182.—Statue in the Boulak Museum. Drawn by Bourgoin.

Fig. 183.—Statue of Ti. Boulak. Drawn by Bourgoin.

A few kneeling statues have also been found. The anonymous personage whose portrait is reproduced in Fig. 185 is upon his knees. His clasped hands rest upon his thighs. His eyes are inlaid; they are formed of numerous small pieces skilfully put together.[2]

There is no less variety in those groups where the sculptor has

[1] *Notice du Musée de Boulak*, No. 772.   [2] *Ibid.*, No. 769.

been charged to represent a whole family reunited in the tomb. Sometimes the husband is sitting and the wife standing. She has her left arm round his neck, the left hand resting on his left shoulder, while with her right hand she holds his right arm (Fig. 88, Vol. I.). Sometimes a father and mother are seated upon the same bench, but here too the woman confesses her dependence on, and shows her confidence in, her master by the same

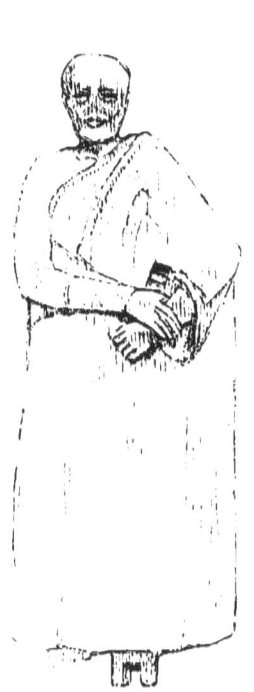
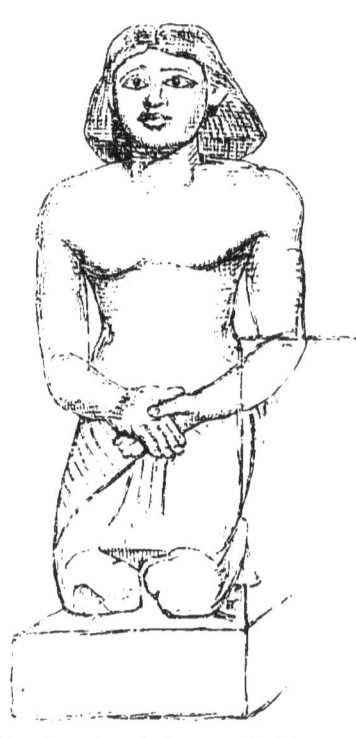

Fig. 184.—Wooden statue, Boulak. Drawn by Bourgoin.

Fig. 185.—Statue in limestone, Boulak. Drawn by Bourgoin.

affectionate gesture (Fig. 186). Both are of the same height, but between them, and leaning against the bench upon which they are seated, appears their child, quite small. His gesture is that to which the Egyptian artist has recourse when he wishes to express early childhood (Fig. 187). We also find the husband and wife standing erect in front of a slab; the relation which they bear to each other is here also indicated by the position of the woman's arms (Fig. 188).[1] Sometimes the woman is altogether absent (Fig. 89, Vol. I.). The head of the family is placed by himself, on a raised seat. In front of this seat, and hardly reaching to their father's knees, are two children, boy and girl, the boy holding the right leg, the girl the left. The boy has the lock of hair pendent

FIG. 185.—Limestone group in the Louvre. Height twenty-eight inches. Drawn by Saint-Elme Gautier.

over the right ear, which, like the finger in the mouth, is a sign of tender years. He is nude; the girl is dressed in an ornamental robe reaching to her ankles. There is a piquant contrast between these two tender little bodies with their childish heads, and the virile power of the father and protector who towers so high above them.

[1] *Notice*, No. 793. These two people were called Nefer-hotep and Tenteta. The latter is also described as *related to Pharaoh*.

These limestone groups do not, as a rule, appear to have been executed with any great care. Their makers do not seem to have taken much pains to give them an individuality of their own; but in spite of this feebleness of execution, they please by their

FIG. 187.—Wooden statuette, Boulak.
Drawn by Bourgoin.

FIG. 188.—Nefer-hotep and Tenteta.
Boulak.

composition. They are well arranged, their attitudes are simple and their gestures expressive. As a whole they have an air of calmness and repose which is thoroughly in accord with the ideas of the Egyptians on the question of life and death.

From the same memphite tombs many limestone statues have been recovered, representing, not the defunct himself, but those who mourn his decease and the crowd of retainers attached to his person. All these are expected to carry on their labours for

FIG. 189.—Limestone statue, Boulak. Drawn by Bourgoin.

FIG. 190.—Limestone statue, Boulak. Drawn by Bourgoin.

his benefit and to be ready to satisfy his wants through all eternity. Here we find one seated upon the ground, his hand upon his head in sign of grief (Fig. 189).[1] There a young man, completely naked, advancing with a sack upon his left shoulder which falls down to the centre of his back. He carries a bouquet

[1] *Notice du Musée de Boulak*, No. 768.

of flowers in his right hand (Fig. 190).[1] A man seated upon the ground holds a vase between his knees, into which he has plunged his right hand (Fig. 191).[2] Another bends over a wide-mouthed jar of mortar in which he is mixing flour and water (Fig. 192). A young woman, in a similar attitude, is occupied over the same task (Fig. 193). Other women are rolling the paste thus obtained on a plank, or rather upon a stone slab, before which they kneel upon the ground. The muscular exertion necessary for the operation is rendered with great skill (Figs. 193 and 194).[3] Women are still to be encountered at Elephantiné and in Nubia, wearing

FIG. 191.—Limestone statue, Boulak. Drawn by Bourgoin.

FIG. 192.—Limestone statue, Boulak. Drawn by Bourgoin.

the same head-dress and carrying out the same operation in the same attitude and with exactly similar utensils. We reproduce two sketches by M. Bourgoin, which show the details of this head-covering, which, among the women of the lower orders, supplied the piece of the wig ; it consists of a piece of stuff held upon the head by a ribbon knotted at the back of the neck (Figs. 196 and 197).

[1] *Notice*, No. 771. This is the person represented in profile in Fig. 47, Vol. I.
[2] *Notice*, No. 766.
[3] The four last quoted figures belong to the series noticed in the Boulak Catalogue under numbers 757 to 764. The statue reproduced in Fig. 197 has been already shown in profile in Fig. 48, Vol. I.

Mariette brought all these figures to Paris in 1878, where they excited the greatest interest among artists and archæologists. They were eminently well fitted to enlighten those who are able to see and to do away with many rooted prejudices. What an abyss of difference they showed between Egyptian art as it used to be defined some thirty years ago and the reality. The stiffness and rigidity which used to be so universally attributed to the productions of the sculptors of Memphis and Thebes, were forgotten

FIG. 193.—Woman kneading dough, Boulak. Drawn by Bourgoin.

before their varied motives and free natural attitudes. The whole of these works, in fact, are imbued with a spirit which is diametrically opposed to the unchanging inflexibility which used to be considered the chief characteristic of Egyptian art. They are distinguished by an extraordinary ease of attitude, and by that curious elasticity of body which still remains one of the most conspicuous physical qualities of the race.

"The suppleness of body which distinguished the female fellah is marvellous. She rarely sits down. When she requires rest she crouches with her knees in the air in an attitude which we should find singularly fatiguing. So too with the men. Their habitual posture corresponds to that shown on the steles: the knees drawn up in front of the face to the height of the nose, or on each side of the head and level with the ears. These attitudes are not graceful, but when the bodies thus drawn together are raised to their full height they are superb. They are, to borrow a happy expression of Fromentin, 'at once awkward and magnificent; when crouching and at rest they look like monkeys; when they stand up they are living statues.'"[1]

FIG. 194.—Woman making bread, Boulak. Drawn by Bourgoin.

This early art never carried its powers of observation and its exactitude of reproduction farther than in the statue of Nem-hotep, which we show in full-face and profile in Figs. 198 and 199. Whether we call him, with Mariette, a cook, or, with Maspero, a master of the wardrobe or keeper of perfumes, it cannot be doubted that Nem-hotep was a person of importance. One of the fine tombs at Sakkarah was his. He certainly did not make his way

[1] GABRIEL CHARMES, *Cinq mois au Caire*, p. 96.

at court by the graces of his person. He was a dwarf with all the characteristics that distinguish those unlucky beings. His head was too large, his torso very long, his arms and legs very short; besides which he was marvellously *dolichocephalic*.

Fig. 195.—Bread maker, Boulak. Drawn by Bourgoin.

The sincerity of Egyptian art is conspicuously shown in its treatment of the foot. Winckelmann noticed that the feet in Egyptian statues were larger and flatter than in those of Greece.

Figs. 196, 197.—Details of head-dresses.

The great toes are straight, no articulations being shown. The second toe is always the longest, and the little toe is not bent in the middle but straight like the others. These peculiarities spring from the Egyptian habit of walking bare-foot on the Nile mud; they are very strongly marked in the feet of the modern fellah.[1]

The general characteristics of these works in the round are repeated in the bas-reliefs of the mastabas at Gizeh and Sakkarah. Of these we have already given numerous illustrations; we shall therefore be content with reproducing one or two which are more than usually conspicuous for their artistic merit.

FIGS. 198, 199.—Nem-hotep; limestone statue at Boulak.

The sculptures of Wadi-maghara and the wooden panels from the Tomb of Hosi are enough to prove that work in relief was as old in Egypt as work in the round. In the mastabas sculptures in low-relief served to multiply the images of the defunct. He is figured upon the steles which occupy the principal wall, as well as in various other parts of the tomb. Sometimes he is shown seated

[1] WILKINSON, *Manners and Customs*, vol. ii. p. 270.

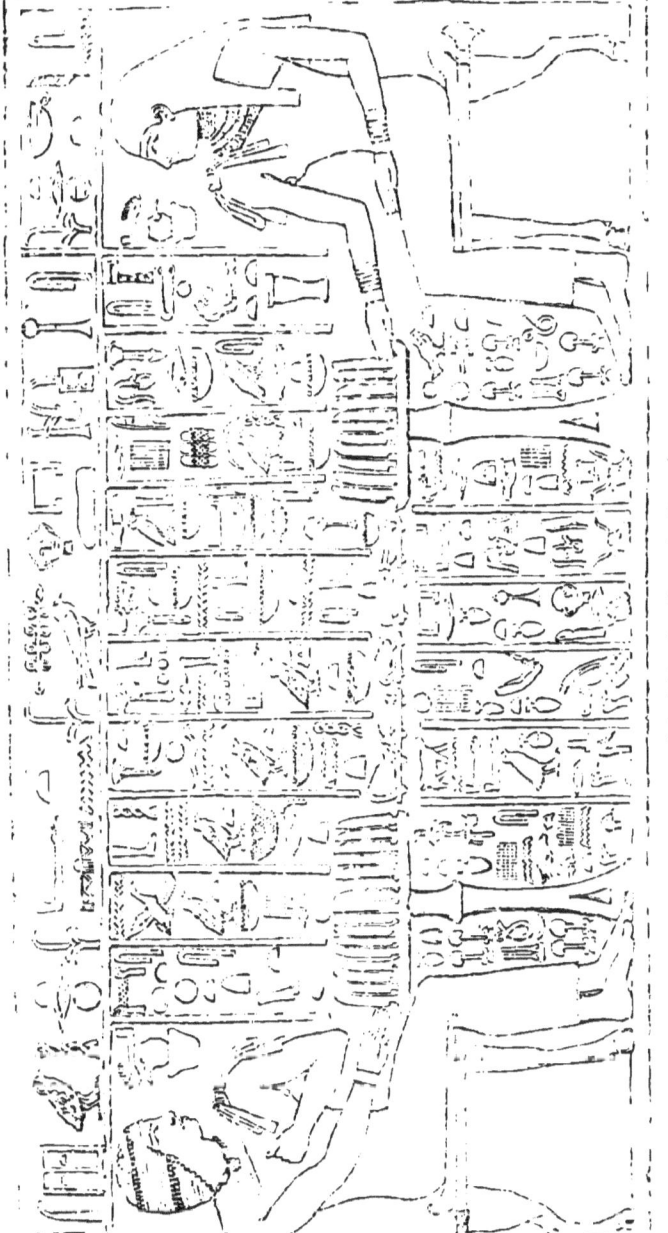

FIG. 200.—Funerary bas-relief; Sakkarah. Drawn by Bourgoin.

before the table of offerings (Fig. 200), sometimes standing upright (Figs. 57 and 120, Vol. I.). But the sculptor did not restrict himself to these two motives. In the preparation and presentation of the funeral gifts he found many themes, to which he was able to give more or less development according to the space at his command.

Even in the earliest attempts that have come down to us, the Egyptian sculptor shows a complete grasp of the peculiar features of the domesticated animals of the country. Men accustomed to the careful study of the human figure could make light of rendering those of beasts, with their more striking distinctions between one species and another. In the time when the oldest existing tombs were constructed, the ass was already domesticated in Egypt. Then as now, he was the most indispensable of the

FIG 201.—Bas-relief from the Tomb of Ti, Sakkarah.

servants of mankind. There were, in all probability, as many donkeys in the streets of Memphis under Cheops as there are now in Cairo under Tewfik. Upon the walls of the mastabas we see them trotting in droves under the cries and sticks of their drivers (Fig. 201), we see the foals, with their awkward gait and long pricked ears, walking by the sides of their mothers (Fig. 202), the latter are heavily laden and drag their steps ; the drivers brandish their heavy sticks, but threaten their patient brutes much oftener than they strike them. This is still the habit of those donkey boys, who, upon the *Esbekieh*, naïvely offer you " M. de Lesseps' donkey." The bas-relief to which we are alluding consists only of a slight outline, but that outline is so accurate and full of character, that we have no difficulty in identifying the ass of Egypt, with his graceful carriage of the head and easy, brisk, and dainty motion.

The same artists have figured another of the companions of man with equal fidelity; namely, the deep-sided, long-tailed, long-horned, Egyptian ox. Sometimes he lies upon the earth, ruminating (Fig. 29, Vol. I.); sometimes he is driven between two peasants, the one leading him by a rope, the other bringing up the rear with a stick held in readiness against any outburst of self-will (Fig. 203). In another relief we see a drove advancing by the side of a canal, upon which a boat with three men is making way by means of pole and paddle. One herdsman walks in front of the oxen, another marches behind and urges them on by voice and gesture (Fig. 204). In another place we find a cow being milked by a crouching herdsman. She seems to lend herself to the operation in the

Fig. 202.—Bas-relief from the Tomb of Ti, Sakkarah.

most docile manner in the world, and we are inclined to wonder what need there is of a second herdsman who sits before her nose and holds one of her legs in both his hands. The precaution, however, may not be superfluous, an ox-fly might sting her into sudden movement, and then if there was no one at hand to restrain her, the milk, which already nears the summit of the pail, might be lost (Fig. 30, Vol. I.).

By careful selection from the sepulchral bas-reliefs, we might, if we chose, present to our readers reproductions of the whole fauna of Ancient Egypt, the lion, hyena, leopard, jackal, fox, wolf, ibex, gazelle, the hare, the porcupine, the crocodile, the hippopotamus, the different fishes in the Nile, the birds in the marshes, the flamingo, the ibis, duck, stork, crane, and goose, the dog and the cat, the goat and the pig. Everywhere we find the same aptitude for summarizing the distinctive characteristics of

FIG. 203.—Sepulchral bas-relief, Boulak.

a species. This accuracy of observation has been recognized by every connoisseur who has treated the subject. "In the Boulak Museum," says M. Gabriel Charmes, "there is a row

FIG. 204.—Bas-relief from the Tomb of Ra-ka-pou, Boulak.

of Nile geese painted with such precision, that I have seen a naturalist stand amazed at their truth to nature and the fidelity with which they reproduce the features of the race. Their colours, too, are as bright and uninjured as upon the day when they were last touched by the brush of the artist."[1]

The figures of men and animals to which our attention has been given all belong to the domain of portraiture. The artist imitates the forms of those who sit to him and of the animals of the country; he copies the incidents of the daily life about him, but his ambition goes no farther. All art is a translation, an interpretation, and, of course, the sculptors of the mastabas had their own individual ways of looking at their models. But they made no conscious effort to add anything to them, they did not attempt to select, to give one feature predominance over another, or to combine various features in different proportions from those found in ordinary life, and by such means to produce something better than mere repetitions of their accidental models. They tried neither to invent nor to create.

And yet the Egyptians must have begun at this period to give concrete forms to their gods. In view of the hieroglyphs of which Egyptian writing consisted, we have some difficulty in imagining a time when the names of their deities were not each attached to a material image with well marked features of its own. To write the name of a god was to give his portrait, a portrait whose sketchy outlines only required to be filled in by the sculptor to be complete. Egypt, therefore, must have possessed images of her gods at a very early date, but as they were not placed in the tombs they have disappeared long before our day, and we are thus unable to decide how far the necessity for their production may have stimulated the imaginative faculties of the early sculptors. In presence, however, of the Great Sphinx at Gizeh, in which we find one of those composite forms so often repeated in later centuries, we may fairly suspect that many more of the divine types with which we are familiar had been established. The Sphinx proves that the primitive Egyptians were already bitten with the mania for colossal statues. Even the Theban kings never carved any figure more huge than that which keeps watch over the necropolis of Gizeh (Fig. 157, Vol. I.). But Egypt had other gods than these first-fruits of her reflective powers, than those

[1] GABRIEL CHARMES, *La Réorganisation du Musée de Boulak* (*Revue des Deux Mondes*, September 1, 1880). He is speaking of the fragment which is numbered 988 in the *Notice du Musée*. According to Mariette it dates from a period anterior to Cheops. It was found near the statues of Ra-hotep and Nefert.

mysterious beings who personified for her the forces which had created the world and preserved its equilibrium. She had her kings, children of the sun, present and visible deities who maintained upon the earth, and especially in the valley of the Nile, the ever-threatened order established by their divine progenitors. Until quite recently it was impossible to say for certain whether or no the Egyptians of the Ancient Empire had attempted to impress upon the images of their kings the national belief in their divine origin and almost supernatural power. But Mariette—again Mariette—recovered from the well in the Temple of the Sphinx at Gizeh, nine statues or statuettes of Chephren. The inscriptions upon the plinths of these statues enable us to recognize for certain the founder of the second pyramid.

Most of these figures were broken beyond recovery, but two have been successfully restored. One of these, which is but little mutilated, is of diorite (Fig. 205); the other, in a much worse condition, is of green basalt (Fig. 56, Vol. I.).[1]

An initial distinction between these royal statues and the portraits of private individuals is found in the materials employed. For subjects even of high rank, wood or limestone was good enough, but when the august person of the monarch had to be immortalized a substance which was at once harder and more beautiful was employed. The Egyptians had no marble, and when they wished to do particular honour to their models they made use of those *volcanic* rocks, whose close grain and dusky brilliance of tone make them resemble metal. The slowness and difficulty with which these dense rocks yielded to the tools of the sculptor increased the value of the result, while their hardness added immensely to their chances of duration. It would seem that figures which only took form under the tools of skilful and patient workmen after years of persevering labour might defy the attacks of time or of human enemies. Look at the statue on the next page. It is very different from the figures we have been noticing, although it resembles them in many details. Like many of his subjects the king is seated. His head, instead of being either bare or covered

---

[1] *Notice du Musée de Boulak*, Nos. 578 and 792. The discovery was made in 1860; MARIETTE gives an account of it in his *Lettres à M. de Rougé sur les Résultats des Fouilles entreprises par ordre du Vice-roi d'Égypte.* (*Revue Archéologique*, No. 5, vol. ii. pp. 19, 20.)

with the heavy wig, is enframed in that royal head-dress which has been known, ever since the days of Champollion, as the *klaft*.[1]

FIG. 205. Statue of Chephren. Height five feet seven inches. Boulak. Drawn by G. Bénédite.

It consists of an ample band of linen covering the upper part of the forehead, the cranium, and the nape of the neck. It stands

[1] This is a Coptic word meaning *hood*.

out boldly on each side of the face, and hangs down in two pleated lappets upon the chest. The king's chin is not shaved like those of his subjects. It is adorned like that of a god with the long and narrow tuft of hair which we call *the Osiride beard*. At the back of Chephren's head, which is invisible in our illustration, there is a hawk, the symbol of protection. His trunk and legs are bare ; his only garment is, in fact, the *schenti* about his middle. His left hand lies upon his knee, his right hand holds a rod of some kind. The details of the chair are interesting. The arms end in lions' heads, and the feet are paws of the same animal. Upon the sides are figured in high relief the two plants which symbolize the upper and lower country respectively; they are arranged around the hieroglyph *sam*, signifying *union*.

The other statue, which now consists of little more than the head and trunk, differs from the first only in a few details. The chair is without a back, and, curiously enough, the head is that of a much older man than the Chephren of the diorite statue. This difference makes it pretty certain that both heads were modelled directly from nature.

These royal statues are, then, portraits like the rest, but when in their presence we feel that they are more than portraits, that there is something in their individuality which could not have been rendered by photography or by casts from nature, had such processes been understood by their authors. In spite of the unkindly material the execution is as free as that of the stone figures. The face, the shoulders, the pectoral muscles, and especially the knees, betray a hand no less firm and confident than those which carved the softer rocks. The diorite Chephren excels ordinary statues in size—for it is larger than nature—in the richness of its throne, in the arrangement of the linen hood which gives such dignity to the head, in the existence of the beard which gives length and importance to the face. The artist has never lost sight of nature ; he has never forgotten that it was his business to portray Chephren and not Cheops or Snefrou; and yet he has succeeded in giving to his work the significance of a type. He has made it the embodiment of the Egyptian belief in the semi-divine nature of their Pharaohs. By its size, its pose, its expression and arrangement he has given it a certain ideality. We may see in these two statues, for similar qualities are to be found in the basalt figure, the first effort made by the genius of Egyptian art to escape from mere realism and to bring the higher powers of the imagination into play.

The reign of those traditional forms which were to be so despotic in Egypt began at the same time. The type created by the sculptors of the fourth dynasty, or perhaps earlier, for the representation of the Pharaoh in all the mysterious dignity of his position, was thought satisfactory. The calm majesty of these figures, their expression of force in repose and of illimitable power, left so little to be desired that they were accepted there and thereafter. Centuries rolled away, the royal power fell again and again before foreign enemies and internal dissensions, but with every restoration of the national independence and of the national rulers, the old form was revived. There are variants upon it; some royal statues show Pharaoh standing, others show him sitting and endowed with the attributes of Osiris, but, speaking generally, the favourite model of the kings and of the sculptors whom they employed was that which is first made known to us by the statue of him to whom we owe the second pyramid. The only differences between it and the colossi of Amenophis III. at Thebes are to be found in their respective sizes, in their original condition, and in the details of their features.

The moulds in which the thoughts of the Egyptians were to receive concrete expression through so many centuries were formed, then, by their ancestors of the Ancient Empire. All the later revivals of artistic activity consisted in attempts to compose variations upon these early themes, to remodel them, with more or less felicity, according to the fashion of the day. Style and technical methods were modified with time, but types, that is the attitudes and motives employed to characterise the age, the mental power, and the social condition of the different persons represented, underwent little or no change.

This period of single-minded and devoted study of nature ought also to have transmitted to later times its care and skill in portraiture, and its realistic powers generally, to use a very modern phrase. Egyptian painters and sculptors never lost those qualities entirely; they always remained fully alive to the differences of conformation and physiognomy which distinguished one individual, or one class, from another; but as the models furnished by the past increased in number, their execution became more facile and superficial, and their reference to nature became less direct and continual. Neither the art of Thebes nor that of Sais seems to have produced anything so original and expressive as the two statues from Meidoum or the *Sheik-el-beled*, at Boulak, or the *scribe* in the Louvre.

We may easily understand what surprise and admiration the discovery of this early phase of Egyptian art excited among archæologists. When the exploration of the Memphite necropolis revealed what had up to that time been an unknown world, Nestor L'Hôte, one of the companions of Champollion, was the first to comprehend its full importance. He was not a savant; he was an intelligent and faithful draughtsman and his artistic nature enabled him to appreciate, even better than the illustrious founder of egyptology, the singular charm of an art free from convention and routine. In his letters from Egypt, Champollion showed himself impressed mainly by the grandeur and nobility of the Theban remains; L'Hôte, on the other hand, only gave vent to his enthusiasm when he had had a glimpse of one or two of those mastabas which were afterwards to be explored by Lepsius and Mariette. Writing of the tomb of Menofré, barber to one of the earliest Memphite kings, he says: " The sculptures of this tomb are remarkable for their elegance and the finesse of their execution. Their relief is so slight that it may be compared to that of a five-franc piece. Such consummate workmanship in a structure so ancient confirms the assertion that the higher we mount upon the stream of Egyptian civilization the more perfect do her works of art become. By this it would appear that the genius of the Egyptian people, unlike that of other races, was born in a state of maturity."[1]

"Of Egyptian art," he says elsewhere, " we know only the decadence." Such an assertion must have appeared paradoxical at a time when the Turin Museum already possessed, and exhibited, so many fine statues of the Theban kings. And yet Nestor L'Hôte was right, as the discoveries made since his time have abundantly proved, and that fact must be our excuse for devoting so large a part of our examination of Egyptian sculpture to the productions of the Ancient Empire.

[1] *Journal des Savants*, 1851. pp. 53, 54.

§ 3. *Sculpture under the First Theban Empire.*

After the sixth dynasty comes an obscure and barren period, whose duration and general character are still unknown to egyptologists. Order began to be re-established in the eleventh dynasty, under the Entefs and Menthouthoteps, but the monuments found in more ancient Theban tombs are rude and awkward in an extreme degree, as Mariette has shown.[1] It was not until the twelfth dynasty, when all Egypt was again united under the sceptre of the Ousourtesens and Amenemhats, that art made good its revival. It made use of the same materials—limestone, wood, and the harder rocks—but their proportions were changed. In Fig. 206 a wooden statue attributed to this period is reproduced. The legs are longer, the torso more flexible, than in the statue of Chephren and other productions of the early centuries.

Compared with their predecessors other statues of this period will be found to have the same characteristics. It has been asserted that the Egyptians, as a race, had become more slender from the effects of their warm and dry climate. It is impossible now to decide how much of the change may fairly be attributed to such a cause, and how much to a revolution in taste. Even among the figures of the Ancient Empire there are examples to be found of these slender proportions, but they certainly appear to have been in peculiar favour with the sculptors of the later epoch. Except in this particular, the differences are not very great. The attitudes are the same. See, for instance, the statue in grey sandstone of the scribe Menthouthotep, which was found by Mariette at Karnak and attributed by him to this epoch. Both by its pose and by the folds of fat which cross the front of the trunk, it reminds us of the figures of scribes left to us by the Ancient Empire. The nobler types also reappear. There is in the Louvre a statue in red granite representing a Sebek-hotep of the thirteenth dynasty (Fig. 207). He sits in the same attitude, with the same head-dress and the same costume, as the Chephren of Boulak. There is one difference, however, his forehead is decorated with the *uræus*, the symbol of royal dignity, which

[1] MARIETTE, *Notice du Musée*, etc. *Avant-propos*, pp. 38, 39.

SCULPTURE UNDER THE FIRST THEBAN EMPIRE. 227

Chephren lacks.[1] The dimensions, too, are different. We do not know whether the Ancient Empire made colossal statues of its

FIG. 206.—Wooden statue, Boulak. Drawn by Bénédite.

kings or not, but this Sebek-hotep exceeds the stature of mankind sufficiently to make it worthy of the name.

[1] See PIERRET, *Dictionnaire d'Archéologie*, under the word *Uræus*.

The Louvre possesses another monument giving a high idea of the taste of the sculptors belonging to this period, we mean the red-granite sphinx (Fig. 41, Vol. I.), which was successively appropriated by one of the shepherd kings and by a Theban Pharaoh of the nineteenth dynasty: the ovals of both are to be found upon it. Like so many other things from Tanis, this sphinx must date from a Pharaoh of the thirteenth dynasty. This De Rougé has clearly shown.[1] Tanis seems to have been a favoured residence of those princes, and most of their statues have been found in it. A leg in black granite, now in the Berlin Museum, is considered the masterpiece of these centuries. It is all that remains of a colossal statue of Ousourtesen.[2]

According to Mariette, many of those fine statues in the Turin Museum which bear the names of princes belonging to the eighteenth dynasty, Amenhoteps and Thothmeses, must have been made by order of the princes of the twelfth and thirteenth dynasties. In later years they were appropriated, in the fashion well known in Egypt, by the Pharaohs of the Second Theban Empire, who substituted their cartouches for those of the original owners. On more than one of the statues signs of the operation may still be traced, and in other cases the usurpation may be divined by carefully studying the style and workmanship.[3]

It was in the ruins of the same city that Mariette discovered a group of now famous remains in which he himself, De Rougé, Devéria, and others, recognised works carried out by Egyptian artists for the shepherd kings. These works have an individual character which is peculiar to themselves.[4] They differ greatly from the ordinary type of Egyptian statues, and must have preserved the features of those foreign invaders whose memory was so long held in detestation in Egypt. This supposition is founded upon the presumed identity of Tanis with Avaris, the

[1] *Notice des Monuments exposés dans la Galerie d'Antiquités Égyptiennes, Salle du Rez-de-chaussée,* No. 23.
[2] DE ROUGÉ, *Notice,* etc. *Avant-propos,* p. 6.
[3] MARIETTE, *Notice du Musée,* p. 86.
[4] MARIETTE, *Lettre de M. Aug. Mariette à M. de Rougé sur les Fouilles de Tanis* (*Revue Archéologique,* vol. iii. 1861, p. 97). DE ROUGÉ, *Lettre à M. Guigniaut sur les Nouvelles Explorations en Égypte* (*Revue Archéologique,* vol. ix., 1864, p. 128).— DEVÉRIA, *Lettre à M. Aug. Mariette sur quelques Monuments Relatifs aux Hyqsos ou Antérieurs à leur Domination* (*Revue Archéologique,* vol. iv. 1861, p. 251).—EBERS, *Ægypten,* vol. ii. p. 108.

Fig. 207.—Sebek-hotep III. Colossal statue in red granite. Height nine feet. Louvre. Drawn by Saint-Elme Gautier.

strong place which formed the centre of the Hyksos power for so many generations.

Confirmation of this theory is found in the existence of an oval bearing the name of Apepi, one of the shepherd kings, upon the shoulder of a sphinx from Tanis. The aspect of this sphinx, and the features and costume of certain figures discovered upon the same site and dispersed among the museums of Europe, are said to have much in common with the ethnic peculiarities of the Syrian tribe by which Middle and Lower Egypt was occupied. M. Maspero, however, who has recently devoted fresh attention to these curious monuments, is inclined to doubt the justness of this conclusion. The position of the cartouche of Apepi suggests that it may be due to one of those usurpations which we have mentioned. For the present, therefore, it may be as well to class these monuments simply among the Tanite remains. Tanis, like some other Egyptian cities, had a style of its own, but we are without the knowledge required for a determination of its origin. We shall be content with describing its most important works and with calling attention to their remarkable originality.

The most important and the best preserved of all these monuments is a sphinx of black granite which was recovered, in a fragmentary condition, from the ruins of the principal temple at Tanis (Fig. 208). Three more were found at the same time, but they were in a still worse state of preservation. The fore-part of one of them is figured in the adjoining woodcut.

"There is a great gulf," says Mariette, "between the energetic power which distinguishes the head of this sphinx and the tranquil majesty with which most of these colossi are endowed. The face is round and rugged, the eyes small, the nose flat, the mouth loftily contemptuous. A thick lion-like mane enframes the countenance and adds to its energetic expression. It is certain that the work before us comes from the hands of an Egyptian artist, and, on the other hand, that his sitter was not of Egyptian blood."[1]

The group of two figures upon a common base, which is such a conspicuous object in the Hyksos chamber at Boulak, seems to have had a similar origin. We give a front and a side view of

---

[1] *Notice du Musée de Boulak*, No. 869. Our draughtsman has not thought it necessary to reproduce the hieroglyphs engraved upon the plinth.

Fig. 208.—Sphinx in black granite; from Tanis. Drawn by G. Bénédite.

it (Figs. 210 and 211), and borrow the following description from Mariette.[1]

"Huge full-bottomed wigs, arranged into thick tresses, cover the heads of the two figures. Their hard and strongly-marked features (unfortunately much broken) bear a great resemblance to those of the lion-maned sphinxes. The upper lips are shaven but the cheeks and chins are covered with long wavy beards. Each of them sustains on his outstretched arms an ingenious arrangement of fishes, aquatic birds, and lotus flowers.

"No monument can be referred with greater certainty than this to the disturbed period when the Shepherds were masters of Egypt. It is difficult to decide upon its exact meaning. In spite of the mutilation which prevents us from ascertaining whether they bore the *uræus* upon their foreheads, it cannot be doubted that the originals of the two statues were kings. In after years Psousennes put his cartouche upon the group, which assuredly he would never have done if he believed it to represent two private individuals. But who could the two kings have been who were thus associated in one act and must therefore have been contemporaries?"

FIG. 209.—Head and shoulders of a Tanite Sphinx in black granite. Drawn by G. Bénédite.

This explanation seems to carry with it certain grave objections. It is not, in the first place, so necessary as Mariette seems to think that we should believe them to be kings. Similar objects—fishes, and aquatic flowers and birds—are grouped in the same fashion upon works which, to our certain knowledge, neither come from Tanisn or date from the Shepherd supremacy. Their appearance indicates an offering to the Nile, and we can readily understand how Psousennes claimed the merit of the offering by inscribing his name upon it, even although he were not the real donor.

Mariette does not hesitate to ascribe to the same series a figure discovered in the Fayoum, upon the site of the city

[1] *Notice du Musée de Boulak.* No. 1.

which the Greeks called Crocodilopolis (Fig. 212). He describes it thus :—[1]

"Upper part of a broken colossal statue, representing a king standing erect. No inscription.

"The general form of the head, the high cheek-bones, the thick lips, the wavy beard that covers the lower part of the

FIG. 210.—Group from Tanis; grey sandstone. Drawn by Bourgoin.

cheeks, the curious wig, with its heavy tresses, are all worthy of remark; they give a peculiar and even unique expression to the face. The curious ornaments which lie upon the chest should also be noticed. The king is covered with panther skins; the heads of two of those animals appear over his shoulders.

"The origin of this statue, which was found at Mit-farès in

[1] *Notice du Musée de Boulak*, No. 2.

the Fayoum, admits of no doubt. The kings who decorated the temple at Tanis with the fine sphinxes and groups of fishermen which I found among its ruins, must also have transported the vigorous fragments which we have before our eyes to the other side of Egypt."

Finally, Devéria and De Rougé have suggested that a work of the same school is to be recognized in the fragment of a

FIG. 211.—Side view of the same group. Drawn by Bourgoin.

statuette of green basalt, which belongs to the Louvre and is figured upon page 237.[1] They point to similarities of feature and of race characteristics. The face of the Louvre statuette has a truculence of expression not unlike that of the Tanite monuments, while the workmanship is purely Egyptian and of the best quality; the flexibility of body, which is one of the most

[1] DEVÉRIA, *Lettre à M. Aug. Mariette*, p. 258.—PIERRET. *Catalogue de la Salle Historique.* No. 6.

constant qualities in the productions of the first Theban Empire, being especially characteristic. The king represented wears the *klaft* with the *uræus* in front of it; his *schenti* is finely pleated and a dagger with its handle carved into the shape of a hawk's head is thrust into his girdle. The support at the back has, unfortunately, been left without the usual inscription

FIG. 212.—Upper part of a royal statue. Grey granite. Boulak. Drawn by G. Bénédite.

and we have no means of ascertaining the age of the fragment beyond the style, the workmanship, and the very peculiar physiognomy. Devéria suggests that it preserves the features of one of the shepherd kings, some of whose images Mariette thought he had discovered at Tanis and in the Fayoum.[1]

[1] M. FR. LENORMANT (*Bullctino della Commissione Archeologica di Roma*, fifth year, January to June, 1877) believes that he has discovered in one of the Roman

It cannot be denied that there are many striking points of resemblance between the different works which we have here brought together. Mariette laid great stress upon what he regarded as one of his most important discoveries. This is his definition of the type which the Egyptian artist set himself to reproduce with his habitual exactness: "The eyes are small, the nose vigorous, arched, and flat at the end, the cheeks are large and bony, and the mouth is remarkable for the way in which its extremities are drawn down. The face as a whole is in harmony with the harshness of its separate features, and the matted hair in which the head seems to be sunk adds to the singularity of its appearance."[1]

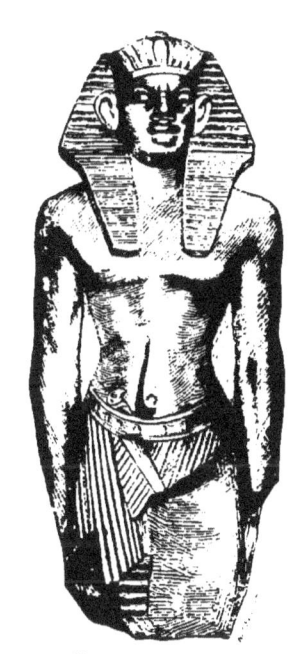

Fig. 213.—Fragmentary statuette of a king; height seven inches. Drawn by Saint-Elme Gautier.

Both Mariette and Ebers declare that this type has been preserved to our day with astonishing persistence. In the very district in which the power of the shepherds was greatest, in the neighbourhood of that Lake Menzaleh which almost bathes the ruins of Tanis, the poor and half savage fishermen who form the population of the district possess the strongly marked features which are so easily distinguished from the rounder and softer physiognomies of the true Egyptian fellah. Ahmes must have been content with the expulsion of the chiefs only of those Semitic tribes who had occupied this region for so many centuries. The mass of the people must have been too strongly attached to the fertile lands where they dwelt to refuse obedience to the conqueror, and more than one immigration.

museums another monument belonging to the same period and to the same artistic group.

[1] *Lettres à M. de Rougé sur les Fouilles de Tanis,* p. 105. (*Revue Archéologique.*)

like that of the Hebrews, may have come in later times to renew the Arab and Syrian characteristics of the race.[1]

Whatever we may think of these conjectures and assertions, the sculptors of the First Theban Empire and of the Hyksos period took up and carried on the traditions of the Ancient Empire. The processes are the same except that in a few particulars they are improved. More frequent use is made of the harder rocks such as granite, basalt, and diorite, and a commencement is made in the art of gem-cutting.

Even the bas-relief carries on the themes which had been in favour in the first years of the monarchy. We have already illustrated two steles of this period (Figs. 87 and 164, Vol. I.). In the second, and especially in the woman, may be noticed those elongated proportions which characterize the sculpture of the first Theban dynasties. Apart from the steles, which come mostly from Abydos, we have few bas-reliefs which may be referred to this epoch. The mastabas with their sculptured walls were no longer constructed, and the most interesting hypogea of the middle Empire, those of Beni-Hassan, were decorated with paintings only. The sepulchral grottos of El-Bercheh possess bas-reliefs dating from the twelfth dynasty, and the quality of their workmanship may be seen in our Fig. 43, Vol. II. The style is less free and more conventional than that of the mastabas. The men who haul upon the ropes and those who march in front of them, are all exact repetitions one of another, causing an effect which is very monotonous. The paintings of Beni-Hassan, which are freer and more full of variety, are more able to sustain a comparison with the decorations of the mastabas. Even then, however, we find too much generalization. Except in a few instances there is a less true and sincere feeling for nature, and a lack of those picturesque motives and movements caught flying, so to speak, by an artist who seems to be amused by what he sees and to take pleasure in reproducing it, which are so abundant in the mastabas.

[1] MARIETTE, Notice du Musée, p. 259. EBERS, Ægypten, vol. i. p. 108.

§ 4. *Sculpture under the Second Theban Empire.*

The excavations at Tanis have helped us to understand many things upon which our information had been and still is very imperfect. We are no longer obliged to accept Manetho's account of the Shepherd invasion. In his desire to take at least a verbal revenge upon the conquerors of his country the historian seems to have greatly exaggerated their misdeeds. We know now not only that the native princes continued to reign in Upper Egypt, but also that the interlopers adopted, in the Delta, the manners and customs of their Egyptian subjects. So far as we can tell, there were neither destructions of monumental buildings nor ruptures with the national traditions. Thus the art of the three great Theban dynasties, from Ahmes to the last of the Rameses, seems a prolongation of that of the Ousourtesens and Sebek-hoteps. There are no appreciable differences in their styles or in their processes, but, as in their architecture, their works of art as a whole show an extraordinary development, a development which corresponds to the great and sudden increase in the power and wealth of the country. The warlike kings who made themselves masters of Ethiopia and of Western Asia, had aspirations after the colossal. Their buildings reached dimensions hitherto unknown, and while their vast wall spaces gave great opportunities to the sculptor they demanded efforts of invention and arrangement from him to which he had previously been a stranger. These great surfaces had to be filled with historic scenes, with combats, victories, and triumphal promenades, with religious scenes, with pictures of homage and adoration. The human figure in its natural size was no longer in proportion to these huge constructions. In order to obtain images of the king which should correspond to the extent and magnificence of the colonnades and obelisks, the slight excess over the real stature of human beings which contented the sculptors of the Ancient Empire was no longer sufficient. Whether they were cut, as at Ipsamboul, out of a mountain side, or, as at Thebes, Memphis, and Tanis out of a gigantic monolith, their proportions were all far beyond those of mankind. Sometimes the mortals who frequented the temples came nearly as high as their knees, but oftener they failed to reach their ankle-bones. The New Empire had a mania for these colossal figures. It sprinkled them over the whole country, but at Thebes they are more thickly gathered than elsewhere. In the immediate neighbourhood of the two seated statues of Amenophis III., the *savants* of the French Commission found the remains of fifteen more colossi.[1]

There were at least as many on the right bank. On the avenue leading through the four southern pylons at Karnak, the same explorers found twelve colossal monoliths, each nearly thirty-five feet high but all greatly mutilated, and the former existence of others was revealed to them by fragments scattered about the ground. They were able to reckon up eighteen altogether on this south side of the building.[2]

Similar stone giants peopled the other religious or political capitals of Egypt—Abydos, Memphis, Tanis, Sais, etc. The largest of all, however, are the colossi at Ipsamboul representing Rameses II. They are about seventy feet high. Among those cut from one enormous block brought from Syene or elsewhere, the best known are those of Amenophis III. at Thebes. They are fifty-two feet high without the pedestal. But the statue of Rameses II., which stood in the second court of the Ramesseum, must have been more than fifty-six feet high, as we may calculate from the fragments which remain. The head is greatly mutilated but the foot is over thirteen feet long.[3]

These statues were generally seated in the attitude which we have already described in speaking of Chephren and Sebek-hotep. Some, however, were standing, such as the colossal figure of Rameses which stood before the Temple of Ptah at Memphis. This figure, which is about forty-four feet high, is cut from a single block of very fine and hard limestone. It lies face downwards and surrounded by palm trees, in a depression of the soil near the village of Mitrahinch. In this position it is covered by the annual inundation. The English, to whom it belongs, have hitherto failed to take possession of it owing to the difficulty of transport, and yet it is one of the most careful productions of

---

[1] *Description de l'Égypte, Antiquités*, vol. ii. p. 182.
[2] *Description. Antiquités*, vol. ii. p. 105.
[3] CH. BLANC, *Voyage dans la Haute-Égypte*, p. 208. It has been calculated that this colossus weighed about 1220 tons.

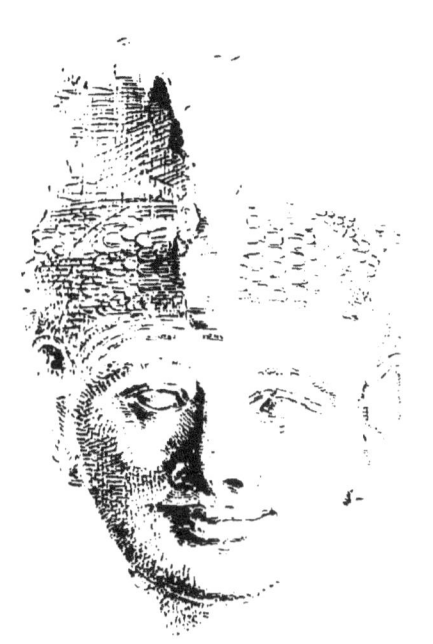

the nineteenth dynasty. The head is full of individuality and its execution excellent.

In spite of their taste for these colossal figures, the Egyptian sculptors of this period rivalled their predecessors in the skill and sincerity with which they brought out their sitter's individuality. It was not, perhaps, their religious beliefs which imposed this effort upon them. The readiness which successive kings showed in appropriating the statues of their ancestors to themselves by simply placing their ovals upon them, proved that the ideas which were attached by the fathers of the Egyptian race to their graven images had lost their force. Effigies which were brought into the service of a new king by a mere change of inscription, were nothing more than monuments to his pride, destined to transmit his name and glory to future generations. The early taste, however, was not extinguished. When the sculptor was charged with the representation of one of those kings who had made Egypt great, or one of the queens who were often associated in the sovereign power, he took the same pains as those of the early Empire to make a faithful copy of his august model.

FIG. 214.—Thothmes III. Boulak. Granite.

Among the monuments of faithful portraiture which this period has left us the statues of Thothmes III. are conspicuous. The features of this prince are to be recognized in a standing figure at Boulak (Fig. 214), but they are much more strongly marked in a head which was found at Karnak and is now in the British Museum (Fig. 215). It formerly belonged to a colossal statue erected by that prince in the part of the temple built by himself.

The features seem in no way Egyptian. The form of the nose, the upturned corners of the eyes, the curves of the lips, and the general contours of the face are all suggestive of Armenian blood.[1] Others have thought it showed traces of negro descent. In the first-named statue these characteristics are less conspicuous because its execution as a whole is less careful and masterly. The same physiognomy is to be found in a porphyry sphinx belonging to the Boulak collection.[2]

There is a strong contrast between the features of Thothmes and those of Amenophis III. the founder of Luxor. Of this we may judge by a head, as well preserved as that of Thothmes, which was found behind one of the statues of Amenophis at Gournah. It also is in the British Museum. The face is long and finely cut, with an expression and general appearance which we should call *distinguished;* the nose is long and thin; the chin well chiselled and bold in outline.[3]

Obliged to draw the line somewhere we have not reproduced this figure, but in Plate XI. we give a female head, discovered by Mariette at Karnak, and believed to be that of Taia, the queen of Amenophis III. Whether rightly named or not, this colossal fragment is one of the masterpieces of Egyptian sculpture.[4]

Mariette enumerates various reasons for believing Taia to have been neither of royal nor even of Egyptian blood. She might have been Asiatic; the empire of her husband extended as far as Mesopotamia. The point has little importance, but as M. Charmes says, "when we stop in admiration before the head of Taia, at Boulak, we feel ourselves unconsciously driven by her charms .... to forge a whole history, an historical romance, of which her enigmatic personality is the centre and inspiration, and to fancy her the chief author of these religious tragedies which disturbed her epoch and left a burning trace which has not yet disappeared."[5]

M. Charmes here alludes to the changes which Amenophis IV.

---

[1] GABRIEL CHARMES, *La Réorganisation du Musée de Boulak.*
[2] MARIETTE, *Notices du Musée,* Nos. 3 and 4.
[3] The head of Amenophis III. may be recognized in the bas-relief reproduced in our Fig. 33, Vol. I. The fine profile and large well-opened eye strongly resemble those of the London statue.
[4] MARIETTE, *Voyage dans la Haute-Égypte,* vol. ii. p. 31.
[5] G. CHARMES, *De la Réorganisation du Musée de Boulak.*

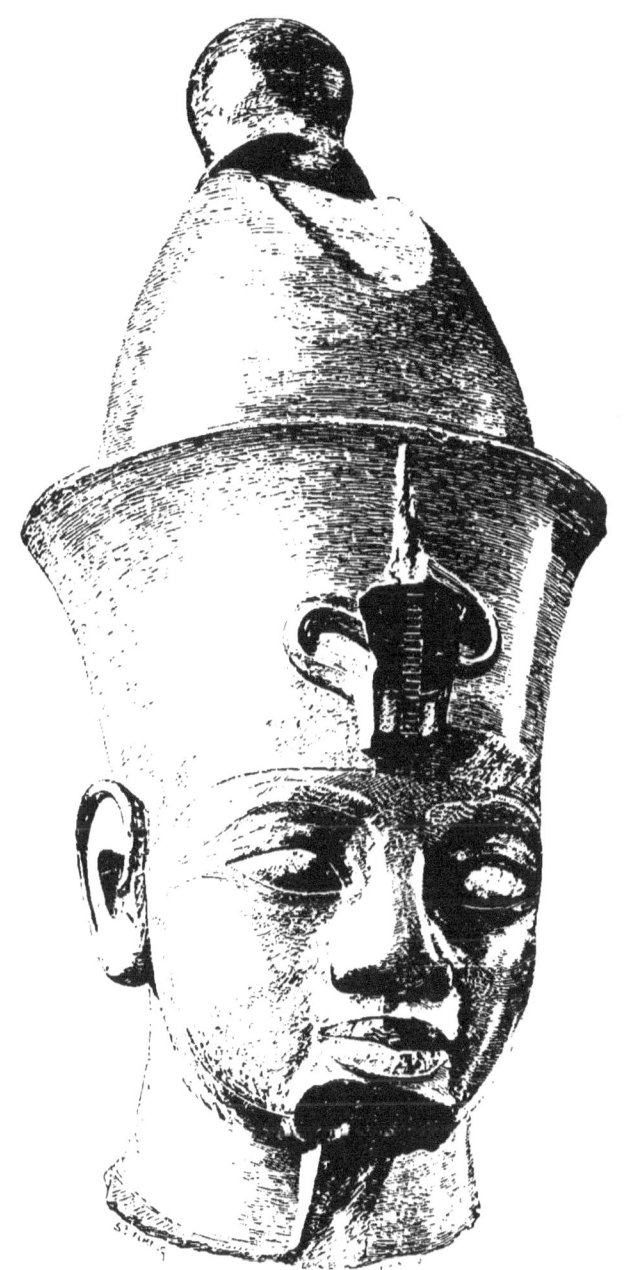

Fig. 215.—Thothmes III. British Museum. Red granite. Drawn by Saint-Elme Gautier.

wished to introduce into the national religion when he attempted to destroy the name and images of Amen, and to replace them with those of a solar god, who was represented by a symbol not previously encountered in the monuments (Fig. 2). If Mariette's hypotheses remain uncontradicted by later discoveries, we may admit Taia to be the mother of Amenophis IV., and to her influence in all probability would her son's denial and persecution of the great Theban deity be due. Our present interest, however, is with the features of Amenophis. They have been faithfully handed down to us by the artists employed at Tell-el-Amarna.[1] By the help of these bas-reliefs a statuette in yellow steatite, now in the Louvre (Fig. 216), has been recognized as a portrait of this Pharaoh. Its workmanship is very fine.

Some have thought that in these bas-reliefs, and in the Louvre statuette, the "facial characteristics and the peculiar shapes of breast and abdomen by which eunuchs are distinguished, are to be found."[2] On the other hand, we know that while still very young Amenophis IV. married the queen Nowertiouta, and that he had seven daughters by her. "It is probable, therefore, that if the misfortune alluded to really befell him, it was during the wars waged by Amenophis III. against the negro races of the south." In any case, Amenophis IV. bore no resemblance to any one of the long procession of princes whose portraits have come down to us, from the early dynasties of the Ancient Empire to the Roman conquest. Lepsius devotes a series of plates to the iconography of the Egyptian kings, and among them all we find nothing that can be compared to the almost fantastic personality of Amenophis, with his low, unintellectual forehead, his pendulous cheeks, his feminine contours, and his general expression of gloom and melancholy. The fidelity with which all these unpleasing features are reproduced is extraordinary, and can only be accounted for by the existence of a tradition so well established that no one thought of breaking through it, even when the portrait of a semi-divine monarch was in question.

There are other works dating from this period which show the same desire for truth at any price. One of the series of bas-reliefs discovered by Mariette in the Temple of Dayr-el-Bahari

---

[1] *Denkmaeler*, vol. vi. plates 91-111. The curious ugliness of this king is most clearly shown in plate 109.

[2] MARIETTE, *Bulletin Archéologique de l'Athenæum Français*, 1855, p. 57.

may be given as an instance. The subject of these reliefs is the expedition undertaken by the regent Hatasu against the country of Punt.[1]

"In the most curious of these sculptures the savage chief advances as a suppliant. His wife walks behind him. Her hair

FIG. 216.—Statuette of Amenophis IV. Height twenty inches. Louvre. Drawn by Saint-Elme Gautier.

is carefully dressed and plaited into a thick tail at the back; a necklace of large discs is round her neck. Her dress is a long yellow chemise, without sleeves, and reaching to the middle of her legs. Her features are regular enough, but virile rather than

MARIETTE, *Notice du Musée*, No. 922, and *Dayr-el-Bahari*, plates.

feminine, and all the rest of her person is repulsive. Her arms, legs, and chest, are loaded with fat, while her person projects so far in the rear as to result in a deformity over which the artist has dwelt with curious complacence." The legs, so far as the chemise allows them to be seen, are so large that they suggest incipient elephantiasis. The Egyptian artist was induced, no doubt, to dwell upon such a monstrosity by the instructive contrast which it presented with the cultivated beauty of his own race.[1]

Realist as he was when he chose to take up that vein, the Egyptian sculptor attained, however, to a high degree of grace and purity, especially in his representations of historic and religious scenes. When he had not the exceptional ugliness of an Amenophis IV. to deal with, he gave to the personages in his bas-reliefs a look of serious gravity and nobility which cannot fail to impress the greatest enthusiast for Greek models. He was no longer content with the sincere imitation of what he saw, like the artists of the Early Empire; his efforts were directed to giving everlasting forms to those superhuman beings, the Egyptian gods and Egyptian kings, with their sons and favourites, who lived in hourly communion with them. Egyptian art at last had an ideal, which it never realized with more success than in certain bas-reliefs of this epoch.

Mariette quotes, as one of the most learned productions of the Egyptian chisel, a bas-relief at Gebel-Silsilis representing a goddess nourishing Horus from her own breast. "The design of this composition is remarkable for its purity," he says, "and the whole picture breathes a certain soft tranquillity which both charms and surprises a modern connoisseur." [2]

We have not reproduced this work, but an idea of its style and composition may be formed from a bas-relief of the time of Rameses II., which we have taken from the speos of Beit-el-Wali (Fig. 255, Vol. I.). The theme is the same. A scene of adoration taken from a pier at Thebes (Fig. 176, Vol. I.) and, still more, a fine bas-relief in which Amenophis III. does homage to Amen, to

[1] MARIETTE, *Dayr-el Bahari*. p. 30, believed that Punt was in Africa, probably in the region of the Somali. He quotes various passages from the writings of modern travellers to show that this strange obesity is rather an African than an Arabian characteristic. See SPEKE's description of the favourite wife of Vouazerou, *Discovery of the Source of the Nile*, chap. viii., and SCHWEINFURTH's account of the Bongo women, *Heart of Africa* (3rd edition) pp. 136 and 137.

[2] MARIETTE. *Itinéraire*, p. 246.

whom he is presented by Phré, may also be compared with the work at Gebel-Silsilis. The movements are free and elegant, and nothing could be more expressive than the gestures of the two deities, than the attitude, at once proud and respectful, of the kneeling prince. The whole scene is imbued with sincere and grateful piety (Fig. 33, Vol. I.).

We find the same theme, with some slight variations, in the bas-relief at Abydos figured on page 390, Vol. I. The sculptures in the temple with which Seti I. adorned this city may be considered the masterpieces of Egyptian art in their own *genre*. Their firm and sober execution, and the severe simplicity of their conception, are well shown in our third plate. This royal figure, which we were compelled to detach from its companions in order that we might give it on a scale large enough to be of service, forms part of a composition which has been thus described by M. Charles Blanc : " Seated upon the round base of a column, we examined the noblest bas-reliefs in the world. Seti was present in his own temple. His noble head, at once human and heroic, mild and proud, stood out from the wall and seemed to regard us with a gentle smile. A wandering ray of sunlight penetrated into the temple, and, falling upon the gentle salience of the sculptured figures, gave them a relief and animation which was almost illusive. A procession of young girls, whose graceful forms are veiled only by their chastity, advance towards the hero with as much freedom as respect will allow. . . . Their beauty attracts us while their dignity forbids all approach. The scene lives before us, and yet the stone is but grazed with the chisel and casts but the gentlest shadow. But the delicacy of the workmanship is combined with such vigour of design and such true sincerity of feeling that these young women, who represent the provinces of Egypt, seem to live and breathe before us."[1]

The same qualities are found, though in less perfection, in those bas-reliefs which commemorate the conquests and military exploits of the great Theban Pharaohs on the pylons and external faces of the temple walls. The space to be covered is larger, the scene to be represented more complicated, than in the religious pictures, which, as a rule, include very few actors. The artist is no longer working for a narrow audience of gods, kings, and priests. His productions are addressed to the people at large, and he attempts

[1] CH. BLANC, *Voyage dans la Haute-Égypte*, p. 263.

therefore to dazzle and astonish the crowd rather than to please the more fastidious tastes of their social leaders. His execution is more rapid and less thoughtful, as may be seen in our illustrations taken from the battle scenes of Karnak, Luxor, the Ramesseum, and Medinet-Abou (Figs. 13, 85, 173, 174, 253, and 254, Vol. I.). In each of these scenes there is a central figure to which our attention is immediately attracted. It is that of the king, and is far larger than those of his subjects and enemies.

Sometimes he is on foot, his threatening mace raised above the heads of his prisoners, who kneel before him and raise their hands in supplication, as in a fine bas-relief at Karnak (Fig. 85, Vol. I.) ; more often he is represented standing in his chariot and dominating the tumult about him like a demi-god, driving a panic-stricken crowd before him sword in hand, or about to cleave the head of some hostile chief, whose relaxed members seem already to have felt the mortal stroke (Fig. 13, Vol. I.). Elsewhere we see him bending his bow and launching his arrows against the flying barbarians (Fig. 174, Vol. I.). "We could never look at this beautiful figure without fresh admiration," say the authors of the *Description*, "it is the Apollo Belvedere of Egypt."[1] Again we see the king returning victorious from his wars, long rows of prisoners march behind and before him, their hands tied at their backs and attached by a rope to the chariot of the conqueror. The horses which, in the battle scenes, we saw rearing and trampling the dead and dying beneath their feet, advance quietly and under the control of the tightened rein, and their dainty walk suggests that they too have a share in the universal satisfaction that follows a war well ended.

In all these reliefs the principal figure, that of the prince, is free and bold in design, and full of pride and dignity. These characteristics are also found in some of the secondary figures, such as those soldiers of the enemy who still resist, or the prisoners who resign themselves to the sovereign's mace (Figs. 13 and 85, Vol. I.). But the wounded and fugitives in these battle pictures are curiously confused in drawing and arrangement. If we take these little figures separately many of them are drawn and modelled well enough, but, taken as a whole, they are huddled up into far too narrow a space, and seem heaped upon each other in impossible fashion. The Egyptian sculptor has been fired with

[1] *Antiquités*, vol. ii. p. 110.

the desire to emulate with his chisel the great deeds of his royal master, and, in his ignorance, he has passed the limits which an art innocent of perspective cannot overleap without disaster.

The persistent tendency towards slightness of proportion, which we have already noticed in speaking of the First Theban Empire, is even more conspicuous in the figures of these reliefs than in the royal statues (Figs. 13, 50, 53, 84, 165, and 175, Vol. I.). Neither in these historical bas-reliefs, nor in those of the tombs, do we ever encounter the short thickset figures which are so common in the Ancient Empire.

In the paintings and bas-reliefs of Thebes this slenderness is more strongly marked in the women than in the men, and everything goes to prove that it was considered essential to beauty in the female sex. Goddesses and queens, dancing girls and hired musicians, all have the same elongated proportions. This propensity is more clearly seen perhaps in the pictures of the Almees and Gawasi of Ancient Egypt than anywhere else. Look, for instance, at our reproduction of a bas-relief in the Boulak Museum (Fig. 217). It represents a funeral dance to a sound of tambourines, accompanied in all probability by those apologetic songs, called θρένοι by the Greeks, of which M. Maspero has translated so many curious fragments.[1] All these women, who are practically naked in their long transparent robes, wear their hair in thick pendent tresses. Two young girls, quite nude, seem to regulate the time with castanets. A number of men, coming from the right, appear to reprove by their gestures the energetic motions of the women. This bas-relief is an isolated fragment, and without a date. It was found in the necropolis of Memphis and from its style Prisse ascribes it to the nineteenth dynasty, " a time when artists were mannered in their treatment of the female form, combining great softness of contour with an impossible slenderness of build. The execution is careless, but the movements and attitudes are truthful enough."[2] Our Plate XII. shows figures of the same general proportions, though rather better drawn.

---

[1] MASPERO, Études sur quelques Peintures Funéraires. Mariette, in describing this bas-relief (Notice du Musée, No. 903), observes that these funeral dances are still in vogue in most of the villages of Upper Egypt. The bas-reliefs from Sakkarah could not, however, as he says, render the piercing shrieks with which these dances are accompanied.

[2] PRISSE, Histoire de l'Art Égyptien. Text, p. 418. This bas-relief has also been reproduced by MARIETTE, Monuments Divers, pl. 68.

This curious mannerism began to establish itself during the first renascence of Egyptian art under the twelfth dynasty. It was to last, and even to grow more conspicuous, until the centuries of final decadence. The growing influence of conventionality is to be seen in other signs also. As art repeated and multiplied its representations, and the spaces which it had to decorate increased in number and size, it had at its disposal, as we may say, a larger number of moulds and made more frequent employment of certain groups and figures which were repeated without material change. In the decorations of this period we find long rows of figures which are practically identical with each other. They look as if they had been produced by stencil plates. With all their apparent richness and their wealth of imagery the sculpture and painting of Thebes show a poverty of invention which is not to be found in the art of the early dynasties.[1]

The gradual falling off in their powers of observing and reproducing natural forms is singularly well shown in their imperfect treatment of those animals which had been unknown to their predecessors. The horse does not seem to have been introduced into Egypt until the time of the shepherd kings, but he soon conquered a high place among the servitors of the upper classes of Egyptians. He became one of the favourite themes of contemporary art. In all the great pictures of battle he occupies a central position, and he is always associated with the prowess of the sovereign. And yet he is almost always badly drawn. His movement is sometimes not without considerable vigour and even nobility, but his forms lack truth, he is generally far too thin and elongated. His head is well set on and his neck and shoulders good, but his body is weak and unsubstantial (Figs. 13 and 174, Vol. I.). The bad effects of conventionality are here strongly felt. The same horse, in one of the two or three attitudes between which the Egyptian sculptor had to choose according to the scene to be treated, appears everywhere. The sculptors of the Memphite tombs saw with a very different eye when they set themselves to surround the doubles of their employers with the

---

[1] Some of our illustrations allow the justice of this observation to be easily verified (Figs. 172, 253, and 254, Vol. I.). In one of these the porters and in another the prisoners of war seem to be multiplied by some mechanical process. A glance through the *Denkmæler* of Lepsius leaves a similar impression. We may mention especially plates 34, 35, 175, 125, and 135 of the third Part.

FIG. 217.—Funeral Dance. Bas-relief in limestone. Boulak. Drawn by Bourgoin.

images of the domestic animals to whom they were accustomed in life.

The difference can be seen, however, without going back to the Ancient Empire. Compare the great historical bas-reliefs of the temples and royal cenotaphs with the more modest decorations of certain private sepulchres, such as those which were found in the tomb of Chamhati, superintendent of the royal domains under the eighteenth dynasty (Fig. 218). The sculptors return with pleasure to those scenes of country life of which the pyramid builders were so fond. The fragment we reproduce shows the long row of labourers bending over their hoes, the sower casting his seed, the oxen attached to the plough and slowly cutting the furrow

FIG. 218.—Bas-relief from the tomb of Chamhati, Boulak.

under the whip and voice of their drivers. Neither men nor beasts are drawn with as sure a hand as in the tomb of Ti, but yet the whole appears more sincere than productions of a more official kind. The oldest and most faithful assistant to the Egyptian fellah, the draught ox, is at least much more like nature than the charger of the Theban battle pictures.

The dangers of routine and of a conventional mode of work seem now and then to have been felt by the Theban artists. They appear to have set themselves deliberately to rouse attention and interest by introducing foreign types into their eternal battle pieces, and by insisting upon their differences of feature, of complexion, of arms and costume. They were also fond of depicting other countries and the strange animals that inhabited them, as in the bas-relief which shows a giraffe promenading among tropical palms.[1] But in spite of all these meritorious efforts, they do not touch our feelings like the primitive artists of Gizeh and Sakkarah, or even of Beni-Hassan. Try as they will, they cannot conceal that soulless and mechanical facility which is so certain to fatigue the spectator. If we turn over the pages of Lepsius, we always find ourselves dwelling with pleasure upon the sculptures from the mastabas, in spite of their apparent similarity, while we have soon had enough of the pompous and crowded bas-reliefs from Karnak, Luxor, the Ramesseum and Medinet-Abou.

These defects are less conspicuous in figures in the round, and especially in the statues of kings. I do not know that the sculptors of the Setis and the Rameses ever produced anything equal to the portraits of Thothmes, Amenophis, and Taia, but there are statues of Rameses II. intact, which may be reckoned among the fine examples of Egyptian art. The features of no prince that ever existed were reproduced more often than those of this Rameses, who built so much and reigned so long. These reproductions, as might be supposed, differ very greatly in value.

In the huge colossi which sit before the Great Temple at Ipsamboul (Fig. 248, Vol. I.), the limbs are not modelled with the careful precision which would be required in the case of a life-size statue. The arms and legs appear rather heavy on close inspection, and in a photograph those parts which are nearest to the camera, namely, the legs and the knees, seem too large for the rest of the figure. But the heads are characterized by a breadth and freedom of execution which brings out the desired expression with great effect when looked at from a proper distance. This expression is one of thoughtful mildness and imperturbable serenity. It is exactly suited to the image of a deified king, sitting as eternal guardian of the temple which his workmen had hewn out in the bowels of the mountain.

Some discrimination must be exercised between the statues of Rameses which approach the natural size. We do not look upon his portrait when a child, which is now in the Louvre, as a

---

[1] So, at Dayr-el-Bahari the decorator has taken pains to give accurate reproductions of the fauna and flora of Punt. See the plates of MARIETTE (*Dayr-el-Bahari*) and the remarks of Prof. EBERS (*Ægypten*, vol. ii. p. 280).

masterpiece (Fig. 219). The noble lines of the profile, recalling his father Seti, are indeed his, but the eye is too large and the

FIG. 219.—Portrait of Rameses II. while a child, actual size. Limestone. In the Louvre.

hands are treated with an elegance which is more than a little mannered. The uraeus on his brow and the titles engraved by his side show that he was already king, but we can see that he was still very young, not so much by the juvenile contours of his body, as by the finger in his mouth and the lock of hair hanging upon his right shoulder. A statue at Boulak (Fig. 220) shows signs of carelessness rather than of affectation. In it Rameses is still a young man. The eyes, the small mouth, the calm and smiling visage, are all well modelled, but the legs are quite shapeless.

Fig. 220.—Statue of Rameses II. Boulak.

Some good bas-reliefs date from this reign. Among others we may name those prisoners of war bound together, which Champollion copied from the plinth of a royal statue in the Ramesseum (Fig. 221). The race characteristics are very well marked. The prognathous negro, with his thick lips, short nose, sloping brow, and woolly poll; the Asiatic, an Assyrian perhaps, with his regular, finely-chiselled profile and his knotted head-dress, are easily recognized. The movement of these two figures is also happy, its only defect is its want of variety. The same remarks may be applied to those sculptures on the external walls of the small temple at Abydos, which represent the soldiers belonging to the legion of the Chardanes or Sharuten, the supposed ancestors of the Sardinians. Their picturesque costume and singular arms have been described more than once. A metal stem and a ball between two crescent-shaped horns surmount their helmets; they are tall and slender, with small heads and short round noses.[1]

The finest statue of Rameses II. that has come down to our time is, perhaps, the one in the Turin Museum (Fig. 222). Its

FIG. 221.—Prisoners of war; Ramesseum. From Champollion, pl. 322.

execution is most careful, and its state of preservation marvellous. The head is full of individuality and distinction. One of the king's sons is shown, on a very small scale, leaning against the foot of his father's seat.

Boulak possesses the upper part of a broken statue of Rameses, which is not inferior to this in artistic merit. The contours are singularly pure and noble.

Most of those who are authorities on the subject agree that art fell into decay towards the end of Rameses the second's long reign of sixty-seven years. Carried away by his mania for building, the king thought more of working rapidly than well. In his impatience to see his undertakings finished, he must have begun by using up

[1] CH. BLANC, *Voyage dans la Haute-Égypte*, p. 74. pl. 31.

the excellent architects and decorative artists left to him by his father. He left them no time to instruct pupils or to form a school, and so in his old age he found himself compelled to employ mediocrities. "The steles, inscriptions, and other monuments of the last years of Rameses II. are to be recognized at a glance by their detestable style," says Mariette.[1] With the fine bas-relief at Abydos which is reproduced in our Plate III., Vol. I., Mariette contrasts another which is to be found in a neighbouring hall and represents Rameses II. in the same attitude. In the former, the figure of Seti is expressed in the most delicate low relief, in the latter the contours of Rameses are coarsely indicated by a deeply-cut outline.[2] So too M. Charles Blanc: "As we pass from the tomb of Seti I. to those of Seti II. and Rameses IV., the decadence of Egyptian art makes itself felt, partly in the character of the pictures, which no longer display the firmness, the delicacy, or the significance, of those which we admired in the tomb of the first-named monarch, partly in the exaggerated relief of the sculptures."[3]

Unless Mariette was mistaken in his identification of one of the most remarkable fragments in the Boulak Museum, Thebes must have possessed first-rate artists even at the death of Rameses. M. Charmes thus speaks of the fragment (Fig. 223) in question: "By a happy inspiration, Mariette has given the bust of Queen Taia a pendant which equals it in attractiveness, which surpasses it, perhaps, in delicacy of treatment . . . . it is the head of a king surmounted by a huge cap which weights it without adding to its beauty. It formerly belonged to a statue which is now broken up. The young king was standing; in his left hand he held a ram-headed staff. . . . It is impossible to give an idea of the youthful, almost childish grace, of the soft and melancholy charm in a countenance which seems overspread with the shadow of some unhappy fate. How did its author contrive to cut from such an unkindly material as granite, these frank and fearless eyes, that slender nose with its refined nostrils, and these lips, which are so soft and full of vitality, that they seem modelled in nothing harder than wax. We are in presence of one of the finest relics of Egyptian sculpture, and nothing more exquisite has been

---
[1] MARIETTE, *Voyage dans la Haute-Égypte*, vol. i. p. 72. Plates 23 and 24.
[2] CHAMPOLLION makes the same remark (*Lettres d'Égypte et de Nubie*, p. 326).
[3] CH. BLANC, *Voyage dans la Haute-Égypte*, p. 178.

FIG. 222.—Statue of Rameses II. in the Turin Museum. Granite. Drawn by Saint-Elme Gautier.

produced by the art of any other people. The inscription is mutilated by a fissure in the granite, but Mariette believes that the statue represents Menephtah, the son of Rameses II."[1]

FIG. 223.—Head of Menephtah, Boulak. Drawn by Saint-Elme Gautier.

There is a colossal statue of Seti II., the son of this Menephtah, in the Louvre (Fig. 224). Although the material of which it

[1] GAB. CHARMES, *De la Réorganisation du Musée de Boulak.*- MARIETTE, *Notice*, No. 22.

FIG. 224.—Seti II. Sandstone statue, fifteen feet high. Louvre. Drawn by Saint-Elme Gautier.

consists, namely sandstone, is much less rebellious than granite, the features, which have a family resemblance to those of Menephtah, are executed in a much more summary fashion than in the Boulak statue, and yet the execution is that of a man who knew his business. The modelling of the muscular arms is especially vigorous.[1]

There are hardly any royal statues left to us which we can ascribe with certainty to the twentieth dynasty, but at Medinet-Abou, both on the walls of the temple and in the Royal Pavilion there are bas-reliefs which show that the sculpture of Rameses III., the last of the great Theban Pharaohs, knew how to hold its own among the other glories of the reign. We have given a few examples of the pictures in which the king is shown as a warrior and as a high priest (Figs. 172 and 173 Vol. I.); other groups should not be forgotten in which he is exhibited during his hours of relaxation in his harem, among his wives and daughters.

Under the last of the Rameses the Egyptians lost their military spirit and, with it, their foreign possessions in the South and East. Inclosed within its own frontiers, between the cataracts in the South and the Mediterranean in the North, and enfeebled by the domination of the priests and scribes, the country became divided into two kingdoms, that of Thebes, under a theocratic dynasty, and that of Tanis in which the royal names betray a strong Semitic influence.

That worship of Asiatic divinities which, though never mentioned in official monuments, is so often alluded to in the steles, must then have taken hold of the people of Lower Egypt. Among these were Resheb, the Syrian Apollo; Kadesh, who bore the name of a famous Syrian fortress, and was but one form of the great Babylonian goddess Anahit, the Anaitis of the Greeks. Kadesh is sometimes represented standing upon a lion *passant* (Fig. 225).

Exhausted by its internal conflicts, Egypt produced few monumental works for several centuries. Many kings, however, of this barren period, and especially Sheshonk, have left at Karnak records of their military victories and of their efforts to re-establish the national unity. After the twenty-fourth dynasty Egypt became the vassal of that Ethiopian kingdom whose civilization was no more than a plagiarism from her own. During the half

---

[1] Louvre. Ground-floor gallery, No. 24

century that this vassalage endured, the southern conquerors gave full employment to such artists as Egypt had preserved. The latter were set to reproduce the features of the Ethiopian kings, but the works which resulted are very unequal in merit.

Sabaco caused the sides of the great door in the pylon of Rameses at Karnak to be repaired. The execution of the figures is by no means satisfactory. "The relief is too bold; the muscular development of the heroes represented is exaggerated to a meaningless degree; coarse vigour has taken the place of graceful strength."[1]

But although these bas-reliefs, the only ones of the period which have been encountered, are evidently inspired by the decadence, the Egyptian sculptors seem to have still preserved much of their skill in portraiture. Mariette believes that a royal head in the Museum at Cairo represents Tahraka, the third of the Ethiopian sovereigns. It is disfigured by the loss of the nose. The remaining features are coarse and strongly marked and the general type is foreign rather than Egyptian.[2] However this may be, it cannot be denied that in the alabaster statue of Ameneritis, which was found at Karnak by Mariette, we have a monument of this phase in Egyptian art remarkable both for taste and knowledge (Fig. 226).[3]

FIG. 225.—The Goddess Kadesh; from Wilkinson, Fig. 55.

During the Ethiopian occupation Queen Ameneritis played

[1] CH BLANC, *Voyage dans la Haute-Égypte*, p. 153.
[2] MARIETTE, *Notice*, No. 20.
[3] MARIETTE, *Notice*, No. 866. There is a cast of this statue in the Louvre, but, like that of the statue of Chephren, which forms a pendant to it, it has been coloured to the hue of fresh butter and the result is most disagreeable. Even when placed upon a cast from an alabaster figure this colour is bad enough, but when the cast is one from a statue in diorite, like that of Chephren, it is quite inexcusable. It would have been better either to have left the natural surface of the plaster or to have given to each cast a colour which should in some degree recall that of the originals and mark the difference between them.

an important *rôle* in the affairs of Egypt. While her brother Sabaco was yet alive she was dignified with the title of regent, later she brought her rights to the double crown of Upper and Lower Egypt to the usurper Piankhi, whom she married and made the father of Shap-en-Ap, who afterwards became the mother of Psemethek I.

The head of Ameneritis is covered with the full-bottomed wig worn by goddesses. She holds a whip in her left hand and a sort of purse in her right; there are bangles upon her wrist and ankles and the contours of her body are frankly displayed beneath the long chemise-like robe, which falls almost to her ankles.

The features are resolute and intelligent rather than beautiful, the squareness of the lower jaw and the firm line of the mouth being especially significant.

We have, then, every reason to believe this to be a good portrait. Both form and expression are just what might be expected in a high-born Egyptian female possessed of sovereign power.

Fig. 226.—Statue of Ameneritis. Alabaster. Boulak. Drawn by G. Bénédite.

The treatment of the body is rather conventional. The bust, so far as it can be traced under the clinging robe, is younger than the head, which is that of a woman in middle life. With these reserves the statue is very pleasing. The arms are a little stiff, but the figure as a whole is characterized by a chaste and sober elegance. The modelling is not insisted upon too much, but its undulating contours are discreetly indicated under the soft though by no means transparent drapery. The whole work is imbued with the spirit of Saite art, an aftermath which was characterized by grace and refinement rather than by freedom and power.

§ 5. *The Art of the Saite Period.*

After the last of the Ramessids the decadence of Egypt was continuous, but in the seventh century B.C. while the Ethiopians and Assyrians contended for the possession of the country, it was particularly rapid. Under Psemethek, however, there was a revival. The foreigners were driven out, the national unity was re-established, and Syria was again brought under the Egyptian sceptre. An artistic renascence coincided with this restoration of political well being, and the princes of the twenty-sixth dynasty set themselves to restore the monuments which had perished during the intestine troubles and foreign inroads. Their attention was mainly directed to the architectural monuments of Lower Egypt; but little now remains of the buildings which drew so much praise from the Greek travellers. Their sculptured achievements have been more fortunate. Their statues were sprinkled over the whole country, and many of them have been found at Memphis, at Thebes, and even among the ruins of cities which have long ago disappeared. Thus we find that most Egyptian collections contain figures which may be assigned to this time, or rather to this school, for the style held its own even as late as the first two or three Ptolemies. Among them may be mentioned the *pastophorus*[1] of the Vatican, the *Arsaphes*[2] of the British Museum, the statues of serpentine found at Sakkarah in the tomb of a certain Psemethek, a high officer under the thirtieth dynasty,[3] and the fine

[1] For the meaning of this word see PIERRET, *Dictionnaire*, &c.
[2] For illustrations of this statue and an explanation of the name here given to it, see BIRCH, *Gallery of Antiquities*. London, 4to.—ED.
[3] MARIETTE. *Notice du Musée de Boulak*, No. 385.

bronzes of Osiris discovered at Medinet-Abou.[1] All the bronzes found in the Serapeum belong to the same category.[2]

By means of secondary remains, such as sphinxes, steles, and scarabs, we can just contrive to get a glimpse at the features of those brilliant sovereigns who, after dazzling Egypt and the surrounding countries early in the seventh century B.C., fell before the first attacks of the Persians.[3] Many of their effigies must have been destroyed by the invaders, either at their first conquest, or during the three subsequent occasions when they were compelled to re-establish their ascendency by force. A similar fate must have overtaken the statues of Inarôs and Nectanebo, who succeeded for a time in restoring the independence of their country. For the whole of this period the royal ·iconography is much more scanty than for the two Theban empires.

We shall not dwell upon the figure in green basalt which stands in the middle of the *Salle Historique* in the Louvre. We know from the inscription upon its girdle that it represents the king Psemethek II. The execution is careful, but the work has suffered great mutilation, the head and parts of the limbs being modern restorations.[4] On the other hand, the two little bronze sphinxes which stand upon the chimney-piece in the same room are in excellent condition. According to De Rougé their heads reproduce the features of Ouaphra, the Apries of the Greeks (Fig. 227).[5] In the ground-floor gallery there are several sphinxes which, according to their inscriptions, should include portraits of some of those princes who between 527 and 332 B.C. temporarily freed Egypt from the Persian yoke; Nepherites, Achoris, Nectanebo, &c. None of them, however, show enough individuality in their features to suggest that they were copied from nature. Their heads are all clothed indiscriminately in the same elegance of contour, and in looking at them we find ourselves far indeed from the admirable portraits of the early empire, or even from that statue of Ameneritis which closes the series of royal effigies.

[1] *Notice*, Nos. 196-7.
[2] *Ibid.* Nos. 105-15.
[3] The Boulak Museum possesses a very fine scarab which shows Nechao between Isis and Neith, one of whom hands him a mace and the other a small figure of Mentou-Ra, the God of Battles. Two chained prisoners are prostrate at the base of the scarab. MARIETTE, *Notice*, No. 556.
[4] PIERRET, *Catalogue de la Salle Historique*, No. 269.
[5] DE ROUGÉ, *Notice Sommaire*, p. 59.

The chief pre-occupation of the Saite sculptor was to obtain suppleness of modelling and an apparent finish of execution, both of which, in his opinion, were effective in proportion as the material used was hard and unyielding.[1] His chisel was employed much more than formerly in fusing together the various layers of muscle which form the walls of the human structure. He did not lay so much stress on the skeleton, or on the leading lines of the figure, as his early predecessors. His care was mainly devoted to rendering the subtle outward curves and contours, and this he often carries to such excess as to produce a result which is simply wearisome from its want of energy and accent. There is a group at Boulak upon which too much praise has been lavished, to which this stricture thoroughly applies. It represents one of the

FIG. 227.—Bronze Sphinx, Louvre. Drawn by Saint-Elme Gautier.

Psemetheks, clothed in a long robe, standing before the goddess Hathor who is in the form of a cow. The head and torso are finely chiselled, but, through an exaggerated desire for elegance, the arms have been made far too long, and the divine cow is entirely without truth or expression. This defect is still more conspicuous in the two figures of Isis and Osiris that were found with this group. Their execution has reached the extremity of coldness through the excessive use of file and sand-paper.[2]

[1] It would appear that wood-carving was never so popular in Egypt as it was under the Second Theban Empire. The numerous wooden statues which fill our museums date from that period. We have given an example of them in Fig. 50, Vol. I.

[2] MARIETTE, Notice du Musée, Nos. 386 and 387. Mariette seems to estimate these two statuettes far too highly.

Sometimes the sculptor knows where to leave off, and the result

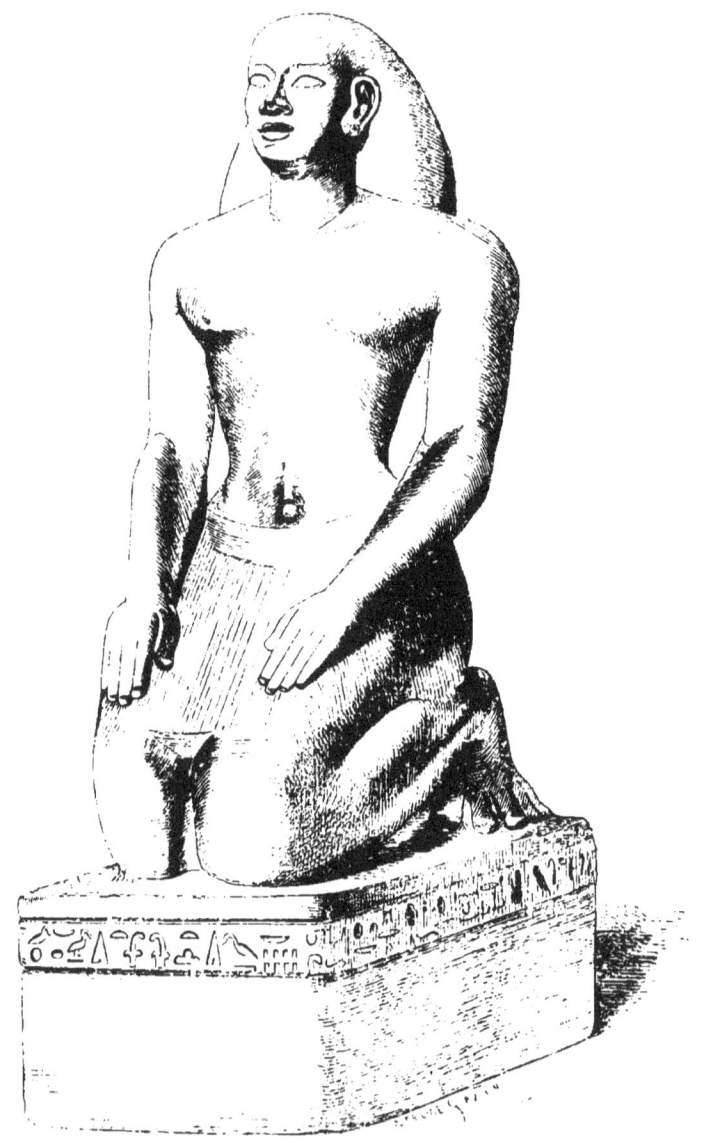

Fig. 228.—Statue of Nekht-har-heb, Louvre. Drawn by Saint-Elme Gautier.

is better. The sandstone statue of Nekht-har-heb, in the Louvre, is one of the best productions of the Saite artists (Fig. 228).[1] The execution of hands and feet is sketchy, and the countenance is without much expression, but the attitudes of the arms and legs,

FIG. 229.—Statue of Horus, Louvre. Drawn by Saint-Elme Gautier.

the modelling of the trunk, and the pose of the head, unite breadth with facility and dignity to such a degree, that we are reminded,

[1] DE ROUGÉ, *Notice des Monuments Exposés au Rez-de-chaussée*, No. 94.

for a moment, of a Greek marble. In spite of the singular attitude there is much in the execution which recalls a much more ancient work, the statue of Ouah-ab-ra, which dates from the twenty-sixth dynasty (Fig. 51, Vol. I.)[1]

Not less remarkable is the headless statue of a personage called Horus, which dates from about the same period (Fig. 229).[2] It is of black granite and yet both limbs and torso are as delicately modelled as if they were of the softest limestone. The attitude of the arms is unusually easy and natural, and the whole figure is freer and less constrained than anything we find in the ancient statues. There is, too, a certain spirit of innovation discoverable in the feet. The toes are well separated and slighty bent, instead of being flat and close together.

Fig. 230.— Bas-relief from Memphis. Length forty inches, height ten inches, Boulak. Drawn by Bourgoin.

The same style, taste, and general tendency are to be found in the steles and in the decoration of the tombs. In a few sepulchral bas-reliefs we can detect a desire to imitate the compositions on the walls of the mastabas. Such attempts were quite natural, and we need feel no surprise that the Egyptians in their decline should have turned to the artistic form and motives which had been invented in their distant and vigorous youth. The old age of many other races has shown the same tendency in their arts and literature.

The beautiful band of sculpture in low relief which was found,

[1] De Rougé, *Notice des Monuments Exposés au Rez-de-chaussée*, No. 91.
[2] *Ibidem*, No. 88.

THE ART OF THE SAITE PERIOD.

together with another very similar to it, at Mitrahineh, upon the site of ancient Memphis, might easily be taken at first sight for a production of the early centuries (Figs. 230 and 231). It formed the lintel to the door of a house dating from the Greek or Roman period, for which purpose it had doubtless been carried off from some tomb.[1] At one end a dignified individual is seated upon a low-backed chair, in his left hand he holds the long wand of office, in his right a ribbon. His name and titles are engraved in front of him: he was a writer, and was called Psemethek-nefer-sam. A scribe bends respectfully before him and introduces a procession of men, women, and children, who bring offerings of various kinds, jars of liquid, coffers, flowers, birds, and calves led by a string. It is the favourite theme of the mastabas over again. The attitudes

FIG. 231.—Continuation of Fig. 230.

are similar, but the execution is different. There is a lack of firmness and rotundity in the modelling, and considerably more striving after elegance. The children especially should be noticed; the fashion in which they all turn towards their elders betrays a desire on the part of the artist to give freshness and piquancy to his composition.

Most of those bronze figures of the gods, which are so plentiful in the European museums, date from this period. We have reproduced several of them in our chapter upon the Egyptian pantheon (Figs. 34-37, Vol. I.). With the advent of Alexander and his

[1] MARIETTE, *Notice du Musée*, Nos. 35-6.

successors, a number of Greek artists became domiciled in Egypt; they employed their talents in the service of the priests and scribes without attempting in any way to affect the religion, the institutions, or the habits of the people. The Egyptian artists were heirs to the oldest of all civilizations, their traditions were so firmly established, and their professional education was so systematic, that they could hardly consent to modify their ideas at the first contact with a race whom they secretly despised, although they were compelled to admit their political and military supremacy. Many years had to pass before Egyptian sculpture, and with it the written character and language, became debased as we find it in certain Roman and Ptolemaic temples. Several generations had to come and go before a hybrid Egypto-Greek style, a style which preserved the most unhappy forms and conventions of Egyptian art while it lost all its native freshness and originality, imposed itself finally upon the country.

The worst of the Saite statues are still national in style. It is an Egyptian soul that inhabits their bodies, that breathes through the features, and places its mark upon every detail of the personality represented. This is no longer the case with the figures which, from the time of Augustus to that of Hadrian, seem to have been manufactured in such quantities for the embellishment of Roman villas. Costumes, accessories, and attitudes are all Egyptian, but the model upon which they are displayed is Greek. Until the beginning of the present century archæologists were deceived by the masquerade, and were unable to distinguish between pasticcios, many of which may not even have been made in Egypt, and the really authentic works of the unspoiled Egyptian artists. Such mistakes are no longer probable, but even now it is difficult to say exactly where the art of Sais was blended into that of the Ptolemies. When there is no epigraph upon which to depend the most skilful archæologist may here make mistakes.

There are, however, a few figures in which the influence of the Greek works brought to Alexandria by the descendants of Lagus, may be detected in an incipient stage. The motives and attributes are still purely Egyptian, but the modelling, the carriage of the head, and the attitude are modified, and we see, almost by intuition, that the Greek style is about to smother the Egyptian. This evidence of transition is, we think, very marked in a bronze group of *Isis suckling Horus* in the Louvre (Fig. 55, Vol. I.), and in *Horus enthroned supported by lions* (Fig. 232). And yet the difference

FIG. 232.—Horus enthroned. Bronze. Louvre.

between these things and those which are frankly Græco-Roman is great, and at once strikes those who come upon the latter in the galleries of Boûlak, where they are mixed up with so many creations of Egyptian genius. The distinction is equally obvious in works produced by foreign sculptors established in Egypt, and in those by Egyptians working under Greek masters. Look at the head found at Tanis, which is reproduced both in full face and profile in Fig. 233. It is of black granite, like so many Egyptian statues, but we feel at once that there is nothing Egyptian

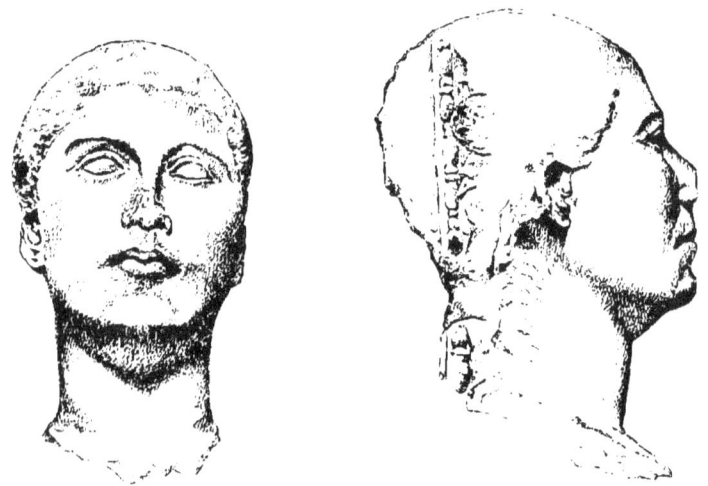

Fig. 233.—Roman head, Boulak. Drawn by Bourgoin.

about it but the material. It is obviously a portrait of a man of mature age ; the face is beardless, the curly hair cut short. During the Greek and Roman period the temple of San was enriched by the statues of private individuals, and doubtless this fragment belonged to one of them. Tradition says that the statue was placed in front of a pier with which it was connected by the Ionic moulding which is still to be traced upon the right side of the head. With this exception the treatment is that of the best Augustan period. The person represented may very well have been one of the first Roman governors of Egypt.[1]

[1] MARIETTE, *Notice du Musée*, No. 18.

§ 6. *The Principal Themes of Egyptian Sculpture.*

When we come to study Greek sculpture we shall find that the masterpieces in which its highest powers are displayed, are statues of divinities, such as the Athenè of the Parthenon and the Olympian Zeus. In our review of the Egyptian works of the same kind we have not had occasion to call attention to a single god or goddess. Their representation was not, as in Greece, the aim of the highest art. The figures of deities were, indeed, numerous enough in Egypt, but the national artist did not show such originality in their conception as in those of kings and private individuals. This phenomenon may seem inconsistent with what we know of the piety of the Egyptians and the place occupied by religion in their daily life ; it is to be easily explained, however, by the origin of Egyptian sculpture and the part which the statues of the gods played in it.

Egyptian art began with portraiture. As soon as it was capable of carving and painting stone it was realistic, not so much by instinct and taste as by duty. After such a beginning it found great difficulty in raising itself above intelligent and faithful reproduction of fact. Such inventive powers as it possessed were spent in creating a type for the royal majesty, and in that case it had concrete reality as a starting point. When it came to representing the gods it had no such help. It could not fall back upon fidelity to fact, and, unlike the Greeks of after ages, it was unable to give them distinction by the superior nobility and dignity of their physical contours and features. It was reduced to differentiating them by the variety of their attributes. By such a proceeding it obtained an almost infinite number of divine types, but each type was only recognizable on condition that its pose and accessories, once determined, should remain without material change. There was none of the mobility and elasticity which distinguishes the dwellers on the Greek Olympus, as may be clearly seen by comparing the poverty and want of variety of a Horus or a Bast with the infinite diversity of an Apollo or an Artemis.

When the Egyptian sculptor had to endow the national gods with concrete forms he found himself, then, in a condition much less favourable than that of his Greek successors. This position, too, was materially affected by the fact that the best site in the temple, the centre of the naos, was reserved for a symbol, sometimes living, sometimes inanimate, which was looked upon as the true representative of the god. It was to this symbol, jealously hidden from all but the high priest and the king, that the prayers of the faithful were addressed. It has been called a survival from the early fetish worship. Perhaps it was so. But at present we are only concerned with its unfortunate results upon artistic development. His statues being excluded from the place of honour, the sculptor was not, as in Greece, stimulated to combine all the qualities ascribed by the nation to its gods in one supreme effort of his knowledge and skill; he was not raised above himself by the desire to produce a work which might give point to the magnificence of a temple and augment the piety of a race.

Mariette was right in insisting upon this difference. "The temples," he says, "hardly contain a statue which is not votive. Sometimes these statues are found irregularly distributed about the foundations or in the sand, sometimes they are of large size and are arranged along the walls, but they hardly ever exceed the life-size of a man. *I cannot say that each temple had a figure which could be specially called the statue of that temple.* The divine images were plentiful enough; but each had its own particular ministration. In the prayers addressed to it the name of its consecrator was always included. *Such a thing as a statue forming the central object of a temple and representing its god without votive appropriation did not, perhaps, exist.*" [1]

Figures of Sekhet, the goddess with the head of a lioness, have been discovered in hundreds in the building at Karnak known as the Temple of Mouth, or Maut. This mine of statues has been worked ever since 1760, and all the museums of Europe have shared the results.[2] Being so numerous these statues could not have reached great excellence of execution. They were

[1] MARIETTE, *Notice du Musée*, p. 16. See also his *Catalogue Général*, c. i.

[2] MARIETTE (*Karnak*, p. 15) calculated that this temple, whose major axis from the pylon to the sanctuary hardly exceeded 300 feet in length, must have contained 572 statues, all in black granite, and differing but little in size and execution. If placed in rows against the walls, and here and there in a double row, their elbows would almost have touched one another. The first and second courts, and the two long corridors which bound the temple to the east and west, were full of them. One of these figures is represented in our Fig. 39, Vol. I.

devotional objects produced in mechanical fashion, and there is little chance of finding a masterpiece of sculpture among them. In an inscription at Karnak we find Thothmes III. boasting of having endowed the temple with a statue of Amen "such that no other temple could show one equal to it."[1] This Amen must have excelled its rivals in richness of material and in perfection of polish. It is unlikely that it was much superior to them in nobility or true beauty.

The position occupied by the statue in the cella of a Greek temple finds something like a parallel, however, in the rock-cut temples of Nubia. We allude to these groups of three or four figures, carved in the living rock, which have been found seated in the farthest recesses at Ipsamboul, Derri, and elsewhere. These figures are now so mutilated that their merit as works of art cannot be decided.

We may safely say that if the temples proper, such as those of Karnak and Luxor, had contained master-statues corresponding in any way to those of the Greeks, they would have been of colossal size. But although the soil of Thebes is almost paved with the fragments of royal colossi, not a single vestige of any gigantic statue of Amen has ever been discovered. All that we know of those few divine statues to which special veneration was paid excludes any idea of size exceeding that of man. The statues of Amen and Khons, at Thebes and Napata, which nodded their approval when consulted by the king as to his future plans, were certainly not colossi.[2] And as for the figure of Khons, which took a voyage into Syria to cure the sister-in-law of one of the latter Ramessids, we can hardly believe it was more than a statuette.[3]

In spite of their number the statues of the gods must have attracted much less attention than those of the kings. The Pharaoh who built a temple filled it with his own effigies; his colossi sat before the gate, they helped to form those structural units which we call Osiride piers, and figures of smaller size were ranged under the porticos. In that part of the Great Temple at Karnak which dates from the eighteenth dynasty, statues of

---

[1] MARIETTE, *Voyage dans la Haute-Égypte*, vol. ii. p. 25.
[2] MASPERO, *Annuaire de l'Association des Études Grecques*, 1877, p. 132.
[3] See the often-quoted story of a voyage taken by a statue of Khons to the country of Bakhtan and its return to Egypt. DE ROUGÉ, *Étude sur un Stèle Égyptienne appartenant à la Bibliothèque Nationale*, 8vo, 1856.

Thothmes III. alone have been found to the number of several dozens; their broken fragments may be identified in every corner.[1]

Among the countless votive offerings with which a great building like that at Karnak was filled, there were a few statues of private individuals. " The right to erect statues in the temples belonged (as we should say) to the crown. We find therefore that most of the private statues found in the sacred inclosures are inscribed with a special formula: ' Granted, by the king's favour, to so and so, the son of so and so . . .' Permission to place a statue in a temple was only given as a reward for services rendered. The temple might be either that of the favoured individual's native town, or one for which he had peculiar veneration. . . . . Civil and foreign wars, the decay of cities, and the destruction of idols by the Christians, have combined to render statues of private persons from public temples of very rare occurrence in our collections." [2]

The tombs were the proper places for private statues; we have seen that at Memphis they were set up in the courtyards and hidden in the serdabs, that at Thebes they were placed, either upright or sitting, in the depths of the hypogea.[3]

Figures in the round, whether gods, kings, or private persons, were always isolated. They were sometimes placed one by the side of the other, but they never formed groups in the strict sense of the word. In the whole of Egyptian sculpture there is but one group, that of the father, mother, and children ; and this was repeated without material change for thousands of years. The Egyptian artist can hardly be said to have composed or invented it ; it was, so to speak, imposed upon him by nature. Those groups which became so numerous in Hellenic art as soon as it arrived at maturity, in which various forms and opposed or complementary movements were so combined as to produce a just equilibrium, are absolutely wanting in Egypt.

The Greeks were the first of the antique races to love the human form for itself, for the inherent beauty of its lines and attitudes. Certain traces of this sentiment are to be found in the decorative art of Egypt, in which motives that are at once ingenious and picturesque are often met with, but it is almost entirely absent from sculpture. Modelled forms are hardly ever

---

[1] MARIETTE, *Karnak*, p. 36. See also his *Abydos, Catalogue Général*, § 2, p. 27.
[2] MASPERO, in the *Monuments de l'Art Antique* of Rayet.
[3] *Description, Antiquités*, vol. iii. p. 41.

anything more than skilful tracings from reality. In the sepulchral system the sculptor supplies relays of bodies, stone mummies which may take the place of the embalmed corpse when it is worn out; in the temples his business is to set up concrete symbols of an idea, emblems of one of the divine powers, or of the majesty of Pharaoh.

The infinite number of combinations which may be obtained by the association of several persons of different ages and sexes in one action, makes the group the highest achievement of an art at once passionate and scientific, such as the sculpture of Greece and Florence. To such a height the Egyptians never soared, but they well understood the more or less conventional methods which are at the command of the sculptor. They produced figures in the round by thousands: most of them were smaller than nature, many were life-size, while a few surpassed it with an audacity to which no parallel can be found elsewhere. Here and there we find a figure, no more than some three or four inches high, to which its maker has contrived to give a freedom of attitude, a breadth of execution, and a nobility of presence which are quite astonishing. Look, for instance, at the reproduction of a little wooden statuette which borders this page (Fig. 234): it is identical in size with the original. Its date is unknown, but we should be inclined to refer it to the Ancient Empire. The air of this little personage is so proud and dignified that he might well be a reduction from a colossus.

FIG. 234.—Wooden statuette belonging to M. Delaroche-Vernet. Drawn by Saint-Elme Gautier.

What we call *busts*, that is, figures which consist of nothing but the head and the upper part of the trunk, were not unknown to the Egyptians. All the descriptions mention the existence in the Ramesseum of two colossal busts of Rameses II., the one in black, the other in a parti-coloured black and red, granite.

It would seem that all the colossi were of stone, especially of the harder kinds. Wood was used for life-size figures and statuettes, particularly the latter. Terra-cotta coated with enamel was hardly used for anything but very small figures. It was the same with bronze, which was seldom employed in large figures. We do not know whether the Egyptians in their days of independence made bronzes as large and larger than life, as the Greeks constantly did. One of the largest pieces known is the Horus in the Posno collection (Fig. 44, Vol. I.). It is about three feet high. It forms a single casting with the exception

FIG. 235.—Bronze cat. Drawn by Saint-Elme Gautier.

of the arms, which were added afterwards. The finish of the head is remarkable, and the eyes appear to have been encrusted with enamel or some other precious material, which has since disappeared. The hands seem to have held some vessel for pouring libations which, being of silver or gold, must have been detached at a very early period. The execution recalls the finest style of the eighteenth dynasty.

The highest use to which sculpture can be put is the rendering of the human figure, but Egyptian sculptors did not disdain to employ their chisels upon the portraiture of those animals which were objects of devotion in their country. We possess excellent representations of most of these; the figure of a cat which we take from the cases of the Louvre is an average specimen (Fig. 235). The lion was equally well rendered. In the bas-reliefs we sometimes find him turned into a sort of heraldic animal by the addition of emblematic designs upon his flanks and shoulders (Fig. 236); but, even where he is most simplified, his outlines and general movements are truthful in the main. Sometimes we find him in full relief, modelled with singular power and sincerity. This is the case with a bronze lion which must once have formed a part of some kind of padlock, if we may judge from the few links of a chain which are still attached to it.[1] Although this animal bears the ovals of Apries, and therefore belongs to the lowest period of Egyptian art, its style is vigorous in no common degree.

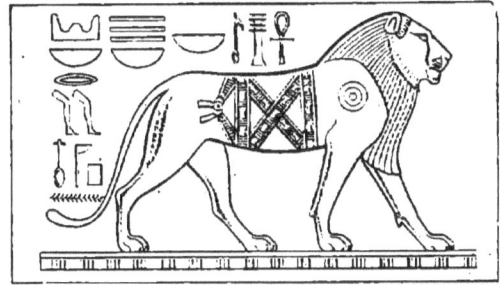

FIG. 236.—Lion, from a Theban bas-relief; from Prisse.

The Egyptians were as much impressed as other eastern peoples by the strength and beauty of these animals, which in their days must have abounded in the deserts of Syria and Ethiopia. They were chosen to be the emblems of royal courage;[2] a lion's head was placed upon the shoulders of Hobs, and that of a lioness upon the shoulders of Sekhet. Finally it was from the lion that the first idea of that fictitious animal which the Greeks called a sphinx, was taken.

"At first the sphinx can have been nothing but a lion placed to guard the entrance to a temple. The combination of a man's

---

[1] MARIETTE, *Notice du Musée*, No. 1010.
[2] At Tell-el-Amarna we find the lion marching by the side of the king (LEPSIUS. *Denkmäler*, vol. vi. pl. 100).

head, which was always that of a king, with a lion's body, must have been a result of the national love for symbolism. The king himself, as represented by this association of physical with intellectual strength, acted as guardian of the building which he had founded. There was a radical distinction between the Greek sphinx and that of the Egyptians. The latter propounded no enigma to the passer-by, and the author of the treatise, *Upon Isis and Osiris* was in sympathy with his times when he wrote: 'There was nothing behind the mysteries of the Egyptians but their philosophy, which was seen as if through a veil. Thus they placed sphinxes before the gates of their temples, meaning by that to say that their theology contained all the secrets of wisdom

FIG. 237.—Bronze lion, Boulak. Drawn by Bourgoin.

under an enigmatic form.' Evidently, the Egyptians did not mean so much as is sometimes thought."[1]

We have already reproduced many examples of what may be called the classic form of sphinx, his head covered with the *klaft* and his paws extended before him (Figs. 41 and 157, Vol. I.). But the type included several secondary varieties. Sometimes the forepaws are replaced by human hands holding symbolic objects (Figs. 227 and 238); sometimes the head of a hawk is substituted for that of a man. The animals which form many of the *dromoi* at Karnak are called crio-sphinxes (Fig. 205, Vol. I.), but the

[1] MARIETTE, *Voyage dans la Haute-Égypte*, vol. ii. p. 9.

name is an unhappy one, because they have nothing in common with a sphinx but the position. They are rams and nothing else.

The Greek word σφίγξ is feminine. The sphinx with female breasts is, however, very rare in Egypt. Wilkinson only knew of one, in which the Queen Mut-neter of the eighteenth dynasty was represented.[1]

The Egyptians were not content with confusing the figures of men and animals in their images of the gods, they combined those of quadrupeds and birds in the same fashion. Thus we sometimes find wings upon the backs of gazelles and antelopes, and now and then a curious animal compounded of a hawk's head and a nondescript body (Fig. 239). Whether such fantastic quadrupeds were consciously and deliberately invented by the Egyptian

FIG. 238.—Sphinx with human hands. Bas-relief; from Prisse.

artists or not, we have no means of deciding. In a period when there was none of that scientific culture which alone enables men to distinguish the possible from the impossible, they may well have believed in winged and bird-headed animals with four legs. For the Greeks of Homer's time, and even for their children's children, the chimera and his kindred were real. They knew where they lived, and they described their habits. In a picture at Beni-Hassan, these imaginary beasts are shown flying before the hunter, and mixed up with the undoubted denizens of the mountains and

---

[1] Upon the significance of the sphinx and its different varieties, see WILKINSON, *Manners and Customs*, etc. vol. iii. pp. 308-312. Wilkinson brings together on a single plate (vol. ii. p. 93) all the fantastic animals invented by the Egyptians. See also MASPERO, *Mémoire sur la Mosaique de Palestrine* (*Gazette Archéologique*, 1879).

deserts.[1] Such representations must have been common upon those objects—partly manufactured in Egypt, partly imitated in Phœnicia—which the enterprising inhabitants of the latter country distributed all over Western Asia, and the basin of the Mediterranean. They had a large share of that mystic and enigmatic

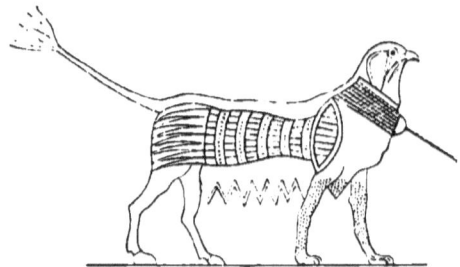

FIG. 239.—Quadruped with the head of a bird. From Champollion, pl. 428 *bis*.

character which has always been an attraction in the eye of the decorator. They may have helped to develop a belief that the curious beings represented upon them existed in some corner of the world, and they certainly did much to form those decorative types which have been handed down through Greece to the modern ornamentist.

§ 7. *The Technique of the Bas-reliefs.*

Work in low relief held such an important place in the affections of the Egyptian sculptor that we must study its processes in some detail.

In the first place, it was almost invariably painted. Those bas-reliefs which show no trace of colour may be looked upon as unfinished.

Secondly, the depth of the relief varied as much as it could, from the almost detached figures of the Osiride piers to the delicate salience of the carvings upon the steles and tomb-walls. A few works in very high relief have been found in the mastabas (Fig. 120, Vol. I.),[2] but they are quite exceptional; the depth is usually

[1] MASPERO, *Les Peintures des Tombeaux Égyptiens et la Mosaïque de Palestrine*, p. 82 (*Gazette Archéologique*, 1879).

[2] See also LEPSIUS, *Denkmæler*, part ii. pl. 11, and a tomb at El Kab (*Eileithyia*). MARIETTE (*Voyage dans la Haute-Égypte*, plate 6 and page 37) cites, as a curious

from two to three millimetres. It is the same with the Theban tombs. It is only in the life-size figures that the relief becomes as much as a centimetre, or a centimetre and a half in depth; articulations, the borders of drapery, and the bounding lines of the contour, are indicated with much less salience.

The processes used in Egyptian reliefs were three in number, one of those three, at least, being almost unknown elsewhere.

The commonest of the three is the same as that in favour with the Greeks, by which the figures are left standing out from a smooth bed, which is sometimes slightly hollowed in the neighbourhood of their contours. When limestone was used, this method was almost always preferred, as that material allowed the beds to be dressed without any difficulty.

Sometimes, on the other hand, the figure is modelled in relief in a sunk hollow, which is from half an inch to an inch and a half deep (Fig. 240). This method of proceeding, which is peculiar to Egypt, was doubtless suggested by the desire to protect the image as much as possible. For this purpose it was singularly efficient, the high "bed" of the relief guarding it both from accidental injury, and from the effects of weather and time. It had one disadvantage, however, in the confusing shadows which obscured a part of the modelling. This process was used, as a rule, for the carvings on granite and basalt sarcophagi (Fig. 195, Vol. I.). It would have cost too much time and labour to have sunk and polished the surrounding surfaces. This method, when once taken up, was extended to limestone, and thus we find, among those objects in the Louvre which were discovered in the Serapeum, a stele of extremely delicate workmanship, representing Amasis in adoration before an apis. The head of Amasis is damaged, and we have preferred to give as a specimen the fine head of Rameses II., chiselled in a slab of limestone, which is also in the Louvre (Fig. 240).

In the third system the surface of the figures and the bed, or field, of the relief are kept on one level. The contours are indicated by hollow lines cut into the stone. In this case there is very little modelling. There is not enough depth to enable the sculptor to indicate different planes, and his work becomes little

example of a bolder relief than usual, the scenes sculptured upon the tomb of Sabou, especially the picture showing the servants of the defunct carrying a gazelle upon their shoulders.

more than a silhouette in which the outline is shown by a hollow instead of by the stroke of a pencil or brush. When more rapid progress than usual had to be made the Egyptian artist was content with this outline. Most of those vast historical and biographical scenes which cover the walls of the Ramesseum and Medinet-Abou (Fig. 173, Vol. I.), were executed by it.

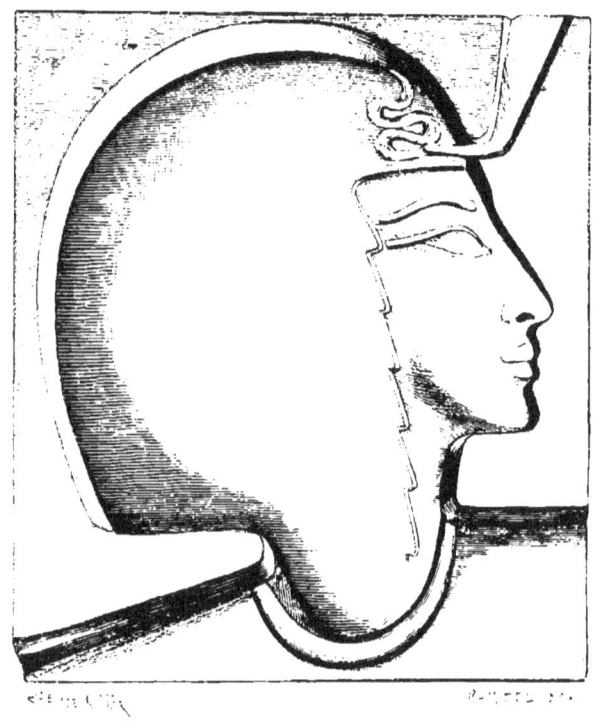

FIG. 245.— Portrait of Rameses II., Louvre. Drawn by Saint-Elme Gautier.

Most of our existing reliefs have come from tombs. In the mastabas their production was easy enough. The sculptor simply carved the faces of their limestone walls. But in the hypogea the difficulties were frequently great, and yet they were always surmounted. The bas-reliefs in such places were, as a rule, on a small scale. Consequently, the knobs of flint and the petrified shells with which the sculptor's chisel was continually coming in contact, must have embarrassed him in no slight degree. Wherever such unkindly lumps were found, they were extracted from the rock, the rough holes which they left were squared and filled up either with a cement which became very hard with time, or with pieces of stone accurately adjusted. In the latter case, the joints have been made with such care that it is very difficult to discover them. In some tomb chambers these insertions are so numerous that they make up not less than a quarter of the whole surface.[1]

As soon as the carvings upon the walls were finished, the latter were covered with a thin layer of stucco. This was hardly ever omitted; it was laid upon rock, cement, and limestone indiscriminately. It afforded a better and a more tenacious ground for coloured decoration than the naked stone.[2]

The principal place in these bas-reliefs is occupied by human figures, and after them by those of animals. The accessories, such as the landscape and inanimate objects are for the most part only slightly indicated, all the labours of agriculture are illustrated, but only so far as the action of man is immediately concerned. There is never more in the way of background than is absolutely necessary for the right comprehension of the scene.[3] The Greeks followed the same rule. In this respect the Egyptians were well advised. Their artistic instincts must have warned them of the true conditions of work in relief, which cannot, without the greatest peril, attempt to rival the complex achievements of painting.

To this practice we might suggest a few exceptions, in certain chiselled pictures at Tell-el-Amarna, and even Thebes itself, in which the artist seems to have amused himself by reproducing the beauties of nature, of groves and gardens surrounding palaces and humbler dwellings, partly for their own sake, partly attracted by some unwonted aspects of the scene which seem to have been borrowed from neighbouring countries.

In most cases the Egyptian sculptor made man the centre and *raison d'être* of his work, and yet, here and there, he shows himself curiously solicitous as to the effective arrangement of the scene

---

[1] *Description de l'Égypte, Antiquités*, vol. iii. p. 42.

[2] BELZONI (*Narrative of the Operations*, etc. pp. 343-365) mentions the presence of this stucco upon the colossi of Rameses at Ipsamboul as well as on the walls of the tombs in the Bab el-Molouk.

[3] This point is very well brought out by RHIND (*Thebes, its Tombs and their Tenants*, etc., pp. 24-25).

about him. It is not without reason, therefore, that some have found in the Egyptian bas-relief, the origin, the first rough sketch, of those landscapes of which *Hellenistic*, or as some would say. *Alexandrian*, art was so fond. One of the most famous of these is the *Palestrina mosaic*, which presents us with an Egyptian landscape during the inundation; its buildings, its animals, and the curious scenes caused by the rising Nile, are rendered with great vivacity.[1]

§ 8. *Gems.*

A highly civilized society like that of Egypt even in the days of the Ancient Empire, must have felt the necessity for some kind of seal. The names and images engraved upon rings must have been used as signatures even at that early date. We know that from that time forward the impressions thus made upon wax and clay were employed in business and other transactions. No engraved stones have come down to us from the early dynasties, and yet their production must have been easy enough to those who carved the diorite statue of Chephren. Under the first Theban Empire, the Egyptians practised the cutting of amethysts, cornelians, garnets, jasper, lapis-lazuli, green-spar and white feldspar, obsidian, serpentine, steatite, rock crystal, red quartz, sardonyx, &c.[2] We do not know whether those early workmen employed the lapidary's wheel or not,[3] but we may safely say that they produced some of the finest works of the kind which are known to us. The annexed illustration of one of the rarest treasures of the Egyptian collection in the Louvre, will bear out our words (Fig. 241).

"A gold ring with a movable square stone, a sardonyx, upon which a personage seated before an altar is engraved with extra-

[1] M. MASPERO was the first to start this theory in his paper entitled *Les Peintures des Tombeaux Égyptiens et la Mosaïque de Palestrine.*

[2] BIRCH, *Guide to (British) Museum*, pp. 70-74. — PIERRET, *Catalogue de la Salle Historique.* Nos. 457, 559. *passim.*

[3] M. SOLDI remarks, in connection with the Mexicans, that they managed to cut the hardest rocks and to engrave finely upon the emerald with nothing but bronze tools. Prescott and Humboldt bear witness to the same fact. The Peruvians also succeeded in piercing emeralds without iron. Their instrument is said to have been the pointed leaf of a wild plantain, used with fine sand and water. With such a tool the one condition of success was time (*Les Arts Méconnus*, pp. 352-359).

ordinary finish. The altar bears the name *Ha-ro-bes*. The figure is clothed in a *schenti*; a thick necklace is about his neck : his hair is in short thick curls : his legs are largely and firmly drawn.

"We are helped to the date of this little work by the engraving on the reverse, which represents a king wearing the red crown and armed with a mace, with which he is about to strike an enemy whom he grasps by the hair. The name of this king is engraved beside him : *Ra-en-ma*, that is Amenemhat III. The workmanship of this face is, perhaps, inferior to that of the obverse, the forms are comparatively meagre and dry ; it is however far from being bad."[1]

The cornelian statuette of Ousourtesen I., which the Louvre has unhappily lost, belonged to the same period. In the three days of

FIG. 241.—Intaglio upon sardonyx, obverse. Louvre collection. Twice the actual size.

FIG. 242.—Reverse of the same intaglio.

July, 1830, a terrible fire was directed upon the crowd by the Swiss stationed in the colonnade of the Louvre. The assailants succeeded, however, in penetrating into the palace and invading the galleries. After their final retirement the only thing which was ascertained beyond a doubt to be missing, was this little statuette, which has never been heard of since. It was equally valuable for its rarity and the beauty of its workmanship.[2]

The artists of the Second Theban Empire do not seem to have excelled those of the first, but their works have come down to us in much greater numbers. The Louvre possesses a considerable number of rings engraved with the names Thothmes, Amenophis,

---

[1] PIERRET, *Catalogue de la Salle Historique*. No. 457.
[2] A description of it will be found in CHAMPOLLION. *Notice Descriptive des Monuments Égyptiens du Musée Charles X.*, 2nd edition, 1827. p. No. 14, p. 55.

and others belonging to the eighteenth and nineteenth dynasties. Their character may be divined from two examples.

"In 1877 the Louvre obtained the stone of a ring finely engraved on each side with representations of the Pharaoh Thothmes II. It is a green jasper, quadrangular in shape. On one side the Pharaoh, designated by his name *Aa-kheper-ra*, has seized a lion by the tail and is about to strike it with his mace.

Fig. 243.—Intaglio upon jasper. Louvre. Actual size.

Fig. 244.—Reverse of the same intaglio.

This scene is emblematic of the victorious and fearless strength of the sovereign. Its rarity is extreme. Its significance is enforced by the word *kuen* or valour (Fig. 243). On the other side Thothmes is shown discharging his arrows from the commanding height of his chariot against the enemies who face him; one falls backwards, another is being trampled under the feet of the king's horses (Fig. 244). Such a representation is common enough upon

Fig. 245.—Seal of Armais. Louvre. Actual size.

the outsides of the temples, but it is not often found upon little objects like these."[1]

Sometimes the ring is all of one material, characters and figures being cut in the metal of which it consists. It is so in the case of

---

[1] P. Pierret, *Une Pierre Gravée au Nom du Roi d'Égypte Thoutmès II.* (*Gazette Archéologique*, 1878, p. 41). This stone is placed in Case P of the *Salle Historique* in the Louvre. M. Lenormant has kindly placed at our disposal the *clichés* of the double engraving which was made for M. Pierret's article.

the most conspicuous object among the Egyptian jewels in the Louvre (Fig. 245), an object which can never have been intended for the finger; it is too large: it must have been made for use only as a seal. It is thus described by M. Pierret: "Seal formed of a ring and movable bezel, both of gold. Upon one face of the bezel the oval of King Armais, the last prince of the eighteenth dynasty, is engraved. Upon the other a lion *passant*, the emblem of royal power; it is surmounted by the words *Nep-khopesch*, lord of valour. Upon the third and fourth sides are a scorpion and a crocodile respectively. The execution of this little work is admirable; the design and action of the lion are especially fine."[1]

The ring given by Pharaoh to Joseph as a sign of the authority delegated to him, may have been such as this.[2] The cheapest rings had bezels of faience or schist covered with enamel. The scarabs were cut as a rule from soft stone.

In gem-cutting the Egyptians made use both of the intaglio process and of relief, but the greater fitness of the former for the work to be done by a signet made it their especial favourite. They were ignorant of the process we call cameo, in which the differently coloured layers of the sardonyx are taken advantage of to produce contrast of tint between the relief and its bed.

A few Egyptian cylinders, in earthenware or soft stone enamelled, are known. They bear royal ovals: the British Museum has one which seems to date from the twelfth dynasty. Their employment seems never to have become very general.[3]

§ 9. *The Principal Conventions in Egyptian Sculpture.*

Whether it were employed upon wood, upon limestone, or upon the harder rocks, whether it were cutting colossi in the flanks of the sandstone hills, or carving the minute images of its gods and kings in the stone of a signet ring, the art of Egypt never shook itself free from those intellectual conceptions which were impressed upon its first creations; it remained true to the

---

[1] PIERRET, *Catalogue de la Salle Historique*, No. 481.
[2] Genesis xli. 42.
[3] BIRCH, *History of Ancient Pottery*, p. 72. PIERRET, *Catalogue de la Salle Historique du Louvre*, Nos. 499, 500, 505.

tendencies of its infancy ; it preserved the same fundamental qualities and defects; it looked upon nature with the same eyes, and interpreted her in the same fashion, from the first moment to the last.

These methods and processes, and the conventionalities of artistic interpretation which maintained themselves through all the changes of taste, have still to be considered. They are the common features by which works which differ greatly in execution are brought into connection, and are to be found as clearly marked in a statue dating from the time of Amasis and Nectanebo as in one from the Ancient Empire.

Some of the conventions of Egyptian art are to be explained by the constitution of the human mind and by the conditions under which it works when it attempts plastic reproductions for the first time ; others appear to spring from certain habits of thought peculiar to Egyptian civilization. There is yet a third class which must be referred to purely technical causes, such as the capabilities of the materials and tools employed. The influence which these exercised over the artistic expression of thought has been too often underrated. We shall endeavour to recognize their full importance.

When we glance at an Egyptian bas-relief, we perceive in it certain imperfections of rendering which we may have often noticed before, either in the early works of other races or in the formless designs which quite young children scribble upon paper. The infancy of art and the art of infancy have much in common.

We are accustomed to processes which are scientifically exact. Profiting by the accumulated learning of so many centuries even the school-boy, among us, understands perspective. We are, therefore, apt to feel too much surprise at the awkwardness and inaccuracy which we find in the works of primitive schools, in transcripts produced by man in the presence of nature without any help from the experience of older civilizations. If we wish to do justice to those early artists, we must endeavour to realize the embarrassment which must have been theirs, when they attempted to reproduce upon a flat surface those bodies which offered themselves to their eyes with their three dimensions of height, width, and depth, and with all the complications arising from foreshortening and perspective, from play of light and shade, and from varied colour. Other perplexities must have arisen from the intersection and variety of lines, from the succession of planes, from the necessity for rendering or at least suggesting the thickness of objects!

When the desire to imitate natural objects began to make itself felt in man he received his first drawing lesson from the sun. Morning and evening its almost horizontal rays threw his silhouette sharply upon the white rocks and walls, and nothing was easier than to fix the outline of the image thus projected with a piece of charcoal or burnt wood; after this beginning it was easy to imitate such a sun-picture either in large or in small. Such figures were of necessity profiles, as the silhouette given by a head viewed in front would be very uncertain and indistinct.

The profiles of men and of the lower animals must, then, have played a chief part in these early efforts towards design. In this there is nothing at variance with our daily experience. The back view need hardly be taken into account, and there are two lateral positions, the right and left profiles, against one for the front face. Finally, the fact that the front face consists of two parts which have to be kept in absolute symmetry with one another, makes it much more difficult of treatment by the novice. Even in the productions of skilful artists we often find that this symmetry has been missed. It is the profile that is first attacked by beginners in the art of drawing, and it is the profile which always remains most comprehensible for simple intelligences. The fellah who is present at the opening of one of those tombs which were constructed by his remote ancestors, at once recognizes the animals represented and the meaning of their attitudes and grouping. Wilkinson noticed this on several occasions. But if an European drawing be shown to the same man, he will be hopelessly bewildered by the foreshortening, the perspective, and the play of light and shade. He will no longer be able to distinguish a bull from a horse or an ass.

In their bas-reliefs, and in their paintings, the Egyptian artists made almost exclusive use of the profile,[1] but, by a singular compromise, we sometimes find it combined with an attitude of

---

[1] In turning over the leaves of Champollion we have found but two exceptions to this rule. In the Temple of Seti, at Gournah, that king is shown, in a bas-relief, in the act of brandishing his mace over the heads of his prisoners. The group is the usual one, but in this case two of the vanquished are shown in full face (pl. 274). At the Ramesseum, also, one man in a long row of prisoners is shown in a similar attitude (pl. 332).

body which would strictly require a full, or at least a three-quarter face. The silhouette in its integrity seems to have been thought insufficient, and the desire to reproduce a more complete image led them to invent the compromise in question.

In Egyptian profiles the eye is drawn as if for a full face. It has been asserted that this is the result of profound calculation, that, " in spite of facts, the Egyptian painter chose to give predominant importance to that organ in the human visage which is the window of the soul."[1] We believe that the true explanation is rather more simple. While the lines of the nose and mouth are more clearly marked in the profile than in the front face, it is in the latter only that the eye is able to display its full beauty. When seen from the side it is small, its lines are short and abrupt, and the slightest change in the position of the head affects its contours in a fashion which is very puzzling to the unlearned artist. When a child attempts to draw a head it gives their true form to the lips and the nose, but in nine cases out of ten it draws the eye as if seen in full face; and art in its childhood did as children do still.

We find a similar want of concord between the trunk and the limbs. Feet and legs are shown in profile while the body to which they belong stands squarely facing us. Both the shoulders are seen in equal fulness, and the attachment of the arms is often faulty (Fig. 246). Sometimes they seem to be broken at the shoulder. Again, the hands are nearly always in such a position as to exclude all doubt as to the number of fingers they possess.

It appears, therefore, that the artist chose the aspect which seemed to him the most natural for each part of the body. It was the resulting contradiction that was against nature. The feeling from which it sprang was identical with that which led Egyptian artists to make what we may call " projections " when they wished to represent buildings. The fixed idea of the draughtsman was to show all the sides of his object at a glance, to exhibit details which in reality were partly hidden by each other. Thus we find that, in certain bas-reliefs, both clothes and the nudity which those clothes were intended to cover are carefully portrayed. In a bas-relief at Tell-el-Amarna, a queen who is waiting on Amenophis IV. is dressed in a long robe reaching to her feet, and yet all her forms

---

[1] CH. BLANC, *Grammaire des Arts du Dessin.* p. 469.

are rendered with as much care and detail as if there were no veil between their beauty and the eye of the spectator (Fig. 247).

An arbitrary combination of a similar character is employed by the Egyptian artist when he wishes to show a number of persons behind one another on a horizontal plane; he places them vertically one above the other. The great battle pictures at Thebes are an instance of this (Fig. 13, Vol. I.). Enemies still fighting are mingled with dead and wounded into one confused heap in front of Pharaoh's car, and reach from top to bottom of the relief. The same convention is to be found in the ranks of prisoners, workmen, or

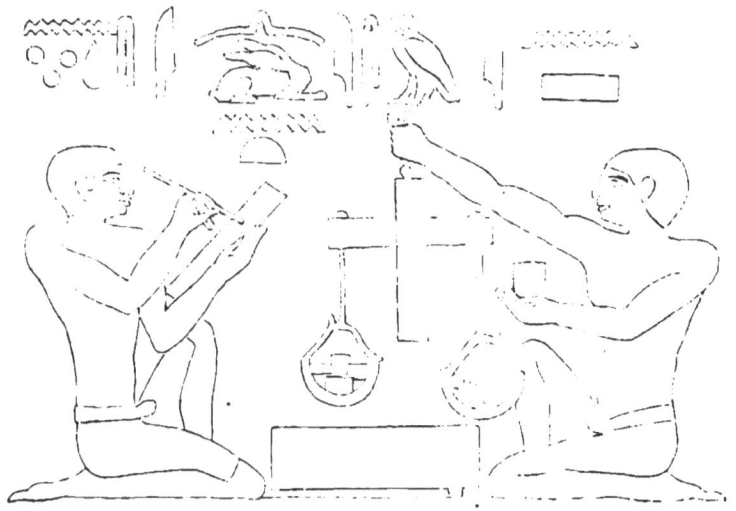

FIG. 246.—Bas-relief from Sakkarah. Fifth dynasty.

soldiers, marching over a flat surface; they are arranged in a kind of echelon upon the field of the relief (Fig. 42).[1]

[1] For other conventional methods, of a similar though even more remarkable kind but of less frequent occurrence, see WILKINSON, *Manners and Customs*, etc., vol. ii. p. 295. The same ruling idea is found in those groups in the funerary bas-reliefs, which show husband and wife together. The wife's arm, which is passed round the body of the husband, is absurdly long (LEPSIUS, *Denkmæler*, part 11. plates 13, 15, 91, 105, etc.; and our Figs. 164 and 165, Vol. I.). This is because the sculptor wished to preserve the loving gesture in question without giving up the full view of both bodies to which his notions committed him. One could not be allowed to cover any part of the other, they could not even be brought too closely together. They were placed, therefore, at such a distance apart that the hand which appears round the husband's body is too far from the shoulder with which it is supposed to be connected.

Faulty though these conventions seem to us, they did not disturb the Egyptian spectator. He was familiar with them by long usage, and his intellect easily re-established the true relation between the various parts of objects so strangely distorted. Even as art matured and as, in some respects, the skill of the Egyptian sculptor increased, he never felt himself impelled to abandon these primitive methods of interpretation. Graphic conventions are

FIG. 247.—The Queen waiting on Amenophis IV.; Tell-el-Amarna. From Prisse.

like those belonging to written and spoken language ; when once established, even those which seem most absurd to the stranger are rendered acceptable by habit, and the native does not even suspect the existence of anomalies which bewilder the foreign visitor.

Speaking generally, we may say that there is no perspective in Egyptian paintings and reliefs. And yet we find sincere efforts to render things in a less arbitrary fashion in certain works dating from the Second Theban Empire. Look, for instance, at the attempt made by an artist in the tomb of Chamhati to show five persons walking almost in line. Instead of being one above another they are on one level (Fig. 248). One of the five is rather behind the rest; the head and most of his body are visible. The other four advance to their front. In order that they may all be seen, the sculptor has shown them as they would appear to one standing on their right and slightly in front; the relief,

FIG. 248.—Bas-relief from the eighteenth dynasty. From Prisse.

therefore, has four planes. The three farther figures are shown by the contours alone. This is perspective, although it is hardly correct. The retreating line of polls sinks as it should, but so do the elbows, and they ought to rise.

This relief gives evidence of considerable progress and, supposing it to be the first of its kind, the sculptor who made it would deserve the credit of having breathed a new life into Egyptian art. But he was not the first; others had made use of the same method, but always within strictly defined limits. It was employed when a few persons had to be brought in who were all in one attitude and making the same gesture,[1] but it was never used as a starting-point for modifications upon the traditional modes of rendering either isolated figures or groups of figures. The Egyptians made use of these until the last days of their civilization without ever appearing to suspect their childish character.

In the case of animals, a firmly-drawn profile was enough to make them easily recognizable. And yet, even in the time of the Ancient Empire, we find distinct efforts to give some variety to these silhouettes. Sometimes the oxen turn their heads towards the spectator, sometimes they swing them round to their flanks, as if to chase away the flies : but even then the heads are shown in profile.[2] At Beni-Hassan we find an advance upon this. In a hunting scene, a lion, who has just brought down an ibex, is shown full face,[3] but neither here or anywhere else has an attempt been made to draw the body of the animal otherwise than in profile.

In his family groups the Egyptian sculptor marked the superiority of the husband and father in a similarly naïve fashion. He made him much taller than the persons about him. The same contrivance was employed to mark the distinction between gods or kings and ordinary men, and between the latter and animals (Fig. 57, Vol. I.). This solution of the problem is universal in the infancy of art. It was adopted by the Assyrians, the Persians, the primitive Greeks, and our own ancestors of the middle ages. It is easier to give a figure double or threefold its proper size than to add greatly to the dignity and nobility of its character.

In their desire to evade difficulties, the Egyptians slurred over distinctions upon which a more advanced art would have insisted. For them every man was in the prime of life, every woman possessed of the elegant contours of a marriageable virgin. In their work in the round they proved themselves capable of bringing out individuality, but they restricted their attentions to the face and hardly attempted to show how the passage of years affects the contours and the firmness of flesh in both sexes. In their

---

[1] Our Fig. 216 gives another instance of the employment of this method, and even in the time of the Ancient Empire the idea had occurred to the Egyptian artists (Fig. 200).
[2] LEPSIUS, *Denkmæler*, part ii. pl. 47 and 61.
[3] WILKINSON, *Manners and Customs*, etc. vol. ii. p. 88.

bas-reliefs and pictures, they employed outline only. The substance of their figures was modelled neither materially nor in colour. With such feeble resources as these the artist would have had great difficulty in suggesting all the differences of age. He therefore took a middle course. To each sex he gave that appearance which seemed best calculated to bring out its peculiar beauties. The one he portrayed in the fulness of manhood, the other as a young girl. When it was necessary to determine the age of his subject with some precision he took refuge in such conventional signs as the finger in the mouth and the long lock of infancy (Fig. 249).

The sculptors of the Ancient Empire, who laid such stress upon exact resemblance, seem to have now and then attempted to mark the advancing age of their models. The head of the great statue of Chephren is that of a man still young (Fig. 204); that of another statue of the same king betrays the approach of old age. This example does not seem to have been followed in later ages. We are tempted to think that each sovereign on his accession to the throne employed some artist of note to make his portrait. The latter would set himself to work; would study his model at first hand, for Pharaoh would perhaps condescend to sit to him; would bring out the peculiarities of visage which he saw, and over the whole face and form of the king would spread that air of flourishing vigour and youth which is common to nearly all the royal statues. An image would be thus elaborated which should combine both the truth of portraiture with the conventional semi-divine type. With the passage of time, according to the talent of the artist, and perhaps to the character of the royal features, one of these elements would encroach upon the other. But once established this image would become a kind of official and authentic standard of the royal appearance, and would serve as a model for all who might be charged during the rest of the reign with the reproduction of the king's person.

FIG. 249.—Horus as a child, enamelled earthenware. Actual size. Louvre.

There are many facts which support this hypothesis. Among the countless images of Rameses II. for instance there are some which according to their inscriptions must have been executed when he was at least eighty years old; and yet they show him as a young man.

Almost the same thing takes place in our own times. In monarchical states the sovereign appears upon the coinage as he was at his accession. His features and the delicacy of his skin are unaffected by the years, for the die made in his youth has to serve for his old age. We may almost say the same of the statues and busts in which the royal features are repeated in the public buildings and public places of the capital. A single portrait which has once been moderately faithful is repeated to infinity. We find it everywhere, upon paper, and canvas, and plaster, and marble, multiplied by every process that science has given to art. It keeps its official and accepted authenticity long after age, care, and disease, have made its original unrecognizable.[1]

There is one convention peculiar to Egyptian art which is not to be accounted for so easily as the last named. So far as we know, no reason has ever yet been given for the almost invariable habit of making such figures as are supposed to be walking thrust their left legs forward. Almost the only exceptions are in the cases of those figures in the bas-reliefs which are turned to the spectator's left. The right leg is then thrust forward (Figs. 18, 24, &c., Vol. I.). Among works in the round there is hardly an exception to the ordinary rule. Are we to look upon it as the effects of caprice? of accident confirmed into a habit? Or was it a result of a superstition analogous, or, rather, contrary to that of the Romans? The latter always took care to cross a threshold with the right foot foremost; in Egypt they may have attached the same ideas to the left foot. Egyptologists should be able to tell us whether there is anything in the texts to suggest the existence of such a superstition.

Apart from its ethnic characteristics, the work of the Egyptian sculptor is endowed with a peculiar physiognomy by a certain stiffness and rigidity which it hardly ever succeeds in shaking

---

[1] M. ÉMILE SOLDI (*La Sculpture Égyptienne*) tells us that during the reign of Napoleon III. such representations of the Emperor as were not taken from the portrait by Winterhalter were forbidden to be recognized officially.

off, even when it represents figures in motion. A support in the shape of a column at the back is nearly always introduced; the arms are held close to the sides; a huge head-dress often enframes the head and hangs down upon the shoulders in two equal masses; a long and narrow beard springs from under the chin and lies upon the chest.

Freedom and variety of attitude is equally absent from the seated statues. The knees are brought together and the hands supported upon them. We never find an arm raised, a hand opened as if to give force to speech, or a leg stretched out to relieve the stiffness of the lines. There is no striving for that suppleness of limb and variety of pose which the Greeks contrived to obtain even in their Iconic figures. The face is often full of animation and individual vitality, the modelling of the trunk and limbs marvellously true and broad, but the body as a whole is too symmetrical in action and entirely without *abandon*. The natural movements which spring from ease and liberty are never employed. Forced and conventional attitudes are universal.

A reason for this has been sought in the supremacy of the sacerdotal caste. The priests, we are told, must soon have adopted such a type, or rather several varieties of such a type, as seemed to them expressive of their own ideas of man when deified by death, of the king as the son of the gods, of the gods themselves as the protectors of the Egyptian race. They imposed the perpetuation and constant reproduction of this type upon artists as a sacred duty, and thus the Egyptian style was *hieratic* in its origin and essence.

Such an assertion is easily made. *Hieratic* is one of those convenient adjectives whose vagueness discourages critical examination. What evidence is there that ancient Egypt was ever a theocracy, in the proper sense of the word? Only once, during so many centuries, did the Egyptian priests attempt to encroach upon the privileges of the king. Towards the close of the twentieth dynasty the prophets of Amen, at Thebes, tried hard to substitute their own authority for that of the last of the Rameses,[1] but the success of their usurpation was very shortlived. In Ethiopia alone, among a people much less highly civilized, sacerdotalism seems to have acquired an uncontested pre-eminence. In Egypt the king was always the first of the

[1] MASPERO, *Histoire Ancienne*, p. 272.

priests. With the help of an army of scribes and officials he governed the country and made war; he initiated and carried on great public works; he developed the industry and commerce of his subjects. Trade and conquest brought him into relation with surrounding peoples, and from them he recruited his armies and obtained agents of every kind.

The active and warlike heads of a great empire like this were never the slaves of a despotic clergy. Such a society never allowed the mechanical reproduction of orthodox types to be forced upon its artists, until, indeed, its final decadence deprived it of all power to invent new forms. We have seen how great was the variety of plan and decoration in Egyptian religious architecture, from the marked simplicity of the temple near the sphinx, to the sumptuous majesty of the Theban buildings and the elegance of those of Sais. The style and taste of Egyptian sculpture underwent a change at each renascence of art. Why, then, did its practitioners remain faithful to certain conventional methods of interpretation, whose falsity they must have perceived, while they modified their work in so many other particulars? No text has ever been put before us, I will not say from a Greek, but from an Egyptian source, which suggests that their hands were less free from religious prescription than those of the architects.

We agree with M. Émile Soldi, who was the first to throw doubt upon the accepted theories, that the explanation of the apparent anomaly is to be sought elsewhere.[1] The tyranny from which the Egyptian sculptor never succeeded in completely freeing himself was not that of the priests but of the material in which he worked. Aided by his personal experience M. Soldi has put this fact very clearly before us. Being at once a sculptor, a medallist, and an engraver upon precious stones, he is enabled to judge at first hand of the influence which the material or tool employed may exercise over the style of a work of art. The style of such a work is the complex product of numerous and very different factors. To determine the part played by each of these factors is not always easy; there are too many opportunities for error. We believe, however, that certain of the most peculiar and persistent characteristics of Egyptian sculpture are due

[1] ÉMILE SOLDI, *La Sculpture Égyptienne*, 1 vol. 8vo, 1876, copiously illustrated. (Ernest Leroux.)

to the hardness of their material and the imperfection of the tools employed.

We know the connection between the funerary statues of the Egyptians and their second life; while those statues endured, the existence of the double was safe guarded. The more solid the statue, the better its chance; if the former was indestructible the life dependent upon it would be eternal. It was under the impulse of this idea that the Egyptians of the Ancient Empire attacked such unkindly materials as granite, diorite, and basalt. Such statues were beyond the reach of private individuals. They were reserved for royalty. Of all the works of the sculptor they were the most carefully and admirably wrought. They set the fashion, and helped to create those habits which did not lose their hold even when less rebellious substances came into use. How did they contrive to cut such hard rocks? Even in our time it can only be done by dint of long and painful labour and with the aid of steel chisels of the finest temper. The workman is obliged to stop every minute to renew the edge of his instrument. But it is agreed on all hands that the contemporaries of Chephren had to do without steel chisels. Egyptologists still discuss the question as to whether the Egyptians made use of iron or not, but even those who believe that its name occurs among the hieroglyphs admit that its introduction was late and its employment very restricted.[1] The weapons and tools of the early Egyptians were of bronze when they were not of stone or hardened wood; and it has never been proved that either the Egyptians or any other ancient people understood how to temper that metal in such a fashion that its hardness approached that of steel. Modern science has in vain searched for this secret.[2] In any case it is only in a few rare instances, and upon remains from the New Empire, that the peculiar markings left by the chisel have been discovered. Those statues and sarcophagi which have been cut from igneous rocks still bear traces which may be recognized by the eye of the connoisseur, of the processes which were employed by their makers.

---

[1] See the note of M. CHABAS, "*Sur le nom du fer chez les Anciens Égyptiens.*" (*Comptes Rendus de l'Académie des Inscriptions.* January 23, 1874.)

[2] Certain alloys, however, have recently been discovered which give a hardness far above that of ordinary bronze. The metal of the Uchatius gun, which has been adopted by Austria, is mixed, for instance, with a certain quantity of phosphorus.

"Granite," says M. Soldi, "is most easily worked by hammering its surface. To begin with, a heavy tool called a *point* is brought into play. This is driven into the material by repeated blows from the hammer, starring the surface of the granite, and driving off pieces on all sides. We believe that this *point* was the habitual instrument of the Egyptians, not only in roughing out their blocks, but even in modelling a head-dress or sinking a hieroglyph. Such a tool could not trace clear and firm contours like those of the chisel, and the peculiar character of its workmanship is to be easily recognized in the broken and irregular outline of many of the monuments in the Louvre."

Another tool employed upon granite in these days is a kind of hammer, the head of which consists of several *points* symmetrically arranged. We may judge of its effects by the appearance of our curb stones, which are dressed by it; there is nothing to show that it was used by the Egyptians. A kind of hatchet with two blades is also used for the same work, and it appears to have been employed by the Egyptians, "who used it hammer fashion, beating the surface of the material, and driving off chips of various sizes according to the weight of the instrument. By these means the desired form could be given with sufficient rapidity and precision to make the chisel superfluous." Most of the Egyptian statues in hard stone seem to have been modelled by the help of an instrument of this kind.

"The surfaces produced by such tools as these had to be polished, the sketchy roughness left by the *point* had to be taken down; we find therefore that the Egyptians always polished their statues."

The Egyptians do not seem to have known either the *file* or the *rasp*, a variety of file which is now greatly employed. The dry markings left by those tools are nowhere to be seen. In the case of broad surfaces it is probable that a polish was given by hand boards sprinkled with powdered sandstone and wetted through a hole in the middle. Flat stones may have sometimes replaced these wooden disks. When a more brilliant polish was required, emery must have been used. This substance was found in abundance in the islands of the Archipelago, and must have been brought to Egypt by the Phœnicians. Without it the Egyptian artists could not have produced their engraved gems.

By dint of continually retempering the bronze and renewing its edge, the sculptors of the New Empire succeeded in cutting hieroglyphs upon a certain number of works in the harder rocks. Perhaps, too, iron may by that time have come into more general use, and they may have learnt how to give it extra hardness by tempering. But when granite and kindred materials had to be cut, the work was commenced with point and hammer as above described. In the case of some of those very large figures which had been rather roughly blocked out in the first instance, the final polishing has not quite obliterated the hollows left by those rude instruments in the stone, especially where the journeyman has struck a little too hard. An instance of this may be seen on the red granite sphinx in the Louvre (Fig. 41, Vol. I.).

M. Soldi is inclined to think that at one period at least the Egyptians used stone weapons rather than metal ones in their attacks upon the harder rocks. He tells us that he himself has succeeded in cutting granites of various hardness with a common flint from the neighbourhood of Paris. He has done the same with diorite, both by driving off small chips from it and by pulverizing its surface with the help of jasper. "This method," he adds, "is excessively long and tedious, and the jasper, though harder than the diorite, is greatly damaged in the process. But yet it proves that a statue may be produced in such fashion, by dint of a great consumption of time and patience."[1] We must also remember that the hardest rocks are easier to cut when they are first drawn from the quarry, than after they have been exposed for a time to the air.

The colours in the bas-reliefs are too much conventionalized to be of any use in helping us to determine the material of which Egyptian implements were made. But the forms of all the tools of which we have been speaking are to be found there. A bas-relief in the tomb of Ti, in which the manufacture of sepulchral statues is shown, is the oldest monument which may be quoted in support of our remarks (Fig. 250). On the left two journeymen are roughly blocking out a statue. Each holds in his left hand [2] a long and slender tool which cannot be other than a chisel; this he strikes with a hammer. Two more are at work polishing another statue, upon which the chisel has finished its work. It is impossible to say whether the egg-shaped tools which they use are of

[1] SOLDI, *Les Arts Méconnus*, p. 492. (1 vol. 8vo. Leroux. 1881.)
[2] It has escaped M. Perrot's notice that one is left-handed.—ED.

stone or wood. As for the statues themselves they must be limestone figures similar to those which were actually found in the tomb of Ti (Fig. 183). In the tomb of Obai, at Gournah, we see a sculptor modelling the fore-paws of a lion (Fig. 251). His blows are vertical instead of horizontal, but his instruments are identical with those shown in the tomb of Ti. From the fifth dynasty to the time of the Rameses, the same bronze chisel and pear-shaped mallet had held their own.[1]

Two paintings at Thebes show us the process of executing a royal colossus in granite (Figs. 252 and 253). Standing upon the plinth and upon the planks of a scaffold, several workmen do their best to hasten the completion of the work, which is already far advanced. Seated upon the topmost pole of the scaffold one

FIG. 250.—Bas-relief from the tomb of Ti.

workman is busy polishing the front of the pschent; another stands behind the image, and, holding his palette in one hand and his brush in the other, spreads his colours upon its posterior support. It may be asked what the man is doing who is engaged with both hands upon the chest of the statue. For an answer to that question we must turn to the second picture, in which we are shown a seated colossus under the hands of its makers. The workman who kneels before its head is making use of two implements. With his left hand he applies to the face of the statue a pointed instrument, which he is about to strike with the object

---

[1] Upon the different kinds of chisels used by the Egyptian sculptors, see SOLDI, *La Sculpture Égyptienne*, pp. 53 and 111. He includes the toothed chisel and the gouge.

held in his right. This action will cause splinters to fly from the granite. These two instruments are the same as those wielded by the workman who leans upon the chest of the standing colossus. The latter seems, however, to pause for a moment's consideration before proceeding with his work. One of these tools is the *point* of stone or metal, the other acts as mallet or hammer. The same tool is to be recognised in the hand of the man who is at work upon the seat of the statue; he, however, uses it without any hammer.[1] Leaning upon one of the cross-pieces of the scaffolding he beats with all his force upon the stone. The work was perhaps

FIG. 251.—Bas-relief at Thebes (Champollion, pl. 180).

begun in this fashion. In the same tomb the representation of a sphinx receiving the final touches which is figured above occurs (Fig. 254). In this painting the polishing tool is a disk, similar to that in use by one of the workmen in Fig. 253. The figure on the left carries in a saucer the powder used for polishing the granite. In his right hand he holds a kind of brush which was used for spreading the powder upon the surfaces to be rubbed.

[1] This man's attitude, the shape of the tool in question, and the general significance of the composition, seem rather to suggest that he is giving the final polish to the surface of the statue. Compare him with the pschent-polisher in Fig. 252.—ED.

Fig. 255 shows a workman fashioning a *tet* with a kind of hatchet or mattock, which he uses much as if it were a mallet.

The only doubt that remains is as to the *material* employed by the Egyptian sculptors in their attacks upon the granite. Were

FIG. 252.—From a painting at Thebes (Champollion, pl. 161).

their mallets and *points* of stone or of metal? They could only dispose of instruments which, with the exception of the chisel, were incompatible with really delicate workmanship. With the latter instrument the skilful carver can obtain any effect he requires from a material which is neither too hard nor too soft—such as marble; but the rocks from which the Egyptians struck their finest work do not lend themselves kindly to the chisel. To

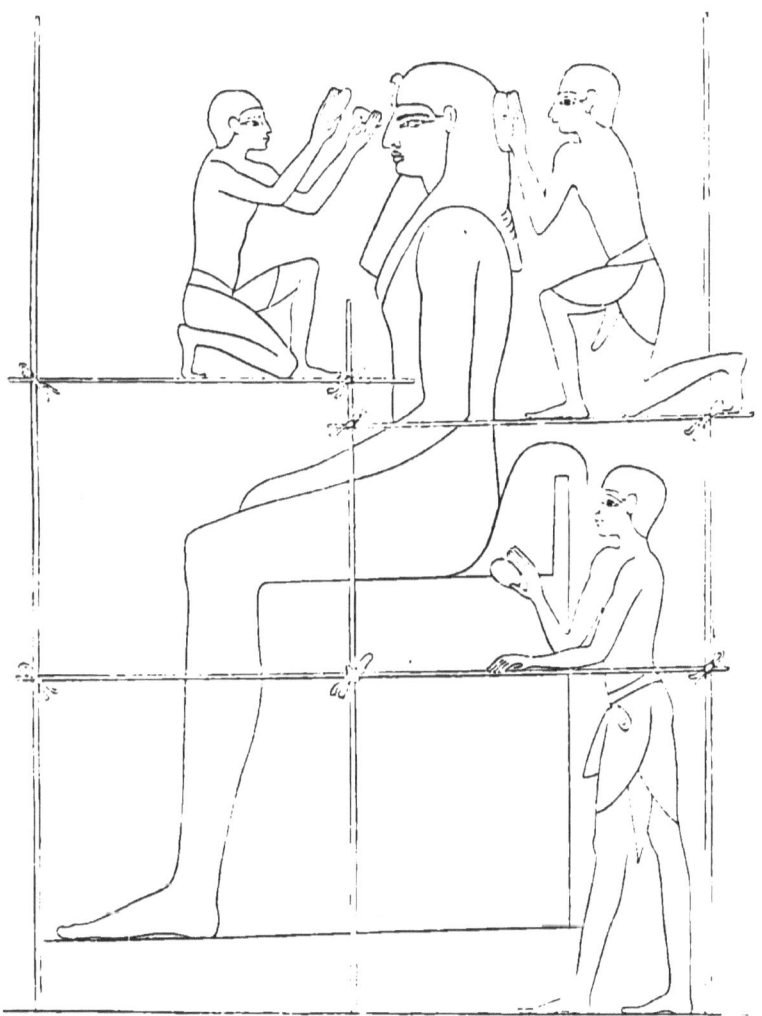

FIG. 253.—Painting at Thebes (Champollion, pl. 161).

obtain the effects required they had to expend as much time and patience upon them as upon their works of architecture. But in spite of the industry and skill of workmen who did not count their hours, there must always have been a certain inequality and rudeness in works carried out by instruments that bruised and shattered rather than cut. The stubbornness of the material, and the defects of the tools employed, had a double consequence. In order to avoid all danger of spoiling his figure when roughing it out, the artist was compelled to err on the side of over solidity and heaviness; he was obliged to multiply the points of support, and to avoid anything like delicacy or slightness of parts. On the other hand, he was forced to fine down and almost to obliterate the suggestive contours of the living form by the final polish, in order to correct the irregularities due to the rude and uncertain nature of his implements.

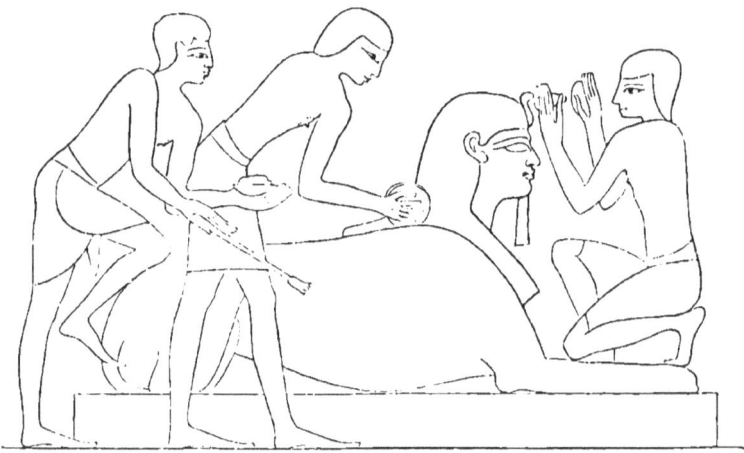

FIG. 254.—Painting at Thebes (Champollion, pl. 161).

All this explains the absolute necessity for the supporting blocks reserved by the Egyptian sculptor at the back of his statues, and for the great massiveness of their forms. To begin with, the comparative slenderness of the attachment between the head and the body was an element of danger. The repeated blows struck by the mallet upon the point might break it off unless precautions were taken. We find, therefore, that the *klaft* head-dress was introduced as often as possible. Its large ends fell down upon each breast, and acted as buttresses to the head. When the *klaft* was not used the hair was brought together in a solid mass, and, falling to the shoulders, gave strength to the neck. We may say the same of the long and thick beard, the shape of which was modified under the pressure of the same necessity. It is never disengaged and turned up at the end, as we see it in the paintings. .... The head covering, which is sometimes very tall and slender, is always supported at the back for nearly the whole of its height and width. The figure itself is supported either at the back or the side by a pier of varying thickness. . . ."[1] The stone is left between the two legs when one is thrust forward, between the arms and the side, and in the hollows above the hips. Nothing could have been easier than to remove these masses, after the work was otherwise complete, by means of the drill. But that

FIG. 255.—Painting at Thebes (Champollion, pl. 186).

instrument, by which the necessary holes could have been made without dangerous shocks, was certainly unknown to the Egyptians. They could only have removed the masses in question by the striking processes we have mentioned, processes which might result in the breaking of an arm or a leg. The hardest materials are also, in a sense, the most brittle. If it was difficult for the sculptor to free the limbs and head of his statue from the rock in which they were partly imprisoned, how much more difficult, nay, how impossible, it must have been to give them any energetic movement—that of running, for instance, or fighting. The beauty

[1] E. SOLDI, *La Sculpture Égyptienne*, pp. 41, 42.

and expressiveness of such movements did not escape his observation, but a want of material resources compelled him to forego their reproduction.

The truth of these observations is confirmed by the fact that when the chisel came to be used upon less unkindly materials, the Egyptian sculptor shook himself free of more than one of those despotic conventions which tyrannized over the makers of the royal colossi. The wooden statues have no supporting mass at the back or side; the legs are separated and free; the arms are no longer fixed to the sides, but are often bent into easy positions (Fig. 7, Vol. I., and Fig. 178). We may say the same of bronze (Figs. 179 and 180). We may judge of the freedom which was often given to works in the latter material by the beautiful little statuette figured upon this page (Fig. 256). The limestone figures are not so free. Convenient instruments for ridding them of superfluous stone were wanting, and, moreover, there was a certain temptation to imitate those statues in the harder rocks which were looked upon as the highest achievements of the national art. The figures were often supported by a mass of stone in which the posterior surfaces of the legs were imbedded.

FIG. 256.—Bronze statuette. Actual size. Boulak.

Sometimes, however, this support was absent, and in that case attitudes became extremely various (Fig. 48, Vol. I., and Figs. 192, 194, 195, Vol. II.), perfect ease and suppleness being often attained. Further confirmation of our theory is afforded by those little ornamental articles which may be referred to the industrial rather than the fine arts. In them we find the figures of men and animals introduced with the most playful and easy skill. The spontaneity of their grouping and the facility with which the most lively actions are pressed into the service of the artist, are remarkable. The graceful and almost athletic figures of swimming girls which form

THE PRINCIPAL CONVENTIONS IN EGYPTIAN SCULPTURE. 313

the handles of so many perfume spoons may be given as instances of this (Fig. 257). The qualities which are so conspicuous in these little works are absent from the official and monumental art of Egypt, because the materials and tools employed hindered their development and prevented the happy genius of the Egyptian people from reaching complete fruition.

This influence is to be recognized in the modelling as well as in the pose of Egyptian statues : their general forms are fairly well understood and expressed, but there is none of that power to suggest the muscles under the skin, and the bones under the muscles, which distinguishes Greek sculpture. The suppleness and elasticity of living flesh are entirely wanting. Everything is in its place, but details are as much suppressed as if the work were to be seen at a distance at which they would be invisible.

The admirable portraits which have been unearthed in such numbers and the skilful modelling of many an isolated work, prove that it was neither the power of observation nor that of manipulation that was wanting. Why, then, was it that the Egyptians failed to advance farther upon the road that led to mastery in their art ? It was due to their infatuation for granite. Even when they worked in soft stone their manipulation was governed by the capabilities of the more stubborn material. The chisel alone can give those truthful and delicate contours without which no sculpture can reach perfection, and the chisel could hardly be used on any material but limestone or wood. The granite or basalt statue, roughly blocked out with tools which imperfectly obeyed the hand, could only be

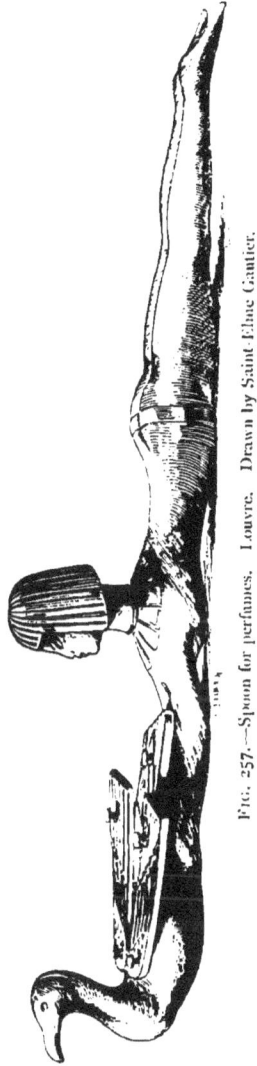

FIG. 257.—Spoon for perfumes. Louvre. Drawn by Saint-Elme Gautier.

brought to completion with the sand or emery of the polisher. No refinement of execution could be hoped for under such conditions. Every surface was flattened and every expressive ridge smoothed down, and the appearance of superficial finish thus obtained involved many sacrifices.

The abuse of this latter process is one of the great defects of Egyptian technique ; but there was another, and, perhaps, more potent cause of failure. The method of writing adopted by the Egyptians, and elaborated at a very early date, must have had a greater effect upon their plastic arts than has generally been supposed. The characters employed by them, at least in monumental situations, were not merely symbols of sounds, as the characters of later syllabic or alphabetic forms of writing became ; they were direct images of objects. Practical requirements soon led to the simplification of such objects, to the suppression of all details beyond those necessary for identification. The figures employed were thus soon reduced to mere empty outlines. Shadow and colour, all those details which distinguish the species of a genus and the individuals of a species, were carefully and systematically eliminated. The sign which stood for a lion or a man, was the same for all lions and all men, although between one man or one lion and another there are differences of stature, of age, of colour, of strength, and of beauty.

Now, in the early ages of Egyptian civilization, when the hieroglyphs in the Memphite necropolis were chiselled in relief, the same hand must have been employed upon the portraits of any particular inhabitants of a tomb and upon the inscriptions which accompanied them. Thus we find upon the panels from the tomb of Hosi (Figs. 174-6), that there is no appreciable difference between the technique of the figures and of the accompanying characters. The same firm and lively handling is visible in both. The images which play the part of written characters are much smaller than the three portraits, and that is all. The crafts of scribe and sculptor were thus combined in one man ; his chisel traced indifferently funerary portraits and hieroglyphs. When the use of papyrus led to much and rapid writing, the two professions were separated. The scribe wrote sometimes with the *kalem* upon papyrus, sometimes with the brush or the point upon wood, stucco, or stone. But he always found enough to do in his own profession without combining it with another.

Sculptors and painters multiplied on their side with the multiplication of the royal and divine images; they represented the king fighting against the enemies of Egypt or returning thanks to the gods for their assistance, and the king's subjects accompanying him to battle, or busied over the varied labours of a civilized society. They had to observe life and to study nature. By dint of so doing they created a style, a certain method of looking at and interpreting natural facts which became common to all the artists of Egypt. One of the most striking features of this style is the continual endeavour to strip form of all that is accidental and particular, to generalize and simplify it as much as possible, a tendency which finds a very natural explanation in the early endeavours of the Egyptians to represent, in their writing, the concrete shapes of every being in earth or sky. This habit of making plastic epitomes of men and animals, and even of inanimate things, was confirmed by the persistent use of ideographic characters during all the centuries of Egyptian civilization. The profession of the scribe was in time separated from that of the sculptor, but the later preserved some of the marked characteristics which it put on before this division of labour was finally established. The Egyptian eye had become accustomed to see things represented in that simplified aspect of which the hieroglyphs are so striking an example, and to deprive individuals, by a kind of unconscious abstraction, of those details by which they stood out from their species as a whole.

The most original features of Egyptian sculpture and its arrested development must, then, be referred, on the one hand to the nature of the materials employed, and, on the other, to the habits contracted during many centuries of ideographic writing.[1] It has long been the fashion to attribute capital importance to what is called a canon, in describing the origin of the Egyptian style. The ideas which have been published on this question seem to us manifestly exaggerated; we must examine them a little closely.

The word *canon* comes from the Greek κάνων, a *rule*. As applied to the arts it has been defined as "a system of measurements by the use of which it should be possible to tell the size of any part by that of the whole, or the size of the whole by that of

[1] M. CH. BLANC had a glimmering of the great influence exercised over the plastic style of Egypt by the hieroglyphs; see his *Voyage dans la Haute-Égypte*, p. 354.

any one of its parts."[1] The idea of proportion, upon which every canon must rest, is a creation of the brain. A canon, therefore, is the result of those searching and comprehensive generalizations of which only races with great intellectual gifts are capable. Each of the arts may have its canon, or rule of proportion, establishing a proper relation between all the elements of its creations and easily expressible in figures.

The finest examples of a canon as applied to architecture are furnished by the Greek orders. Given the smallest member of an Ionic or Doric order, the dimensions of all the other members of the column and its entablature may be calculated with almost complete accuracy. There is nothing of the kind in Egyptian architecture. There is no constant proportion between the heights and thicknesses of the shaft, the capital, and the entablature; there is no constant relation between their shapes. In a single building, and in a single order, we find proportions varying between one hall or court and another.

The word *canon* has an analogous sense when applied to sculpture. We establish a canon when we say that a figure should be so many heads high, and that its limbs should bear a certain proportion to the same unit. It would be the same if, as has often been proposed, the medius of the hand were erected into the unit of measurement, except that the figure would then be divided into a larger number of parts. Both ancients and moderns have investigated this question, but we need not dwell upon the results of their inquiries. The Greeks had the canon of Polycletus; the Romans that of Vitruvius, while Leonardo da Vinci set an example to the numerous artists who have investigated the question since his time.[2]

Had the Egyptians a canon ? Did they choose some one part of the human body and keep all the other parts in a constant mathematical relation with it ? Did their canon, if they had one, change with time ? Is it true that, in deference to the said canon, all the artists of Egypt living at one time gave similar proportions to their figures ?

It has sometimes been pretended that in each century the priests decided upon the dimensions, or at least upon the proportions,

---

[1] *Dictionnaire de l'Académie des Beaux-Arts*, under the word *Canon*.

[2] These researches are described in the chapter entitled *Des Proportions du Corps Humain* of M. CH. BLANC's *Grammaire des Arts du Dessin*, p. 38.

to be given by artists to their figures. Such an assertion can hardly be brought into harmony with the facts observed.

The often quoted words of Diodorus have been taken as a text: "The Egyptians claim as their disciples the oldest of the Greek sculptors, especially Telecles and Theodoros, both sons of Rhæcos, who executed the statue of the Pythian Apollo for the inhabitants of Samos. Half of this statue, it is said, was executed at Samos by Telecles, the other half at Ephesus by Theodoros, and the two parts so exactly fitted each other that the whole statue appeared to be the work of a single sculptor. After having arranged and blocked out their stone, the Egyptians executed the work in such fashion that all the parts adapted themselves one to another in the smallest details. To this end they divided the human figure into twenty-one parts and a quarter, upon which the whole symmetry of the work was regulated."[1]

We may ask what authority should attach to the words of Diodorus, a contemporary of Augustus, in a matter referring to the Pharaonic period. But when the monuments began to be examined it was proclaimed that they confirmed his statements. Figures were found upon the tomb-walls which were divided into equal parts by lines cutting each other at right angles. These, of course, were the canonical standards mentioned by Plato and Diodorus.

Great was the disappointment when these squares were counted. In one picture containing three individuals, two seated figures, one beside the other, are inscribed in fifteen of the squares ; a standing figure in front of them occupies sixteen.[2] Another figure is comprised in nineteen squares.[3] In another place we find twenty-two squares and a quarter between the sole of the foot and the crown of the head.[4] In yet another, twenty-three.[5] As for the division given by Diodorus, it never occurs at all, and in fact it is hardly to be reconciled with the natural punctuation of the human body by its articulation and points of section.

[1] DIODORUS, i. 98, 5-7.
[2] LEPSIUS, *Denkmæler*, part iii. plate 12.
[3] *Ibid.* plate 78. It is in this division into nineteen parts that M. Blanc finds his proof that the medius of the extended hand was the canonical unit. (*Grammaire*. &c. p. 46.)
[4] At Karnak, in the granite apartments. See CHARLES BLANC, *Voyage de la Haute-Égypte*, p. 232. Two figures upon the ceiling of a tomb at Assouan are similarly divided. [5] LEPSIUS, *Denkmæler*, part iii. p. 282.

To surmount the difficulty the theory of successive canons was started ; some declared for two,[1] some for three.[2] This theory requires explanation also. Do its advocates mean that in all the figures of a single epoch there is a scale of proportion so constant that we must seek for its cause in an external peremptory regulation ? If, however, we doubt the evidence of our eyes and study the plates in Lepsius or the monuments in our museums, measure in hand, we shall see at once that no such theory will hold water. Under the Ancient Empire proportions varied appreciably between one figure and another. As a rule they were short rather than tall ; but while on the one hand we encounter certain forms of very squat proportions, amounting almost to deformity (Fig. 120, Vol. I.), we also find some whose forms are very lengthy (Fig. 101, Vol. I.). The artists of Thebes adopted a more slender type, but with them too we find nothing like a rigorous uniformity. Again, the elongation of the lower part of the body is much more strongly marked in the funerary statuettes (Fig. 50, Vol. I.) and in the paintings (Plate XII.) than in statues of the natural size (Figs. 211, 216) and in the colossi. If there had been a canon in the proper sense of the term its authority would have applied as much to those statuettes and bas-reliefs as to the full-sized figures. But, as a fact, the freedom of the artist is obvious; his conception is modified only by the material in which he worked. He could not make a great statue in stone too slender below, as it would want base and solidity ; but as soon as he was easy on that score he allowed himself to be carried away by the temptation to exaggerate what seemed to him an especially graceful feature.

We see, then, that art in Egypt went through pretty much the same changes and developments as in other countries in which it enjoyed a long and busy life. Taste changed with the centuries. It began by insisting on muscular vigour, as displayed in great breadth of shoulder and thickset proportions generally. In later years elegance became the chief object, and slenderness of proportion was sometimes pushed even to weakness. In each of these periods all plastic figures naturally approached the type which happened to be in fashion, and in that sense alone is it

---

[1] ENERS, *Ægypten*, vol. ii. p. 54. PRISSE, *Histoire de l'Art Égyptien*, text, pp. 124-128.

[2] LEPSIUS, *Ueber einige Kunstformen*, p. 9. BIRCH, in WILKINSON's *Manners and Customs*, vol. ii. LEPSIUS, *Denkmæler*, part ii. pl. 9, p. 270, note 3.

just to assert that Egyptian art had two different and successive canons.

The question as to whether the Egyptians ever adopted a unit of measurement in their rendering of the human figure or not, is different. Wilkinson and Lepsius thought they had discovered such a unit in the length of the foot, Prisse and Ch. Blanc in that of the medius. There is nothing in the texts to support either theory, and an examination of the monuments themselves shows that sometimes one, sometimes the other of the two units, is most in accordance with their measurements. Between the Ancient Empire and the New proportions differed so greatly that it is impossible to refer them to one unit. Among the works of a single period we find some that may be divided exactly by one of the two; others which have a fraction too much or too little. It has not yet been proved, therefore, that the Egyptians ever adopted such a rigorous system as that attributed to them. Like all races that have greatly practised design, they established certain relations between one part of their figures and another, relations which gradually became more constant as the national art lost its freedom and vitality; and they arrived at last at the mechanical reproduction of a single figure without troubling themselves to calculate how many lengths of the head, the nose, the foot, or the medius, it might contain. Their eyes were their compasses, and they worked—at least under the New Empire and during the Græco-Roman period—from models which represented the experience of the past. It is therefore unnecessary to search for an explanation of the uniformity which characterises their works in the following of a rigid mathematical system; we must be content to see in it the natural result of an artistic education into which, as the centuries succeeded one another, the imitation of previous types, and the application of traditional recipes entered more and more.

As for the designs traced within lines which cross each other at regular intervals, they can be nothing but drawings squared for transferring purposes. *Squaring* is the usual process employed by artists when they wish to repeat a figure in different dimensions from those of the original. Having divided the latter by horizontal and perpendicular lines cutting each other at regular intervals, they go through the same operation upon the blank surface to which the figure is to be transferred, making the lines equal in number to those upon the original, but the resulting squares larger if the copy is to be larger, smaller if it is to be smaller, than that original. Egyptian decorators often made use of this process for the transference of sketches upon papyrus, stone, or wood, to the wall. Of this practice we give two examples. The first is an elaborate composition in which several modifications and corrections of lines and attitudes may be traced (Fig. 258); the second is an isolated figure (Fig. 259). In each case the figures extend vertically over nineteen squares. The first dates from the eighteenth, the second from the nineteenth dynasty.[1]

FIG. 258.—Design transferred by squaring. From Prisse.

The same device is sometimes made use of to transfer heads, and even animals, from a small sketch to the wall. In the tomb of Amenophis III., in the Bab-el-Molouk, there is a fine portrait of a prince thus squared ;[2] at Beni-Hassan we find a cow and an antelope treated in the same fashion.[3]

Traces of another and yet more simple process are to be found. Before drawing the figures in his bas-reliefs the artist sometimes marked in red on the walls the vertical and horizontal lines which would give the poise of the body, the height of the shoulders and armpits, and of the lower edge of the drawers. The positions of secondary anatomical points were marked upon

[1] PRISSE, *Histoire de l'Art Égyptien.* [2] LEPSIUS, *Denkmaeler,* part iii. pl. 70.
[3] *Ibid.* plate 152.

these lines, and the whole formed a rough guide for the hand of the designer.[1]

The fact that these lines and squares are only found upon a small number of paintings and bas-reliefs does not prove that their employment was in any way exceptional. It is probable that one of the two processes was generally used, but that the colour spread both upon figures and ground hides their traces. The few pictures in which they are now to be traced were never completed.

Most of the painters and sculptors to whom the decorations of tombs and temples were confided must have had recourse to these contrivances, but here and there were artists who had sufficient skill and self-confidence to make their sketches directly upon the wall itself. More than one instance of this has been discovered in those Theban tombs whose decorations were left unfinished. In a few cases the design has been made in red chalk by a journeyman and afterwards corrected, in black chalk, by the master.[2]

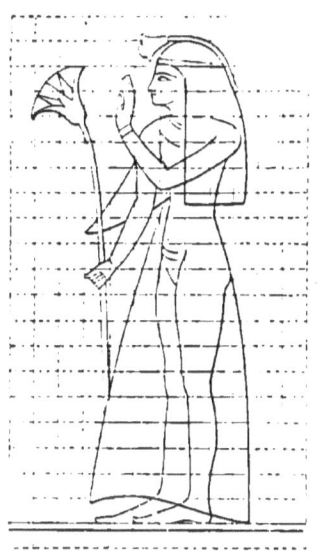

FIG. 259.—Design transferred by squaring. From Prisse.

As the bas-relief was thus preceded by a sketch which was more or less liable to modification, it would seem probable that a similar custom obtained in the case of the statue. It appears especially unlikely that those great figures in the harder

---

[1] PRISSE, *Histoire de l'Art Égyptien*, text, p. 123. LEPSIUS, *Denkmæler*, pl. 65.

[2] Upon the preparation of the bas-relief, see BELZONI, *Narrative of the Operations*, etc. p. 175.

PRISSE gives several interesting examples of these corrected designs, among others a fine portrait of Seti I. (*Histoire*, etc. vol. ii.)

"Examples of these corrections are to be found in sculpture as well as in painting. Our examination of the sculptures at Karnak showed that the artist did not always follow the first sketch traced in red ink, but that as the work progressed he modified it, and allowed himself to be guided, to some extent, by the effects which he saw

rocks which represented such an enormous outlay of manual labour, would be attacked without some guide which should preserve them from the chance of ruin by some ill-considered blow. Did the Egyptian sculptor begin, then, with a clay sketch? There is no positive information on the subject, but in all those numerous bas-reliefs which represent sculptors at work, there is not one in which the artist has before him anything in the shape of a model or sketch to guide him in his task. It is possible that the sameness of his statues, especially of his colossal figures in granite or sandstone, enabled the Egyptian to dispense with an aid which the infinite variety of later schools was to render necessary.

The Egyptian sculptor was contented with a few simple attitudes which he reproduced again and again. He doubtless began by marking the salient points and relative heights of the different parts upon his block. The rock was so hard that there was little risk of his journeymen spoiling the material by taking away too much, supposing them to be carefully overlooked. Marble would have been far more liable to such an accident. Even Michael Angelo, when he worked the marble with his own hands, spoilt more than one fine block from Carrara.

Although we have no evidence to show that the Egyptians understood the use of clay models, we have some idea of the process by which they were enabled to do without them, and of the nature of their professional education. The chief Egyptian museums possess works which have been recognized as graduated exercises in the technique of sculpture. They are of limestone, and of no great size—from four to ten inches high. The use of these little models is shown to have been almost universal by the fact that Mariette found them on nearly every ancient site that he excavated. Their true character is beyond doubt.[1] At Boulak there are twenty-seven sculptured slabs which were found at Tanis. One is no more than a rough sketch, just begun. By its side is a completed study of the same subjects. Some of these slabs are carved on both sides; on others we find one motive

growing under his hands. The western wall of the hypostyle hall contains many instances of this. It is decorated with sculptures on a large scale, in which the lines traced by the chisel differ more or less from those of the sketch. (*Description, Ant.* vol. ii. p. 445.)

[1] MARIETTE, *Notice du Musée.* Nos. 623-688.

THE PRINCIPAL CONVENTIONS IN EGYPTIAN SCULPTURE. 323

treated twice, side by side, once in the state of first sketch, and again as a finished study. The plaques which bear the heads of cynocephali, of lions and lionesses, are remarkable for the freedom of their execution (Figs. 260, 261, and 262).[1] The same

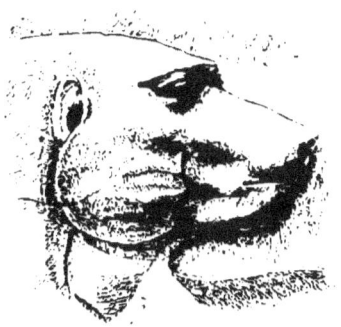

FIG. 260.—Head of a Cynocephalus.

may be said of fifteen royal heads found at Sakkarah. They should be examined together. They range[2] in order from No. 623, which is a roughly-blocked-out sketch, to 637, a finished head.

FIG. 261.—Head of a Lion.   FIG. 262.—Head of a Lioness.

One of these models is divided down the middle, so as to give accent to the profile. A few of them are squared in order to test the proportions. But even here no canon of proportion is to be

[1] Nos. 652-654 of the *Notice du Musée*.   [2] In the Boulak catalogue.

found. "If the squares were based upon some unchanging unit, they would be identical in every model in which they occur. But in one of these heads we find three horizontal divisions between the uræus and the chin; in another four. In most cases the number of the squares seems to have been entirely due to the individual caprice or convenience of the artist. There are but two examples in which another rule seems to have been followed; in them the proportions of the squares are identical, and their intersections fall upon the same points. All that may be fairly deduced from this, however, is that they are the work of the same hands."[1] A second series of royal heads was found at Tanis; others have been discovered in the Fayoum. Boulak also possesses models of the ram, the jackal, and the uræus, of arms, legs, hands, &c. Upon a plaque from Tanis the figure of Isis appears twice, once as a sketch and once as a finished study.

From the style of these remains Mariette is disposed to think that they were not earlier than the Saite epoch. As the Egyptian intellect gradually lost its inventive powers, the study of such models as these must have played a more and more important part in artistic education; but we have no reason to believe that their use was confined to the later ages of the monarchy. As artists became accustomed to reproduce certain fixed types, they gradually lost their familiarity with nature, and their works became ever more uniform and monotonous. This tendency is to be easily recognized in Egyptian work long before the days of Amasis and the Psemethcks; in some degree it is found even in the productions of the Ancient Empire. The use of the models in question may have become general at the beginning of the Middle Empire. But their introduction was not due to the priests, but to the masters in the arts, who saw that they offered a sure and rapid method of instructing their scholars.

Yet one more cause of the monotony of type which distinguished Egyptian art after its first renascence remains to be noticed. The Egyptians were fully conscious of the great antiquity of their civilization. They thought of other nations much as the Greeks and Romans of a later age thought of those whom they called barbarians. When the scribes had to speak of foreigners they

---

[1] MARIETTE, *La Galerie de l'Égypte Ancienne à l'Exposition du Trocadéro*, pp. 69, 70.

made use of a complete vocabulary of contemptuous terms, and, as always occurs, the pride of race upon which they were based long survived the condition of things which formed its justification. The Greek conquest was necessary to cure the Egyptians of their disdain, or, at least, to compel them to hide it. Now the visible sign of their superiority was the beauty of the national type, as elaborated by judicious selection and represented in art since the earliest days of the monarchy. The Egyptian was proud of himself when he compared the refined features of his gods and kings, their graceful attitudes and smiling looks, with the thick and heavy lines of the negro or the hard and truculent features of the Libyan and the Syrian nomad. In attempting to innovate, some danger of lowering the nobility of the type would be incurred. The pressure of neighbouring races ended by throwing back the Egyptian frontiers. At one time they were forcibly curtailed by victorious invasion; at others they were weakened here and there, allowing the entrance of the shepherds, of foreign merchants, and of mercenaries of various nationalities. The purity of the Egyptian blood was menaced, and at all hazards it was necessary to preserve without alteration the ideal image of the race, the concrete emblem of its glorious past and the pledge of its high destinies. It was thus that in Egypt progress was hampered by fear of retrogression. Perfection is impossible to those who fear a fall.

Another obstacle that helped to prevent the Egyptians from reaching the perfection which their early achievements seemed to promise, was their love for colour. They did not establish a sufficiently sharp line of demarcation between painting and sculpture. They always painted their statues, except when they carved them in materials which had a rich natural hue of their own, a hue to which additional vivacity was given by a high polish. By this means varied tints were obtained which were in harmony with the polychromatic decoration which was so near their hearts. Their excuse is to be found in their ignorance of statuary marble and of the clear and flesh-like tones and texture which it puts on under the sculptor's chisel.

The Egyptians, however, never committed the fault of colouring their statues in an imitative fashion, like those who make wax figures. Their hues were always conventional. Moreover, they were never either broken or shaded, which is sufficient to show that no idea of realistic imitation was implied in their use.[1] Sculpture is founded upon an artificial understanding by which tangible form and visible colour are dissociated from each other. When the sculptor looks to the help of the painter he runs great risk of failing to give all the precision and beauty of which form by itself is capable, to his work. Even the Greeks did not grasp this truth at once. The Egyptians had at least a glimmering of it, and we must thank them for having employed polychromy in their sculpture in a discreet fashion.

§ 10. *The General Characteristics of the Egyptian Style.*

We have attempted to give an idea of the origin of Greek sculpture, of its development and its decadence. We have noticed those slow changes of taste and style which sometimes required a thousand years for their evolution, for a century in Egypt was hardly equal to a generation elsewhere. After proving that Egypt did not escape the universal law of change, we studied the methods and conventions which were peculiar to her sculptors and impressed their works with certain common characteristics. The union of these characteristics formed the Egyptian style. We must now define that style, and attempt to make its originality clear to our readers.

In its commencement Egyptian art was entirely realistic. It was made realistic both by the conceptions which presided at its birth and by the wants which it was called upon to satisfy. The task to which it applied itself with a skill and conscience which are little less than marvellous, was the exact representation of all that met its vision. In the bas-relief it reproduced the every-day scenes of agricultural life and of the national worship; in the statue it portrayed individuals with complete fidelity. But even in those early ages imagination was not asleep. It was continually seeking to invent forms which should interpret its favourite ideas. It figured the exploits of the king, the defender of the national civilization, in the form of a warrior brandishing his mace over the heads of his enemies. In the royal statues everything combined to mark the gulf between the Pharaoh and his subjects, their materials,

---

[1] CH. BLANC, *Voyage de la Haute-Égypte*, p. 99.

size, attitude, and expression, although in natural life there can have been no such distinction. Finally the Great Sphinx at Gizeh is sufficient to prove that the Egyptians, in their endeavour to make the great deities whom they had conceived visible to the eye, had attempted to create composite types of which the elements were indeed existent in nature, but separate and distinct.

After the first renascence their imaginations played more freely. They multiplied the combinations under which their gods were personified. They transformed and idealized the human figure by the gigantic proportions which they gave to it in the seated statues of the king, and in those upright colossi in which the majesty of Pharaoh and the divinity of Osiris are combined in one individual. The sculptors portrayed the king in attitudes which had never been seen by mortal eyes. Sometimes he is seated upon the knee of a goddess and drawing nourishment from her breast; sometimes he bends, like a respectful and loving son, before his father Amen, who blesses him, and seems by his gesture to convey to him some of his own omnipotence and immortality. Again he is presented to us in the confusion of battle, towering so high above his adversaries that we can only wonder how they had the temerity to stand up against him. Events hardly passed thus in those long and arduous campaigns against the Khetas and the *People of the sea*, in which more than one of the Theban Pharaohs spent their lives. Victory, when it was victory, was long and hotly disputed. Superiority of discipline and armament told at last and decided the contest in favour of the Egyptians, who were inferior in strength and stature to most of their enemies, especially to those who came from Asia Minor and the Grecian islands.

It is hardly just, therefore, to say, as has been said,[1] that " Egyptian art had only one aim, the exact rendering of reality ; in it all qualities of observation are developed to their utmost capabilities, those of imagination are wanting." Egyptian art is not like the sensitized plate of the photographer. It does not confine itself to the faithful reproduction of the objects placed before it. Painters and sculptors were not content, as has been pretended, with the art that can be *seen*, as opposed to the art that can be *imagined*, and an injustice is done to them by those who would confine the latter to the Aryan race. The apparent precision of such an assertion makes it all the more misleading.

[1] E. Melchior de Vogüé, *Chez les Pharaons*.

Egyptian art was realistic in its inception and always remained so to a certain degree, but with the passage of time the creative intellect began to play a part in the production of plastic works; it added to and combined the elements which it took from nature, and thus created imaginary beings which differed from natural fact by their proportions, their beauty, and their composition. The Egyptian artist had his ideal as well as the Greek.

In saying, then, that the art of Egypt was realistic, we have only laid the first stone of the definition we wish to establish. Its original character was, perhaps, still more due to another feature, namely to its elimination or suppression of detail. This elimination, far from diminishing with time, went on increasing as the country grew older. It may be traced to the action of two causes. In the first place, the influence of the ideographic writing upon the national style can hardly be exaggerated. The concrete images of things could only be introduced into it by means of simplification and generalization. In such a school the eye learnt to despoil form of all those details which were merely accidental, of all that made it particular. It sought for the species, or even the genus, rather than the individual. This tendency was increased by the peculiar properties of the materials upon which the Egyptians lavished their skill and patience. The harder rocks turned the edges of their bronze chisels, and compelled them to choose between roughly-blocked-out sketches and a laborious polish which obliterated all those minor details of modelling which should vary according to the sex, the age, and the muscular exertion of the persons represented. We see, then, that the rebellious nature of the granite, and the imperfect methods which it imposed, completed the lessons begun by that system of figured writing which dates from the remotest periods of Egyptian civilization.

There is an obvious contradiction between the tendency which we have just noticed, and those habits of realistic imitation whose existence has been explained by the desire to secure a posthumous existence for the dead. The history of Egyptian sculpture, is, in fact, the history of a contest in the mind of the artist between these two opposing forces. In the early years of the monarchy, his first duty was to supply a portrait statue, the chief merit of which should lie in the fidelity of its resemblance. Of this task he acquitted himself most skilfully and conscientiously, reproducing every individual peculiarity, and even deformity of his model. His chief attention was given to the face, as being the member by which men are principally distinguished one from another. Even then, and in the funerary statues, the body was much more general in its forms than the head. In the course of succeeding ages the sculptor was able, whenever he wished to make a faithful portrait either of an individual man or of a race, to bring this faculty into play and to clearly mark the differences between races or between the individuals of a race, by the varying character of the head. But yet his art showed an ever increasing tendency to follow the bent which had been given to it by the practice of glyptic writing, and by the long contest with unkindly materials. After the close of the Ancient Empire Egyptian art became ambitious of a higher style. Under the Theban Pharaohs it worked hard to attain it, and it knew no better means to the desired end than the continual simplification and generalization of form.

This is the great distinguishing characteristic of the Egyptian style. The uniformity, stiffness, and restraint of the attitudes, the over-rigorous symmetry of the parts and of the limbs, and the close alliance of the latter with the bodies, are only secondary features. We shall find them in the works of every race compelled to make use of materials that were either too hard or too soft. Moreover, these are the constant characteristics of archaic art, and it must not be forgotten that even in Egypt many wooden and limestone figures have been unearthed which surprise us by the freedom of their attitudes and movements. The true originality of the Egyptian style consists in its deliberately epitomizing that upon which the artists of other countries have elaborately dwelt, in its lavishing all its executive powers upon chief masses and leading lines, and in the marvellous judgment with which it seizes their real meaning, their proportions, and the sources of their artistic effect.

As figures increased in size this tendency towards the suppression of detail increased also, and so too did their fitness for the architectonic *rôle* they had to play. The colossi which flank the entrances to an Egyptian temple have been often criticised from an erroneous standpoint. They have been treated as if they were meant to be self-sufficient and independent. Their massiveness and want of vitality have been blamed; it has been said that the seated figures could not rise, nor the standing ones walk. To form a just estimate of their merit we must take them with the monuments of which they formed a part. We must rouse our imaginations, and picture them to ourselves with their flanking colonnades about them, with the pylons at their backs, and the obelisks at their sides. We must close our eyes for a moment and reconstruct this combination of architectural and sculpturesque lines. We shall then readily perceive how entirely these colossi were in harmony with their surroundings. Their vertical and horizontal lines echoed those of the monument to which they were attached. The rhythm of the long colonnades was carried on by their repetition of a single attitude, while their colossal dimensions and immovable solidity brought them into complete accord with the huge structures by which they were surrounded. It has been said that, more than any of its rivals, " the architecture of Egypt impresses us with the idea of absolute stability, of infinite duration." Could anything be in more complete harmony with such an art than the grave and majestic attitudes of these seated Pharaohs, attitudes which from every line breathe a profound calm, a repose without change and without end.

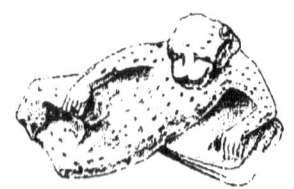

CHAPTER IV.

PAINTING.

§ 1. *Technical Processes.*

MOST of our observations upon Egyptian sculpture are applicable to the sister art of painting. The conventions which form the characteristic originality of the Egyptian style were established by the sculptor ; but when the artist had to draw the outline of a form, and to fill it in with colour instead of cutting it upon the naked surface of the wall, the difference of process did not affect his method of comprehending and interpreting his models. We find the same qualities and the same defects. The purity of line, the nobility of pose, the draughtsmanship at once just and broad, the ignorance of perspective, and the constant repetition of traditional attitudes are found in both methods. Painting, in fact, never became an independent and self-sufficing art in Egypt. It was commonly used to complete sculpturesque effects, and it never freed itself from this subordination. It never attempted to make use of its own peculiar resources for the expression of those things which sculpture could not compass—the depths of space, the recession of planes, the varieties of hue which passion spreads over the human countenance, and the nature and intensity of the feelings which are thus betrayed. We may say that it is only by some abuse of terms that we can speak of *Egyptian painting* at all. No people have spread more colour upon stone and wood than the Egyptians ; none have had a more true instinct for colour harmony ; but yet they never attempted to express, by the gradation of tone, by the juxtaposition or superposition of tints, the real aspects of the surfaces which present themselves to our eyes, aspects which are unceasingly modified by the amount of light or shadow, by distance and the state of the atmosphere. They had not the least glimmering of what we call chiaroscuro or of aerial perspective.

Their painting rests upon conventions as audacious as those of their sculpture. In it every surface has an uniform and decided value though in nature everything is shaded. A nude figure is all one colour—dark for a man, light for a woman. A drapery has but one tone, the artist never seeming to trouble himself whether it be in light or shadow, or partly in one partly in the other. In a few plates in Lepsius, and still more in Prisse,[1] there are suggestions that an artist here and there, more skilful than his rivals, understood that values differed, and distinguished in his more careful work between colour in shadow and colour in light. One or two contours appear to hint at the rotundity of chiaroscuro. In accepting such a suggestion, however, we should be making a mistake against which we have been warned even by such early travellers as the authors of the *Description*.[2] The effects in question must be placed to the credit of the sculptor. The images in which they appear are painted bas-reliefs, and the slight shadow thrown by their salient grounds gives an appearance of half-tint to their contours. Wherever pictures are without relief there is no such appearance, and yet changes of value would in them be more useful than elsewhere.

To place unbroken colours in juxtaposition to each other without transitions is to illuminate; it is not painting in the true sense of the word, and its practitioner is an artisan rather than an artist. The artist is he who traces the design upon the walls, who, chalk in hand, sketches the forms of men and women and the lines of the ornament. Many of these sketches are admirable for the freedom and breadth of their outline. The portrait of Amenophis III. which is to be seen in his tomb in the Bab-el-Molouk is a good example of these master-studies (Fig. 263). When nothing interfered to prevent the completion of the work, the painter came with his palette and brushes to spread colour over the spaces enclosed by these lines. Nothing could be easier than his task. He was only required to lay his colours smoothly, and to avoid overpassing the boundaries laid down for him. The hues of the flesh and of the draperies were fixed in advance as well as those of the various objects which were repeatedly introduced in such works.

[1] Vol. ii. plates 41, 66, and 70. [2] *Description, Antiquités*, vol. iii. p. 45.

At Beni-Hassan, and in several of the Theban tombs, there are representations of the painter at work. When he had to spread a single tint over a large surface—brown, for instance, upon the whole superficies of a limestone statue—we see him seated upon a kind of stool, his pot of colour in his left hand, his brush in his unsupported right (Fig. 54 Vol. I.,). Sometimes his work was more complicated than this. There are a few royal portraits, and a few scenes with numerous actors, in which the whole scale of

FIG. 263.—Outline for a portrait of Amenophis III. Champollion, pl. 232.

tints at his command must have been required. He then makes use of a palette. Specimens of these palettes are to be seen in every museum. They are rectangular pieces of wood, of alabaster, or of enamelled earthenware. They usually have seven little colour cups, but a few have as many as eleven or twelve. Small *styles*, as large as a crow-quill, have been found with these palettes. The use of these has been much discussed. Prisse cut one and steeped it in water. It was then discovered that the reed of which it was composed became a brush when its fibres were thus softened by moisture.[1] None of the large brushes which must have been used to spread the colour over considerable surfaces have been discovered, but Prisse believes that they too must have been made of fibrous reeds, such as the sarmentose stems of the *Salvadora persica*. Others think that for such purposes the hair pencil must have been employed.

Cakes of colour have sometimes been found in the tombs, together with earthenware mortars and pestles for grinding them. The tints usually employed were *yellow*, *red*, *blue*, *green*, *brown*, *white*, and *black*. These correspond to the seven cups hollowed in most of the palettes. They each included several varieties. Some of these colours were vegetable, such as indigo; others— and these more numerous—were mineral. Among the latter is a certain blue, which has preserved all its brilliancy even after so many centuries. Its merits were extolled by Theophrastus and Vitruvius. It is an ash with wonderful power of resisting chemical agents, and neither turning green nor black with exposure to the air. It must have been composed, we are told, of sand, copper-filings, and subcarbonate of soda reduced to powder and burnt in an oven. Copper is also the colouring principle, at least in our days, of those greens which are more or less olive in tone. Different shades of red, yellow, and brown, were obtained from the ochres. Their whites, formed of lime, of plaster, or of powdered enamel, have sometimes preserved a snowy whiteness beside which our whitest papers seem grey.[2] As for violet, Champollion tells us that no colour used by the ancients had that value. In those few bas-reliefs in which it is now found, it is a result of the changes which time has spread over surfaces

---

[1] PRISSE, *Histoire de l'Art Égyptien*, text, p. 289.

[2] Fuller details as to the composition of these colours are given in PRISSE, *Histoire de l'Art Égyptien*, text, pp. 292-295. A paper written by the father of Prosper Mérimée and printed by Passalacqua at the end of his *Catalogue* (pp. 258, *et seq.*) may also be consulted with profit; its full title is *Dissertation sur l'Emploi des Couleurs, des Vernis, et des Émaux dans l'Ancienne Égypte*, by M. MÉRIMÉE, *Secrétaire Perpétuel de l'École Royale des Beaux-Arts*. This paper shows that M. Mérimée added taste and a love for erudition to the talent as a painter which he is said to have possessed. BELZONI shows that the manufacture of indigo must have been practised by the ancient Egyptians by much the same processes as those in use to-day (*Narrative of the Operations*, etc. p. 175). See also WILKINSON, *Manners and Customs*, etc. vol. ii. p. 287.

originally gilded. The hue in question is caused, we are told, by the mordant or other preparation upon which the gold was laid.[1]

In the Theban tombs the figures are first drawn and then painted upon a fine coat which has all the polish of stucco. It seems to consist of a very fine plaster and a transparent glue. It is still white where no tint has been laid upon it; here and there its shining surface is still undimmed.[2] When the pictures were executed upon wood or, as in the mummies, upon linen laid down upon a thin layer of plaster, a preparatory coat of white was always spread in the first instance. The tints became more brilliant over such a coat, the most opaque being in some degree transparent.[3]

The paintings are, as a rule, free from cracks. The colours seem to have been mixed with water and some flexible gum like tragacanth.[4] M. Hector Leroux, who took impressions of many bas-reliefs during his visit to Egypt, is inclined to believe that the Egyptians sometimes mixed honey with their colours, as the makers of water-colours do now. In some of the tombs the painting became sticky when he laid his moistened paper upon their surfaces. In others no amount of wetting affected the surface of the colours, which remained as smooth and hard as enamel. Some Egyptian paintings are covered with a resinous varnish which has blackened with time and spoilt the colours upon which it is laid.[5] The same varnish was used for the mummy cases and gives them the dark hue which they now present. A few exceptionally well preserved examples permit us to suppose that their colours when fresh must have been much lighter in tone and more brilliant than they now appear. No such precaution was taken, as a rule, in the case of the frescos. Their surfaces were left free from a substance that could so greatly alter with time, and thanks partly to this, partly to the equality of temperature and to the dryness and tranquillity of the air, they have retained an incomparable freshness. The centuries

---

[1] CHAMPOLLION, *Lettres d'Égypte et de Nubie*, p. 130.
[2] *Description, Ant.* vol. iii. p. 44.
[3] MÉRIMÉE. *Dissertation sur l'Emploi des Couleurs*, p. 130.
[4] MÉRIMÉE. *Dissertation*, etc. Champollion uses the term *gouache*, body colour, in speaking of these paintings, but as the characteristic of that process is that every tint is mixed with white, there is some inaccuracy in doing so.
[5] PRISSE. *Histoire de l'Art Égyptien*, text. p. 291.

have passed gently over them, but since all the world has taken to visiting Egypt, including even the foolish and ignorant, they have suffered greatly from the barbarity of tourists. Of this the state of those beautiful decorations in the tomb of Seti which have excited the admiration of all cultivated travellers, is a painful instance.

Several mummy masks are in existence which prove that encaustic painting, in which naphtha and wax were used, was employed by the Egyptians;[1] but this process does not seem to have been developed until after the Macedonian conquest. Speaking generally, we may say that the Egyptian method was *distemper.*

The Egyptians produced easel pictures as well as wall paintings. In one of the Beni-Hassan tombs two artists are represented painting animals upon a panel.[2] Herodotus tells us that Amasis presented his portrait to the people of Cyrene.[3] Supposing it to be the work of a native artist, we may fomr some idea of its character from the Egyptian portraits, dating from the Roman epoch, which are now in the Louvre. Doubtless the portrait of Amasis was very different in style from these productions of the decadence; but it is probable that, like them, it was painted upon a cedar panel.

We have no reason to believe that the Egyptians ever succeeded in crossing the line which separates illumination from painting. The convention which saw only single flat tones on every surface being once adopted, it was sometimes pushed to extraordinary lengths. Not content with ignoring the varieties of tone and tint which nature everywhere presents, the Egyptian artists sometimes adopted arbitrary hues which did not, even faintly, recall the actual colours of the objects upon which they were used. As a rule they represented the female skin as a light-yellow, and the male as a reddish-brown. This distinction may be understood. Besides its convenience as indicative of sex to a distant observer, it answers to a difference which social habits have established in every civilized society. More completely covered than men and less in the open air, the women, at least those of the upper classes, are less exposed to

---

[1] PRISSE, *Histoire,* etc. text, p. 291.
[2] WILKINSON, *Manners and Customs,* etc. vol. ii. p. 294.
[3] HERODOTUS, ii. 182.

the effects of sun and wind than men. Their skins are usually fairer. In northern climates they are whiter, in southern less brown. We are surprised therefore to find that in the small temple at Ipsamboul the carnations of male and female, whether they be kings and queens or gods and goddesses, are all alike of a vivid yellow, not far removed from chrome.[1] Those divinities who have the limbs and features of man, such as Amen, Osiris, Isis, and Nephthys, should, we might think, be subject to the same rule as the images of men and women, and in most cases it is so. But, on the other hand, the painter often endows them with skins of the most fanciful and arbitrary hue. At Ipsamboul there is an Amen with a blue skin,[2] and, again, an Amen and an Osiris which are both green.[3] At Philæ we find numerous examples of the same singularity.[4] At Kalabché, in Nubia, there are royal figures coloured in the same fashion.[5]

Exceptional though they may be, these curious representations help us to understand the Egyptian method of looking at colour. They did not employ it like the modern painter, in order to add to the illusion; they used it decoratively, partly to satisfy that innate love for polychromy which we have explained by the intensity of a southern sun, partly to give relief to their figures, which would stand out more boldly from the white ground when brilliant with colour than when they had to depend solely upon their slight relief. In the interior of the figure colour was used to distinguish the flesh from the draperies, and to indicate those enrichments in the latter which made up the elegance of the Egyptian costume. A good example of this way of using colour is seen in the tomb of Amenophis III., which contains the portrait of Queen Taia reproduced in our Fig. 264.[6]

---

[1] There are other exceptions to the ordinary rule. In a fine bas-relief in the Louvre, representing Seti I. before Hathor, the carnations of the goddess are similar to those of the Pharaoh; they are in each case dark red (basement room, B, 7).

[2] CHAMPOLLION, *Monuments de l'Égypte et de la Nubie*, pl. 11. Blue was the regular colour for Amen when represented with a complete human form; when he was ram-headed he was generally painted green (see CHAMPOLLION, *Panthéon Égyptien*. No. 1; PIERRET, *Dictionnaire Archéologique*; and pl. 2, vol. i. of the present work).—ED.

[3] *Ibid.* pl. 59.   [4] *Ibid.* plates 71, 76, 78, 91.   [5] *Ibid.* pl. 154.

[6] We place this portrait of Taia in our chapter on painting because its colour is exceptionally delicate and carefully managed (see PRISSE, text, p. 421). The original is, however, in very low relief, so low that it hardly affects the colour values.

We find, too, that in pictures in which people of different races are brought together, the artist employs different tones to mark their varied hues. In a tomb at Abd-el-Gournah, in which the construction of a building is represented, the workmen, who are doubtless slaves or prisoners of war, have not all skins of one colour; some are light yellow, some light red, while others are reddish-brown. We are led to believe that this is not merely the result of caprice on the part of the painter, by the fact that the men with the light yellow skin seem to have more hair on their chests and chins than the others. They come, no doubt, from northern latitudes, whose inhabitants are more hairy than the southerners.[1] The negroes are made absolutely black,[2] the Ethiopians very dark brown.[3]

But although the Egyptian painter made no attempt to imitate the hues of nature in their infinite variety, we find a curious effort in certain Theban paintings to reproduce one of those modifications of local tone which were to attract so many artists of later times. The flesh tints are brown where they are uncovered, and light yellow where they are veiled; the painter thus attempting to show the warm skin shining through the semi-transparence of fine linen.[4]

This is, however, but an isolated attempt, and it does not affect the truth of our description of Egyptian painting, and of its conventional methods of using colour. The observations we have made apply equally justly to coloured bas-reliefs and to paintings properly speaking. The latter are only found in the tombs. In the temples the figures which compose the decoration are always engraved upon the walls in some fashion before they are touched with colour, and the office of the painter was restricted to filling in the prepared outlines with colour. It is the same, as a rule, with the steles; but a few exist upon which the painter has had the field to himself. The papyri, too, were illustrated by the artist in colour. Those elaborate examples of the *Ritual of the Dead*, which come from the tombs of princes and of rich subjects, are full of carefully executed vignettes (Figs. 97 and 184, Vol. I.).

It is easy to understand why the painter reserved himself for

---

[1] LEPSIUS, *Denkmæler*, part iii. pl. 40, cf. pl. 116.   [2] *Ibid.* pl. 117.
[3] See the Ethiopians in the painting from the tomb of Rekmara, which is reproduced in WILKINSON, vol. i. plate 2.
[4] LEPSIUS, *Denkmæler*, part iii. pl. 216.

the tomb. The pictures upon the external walls of the temples and upon the pylons were seen in the full glare of a southern sun; so too, at least for a part of the day, were those upon the walls of the courtyards, and upon the shafts of their surrounding columns. Even in the interior many of the decorations would receive direct

FIG. 264.—Portrait of Queen Taia. From Prisse.

sunlight from the claustra of the attic, others would be subject to friction from the hands and garments of visitors. Painting by itself would be unfitted for such situations. It would either have its effect destroyed by the direct light, or its colours dulled and damaged by constant touches. Figures carved in the substance of the walls would have a very different duration. When their colours paled with time, a few strokes of the brush would be sufficient to renew their youth, and the combination of colour with relief would give a much more telling result than could be obtained by the use of the latter alone.

With the tomb it was very different. In its case neither violent changes of temperature, nor friction, nor the rays of a dazzling sun were to be feared. Its doors were to be ever closed, and the scenes which were entrusted to its walls were to have no spectator but the dead man and his protecting Osiris. To carry out the whole work with the brush was quicker than to associate that instrument with the chisel, and we need therefore feel no surprise that many tombs were so decorated.

These paintings are in no way inferior to the sculptural works of the same period; the outlines of both must, in fact, have been traced by the same hands. The wielders of the chisel and brush must have been nothing more than journeymen or artisans ; the true artist was he who traced upon the wall the outline which had afterwards to be filled in either in relief or in colour.

We should have liked to have reproduced the best of these paintings with all their richness and variety of tint, but we had no original studies of which we could make use, and, as in the painted architecture, we saw no great advantages to be gained by copying the plates of Champollion, of Lepsius, or of Prisse. The processes which they were compelled to employ have in many cases visibly affected the fidelity of their transcriptions. We have therefore felt ourselves compelled, much to our disappointment, to trust almost entirely to black and white. We have, however, been careful to preserve the relative values of the different tones. Those who have seen Egyptian paintings in the original, or even in the copies which hang upon the staircase of the Egyptian museum in the Louvre, will be able to restore their true colours to our engravings without difficulty; the flesh tints, light or dark according to circumstances, the blackness of the hair, the whiteness of linen cloth and of the more brilliant colours, the reds and blues which adorn certain parts of the draperies and certain details of furniture and jewellery, may all be easily divined.

Our plates, though less numerous than we could have wished, will help the reader to restore the absent colour. Plate II., in the first volume, gives a good idea of the scale of tints used in the painted bas-reliefs of the temples; we have every reason to believe it accurate.[1] The plate which faces page 334 is a faithful reproduction of a fragment in the Louvre. It comes from a Theban tomb, and shows the elegance and refinement of the contours which the painter had to fill up. The colour has faded, but the most interesting point in all these pictures is the outline, in which alone real artistic talent and inventive power are displayed. Finally, our Plates III. and IV., drawn and coloured from notes and sketches made upon the spot by M. Bourgoin, represent the polychromatic decoration of the Ancient Empire as it was left by those who decorated the tomb of Ptah-hotep. In this case at least we know that we possess the true value of the tones brought together by the artist, for the mastaba in question is one of those which the desert sands have most completely preserved.

§ 2. *The Figure.*

In the mastabas colours are applied to figures in relief. It is not till we reach the first Theban Empire, in the tombs at Beni-Hassan, that we find real paintings in which the brush alone has been used.

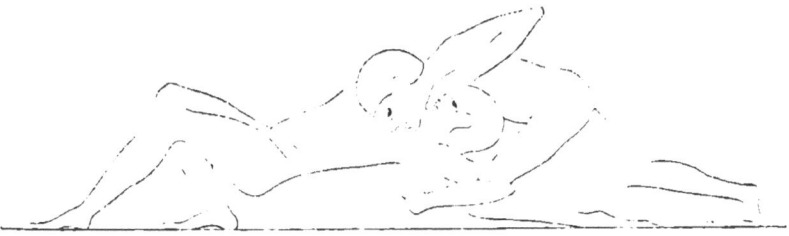

FIG. 265 —Painting at Beni-Hassan. Champollion, pl. 374.

We have already described the style and character of the paintings at Beni-Hassan. In most cases the outlines prepared for the painter do not differ from those meant for the sculptor.

---

[1] The materials for this plate were borrowed from the *Description de l'Égypte*. In the complete copies of that work the plates were coloured by hand, with extreme care, after those fine water-colours the most important of which are now in the *Cabinet des Estampes* of the *Bibliothèque Nationale*. The colours thus applied are far nearer the truth than those of the chromo-lithographs in more modern publications.

We have already reproduced many works in outline in which there is nothing to show whether they are paintings or bas-reliefs. Their execution is almost identical (see Figs. 2, 5, 25, 98, 170, Vol. I. ; Figs. 25, 26, 31, Vol. II). It is the same with the two

FIG. 266.—Painting at Beni-Hassan. Champollion, pl. 371.

wrestling scenes which we take from the frescos in which all the gymnastic exercises then in vogue are represented (Figs. 265 and 266), and with the charming group formed by an antelope and a man stroking his muzzle (Fig. 267).

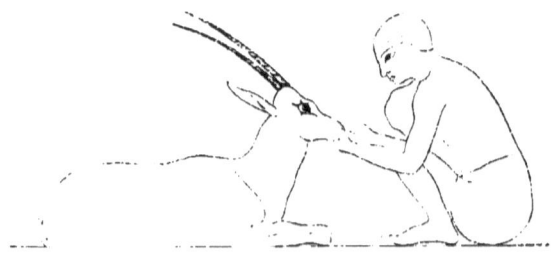

FIG. 267.—Painting at Beni-Hassan. Champollion, pl. 359.

Even at Beni-Hassan, however, there are a few paintings in which the peculiar and distinguishing characteristics of that art are to be found. The group of singers and musicians figured on this page is an instance in point. Two of the heads are shown in full face, a view which we hardly ever meet with in the bas-reliefs. The hair and the draperies are also treated in a fashion

FIG. 268.—Painting at Beni-Hassan. Champollion, pl. 377 *ter*.

quite different from that of sculpture, at least in the case of the two musicians on the right. Their twisted tresses seem to be thrown into disorder by the energetic movements of their heads,

FIG. 269.—Painting at Thebes. From Horeau.

which they seem to sway in time to the music of the flute, which is also marked by the hands of two members of the party. The deep shadows cast by their hair give a strong relief to the oval contours of the two faces which look out of the picture. The execution of the drapery is governed by the same idea, its numerous small folds are suggested by lines at slight intervals.

In the whole series of Egyptian wall-paintings I know of nothing which is more truly pictorial in character than this picture. A

FIG. 270.—Painting at Thebes. From Prisse.

careful study of it might well lead us to believe that its painter deliberately set himself to cast off traditional methods, and to obtain all the effect that the skilful use of colour can give. But the seed thus cast did not spring up. Theban painting is not an advance upon that of Beni-Hassan. It hardly ever attempts the full face. It is only here and there that we can point to a work in which the brush seems to have dwelt upon a few details

FIG. 271.—Harpist. From the *Description*.

that would be rendered in a more summary fashion by the chisel. The mandore player in Fig. 270, who comes from the same hypogeum at Abd-el-Gournah as the Amenophis III. upon the knees of a goddess in Fig. 24, is one of these rare instances. The hair, plaited into narrow tresses and retained in place by a long comb, is carried out with quite unusual care. The areolæ of the breasts are very clearly marked, a detail which Prisse says he never met with elsewhere.[1]

FIG. 272.—European prisoner. From Champollion.

FIG. 273.—Head of the same prisoner.

The slender proportions which we have already noticed as characteristic of this period are here strongly marked. They are also conspicuous in the figures in Plate II. This is a funerary scene. Three women stand before the defunct; one hands the cup for the libation, the two others play upon the flute and the harp respectively.

This fragment must have formed part of a funerary scene similar to that put before us in full by a painting in one of the tombs in the *Valley of Queens* at Thebes. We there see women

[1] PRISSE, *Histoire de l'Art Égyptien*, text. p. 424.

with offerings and others playing upon musical instruments, advancing towards the deceased, who has his daughter upon his knees and his wife seated at his right hand (Fig. 269).

The two often reproduced players upon the harp in the tomb of Rameses III. (long called *Bruce's Tomb*, after its discoverer) belong to the same class of representations (Fig. 271). Robed in a long black mantle, the musician abandons himself entirely to his music. The draughtsmanship of the arms is faulty, but the pose of the figure is natural and life-like. The harp is very richly ornamented :

FIG. 274.—Ethiopian prisoner. Champollion, pl. 932.

FIG. 275.—Head of the same prisoner.

its base terminates in a royal head rising from a circlet of ample necklaces. The wood seems to be inlaid with colour.

Among the most interesting of the painted figures in the royal tombs are the prisoners of war and other representations of foreign and conquered races. We reproduce two of these figures from the tomb of Seti I. In order that the care expended by the artist both on the costumes and upon the peculiar characteristics of the physiognomies may be appreciated, we have given their figures at full length, and also their heads upon a larger scale.

The first of these two prisoners must have been a European,

according to Champollion. His white skin, his straight nose, and the tattooing upon his arms all help to prove this (Figs. 272 and 273). He is dressed in a long robe, bordered with a rich fringe and covered with ornaments. This robe is held up by a large knot over the left shoulder, but it leaves one half of his body without a covering. His profile is very curious ; the nose is large and

FIG. 276.—Winged figure. *Description*, vol. ii. pl. 92.

aquiline, his beard curled and wavy, and down by his right ear hangs one of those side locks which were, in Egypt, the peculiar property of infancy. Long tresses hanging down on each side of the brow, and two fringe-like bands passing round the head complete this strange head-dress.

The individual in the second figure appears to be an Ethiopian

(Figs. 274 and 275). His costume is comparatively simple. It consists of a pair of drawers kept in place by a wide band like a baldrick, which is passed over the left shoulder and tied round the loins. The end of this baldrick hangs down between the legs; it is decorated with rosettes and edged with a band upon which circular ornaments are scattered. The almost negro features are similar to those represented in the bas-relief at the Ramesseum which is reproduced in Fig. 221. The shape of the head-dress, too, is similar. The artist has had some difficulty with the woolly hair, and has attempted to render its appearance by a series of knots strung together. In this part of the picture, as in Fig. 273, there is some conventionality, but in the outline of the figure and especially of the face, we find the characteristic genius of Egyptian art, the power to create types which are at once life-like and general, to epitomize all those attributes which constitute a species and allow it to be defined.

Fig. 277.—Winged figure. *Description*, vol. ii. pl. 87.

The scenes represented upon the walls of the tomb may be divided into two groups: those which are more or less historical, and those which are purely religious or mystical. Among the latter the figures of winged goddesses, of Isis and Nephthys, are frequently encountered. They are either seated or standing, carved upon the sarcophagi or painted upon the wooden mummy cases. One wing is always raised, the other lowered (Figs. 276 and 277). The artists of other Oriental races, and even of the Greeks themselves, loved to endow the figures of men and animals with wings. Egypt was the first to carry out this idea, and the winged figures which had a definite meaning when used in the tombs, came at last to be employed as mere decoration upon the industrial products which she exported through the Phœnicians. Fig. 277 comes from a royal tomb, and it shows how these winged goddesses were sometimes combined with motives, which were either purely decorative or easily used for decorative purposes. Like sphinxes and griffins, these composite forms amused the eye and were soon seized upon by the ornamentist, while their wings, which could be either closed or expanded, were useful for covering large spaces and helping to "furnish" the decoration.

§ 3. *Caricature.*

We have shown the artists of ancient Egypt making naïve and sincere transcripts of reality; we have shown them, in their religious and historical scenes, inventing motives, creating types, and even aspiring to the ideal; we have yet to show that they understood fun and could enjoy a laugh. Without this last quality their art would hardly be complete. In the royal tombs at Thebes we find a lion and a donkey singing to their own accompaniment on the harp and lyre respectively.[1] This particular bent of the Egyptian artist is seen at its best, however, in a group of remains which are called the *Satirical Papyri,* and apparently date from the nineteenth dynasty. The Egyptians, like the Greeks after them, seem to have understood that sculpture properly speaking, the art that produces figures of large size from such materials as bronze and marble, does not lend itself to the provocation of laughter by the voluntary production of ugliness and deformity. They also perceived that such subjects were equally ill-adapted for wall paintings, whether in tombs or palaces. Among them, as among the Greeks, the grotesque was only allowed to appear where the forms were both very much smaller than life and considerably generalized. The designs traced with a light and airy hand upon such papyri as that of which the Turin Museum possesses an important fragment are examples of this treatment.

The drawings in this papyrus are not caricatures as we now understand the word. Caricature is an exaggerated portrait; it

[1] JOHN KENRICK, *Ancient Egypt under the Pharaohs,* vol. i. pp. 269, 270.

founds itself upon reality while turning it into ridicule by the accentuation of its most laughable features. But the drawings in this manuscript are inspired by the same ideas and the same intellectual bent as our modern caricatures. They respond to the universal taste of mankind for the mental relaxation afforded by parody, for the relief from the serious business of life which is to be found in comedy and burlesque. Ancient Egypt was a merry country. Its inhabitants were as pleased as children over the simplest and most homely jokes; jests, fantastic tales, and fables in which animals acted like men and women, were as popular with them as with their successors in civilisation. Their comic artists were especially fond of treating scenes of this last description, and their works often remind us of those produced in much later times for the illustration of Æsop or La Fontaine.

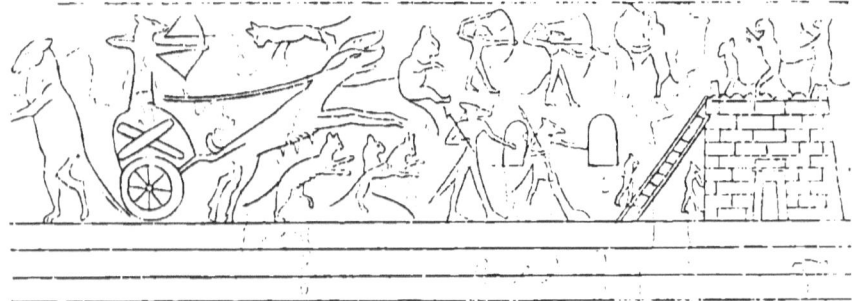

FIG. 278. Battle of the Cats and Rats. From Prisse.

Prisse reproduces the most interesting part of the Turin papyrus, and we have copied a fragment of his plate (Fig. 278). "In the first group, four animals—an ass, a lion, a crocodile, and a monkey—make up a quartette, playing on such musical instruments as were then in fashion. Next comes an ass dressed, armed, and sceptred like a Pharaoh; with a majestic swagger he receives the offerings brought to him by a cat of high degree, to whom a bull is proud to act as conductor. At the side a unicorn seems to threaten a kneeling cat with its harp. . . . . . The scenes drawn below, and on a smaller scale, are no more coherent than these. In the first place we see a flock of geese in open rebellion against its conductors—three cats, one of whom has fallen under the blows of the angry birds. Next we come to a sycamore in which an hippopotamus is perched; a hawk has climbed into the tree by means of a ladder and proceeds to dislodge him; finally, we have a fortress defended by an army of cats, who are without other arms than their claws and teeth, against a storming party of rats provided with arms offensive and defensive, and led by one of their own species, who is mounted on a chariot drawn by two greyhounds.

"The artist's idea—at least in the lower part of the picture—seems to have been to paint the cats defeated by the animals upon which they prey. It is the world turned upside down, or if the painter must be credited with a deeper meaning, it is the revolt of the oppressed against the oppressor."[1]

The lower part of the plate contains a scene of the same kind taken from a papyrus in the British Museum. A flock of geese are being driven along by a cat, and a herd of goats by two wolves with crook and wallet; one of the wolves is playing on the double flute. At the other end there is a lion playing draughts with an antelope.

One of the tombs has upon its walls a picture of a humble and timid cat attempting to propitiate a lion by the offering of a goose.[2]

In the opinion of some these scenes are satires upon royalty and religion. This is an evident exaggeration. We have no reason to suppose that the Egyptian intellect ever arrived at the maturity required for scepticism. Neither the authority of Pharaoh nor that of the priests seems to have ever been called in question. But although their anger was not stirred by the government of the world, they could find something to laugh at in it. In the cat presented to an ass we cannot fail to see a parody of Pharaoh receiving the homage of some vanquished enemy. Still more personal is the cat offering a goose to a lion. The cat can only be that unlucky fellah who, in the Egypt of the Pharaohs as in that of the Khedives, has never succeeded in keeping clear of the bastinado and the *corvée* except by giving presents to the *sheikh* of his village or the *mudir* of the neighbouring town. In laying this scene upon the wall the artist was writing a page of his own biography and of the history of all the people about him. He revenged himself in his own way upon the greedy functionary

[1] PRISSE, *Histoire de l'Art Égyptien*, text, pp. 142, 143.
[2] *Ibid.* p. 144.

to whom he had been compelled to offer the fatlings of his own farm-yard.

FIG. 279.—The soles of a pair of sandals. From Champollion.

Traces of this mocking spirit are to be found in other productions of Egyptian art. Thus the soles of those leathern or wooden sandals which have come down to our times often present

FIGS. 280, 281.—The god Bes. From the Louvre. Actual size.

a group of two prisoners, the one a negro, and the other a native, perhaps, of Libya or Syria. There can be no mistake as to the intentions of the artist. The Egyptian seems to have enjoyed a laugh at the expense of his trembling enemies. Not content with thus treading upon them at every step he took, he added insult to injury by making them grotesque (Fig. 279).

The same spirit may be recognized in those figures of Bes which are so numerous in our museums. It was by mere exaggeration of certain not uncommon features that the figure of this paunchy dwarf was arrived at. His animal grin, beady eyes, flat nose, thick lips, and pendent tongue, his short legs and salient buttocks, make up a sufficiently droll personality (Figs. 280 and 281). The comic intention is very marked in a composition reproduced by Prisse, in which a person of proportions rather less curtailed than those of the ordinary Bes, but endowed with the features, the head-dress, and the lion-like tail of that god, is shown playing upon a cithara.[1]

These productions were not always decent. The Turin papyrus contains a long priapic scene.

§ 4. *Ornament.*

In the painted decorations with which the Egyptians covered every available surface, the figure played a more important part than in the case of any other people. But yet the multiplication of historical, religious, and domestic scenes, the countless groups of gods, men, and the lower animals, had their limits. However great their development might be, these traditional themes could only supply a certain number of scenes, which required, moreover, to be framed. Again, there were certain surfaces upon which the Egyptians did not, as a rule, place figures, either because they would be seen with difficulty, or, as in the case of ceilings, because taste warned them that it would be better to treat such a surface in some other fashion. Between the lofty roofs of the hypostyle halls and the sky which covers our heads the Egyptian decorator established a relationship which readily commends itself to the mind. The ceilings of the temples at Thebes had generally a blue ground, upon which vultures with their great wings outspread, floated among golden stars (Figs. 192 and 282).

[1] PRISSE, *Histoire de l'Égypte*, text, p. 146.

Side by side with the paintings which deal with living form we find those painted ornaments which cover with their varied tints all the surfaces which are not occupied by the figure. This system of ornament went through a continual process of enrichment and complication. Its appearance in the early centuries is well shown in our two Plates, III. and IV.; the first shows the upper, the second the lower part of the western wall in the tomb of Ptahhotep at Sakkarah. They confirm the ideas of Semper as to the origin of ornament.[1] That writer was the first to show that the basket-maker, the weaver, and the potter, originated by the mere play of their busy hands and implements those combinations of line and colour which the ornamentist turned to his own use when he had to decorate walls, cornices, and ceilings. The industries we have named are certainly older than the art of decoration, and

FIG. 282.—Vultures on a ceiling.

the forms used by the latter can hardly have been transferred from it to mats, woven stuffs, and earthen vessels. In the regularity with which the lines and colours of early decoration are repeated it is easy to recognize the enforced arrangement of rushes, reeds, and flaxen threads, while chevrons and concentric circles are the obvious descendants of the marks traced by the finger or rude implement of the potter upon the soft clay.

In these examples the intentions of the decorator are easily grasped. He has begun with a ground of rush-work, like that which is also found in the tomb of Ti.[2] In the compartments

---

[1] SEMPER (G.), *Der Stil in den Technischen und Tektonischen Künsten, oder Praktische Æsthetik.* Munich, 1860-3, 2 vols. 8vo, with 22 plates, some coloured, and numerous engravings in the text.
[2] PRISSE. *Histoire de l'Art Égyptien,* text, p. 418.

between the vertical bars he has imitated the appearance of mat walls, and of windows closed by the same contrivances (see Fig. 165). As if to prevent mistakes, he has been careful to introduce the cords, rings, and lath, by which the lower ends of the mats are kept in place. The design of the ornament is quite similar to those produced to this day by the basket or mat-maker. They are squares, lozenges, and chevrons. In the middle of the lozenges we find little crosses or circles of a different colour, which help to lighten the effect. Each mat has a red border at its lower end, which forms a satisfactory tailpiece, and unites it with the straight lath. There are narrow grooves between the mats in which the chains for drawing the latter up and down seem to be imitated. In any case, this latter detail is copied from the productions of one of the oldest of civilized industries—that of the blacksmith.

FIGS. 283, 284.—Details from the tomb of Ptah-hotep.

Six colours are used in this decoration: black, white, red, yellow, green, and blue. The result is sober, well-balanced, and by no means without harmony.

In other parts of the same tomb we find this taste for literal imitation applied to another theme. As interpreted by the ornamentist, lotus and papyrus were sure in time to put on conventional forms, but here those vegetables found are reproduced with a feeling for truth that could not be excelled by a modern flower painter (Fig. 283).[1] In Fig. 284 a bird among the lotus-stalks is in the grasp of a human hand.

[1] DÜMICHEN, *Resultate der Archæologisch-photographischen Expedition*. Berlin, 1869. folio. part i. plate 8.

The ornamentist also borrowed motives from those robes and carpets of varied colour, which are preserved for us in the paintings (see Fig. 285). But with time and experience his hand became more skilful, his imagination more active, and he was no longer contented to convey his ideas wholesale, from nature on the one hand, and on the other from those humble arts which flourish even in the earliest ages of every civilized society. He learnt to create designs for himself—designs which can certainly not be traced to the mats and tissues which formed his first models. Our Figure 286 will give some idea of the variety of motives to be found upon the panels and ceilings of the tombs and other buildings at Thebes. The chess-board pattern which was so much used during the Ancient Empire, is found here also; but by its side appear patterns composed of frets, meandering lines, and rosettes. Below these, again, are designs in which lines twist themselves into volutes and spirals, crossing each other and enclosing lotus flowers, rosettes, and forms like the shafts of columns. The flowers are in no way imitative; their motives have been suggested, not supplied, by nature. The papyrus may have given the first idea for the sixth of these designs, while in the last we find a motive which afterwards played an important part in Greek and Roman ornament—namely, the skull of an ox. The two specimens of this last-named motive given by Prisse, are taken from tombs of the eighteenth and twentieth dynasties.[1]

FIG. 285.—Carpet hung across a pavilion.

These tombs and the mummy cases they contain are often decorated with symbolic ornament, as well as with geometrical designs and those suggested by the national flora. The compartments of ceiling decorations have scarabs in their centres, and

[1] PRISSE, *Histoire de l'Art Égyptien*, text. p. 369.

FIG. 285.—Specimens of ceiling decorations. From Prisse.

upon the mummy cases it is occasionally substituted for the
uræus-crowned disk in the centre of a huge pair of extended
wings. Beneath it, figures of Isis or Nephthys, the guardians of

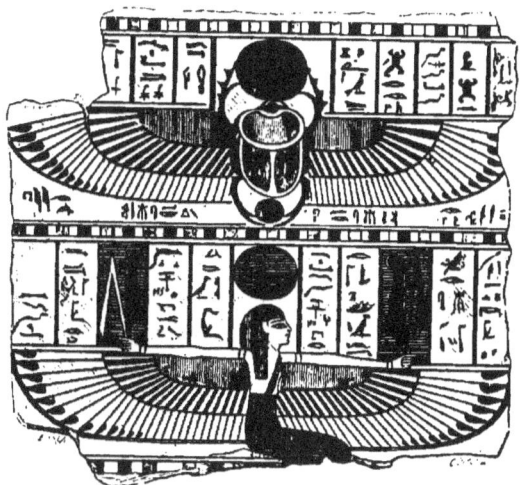

FIG. 287.—Painting on a mummy case. *Description*, vol. ii. pl. 58.

the tomb, are found (Fig. 287). The effect is similar to that of
the winged globes which are found upon cornices. In the latter
the disk which represents the sun is red, and stands boldly out
from the green of the two wings. The latter, again, are relieved

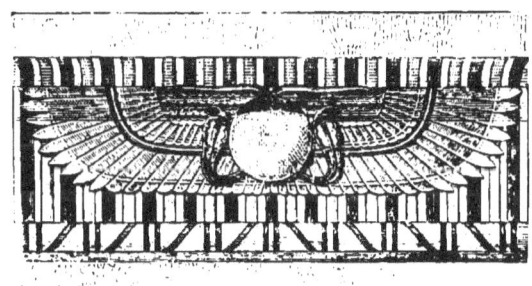

FIG. 288.—Winged globe. From Prisse.

against a striped ground, on which bands of red, blue, and white
are laid alternatively. Thanks to the happy choice of these
colours, the result is excellent from a decorative point of view,

and that in spite of its continual repetition and the simplicity of its lines.

Among the original motives to be found in these paintings, there is yet another which deserves to be named for its uncommon character, we mean those tables for offerings which are shown loaded with vases and other objects of a like nature. As if to mark the importance of the funerary gifts, the stems of these tables are made so lofty that they rise high above two trees, apparently cypresses, which grew right and left of their feet (Figs. 289 and 290).

The Egyptians made use of the afterwards common decorative motive of alternate buds and open blooms of lotus, but they entirely failed to give it the lightness and elegance with which it was endowed by the Greeks. Their buds were poor and meagre, their flowers heavy, and the general design not without stiffness.[1]

The colours are often well preserved, at least in parts, and, as one combination is repeated several times, it is easy to restore the missing parts by reference to those which are intact. The gilding, however, has disappeared, and left hardly a trace behind. Gold was used pretty generally in order to give warmth and brightness. The obelisks, those of Hatasu for instance, were gilded upon all four faces; the winged globe was sometimes gilded,[2] and so were the bronze plates with which the temple doors were covered. The important part played by the gilders, some of whose books of gold have come down to our time,[3] is chiefly known to us by the inscriptions. Their employment may also be divined here and there by the fashion in which the stone has been prepared, sometimes by the peculiar colour effects in certain parts of the bas-reliefs.

In some tombs gold is found in its pure state. During the excavations at the Serapeum, Mariette opened the tomb of Ka-em-nas, a son of Rameses II. When the mummy chamber was entered, the lower parts of the walls and of the mummy cases shone with gold in the candle-light. The floor was strewn with scraps of the same metal, and as many as four books of gold leaf

---

[1] LEPSIUS, *Denkmæler*, part iii. plate 62. PRISSE, *Histoire de l'Art Égyptien*, atlas, plate lettered *Frises Fleuronnées*.

[2] *Description, Antiquités*, vol. ii. p. 533.

[3] There is one of these books in the Louvre (*Salle Funéraire*, case Z); the gold leaf which it contains differs from that now in use only in its greater thickness.

were found in the tomb. Mariette was then in want of funds, and in order that the excavations might proceed, he obtained authority from the French consul to sell this gold, to which of course, no scientific interest was attached. The thick gold mask of the prince and the fine jewelry which adorned his mummy are now in the Louvre.

The mummy's toe-nails, bracelets, and lips, and the linen mask over its face, were very often gilt. The feet are sometimes entirely gilt. So too is the shroud. Those of princes and great personages are sometimes covered with gold from head to foot.

 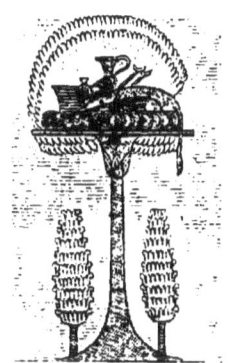

FIGS. 289, 290.—Tables for offerings; from the paintings in a royal tomb.

The Egyptian artisans understood these delicate operations at a very early date. Even in the tombs at Beni-Hassan we find the process of gold-beating illustrated in full. We need hardly say that a decorative industry which disposed of such complete resources, thoroughly understood what we call *graining*, the imitation of the veins and textures of wood, and also those of the different kinds of granite, upon other substances. In more than one instance we find the commoner kinds of stone thus made to look like rarer and more costly materials.

CHAPTER V.

THE INDUSTRIAL ARTS.

§ 1. *Definition and Characteristics of Industrial Art.*

THE expression, *industrial art*, has sometimes been severely criticised, but yet it answers to a real distinction founded upon the nature of things, and we do not see that it could be dispensed with. When the artist sets about making a statue or a picture his only aim is to produce a fine work. He does not take *utility*, in the unphilosophic sense of the word, into account. The task which he sets before himself is to discover some form which shall truly interpret his own individual thoughts and feelings. This done, his end is accomplished. The resulting work of art is self-contained and self-sufficient. Its *raison d'être* is to satisfy one of the deepest and most persistent desires of the human mind, the *æsthetic sentiment*, or *instinct for the beautiful.*

In the industrial arts it is different. When a cabinet-maker or a potter sets to work to produce an easy chair, or a vase, his first idea is to make a chair in which one may sit comfortably, or a vessel to which liquids may be safely entrusted and from which they may be easily poured. At first, the artisan does not look beyond fulfilling these wants, but a time comes, and comes very soon, when he feels impelled to ornament the furniture or pottery upon which he is at work. He is no longer content to turn out that which is merely useful; he wishes everything that comes from his hands to be rich and beautiful also. He begins by adding ornament made up of dots and geometrical lines; this he soon follows up with forms borrowed from organic life, with leaves and flowers, with figures of men and animals; and from an artisan he springs at once to be an artist. But his productions are strictly works of industrial art, and although they may deserve a high place in right of their beauty, that beauty is only in some sort an excrescence, it does not affect the primary object of the matters to which it is applied, although it may greatly increase their value and interest.

In view of this definition, it may be asserted that architecture itself is one of the industrial arts. The first duty of the constructor is to make his building well fitted for the object it has to serve. The house must afford a proper shelter for its inhabitants, the tomb must preserve the corpse entrusted to it from all chance of profanation, the temple must shield the statue or the symbol of the god from curious glances, and afford convenient space for ritual celebrations. These requirements may be fulfilled by edifices which have no pretensions to beauty. With a roof and a certain number of naked walls, it is always possible to cover and enclose a given space, and to divide it into as many portions as may be desired. Such a process has nothing in common with art. Art steps in when the builder attempts to endow his work with that symmetry which does not exclude variety, with nobility of proportion, and with the charm of a decoration in which both painter and sculptor play their parts. The constructor then gives place to the architect. The latter, of course, always keeps the practical end in view, but it is not his sole preoccupation. The house, as he builds it, has to respond to all the wants, intellectual as well as corporeal, of civilized man; the tomb must embody his ideas of death and a future life; the magnificent dimensions and the gorgeous decorations of the temple must give expression to the inexpressible, must symbolize the divine majesty to the eyes of men, and help to make it comprehensible by the crowds that come to sacrifice and pray.

In all this, the *rôle* played by art is so preponderant that it would be unjust to class architecture among the industrial arts. The ambition of those who built the temple of Amen, at Karnak, or that of Athené, on the Acropolis, was to produce a work which should give faithful expression to the highest thoughts which the human mind can conceive. In one sense, architecture may be called the first of the arts. In those great compositions whose remains we study with such reverence, whose arrangements we endeavour with such care to re-establish, it was the architect who determined what part the painter and the sculptor should take in the work, who laid out for them the spaces they were called upon to fill.

Although we shall not include architecture among the industrial arts, the distinction which we have established loses none of its practical importance. We must acknowledge, however, that there are certain classes of objects which lie upon the borderline between the two categories, so that we have some difficulty in deciding whether they belong to fine or to industrial art. The work of some Cellini of ancient times, or of our own day, may be classed, for instance, by its general form and ostensible use, among the more or less utilitarian productions of the goldsmith or silversmith; but, on the other hand, it may be adorned with figures executed in such a fashion that we are tempted to place it among works of sculpture. Rigorous and inflexible definitions have, in fact, to be confined to the exact sciences, such as geometry. In the complexity of life, definitions and classifications can only be adhered to with a reservation. They help the historian to find his way amid the infinite diversity of phenomena, but he is the first to acknowledge that they are far from having an absolute value. They must be taken for what they are worth, simply as methods of exposition, as approximations which are useful and convenient, though more or less imperfect.

We have no intention of writing a history of Egyptian industry. We refer those who require an account of it to the voluminous work of Sir Gardner Wilkinson, where they will find abundant details upon the trades of Egypt and the materials which they employed. We shall be content with selecting a few examples from the chief industries upon which the wealth of Egypt depended, in order to show how her artisans, like those of Greece, sought to give a certain amount of artistic value to every object that left their hands. Forms and motives which we have encountered in the higher branches of art are there again to be found. When civilization is in its first infancy, and the plastic instinct just struggling into life, it is from those handicrafts which may be called elementary or primitive that art borrows its first combinations of line and colour. But afterwards, when art has developed itself and created a style expressive of the national genius, the process is reversed, and the handicraftsman borrows in turn from the artist. In our modern society the use of machines and the division of labour have put a great gulf between the workman and the artist. Among the ancients it was very different. The workman was responsible for his work from inception to completion, and he expended upon it all the inventiveness, taste, and skill, that he possessed. He was not the slave of a machine turning out thousands of repetitions of a single object with inflexible regularity. Every day he introduced, almost without knowing it, some variation upon his work of the day before; his labour was a perpetual improvisation. Under such conditions it is difficult to say where the artist began and where the handicraftsman left off. In spite of the richness and subtlety of their idioms, the classic languages were unable to mark this distinction. In Greek, as in Latin, there was but a single term for two positions which seem to us by no means equal in dignity.

§ 2. *Glass and Pottery.*

The potter's is, perhaps, the oldest of all the crafts. Among the relics of the cave-men and lake-dwellers of the West, the remains of rough pottery, shaped by the hand and dried either by the sun or in the neighbourhood of the domestic hearth, have been found. The Egypt of the earliest dynasties was already more advanced than this. The vases found in the mastabas show by their symmetrical shapes that the potter's wheel was already in use, and by their quality, that, although the Egyptians were content to dry their bricks in the sun, they fired their pottery in kilns and thoroughly understood the process.[1]

Egypt afforded an abundant supply of excellent potter's earth, and her inhabitants, like those of ancient Greece and Italy, employed terra-cotta for purposes to which we should now apply glass, wood, or metal. A good idea of the varied uses to which the material was put may be obtained from the early chapters of the work in which Dr. Birch has traced the history of ancient pottery, with the help of numerous illustrations.[2]

We shall not dwell upon common earthenware. It is represented

[1] The oldest representation of the potter's wheel yet discovered is in one of the paintings at Beni-Hassan. It is reproduced in BIRCH's *Ancient Pottery*. p. 14.

[2] S. BIRCH. *A History of Ancient Pottery, Egyptian, Assyrian, Greek, Etruscan, and Roman*, 1 vol. 8vo, 1873. London, Murray.

by numerous vessels from the most ancient tombs in the Memphite necropolis; they are of a reddish or yellowish colour, and, in spite of the absence of all glaze, they hold water perfectly well. Like Greek vessels of the same kind they have sometimes three ears or handles (Fig. 291). Examples of coupled vessels, like those found in Cyprus, have also been discovered. They communicate with one another by a tube and are kept together by a common

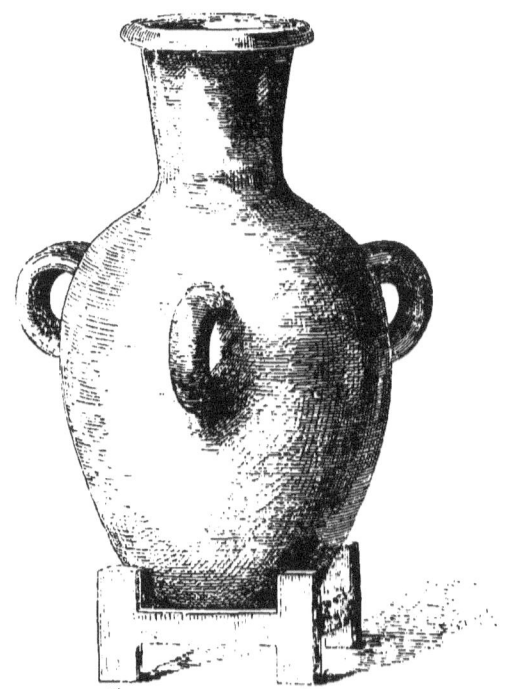

FIG. 291.—Pitcher of red earth. British Museum.

handle (Fig. 292). Of all the representative specimens of earthenware from the mastabas given by Lepsius, there is but one which does not seem to belong to the category of domestic pottery. It is a kind of aryballus, and is gracefully ornamented with interlacing circles.[1] In later times many of these unglazed vases were decorated with the brush, but they were not remitted to the oven after that operation.[2] The colour was therefore without lustre or solidity, and the designs were always very simple. To this

[1] LEPSIUS, *Denkmaeler*, part ii. pl. 153.   [2] BIRCH, *Ancient Pottery*, p. 37.

group belong the vases shaped in the form of men, women, or animals, which are common enough in museums.[1] Sometimes a head, recalling that of the god Bes, is sketched in low relief upon a vase, and in a few instances a pair of small arms complete the fanciful design (Fig. 293).

Another kind of pottery, that known as *Egyptian porcelain*, must be noticed in greater detail. This designation is inexact. The proper name would be *Egyptian faience*. It consists of white sand, gently fused, and overspread with a glaze of coloured enamel. This enamel is composed of flint and soda, with the addition of a colouring

FIG. 292.—Red earthenware. British Museum.

matter. This faience has been fired with such care that it is able to support the high temperature of a porcelain kiln without damage. Vases of many different kinds, enamelled tiles, statuettes (Fig. 294), sepulchral *figurines* (Figs. 96 and 97, Vol. I.), neck ornaments and other articles for decorating the person, amulets (Fig. 295), scarabs, rings, and many other articles were made in this material.

Vases were generally either blue or apple green. A very small number of them were ornamented with figures of men or animals. always treated in a purely decorative fashion. No vase has yet

[1] BIRCH, *Ancient Pottery*, Figs. 23 and 25.

been discovered with any attempt to portray an incident upon it. The figures are never united by a subject. Bouquets of lotus around some central motive are of most frequent occurrence (Fig. 296). Sometimes these flowers are combined with mystic symbols, like the eyes in Fig. 297. These designs, which are in black, are produced by inlaying coloured enamel.

Two of the vases which we reproduce (Figs. 296 and 297) are similar to those shown in the bas-reliefs, in scenes of libation

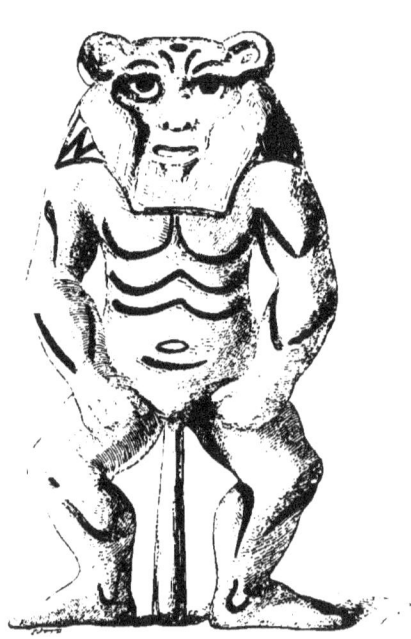

Fig. 293.—Gray earthenware. Boulak.

Fig. 294.—The God Bes. Enamelled earthenware.

to the gods or to the dead. Their form is that of the Greek φιάλη and the Latin *patera*. Numerous bottles have also been found whose general shape exactly resemble that of the Greek ἀρύβαλλος (Fig. 298).

The blue with which these objects are covered has often preserved a brilliance and transparency which could not even now be surpassed. Yellow, violet, and white glazes are also met with, but less frequently. The hieroglyphs which many of them bear prove that the manufacture of these little articles was in full swing under the three great Theban dynasties, that it continued through the Saite period, and that under the Ptolemies, and even later still, it was not extinct. To the same branch of industry belong those tiles of enamelled faience which seem to have been

Fig. 295.—Pendant for necklace. Louvre.

Fig. 296.—Enamelled earthenware. British Museum.

used by the Egyptians from very early times. They were also used by the Assyrians, as we shall see hereafter. "These tiles were used very extensively in eastern and southern countries, and are found both in palaces and in private dwellings. In the

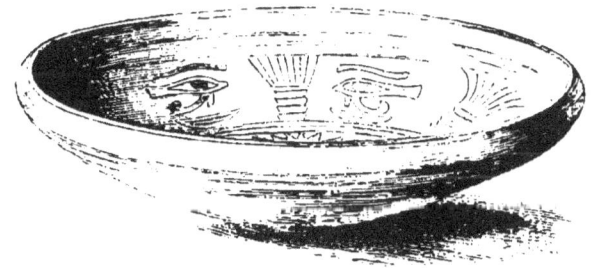

Fig. 297.—Enamelled earthenware. British Museum.

towns of Turkey and of Modern Egypt, in the towns and villages of Algeria and of all the African coast as far as the Straits of Gibraltar, thousands of examples are to be found. The freshness which seems to result from their use and the enduring brilliancy of their colours make these tiles very popular with the inhabitants of hot climates."[1]

We do not know whether these tiles were used for the floors and walls in the dwellings of rich Egyptians or not, but it appears certain that their manufacture was understood even as early as the Ancient Empire. The doorway of a chamber in the stepped pyramid of Sakkarah is enframed with enamelled plaques. A sketch of Perring's, which we reproduce, gives a good idea of this arrangement (Fig. 299).[2] Some of these plaques are now in London, but a still larger number are in the Berlin Museum,

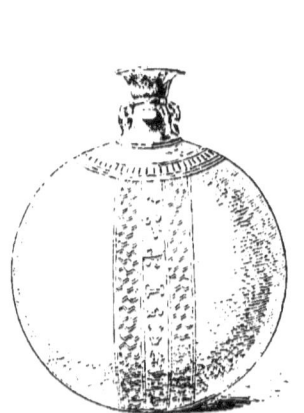

FIG. 298.—Enamelled faience. British Museum.

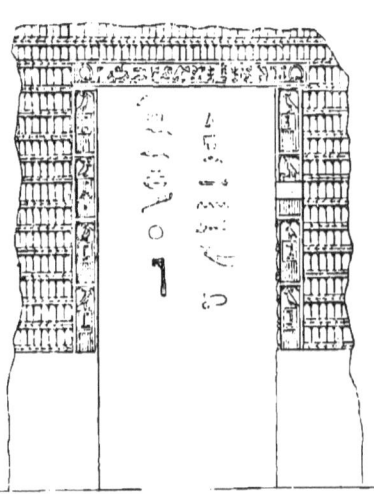

FIG. 299.—Doorway in the Stepped Pyramid at Sakkarah.

where the doorway as a whole has been restored, the missing parts being replaced by copies. Our Figures 300—302 show the back, the front, and the profile, of a single plaque. The obverse is slightly convex, and covered with a greenish-blue glaze ; the reverse has a salient tenon which was held securely by the mortar. Through a small hole in this tenon a rod of wood or metal may have passed which, by uniting all the plaques in each horizontal row, would give additional solidity to the whole arrange-

[1] BRONGNIART, *Histoire de la Céramique*, vol. ii. p. 95.
[2] See also LEPSIUS, *Denkmæler*, part ii. pl. 2, and the *Verzeichniss der Ægyptischen Alterthümer* of the Berlin Museum, 2879, p. 25.

ment.[1] On the backs of several plaques there are marks which seem to be rotation numbers. They are figured in the centre of Perring's sketch. Other bricks from the same doorway are covered with an almost black enamel. They form the horizontal mouldings between the rows of upright bricks, and are decorated with a sort of arrow-head pattern.

This fashion endured throughout the Theban period. The most important relic of it which we now possess is from the decoration of a temple built by Rameses III. to the north-west of Memphis, near the modern Tell-el-Yahoudeh, upon the railway from Cairo to Ismailia. The building itself was constructed of crude brick, the walls being lined with enamelled tiles. The

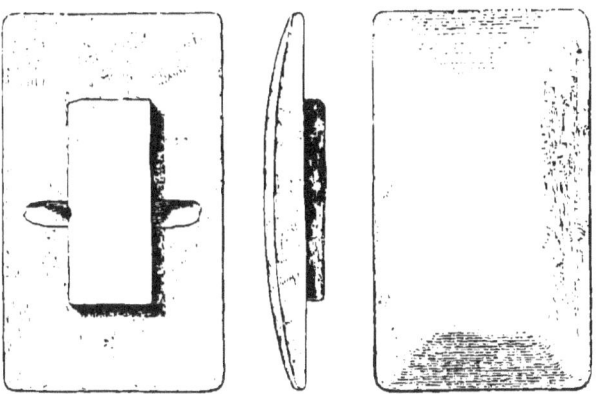

FIGS. 300—302.—Enamelled plaque from the Stepped Pyramid.

royal ovals and titles were cut in the earth before it was fired, and afterwards filled up with an enamel so tinted as to stand out in strong relief from the colour of the brick. Other tiles represent African and Asiatic prisoners. The figures are in relief; the enamel is parti coloured, the hair of the prisoners being black, their carnations yellowish-brown, and certain details of their costume being accentuated by other hues. Dr. Birch reproduces some of these painted reliefs and compares them to the *figurines rustiques* of Bernard Palissy.[2] The principal fragments of this

[1] We owe our ability to give these curious details to the kindness of M. Conze and the officers of the Egyptian museum at Berlin. One of the original fragments brought home by Lepsius was lent to us.

[2] BIRCH, *Ancient Pottery*, p. 50.

decoration are in the store-rooms of the Boulak Museum. They deserve more publicity than they have received. Most of them are purely decorative in character and bear designs of which an idea may be gained from three pieces of faience which are now in the British Museum. Two have graceful rosettes, while the third is covered with a pattern resembling a spider's web (Figs. 303—305).[1]

Certain buildings in Memphis seem to have been decorated in the same fashion. "The most curious thing brought by me from Mitrahineh," writes Jomard, "is a fragment of enamelled and sculptured terra-cotta, which probably belonged to a wall lined with that fine material. It is remarkable for the brilliant blue, the blue of the lapis-lazuli, which covers it. .... The outlines of the hieroglyphs are as firm, and their edges as sharp as if they were the work of a skilful carver, and had never been subjected to the heat of a furnace. They are of blue stucco, inlaid into the

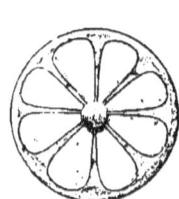 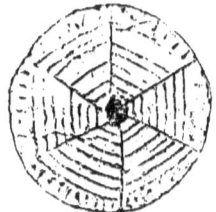 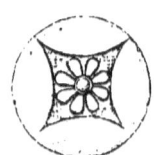

FIGS. 303—305.—Enamelled earthenware plaques in the British Museum.

body of the enamel. I look upon this kind of decoration as analogous to that of the Cairo divans, in which we see walls covered with earthenware tiles which are painted with various ornaments and subjects."[2] Now that attention has been attracted to this kind of decoration, traces of it will no doubt be found at many other points of Ancient Egypt.[3]

[1] I am told that a circular base, like that of a column of a table for offerings, was discovered in the same building. It is entirely covered with this same faience.

[2] *Description, Antiquités*, vol. v. p. 543, and *Atlas*, vol. v. plate 87, Fig. 1.

[3] The collection of M. Gustave Posno, which will, we hope, be soon absorbed into that of the Louvre, contains many enamelled bricks from decorative compositions like those in the stepped pyramid and the temple of Rameses III. (Nos. 8, 9, 11, 20, 58, 59, 60, 61 of the Catalogue published at Cairo in 1874). One of these, which has a yellow enamel, bears in relief the oval and the royal banner of Papi, of the sixth dynasty. Another has the name Seti I.; others those of Rameses III. and Sheshonk. The reliefs upon which prisoners' heads appear must have come from Tell-el-Yahoudeh.

These enamels were not always used upon stone or faience; their charming varieties of tone are also found upon wooden grounds. M. Maspero mentions as an example of this the fragments of a mummy case in the Turin Museum. An inscription upon the wood is surrounded by faience ornament of a very rich colour. Mariette also mentions bronzes in which the remains of enamel and of *pietra dura* inlays are yet to be seen.[1]

Enamel is glass coloured by means of a metallic oxide and spread thinly over a surface, with which it is combined by means of heat. The Egyptians must therefore have understood the manufacture of glass at a very early date. It is represented in the paintings at Beni-Hassan.[2] Workmen are shown crouched by a fire and blowing glass bottles by means of a hollow cane, exactly as they do to this day. This industry continued to flourish in Egypt down to the Roman epoch. The glass manufacturers of Alexandria told Strabo that Egypt possessed a peculiar vitrifiable earth, without which the magnificent works in many-coloured glass could not be executed.[3] It is generally supposed that this "earth" was soda. The Venetians of the middle ages imported the soda required for their glass-making from Alexandria. It is said that Egyptian soda is the best known. It comes from the ashes of a plant called by botanists *Mesem Bryanthemum copticum*.[4]

Vessels of Egyptian glass are to be found in most museums, which recall those of Venice by their bands and fillets of brilliant colours. As for ordinary glass it seems never to have been quite transparent and colourless; it was always tinged with green and slightly opaque. It was upon their productions in colour that the fame of the Egyptian glass-makers depended. They produced vases, cups, paterae, goblets, beads and other ornaments for necklaces and bracelets, amulets and everything else that the material would allow, in prodigious quantities, both for domestic consumption and for exportation. At one time mummies were covered with a kind of garment composed of multitudinous strings of beads.

Statuettes, such as the two figured below, were also made of

---

[1] MARIETTE, *Notice du Musée de Boulak*. p. 69.
[2] WILKINSON, *Manners and Customs*, vol. ii. p. 140.
[3] STRABO, xvi. ch. ii. § 25.
[4] PRISSE, *History de l'Art Égyptien*, text. p. 313.

glass. The larger of the two, which still has the hook, by which it was suspended, in its head, is entirely covered with parti-coloured ornaments similar to those shown upon its right shoulder. Our draughtsman at Boulak had no time to finish the drawing he had begun, and we have reproduced it in its actual condition rather than omit it or have it completed in any degree conjecturally. The details given afford a sufficiently good idea of the motives

FIG. 306.—Glass statuette. Boulak. Actual size.

FIG. 307.—Glass statuette. Boulak. Actual size.

employed by the Egyptian artist. The ornamentation of the other figure is more simple (Fig. 307), but the attitude is the same. There are two colours on the very well modelled head which acts as tail-piece to the *Introduction* in our first volume. The globe of the eye and its contours stand out in black against the yellow of the flesh. The wig is also black.

Nothing can have been more surprising to the ancient traveller who set foot upon the soil of Egypt for the first time, than the vast number of these objects in coloured glass and in green or blue faience. They appeared everywhere; upon the walls of buildings and upon the persons of their inhabitants, upon every article which helped to furnish tombs or temples, palaces or private houses. Everything shone with the brilliant colours of this enamel, whose unchanging brightness was so grateful to a southern eye. It harmonized to perfection with the whiteness of the fine linen worn by the richer classes of Egyptians, and formed happy combinations with the rich red and blue fringes which bordered their robes and girdles. Enamel was much more easily cleaned than cloth. When it was tarnished by dust or dirt, a few drops of water would restore all its brightness. The lavish employment of such a material doubtless did much to give the persons of the Egyptians and their dwellings that neat and smiling aspect which so charmed foreign visitors. Herodotus tells us that one of the features which most strongly warned the traveller that he was in the presence of a very ancient and refined civilization, was the national passion for a cleanliness that was almost too fastidious, for fine linen constantly renewed, for frequent ablutions, for the continual use of the razor. A nation dressed in spotless white, shaved, circumcised and continually washed, afforded a curious contrast to shaggy barbarians clothed in wool that was dirty with long usage. Even in the time of Herodotus more than one tribe of Greek mountaineers was still in existence, that hardly differed in habits and costume from those early ancestors of the Hellenes who, as Homer tells us, "slept upon the bare ground and never washed their feet."

§ 3. *Metal-work and Jewelry.*

Egypt had, perhaps, her age of stone. MM. Hamy and François Lenormant have called attention to the cut and polished flints which have been found in Egypt, and Mariette brought a whole series of them to the Universal Exhibition of 1878. Mariette, however, was careful to remark that some of these flint implements, exactly similar in appearance to those found in the open air, were discovered in the tombs, among the mummies.[1]

[1] MARIETTE, *De la Galerie de l'Égypte Ancienne à l'Exposition Rétrospective du Trocadéro*, 1878, pp. 111, 112. WILKINSON, *The Manners and Customs of the Ancient Egyptians*, etc. vol. ii. p. 261.

These flint knives, therefore, are not necessarily anterior to the commencement of Egyptian history, that is to say to the first dynasties mentioned by Manetho. Moreover, Herodotus tells us that it was with a flint knife that the Egyptian embalmer made his first incision upon the corpse entrusted to him.[1] It would, then, be difficult to distinguish between prehistoric flint objects and those which belong to the civilization whose remains we are now studying, while our examination of the latter leads us quite as deeply into the past as we desire to go.

Even under the earliest dynasties the Egyptians were metalworkers.

Several bronze objects are in existence which date at least from the end of the Ancient Empire,[2] and in the bas-reliefs of the tomb of Ti, we see smiths directing the flame, by means of long tubes, upon the block of metal which they are forging (Fig. 21, Vol. I.). This is a kind of elementary blow-pipe, such as those still used by certain savage tribes.

The Egyptians began by making use of pure copper, which they could obtain from Sinai and other mines within easy reach. Various indications allow us to conclude that they were long ignorant of the fact that by mixing it with a little tin its hardness could be enormously increased.[3] In any case, they had certainly discovered the secret during the fifth, or, at latest, the sixth, dynasty. As to where they found the tin, we can say nothing positively. No deposit of that metal is known either in Egypt or in the neighbouring countries. It may possibly have come from India, passing through various hands on its way. In later years the Phœnicians brought it from Spain and the southern shores of Britain. The metal must then have become common enough, and it was used in large quantities by the Egyptian founders. Thus when the pavement of the room in the north-western corner of the Temple of Rameses III. at Medinet-Abou was raised, nearly a thousand bronze statues, all representing Osiris, were found. The existence of this deposit bears witness to the Egyptian habit of sanctifying the site of a new temple by sowing it broad-cast with sacred images.[4]

[1] HERODOTUS, ii. 86. [2] See page 197.
[3] See BIRCH, notes to Wilkinson's *Manners and Customs*, vol. ii. p. 232, edition of 1878.
[4] MARIETTE, *Itineraire*, p. 210.

Bronze was employed for all kinds of domestic purposes. The graceful mirror-handle reproduced below (Fig. 308) is in the Boulak Museum. So too, are the bronze hair-pin (Fig. 309) and the curiously designed dagger (Fig. 310).

The analysis of various specimens of Egyptian bronze shows that the proportion of tin which it contained was not constant. It varies from about five to fifteen per cent.[1] Traces of iron are also found in it.

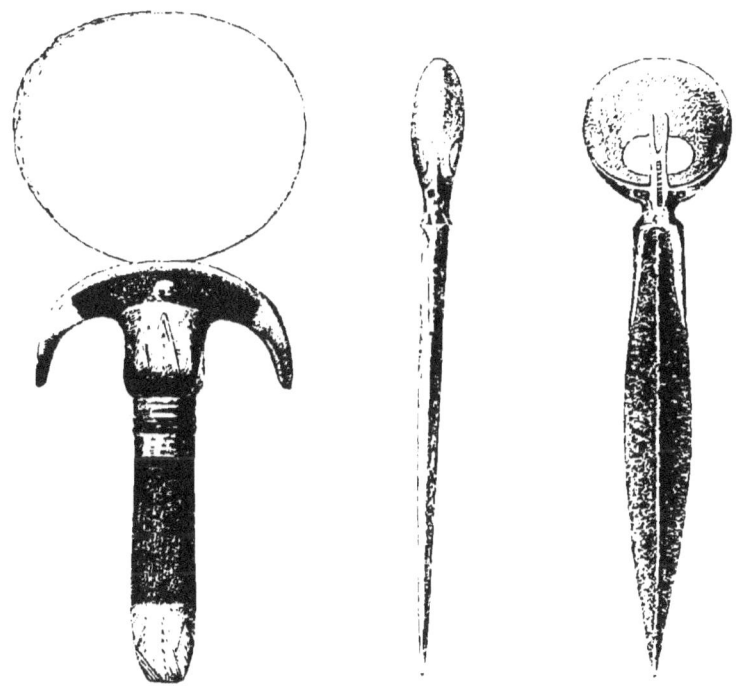

FIG. 308.—Mirror-handle.   FIG. 309.—Bronze hair-pin.   FIG. 310.—Bronze dagger.

The date at which this last named metal was introduced into the country is still matter of dispute. Various facts brought together by Dr. Birch, lead us to think that the Egyptians were acquainted with iron at least as soon as the commencement of the Theban supremacy,[2] but it would seem that they always made a greater use of bronze.

[1] WILKINSON, *Manners and Customs*, etc. vol. ii. pp. 232 and 401.
[2] *Ibid.* vol. ii. pp. 250, 251.

The word that signifies gold appears in the oldest inscriptions, and in the pictures at Beni-Hassan contemporary with the twelfth dynasty the whole process of making gold ornaments is represented.[1] From that time onward the Egyptian Pharaohs caused the veins of quartz in the mountains between the Nile and the Red Sea to be worked ; they also obtained large supplies of the precious metal from Ethiopia. Silver came from Asia. It seems to have been rarer than gold, at least during the last centuries of the monarchy. As Belzoni remarked, while gold is lavished upon the mummies and upon all the sepulchral furniture about them silver is only met with in exceptional cases.[2] In 1878, Mariette exhibited in Paris five massive patera-shaped silver vases, which, from the style of their ornaments, he attributed to the Saite epoch.

The finest specimens of Egyptian jewelry now extant belong to the three great Theban dynasties. We may give as instances the jewels of Queen Aah-hotep, which are among the most precious treasures of the Boulak Museum,[3] and those found in the tomb of Kha-em-uas, son of Rameses II. These are in the Louvre. The splendid breast ornament figured on the opposite page (Fig. 311), is one of them. It is made of lapis-lazuli and gold, and is thus described by M. Pierret : " Jewel in the form of a naos, in which a vulture and an uræus are placed side by side ; above them floats a hawk with extended wings ; in his claws are seals, the emblems of eternity. Under the frieze of the naos an oval with the prenomen of Rameses II. is introduced. Two *tet* are placed in the lower angles of the frame."[4] These jewels were funerary in character. They consist of a little chapel in the middle of which there is usually a scarab—emblem of transformation and immortality—adoring the goddesses Isis and Nephthys. They are called *pectorals* because they were placed upon the bosoms of the dead. Great numbers of them have been

[1] WILKINSON, *Manners and Customs*, vol. ii. pp. 233-237.
[2] BELZONI, *Narrative*, etc. vol. i. p. 277.
[3] MARIETTE, *Notice du Musée de Boulak*, Nos. 810-839. Coloured reproductions of them are published in M. CÉSAR DALY's *Revue de l'Architecture*, a sequel to the *Histoire d'Égypte d'après les Monuments* (published in 1860) of M. ERNEST DESJARDINS.
[4] PIERRET, *Catalogue de la Salle Historique*, Louvre, No. 521. This jewel is reproduced, with many others from the same tomb, in two fine coloured plates in MARIETTE's unfinished work, *Le Sérapéum de Memphis*. Folio, 1857.

found in the tombs, in metal, in wood, and in earthenware; few, however, are as rich as that of Kha-em-uas. Each compartment of the golden frame-work is filled in either with coloured glass or with a piece of some *pietra dura* with a rich hue of its own.

In the same case as this pectoral there are two golden hawks incrusted in the same fashion, which may have belonged to a

Fig. 311.—Pectoral. Actual size. Drawn by Saint-Elme Gautier.

similar jewel. The larger of the two (Fig. 312) has a ram's head.[1] There is a necklace about its throat, and in its talons it grasps a pair of seals, the symbols of reproduction and eternity. The same emblem is held by the smaller hawk (Fig. 313), whose wings form a large crescent.[2]

[1] PIERRET, *Catalogue de la Salle Historique*, Louvre. No. 535.
[2] *Ibid.* No. 534.

Living forms are interpreted in a less conventional fashion in the little monuments which are known as *ægides*, on account of their

FIG. 312.—Golden Hawk. Actual size. Drawn by Saint-Elme Gautier.

shape. This may be seen by reference to one recently acquired by the Louvre (Fig. 314). The name of an Osorkhon of the

FIG 313.—Golden Hawk. Actual size. Drawn by Saint-Elme Gautier.

twenty-second dynasty and that of Queen Ta-ti-bast are on the back. At the top appears the lion-head of the goddess Sekhet, modelled with great skill and freedom, and supported on each side by the head of a hawk; below these comes a plate of gold, entirely covered with fine engraving. A seated figure with expanded wings forms a centre for numerous bands of ornament in which the open flower of the lotus is combined with its buds and circular leaves.

Necklaces are also very rich and various in design. Fig. 315 is the restoration of one which exists in a dislocated state in one of the cases of the Louvre. It is formed of glass beads in four rows, below which hangs a row of pendants, probably charms. The *tet*, the god *Bes*, the *oudja* or symbolic eye, &c., are to be distinguished among them.

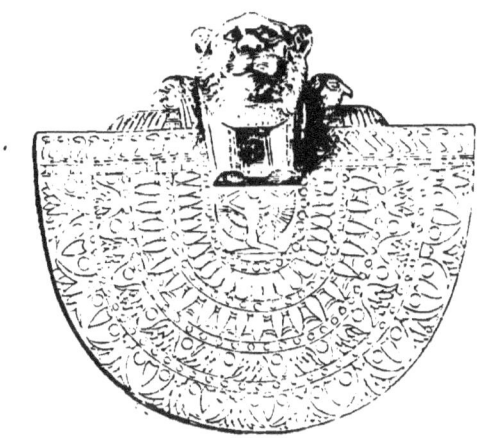

FIG. 314.—Ægis. Louvre. Actual size. Drawn by Saint-Elme Gautier

The beautiful group of Osiris, Isis, and Horus deserves to rank as a work of sculpture (Fig. 316). These little figures are of gold. Osiris is crouching between the other two deities on a pedestal of lapis-lazuli, which bears the name of Osorkhon II. The inscription upon the base consists of a religious benediction upon the same Pharaoh. These little figures are finely executed, and the base upon which the group stands is incrusted with coloured glass.

We have already reproduced specimens of finger rings (Figs. 241 and 243), and the additional examples on page 387 will help to show how varied were their form. Many of these little articles have moveable or rotating stones upon which figures or inscriptions are engraved. Some have this merely upon a flattened or thickened part of the ring, which, again, is sometimes double (Fig. 318). Ear-rings of many different forms have been found; they are ornamented with little figures in relief (Figs. 319 and 320).

Some writers have spoken of the *cloisonné enamels* of Egypt. This expression is inaccurate, as Mariette has observed.[1] There are certainly *cloisons* in many of the jewels above described—such as the pectoral and the two hawks—*cloisons* made up of thin ribs of silver or gold, but these compartments are not combined by firing with the material used to fill them. Where the Chinese place enamel the Egyptians inserted fragments of coloured glass or of such stones as the amethyst, cornelion, lapis-lazuli, turquoise, jasper, &c. The work was not passed through an oven after the insertion of these colouring substances; it was therefore rather a mosaic than an enamel in the proper sense of the term. By an analagous process bronze was damascened with gold and silver, threads of these two metals being inserted in prepared grooves and hammered into place. Mariette has called attention to several bronzes at Boulak thus inlaid with gold,[2] and in the Louvre there is a graceful little sphinx marked with the cartouche of Smendes, which is damascened with silver.

The Egyptians were also workers in ivory, which was obtained in large quantities from Ethiopia. Sometimes they were content with carving it (Fig. 322), sometimes they engraved upon it with the *point* and then filled in the design with black, giving it a forcible relief (Fig. 323). The ivory plaque from Sakkarah reproduced in Fig. 321, deserves to be studied for its technical method, although it dates from the Greek period. The blacks shown in our woodcut are produced in the original by filling up with mastic the hollows made with the *point*.

Famous sculptors were especially fond of working in ivory. Iritesen speaks as follows upon a stele translated by M. Maspero:—"Ah! there is no one who excels at this work except myself and the eldest of my legitimate sons. God decided that he should excel, and I have seen the perfection of his handiwork

---

[1] MARIETTE, *Notice du Musée de Boulak*, No. 388. *Galerie de l'Égypte Ancienne au Trocadéro*, pp. 114, 115.

[2] MARIETTE, *Notice du Musée*, Nos. 107, 108, 131.

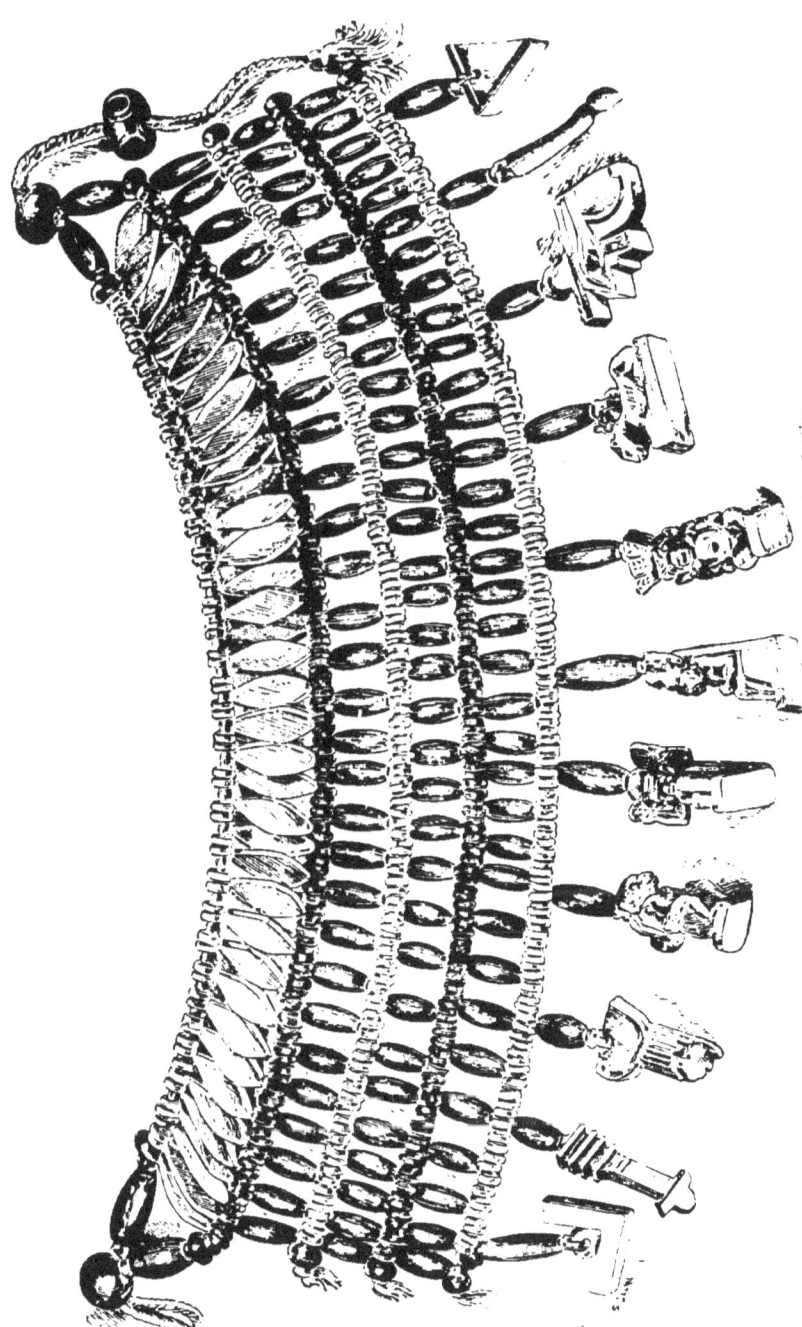

Fig. 315.—Necklace. Louvre. Drawn by Saint-Elme Gautier.

as an artist, as the chief of those who work in precious stones, in gold, silver, ivory and ebony."[1]

FIG. 316.—Osiris, Isis, and Horus.

No traces of amber have been discovered in Egypt, and egyptologists tell us that no word for it is to be found in the language.

FIGS. 317, 318.—Rings. Louvre.   FIGS. 319, 320.—Ear-rings. Louvre.

A complete idea of Egyptian jewelry and work in the precious metals cannot be given without colour ; without its assistance the brilliance, softened into completest harmony by the action of time,

[1] *Transactions of the Society of Biblical Archaeology*, v. part ii. 1877.

which distinguishes the objects of which we have now been speaking, can only be guessed at. Our best advice to those who wish to thoroughly appreciate their beauty, is to examine them in the museums where they are exposed. But even in the black and white of our draughtsman the excellent taste which animated the Egyptian jeweller may be fairly estimated. Other races, the Greeks, for instance, gave more lightness and a more refined grace to their trinkets, but our familiarity with their productions does not prevent us from recognizing the nobility

FIG. 321.—Ivory Plaque. Boulak.

and amplitude of these designs. Their originality, too, is strongly brought out by their affinity to the style and decoration of the great national buildings; we might almost be tempted to think that their designs and colour compositions were supplied by architects.

The same characteristics are to be recognized on the vases figured in the royal tombs at Thebes.[1] They are coloured yellow

[1] See two plates of PRISSE entitled: "*Art Industriel. Vases en Or Émaillé; Rhytons et autres Vases.*"

and blue, and both their form and tint forbid us to suppose that

FIG. 322.—Ivory Castanet. Louvre.

they were of any material but metal, of gilt bronze or gold, or of silver. Incrustations in enamel or coloured *pietra dura* relieve the monotony of the metal surface. Some of these pieces seem to have been very large. Their decoration and design is rich and complex. Flowers and half-opened buds, lions' heads, masks of Bes and of negroes, birds, sphinxes, etc., are introduced. We may presume that such objects were made for presentation to the gods and preservation in treasure-houses ; few of them could have been put to any practical use. The great men of Egypt followed the example of Pharaoh in enriching the temples. The stele of Neb-oua, chief prophet of Osiris in the reign of Thothmes III., runs thus : " I have consecrated numerous gifts in the temple of my father Osiris ; in silver, in gold, in lapis-lazuli, in copper, and in all kinds of precious stones." [1]

§ 4. *Woodwork.*

The Egyptians made great use of wood. Under the Ancient Empire it furnished the material for all their lighter constructions, to which, by the help of colour, great variety and cheerfulness was imparted. Even in those early ages the cabinet-maker or joiner endeavoured to make his work artistic. Various articles of furniture had their feet carved into the shape of lions' paws, or the hoofs of oxen.[2] To judge from certain stone objects preserved in the mastabas, wood, which was comparatively easy to work, must have afforded the material for those skilfully-made and complex pieces of furniture whose forms are preserved for us by paintings from the Theban epoch.[3]

In these pictures the labours of the carpenter (Fig. 324), and those of the cabinet-maker (Fig. 325) are often represented. The specimens of furniture in our modern museums are mostly of a commonplace character, but they are interesting from the light they throw upon the methods of the Egyptian joiners (Fig. 326). The richness and elaboration of Egyptian furniture under the great

---

[1] MARIETTE, *Notice du Musée*, No. 93.
[2] LEPSIUS, *Denkmaeler*, part ii. plates 36 and 90.
[3] Among such objects is a table for libations, which was found in a tomb at Sakkarah. It is supported by two lions, whose pendent tails are twisted round a vase. MARIETTE, *Notice du Musée*, No. 93.

WOODWORK. 391

Theban dynasties can only be estimated from the paintings. We

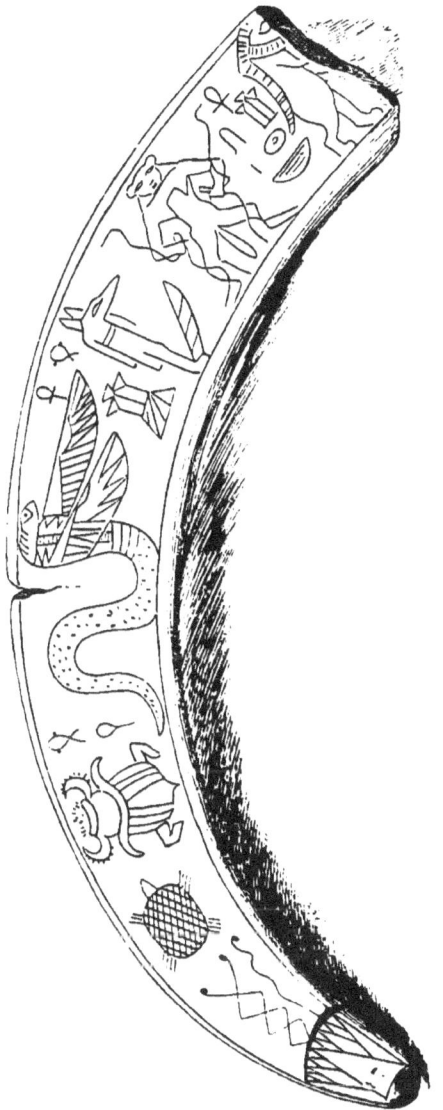

FIG. 323.—Fragment of an Ivory Castanet. Louvre.

have already seen that their musical instruments were elaborately decorated ; the harp of the famous minstrel figured on page 345 is entirely covered with incrustations, and its foot is ornamented with a bust of graceful design. In this luxurious age the arts of

FIG. 324.—Workman splitting a piece of wood. Gournah. From Champollion.

the cabinet-maker must have been carried to a great height. The interior of an ancient Egyptian house must have been very different from the bareness which greets a visitor to the modern

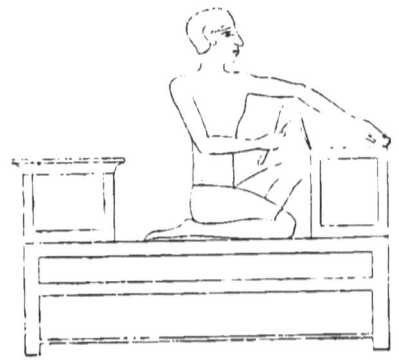

FIG. 325.—Joiner making a bed. From Champollion.

East. Chairs with or without arms, tables of varied form, folding seats, foot-stools, brackets supporting vases of flowers, cabinets in which objects of value were locked up, filled the rooms. The upper classes of Egypt lived a life that was refined and elegant as well as civilized. A great lord of the time of a Thothmes or a Rameses was not content, like a Turkish bey or pacha, with a divan, a few carpets, and a mattress which, after being locked up in a cupboard during the day, is spread upon the floor for his accommodation at night. He had his bedstead, often inlaid with metal or ivory, and, like a modern European, he had other articles of furniture besides.

Several pictures are extant in which Egyptian receptions— Egyptian *salons*—are represented. The company is not crouched upon the earth, in the modern Oriental fashion. Both men and women are seated upon chairs, some of which have cushioned seats and backs.[1]

FIG. 326.—Coffer for sepulchral statuettes. Louvre.

The elegance of these seats may be guessed from the two examples on the next page, one from the tomb of Rameses III. (Fig. 327). the other from that of Chamhati (Fig. 328). They are both royal chairs, or thrones. The smaller chair figures among a number of things presented by Chamhati to his master, Pharaoh, and we need feel no surprise that among the supports of both these pieces of furniture, those crouching prisoners which became about this time such a common motive in Egyptian ornament, are to be found. In the one example, they are incorporated with the carved members which support the seat, in the other they are inserted between the legs, which are shaped respectively like the

[1] See the illustration which EBERS calls *A Reception in Ancient Egypt*. (*Ægypten*, vol. ii. p. 276.)

fore and hind quarters of a lion. Each arm terminates in a lion's head. A crowned, winged, and hawk-headed uræus, some lotus-flowers, and a sphinx with a vanquished enemy beneath his paws, are carved upon either side of the chair. The scheme of decoration as a whole is a happy combination of æsthetic beauty with allusions to the power and success of the king.

These elaborate pieces of furniture are only known to us by the paintings, but when we turn to articles of a less ambitious description, such as toys and what are called *bimbeloterie* in French, and,

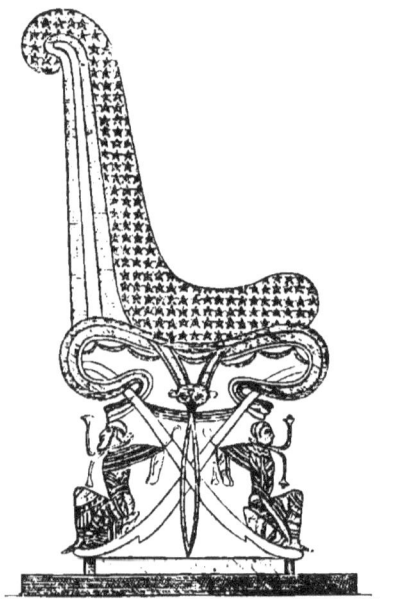

FIG. 327.—Chair. From the *Description*.   FIG. 328.—Chair. From Prisse.

rather helplessly, "fancy articles" in English, we have many fine specimens to turn to. Of these the most conspicuous are those perfume spoons whose handles so often embody charming motives. The more simple examples are ornamented merely with the buds or open flowers of the lotus (Fig. 329). Others, however, have beautifully carved figures. In Fig. 330 we see a young woman picking a lotus bud. Several stalks crowned with open flowers support the bowl, which is shaped like that of a modern spoon, except that its narrow end is turned towards the handle. The attitude and expression of this little figure are very good. The right foot, which is thrust forward, only touches the ground by the toes. The water in which she is about to step may hide sharp flints or unkindly roots, and, with commendable prudence, she begins by testing the bottom. Her legs are bare, because she has raised her garment well above the knee before descending into the marsh. Her carefully plaited hair and her crimped petticoat show that her social condition is good.

Another spoon shows us a musician between stems of papyrus. She stands upright upon one of those boats which were used in the papyrus-brakes (Fig. 331). Her instrument is a long-handled guitar. The musician herself seems to have been one of those dancers and singers whose condition was pretty much the same in ancient as in modern Egypt. Her only garment is a short petticoat knotted about her waist. The bowl of this spoon is rectangular.

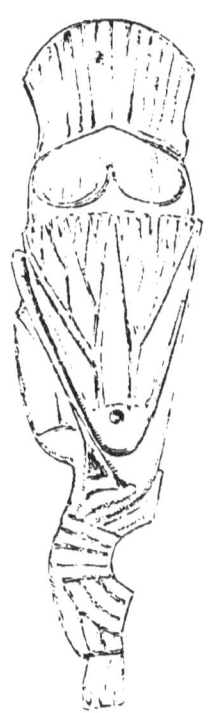

FIG. 329.—Perfume spoon. Boulak. Drawn by Bourgoin.

Another common motive is that of a girl swimming. She is represented at the moment when her stroke is complete; her upper and lower limbs are stretched out to their full extent so as to offer the least possible resistance to the water (Fig. 257). There is a perfume-box in the Louvre which is supported on a figure contrasting strongly with the last described. The box is shaped like a heavy sack, and is supported upon the right shoulder of a slave, who bends beneath its weight. By the thick lips, flat nose, heavy jaw, low forehead, and closely-shaven, sugarloaf head, we may recognize this as yet another of those caricatures of prisoners which we have already encountered in such numbers.[1] A perfume-box at Boulak should also be mentioned. It is in the shape of a goose turning its head backwards. Its wings open and give access to the hollow of the box.

This desire to ornament even the most apparently insignificant

[1] This figure is reproduced in Rayet's *Monuments de l'Art Antique* and described by M. MASPERO. (*Cuillers de Toilette en Bois.*)

objects of domestic use was universal. The sticks which are

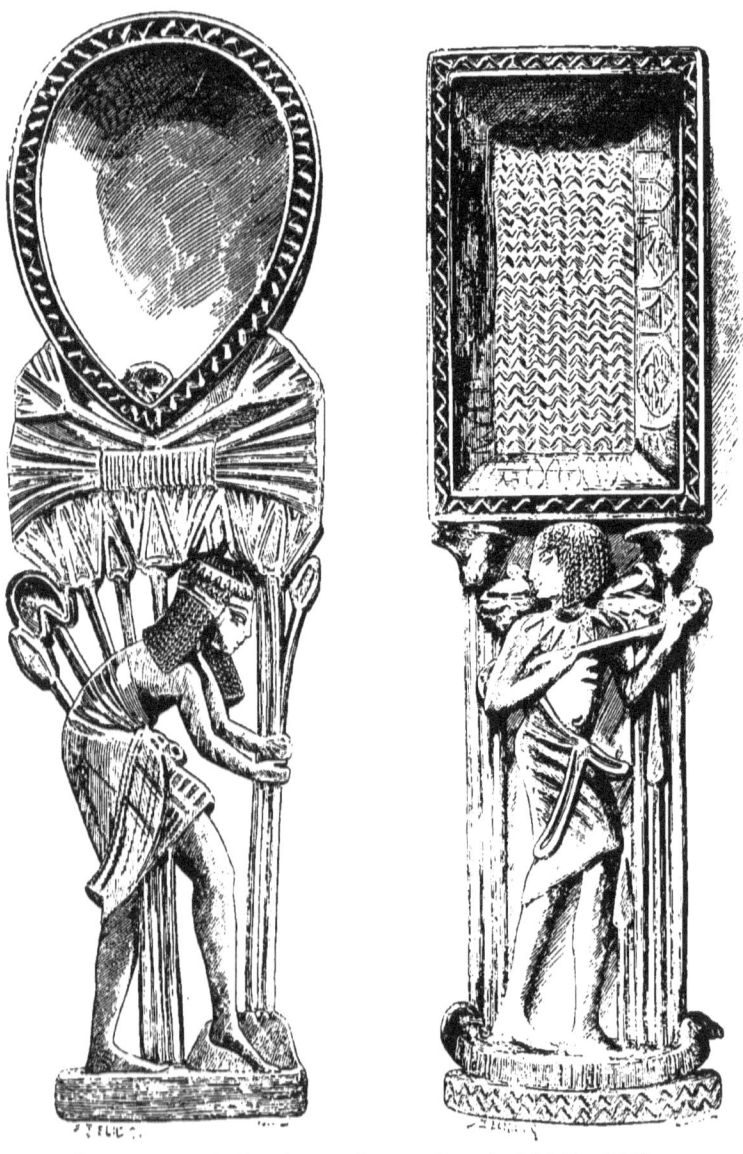

FIGS. 330, 331.—Perfume Spoons. Louvre. Drawn by Saint-Elme Gautier.

shown in the bas-reliefs in the hands of almost every Egyptian of good social position, were generally provided with a more or less richly ornamented head. The simplest terminate in a handle which appears to be modelled after the leaf of the lotus, as it rises above the level of the water, and, before opening to the full expansion, forms an obtuse angle with the stalk which supports it (Fig. 332). Other sticks of a similar shape have an eye painted upon them (Fig. 333). Sometimes the handle is shaped like a lotus-flower surmounted by an oval knob (Fig. 334). Wooden pins have been found with the head of a jackal or some other animal carved upon them (Fig. 335).

Wooden articles were often entirely gilt. A Hathoric capital in the Louvre (Fig. 336) is an instance of this. The outlines of the eyes and eyebrows stand out in black upon the dead gold which covers the rest of this little monument.

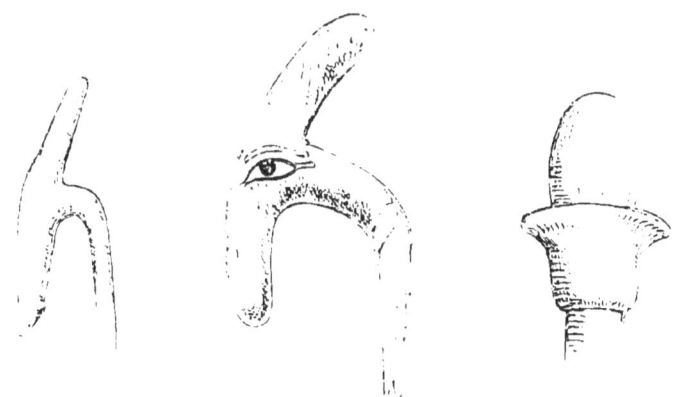

FIGS. 332—334.—Walking-stick handles. Boulak.

The coffin-makers were large consumers of wood. Some mummy cases were of that material, others of a very thick board made up of many layers of linen glued together with such skill and firmness that the resulting substance had all the hardness and resonance of wood. Cases of both kinds were covered with a thin coat of plaster, varnished, and decorated with designs in colour. The thickness of the plaster coat may be easily seen in the numerous cracks which these coffins display.

All the decorative motives which we find traced by the brush or engraved by the chisel upon the walls of buildings and upon works in terra cotta, in metal, and in wood, must have been repeated upon the woven stuffs of the country, and upon those needle embroideries with which they were ornamented. There is nothing in which the superiority of Egyptian manufactures is better shown than in linen cloth. Linen has been recovered from the tombs which is as fine as the best Indian muslin. Some has been found which feels like silk to the touch, and equals the best French *batiste* in the perfection of its weaving. We know from the bas-reliefs and paintings that some Egyptian stuffs had the transparency of gauze. Body-linen was usually of a dazzling

FIG. 335.—Wooden pin or peg. Boulak.

FIG. 336.—Hathoric capital. Louvre.

white, but in some instances it was dyed red, and in others it had borders made up of several bands of red and indigo blue. The designs were either woven in the stuff or applied to it by a process which gave effects not unlike those of our printed cottons. Golden threads were introduced into specially fine tissues. But the great excellence of Egypt in such matters as these was in her needle embroidery. Even during the epoch of Roman supremacy her productions of that kind were eagerly sought after.[1]

[1] MARTIAL, *Epigrammata*, xiv. 150. LUCAN, X. v. 141.

§ 5. *The Commerce of Egypt.*

When, under the great Theban Pharaohs, Egypt found herself impelled, either by force or by inclination, to emerge from her long isolation, her vast internal commerce and her industrial development must have had a greater effect over the foreigners with whom she came into contact than her gigantic buildings, or the colossal statues, bas-reliefs, and paintings with which they were adorned. During the Middle Empire she opened her gates to some extent to certain tribes of Semites and Kushites, who dwelt close to her frontier. After her conquest by the Hyksos, and the establishment, some centuries later, of her own supremacy in Syria, she never ceased to hold intercourse with her neighbours.

Her foreign relations were, however, peculiar in character. During many centuries it never occurred to the worshipper of Osiris that it was possible to live and die out of the sacred valley of the Nile. Thrown by some accident outside those limits which for him coincided with the frontiers of the habitable world, he would have felt as helpless as a Parisian stranded upon some cannibal island. In later years, after about the seventeenth century B.C. the separation between the Egyptians and the people of Western Asia became less complete. The time arrived when Babylon and Greece were in advance of Egypt; but even then the Egyptians shrank from changing their ancient habits. Their well-being in the valley watered by their sacred river was too complete, their pride of race was too great, to allow of their mingling readily with those whom they looked upon as barbarians. Still more effectual was their unwillingness, their fear, to confide their mortal bodies to any other soil but that of Egypt. There alone could they count with certainty upon the care and skill which would preserve it from final destruction. Nowhere but in the *Western Mountain* could they be sure of receiving the necessary offerings and homage. The gods who watched over the mummy, who guided the soul in its subterranean voyage and shielded it during the tests to which it was exposed after death, dwelt in Egypt alone. Military expeditions were pushed into Syria, and even as far as the Euphrates, but no Egyptian crossed the Isthmus of Suez without longing for the day of his return.

He brought back the plunder of his successful combats to the crowded cities of his own country, with their countless monuments and their memories of a glorious past; he could enjoy life only where the tombs of his ancestors and his own *happy dwelling* marked the spot where he should repose when that life had ceased.

By taste, then, the Egyptian was no traveller. But in time the men of other nations came to seek him; they came to buy from him the countless wonders which had been created by his skilful and patient industry. The Phœnician, especially after the beginning of the eighteenth dynasty, took upon himself the useful office of middle-man; in later days, under the Psemetheks and their successors, the Greek came to dispute that office with him. Like the Portuguese and the Dutch in China and Japan, first the Phœnicians and afterwards the Ionians had their *factories* at Memphis and in the cities of the Delta. Thanks to these adroit and enterprising middle-men, Egypt had a large foreign trade without either ships, sailors, or merchant-adventurers. Upon this point much valuable information has been obtained from the texts, but the discoveries of modern archæology have been still more efficient in enabling us to form a true and vivid conception of the trade carried on by the inhabitants of the Nile Valley.

Ever since attention was first drawn to the wide distribution of such objects, not a year has passed without articles of Egyptian manufacture being discovered at some distant point. Syria and Phœnicia are full of them; they have been found in Babylonia and in Assyria, upon the coasts of Asia Minor, in Cyprus, in the islands of the Grecian Archipelago, in Greece itself, in Etruria, in Latium, in Corsica and Sardinia, in the neighbourhood of Carthage; they are, in fact, spread over all Western Asia and the whole basin of the Mediterranean. At the moment when the Phœnicians began to secure the monopoly of this trade the Egyptian workshops had no rivals in the world; and when, after many centuries, other nations began to pour their manufactures into the same markets, they had long to compete in vain against a prestige which had been built up by ages of good work and well earned notoriety.

CHAPTER VI.

THE GENERAL CHARACTERISTICS OF EGYPTIAN ART, AND THE PLACE OF EGYPT IN ART HISTORY.

IN the study which we have now almost completed, we have made no attempt to reconstitute the history of Egypt. We are without the qualifications necessary for such a task. We do not read the hieroglyphs, and are therefore without the key to that great library in stone and wood, in canvas and papyrus—a library which could afford material for thousands of volumes—which has been left to the world by the ancient Egyptians.

Our one object has been to make Egyptian art better known; to place its incomparable age and its originality in a clear light, and to show the value of the example set by the first-born of civilization to the peoples who came after them and began to experience the wants and tastes which had long been completely satisfied in the Valley of the Nile. The importance and absolute originality of the national forms of art were hardly suspected before the days of Champollion; he was something more than a philologist of genius; his intellect was too penetrating and his taste too active, to leave him blind to any of the forms taken by the thoughts and sentiments of that Egypt which was so dear to him. " I shall write to our friend Dubois from Thebes," he says in one of his letters, "after having thoroughly explored Egypt and Nubia. I can say beforehand, that our Egyptians will cut a more important figure in the future, in the history of art, than in the past. I shall bring back with me a series of drawings from things fine enough to convert the most obstinate."[1]

The forecasts of Champollion and Nestor L'Hôte have been confirmed by the excavations of Lepsius and Mariette. The

[1] CHAMPOLLION, *Lettres d'Égypte et de Nubie*, p. 113.

conclusions deduced by the former from their examination of the remains in the Nile Valley have been indirectly corroborated by the discoveries which have successively revealed to us ancient Chaldæa, Syria, Phœnicia, Asia Minor, primitive Greece and Etruria. No one contests the priority of Egypt. It is recognized that its origin dates from a period long antecedent to that of any other race which, in its turn, played the leading *rôle* upon the stage of the ancient world. Justice has been rendered to the richness of its architecture, to the skill of its painters and sculptors, to the inventive fertility of its handicraftsmen and the refinement of their taste. And yet no one had attempted to do for Egypt what such men as Winckelmann and Ottfried Müller did for Greece, Etruria, and Rome. The methods of analysis and critical description which have long been employed with success upon another field, had never been applied to her art as a whole; no one had attempted to trace the steps of Egyptian genius during its long and slow evolution. The difficulties were great, especially when architecture was concerned. The ruins of the Pharaonic buildings had never been studied at first hand with such care as had been lavished upon the classic monuments of Italy and the Eastern Mediterranean. The works to which we have had to turn for information have many plates which make a fine show, which are accompanied with a luxury of detail which is very reassuring, but when we examine them closely we are amazed to find the most unforeseen omissions in their materials both for restorations, and for the reproduction of buildings in their actual condition.

When we attempt to make use of two separate works for the restoration of a temple, we are met with an embarrassment of another kind. Differences, and even actual contradictions, between one author and another are frequent, and that without any new excavations having taken place between-times to account for the inconsistency. Both observers had the same facts under their eyes, and it is often difficult to decide which of the two has observed badly. For one who does not wish to admit pure fancy into his work, all this causes doubts and hesitations which add greatly to the difficulty of his task.

The deeper we penetrate into such studies, the more we regret the insufficiency of the materials, and yet we have thought it imperative that we should fill in the framework of our history. It has one peculiar aspect which distinguishes it from all others:

the Egyptians gave much to their neighbours and received nothing from them, at least, during that period during which the character of their art as a whole was established. The features which are distinctive of Egyptian sculpture and architecture were determined at a time when there were no races in her neighbourhood sufficiently advanced to have influence upon them. This was not the case with Chaldæa and Assyria, at least, to anything like the same extent. Their work, moreover, has come down to us in a very fragmentary condition. Egypt is, then, the only country in which a complete development, begun and carried on solely by the energy and aptitude of one gifted race, can be followed through all its stages. Everywhere else the examples of predecessors or of neighbours have had an influence upon the march of art. They may have accelerated its progress, but at the same time they diverted it in some degree from its natural channel; they may have helped men to do better, it is certain that they led them to do what they would not otherwise have done. The goal may have been reached more quickly by those who had a guide, but it was reached by a path different from that they would have taken had they been left to their own devices. In the Valley of the Nile there was no guide, no precedent to follow. There, and there alone, did the evolution of the plastic faculty preserve a normal organic character from the commencement of its activity almost to its final decease.

From all this it follows that the art history of Egypt may be reviewed in terms more definite, and that the conclusions drawn from it are more certain or, at least, more probable, than that of any other nation. It is, if we may be allowed such a phrase, more transparent. Elsewhere, when we find a new decorative form introduced, or a new style become prevalent, it is always open to us to ask whether they may not have been foreign importations. When such borrowing is suspected we have to trace it to its original source, and often the search is both slow and painful. In the case of the Egyptians such problems have to be solved differently. There is no need to extend one's inquiries beyond the happy valley where, as in an inaccessible island surrounded by a vast ocean of barbarians, they lived for ages whose number can never be guessed. Other civilizations are to be partly explained by those of their predecessors and their neighbours; that of Egypt is only to be explained by itself, by the inherent aptitudes of its people and their physical surroundings. Every element of which the national genius made use was indigenous; nowhere else can the fruit be so easily traced to the seed, and the natural forces observed which developed the one from the other.

Another point of attraction in the study of Egyptian art is that extreme antiquity which carries us back, without losing the thread of the story, to a period when other races are still in the impenetrable darkness of prehistoric times. A glance into so remote a past affords us a pleasure not unmingled with fright and bewilderment. Our feelings are like those of the Alpine traveller, who, standing upon some lofty summit, leans over the abyss at his feet and lets his eye wander for a moment over the immeasurable depths, in which forests and mountain streams can be dimly made out through mist and shadow.

Long before the earliest centuries of which other nations have preserved any tradition, Egypt, as she appears to us in her first creations, already possesses an art so advanced that it seems the end rather than the beginning of a long development. The bas-reliefs and statues which have been found in the tombs and pyramids of Meidoum, of Sakkarah and of Gizeh, are perhaps the masterpieces of Egyptian sculpture, and, as Ampère says, "the pyramid of Cheops is of all human monuments the oldest, the simplest, and the greatest."

The work of the First Theban Empire is no less astonishing. "Twenty-five centuries before our era, the kings of Egypt carried out works of public utility, which can only be compared, for scale and ability, to the Suez Canal and the Mont Cenis Tunnel. In the thirteenth century B.C., towards the presumed epoch of the Exodus and the Trojan war, while Greece was still in a condition similar to that of modern Albania, namely, divided up into many small hostile clans, five centuries before Rome existed even in name, Egypt had arrived at the point reached by the Romans under Cæsar and the Antonines; she carried on a continual struggle against the barbarians who, after being beaten and driven back for centuries, were at last endeavouring to cross all her frontiers at once."[1]

The princes, whose achievements were sung by Pentaour, the Egyptian Homer, had artists in their service as great as those of

---

[1] RHONÉ, *L'Égypte Antique*, extract from *L'Art Ancien à l'Exposition de* 1878.

the early dynasties, artists who raised and decorated the Great Hall of Karnak, one of the wonders of architecture.

It is not only by its originality and age that the art of Egypt deserves the attention of the historian and the artist; it is conspicuous for power, and, we may say, for beauty. In studying each of the great branches of art separately we have endeavoured to make clear the various qualities displayed by the Egyptian artist, either in the decoration of the national monuments or in the interpretation of living form by sculpture and painting. We have also endeavoured to show how closely allied the handicrafts of Egypt were to its arts.

Our aim has been to embrace Egyptian art as a whole and to form a judgment upon it, but, by force of circumstances, architecture has received the lion's share of our attention. Some of our readers may ask why an equilibrium was not better kept between that art whose secrets are the most difficult to penetrate and whose beauties are least attractive, not only to the crowd but even to cultivated intellects, and its rivals.

The apparent disproportion is justified by the place held by architecture in the Egyptian social system. We have proved that the architect was socially superior to the painter and even to the sculptor. His uncontested pre-eminence is to be explained by the secondary *rôle* which sculpture and painting had to fill. Those arts were cultivated in Egypt with sustained persistence; rare abilities were lavished upon them, and we may even say that masterpieces were produced. But plastic images were less admired ·in themselves, their intrinsic beauty was less keenly appreciated, in consequence of the practical religious or funerary office which they had to fulfil. Statues and pictures were always means to an end ; neither of them ever became ends in themselves, as they were in Greece,—works whose final object was to elevate the mind and to afford to the intellectual side of man that peculiar enjoyment which we call æsthetic pleasure.

Such conditions being given, it is easy to understand how painters and sculptors were subordinated to architects. It was to the latter that the most pious and, at the same time, the most magnificent of kings, confided all his resources, and his example was followed by his wealthy subjects ; it was to him that every one employed had to look as the final disposer ; the other artists were no more than agents and translators of a thought which was grasped in its entirety by the architect alone. His work, embellished with all the graces of a decoration which reckoned neither time nor materials, formed a homogeneous and well-balanced whole. It was in inventing, in bringing to perfection, and in contemplating such a work that the Egyptian mind gave itself up most completely to love for beauty. If we take an Egyptian building in its unity, as the product of a combined effort on the part of a crowd of artists labouring under the directing will of the architect, we shall no longer feel surprise at the space demanded by our study of his art.

The Egyptian temple of the Theban period, as we know it by our examination of Karnak and Luxor, the Ramesseum and Medinet-Abou, gives us the best and highest idea of the national genius. We have had nothing more at heart than the restoration of these edifices by the comparison of all available materials; we have endeavoured to re-establish their general arrangements, to describe their distinctive features, and to grasp their original physiognomies as a whole. But while making this effort we could never succeed in banishing the Greek temple from our minds. In vain we may try to judge the art of each people entirely on its own merits; such comparisons are inevitable, and without dwelling upon the question we shall devote a few words to it.

The differences are considerable and are all to the advantage of the Greek creation. Its nobility is more intimate and smiling; the genius of man has there succeeded better in giving to his work that unity which nature imprints on its highest productions, an unity which results from the complete alliance between different organs, and allows neither the subtraction of any part nor the addition of any novel element.

These contrasts may be explained to a certain extent by the religion of Greece and its social system. At present it is enough to point out their existence.

This superiority of the Greek temple will hardly be contested, but after it that of Egypt is certainly the most imposing and majestic product of ancient art. The religious buildings of Chaldæa, Assyria, Persia, Phœnicia, and Judæa, have left but slight remains behind them, and the information which we possess as to their proportions and general arrangements is obscure and incomplete. But we at least know enough to sketch out a parallel which is all to the honour of Egypt. Some of these eastern temples, being entirely composed of inferior materials, never had the richness and variety presented by the monuments of Memphis and Thebes. Others were but more or less free imitations of Egyptian types. Suppose that temple of Bel, which was one of the wonders of Babylon, still standing upon the great plains of Mesopotamia; it would, in spite of its height and its enormous mass, in spite of the various colours in which it was clothed, appear cold and heavy beside Karnak in its first glory, beside the imposing splendours of the Hypostyle Hall.

Until the rise of Greek art, the artists of Egypt remained, then, the great masters of antiquity. Her architecture, by the beauty of its materials, by its proportions, by its richness and variety, was without a rival until the birth of the Doric temple. Her sculptors betrayed a singular aptitude in grasping and interpreting the features of individuals or of races, and they succeeded in creating types which reached general truth without becoming strangers to individuality. Their royal statues were great, not so much by their dimensions as by the nobility of their style, and their expression of calm and pensive gravity. The existence of a few child-like conventions, from which they never shook themselves free, cannot prevent us from feeling deep admiration for the insight into life, the purity of contour, the freedom and truth of design which distinguish their bas-reliefs and paintings. Egyptian decoration is everywhere informed by a fertile invention and a happy choice of motives, by a harmony of tints which charms the eye even now, when the endless tapestry with which tombs and houses, palaces and sanctuaries, were hung, is rent and faded. The smallest works of the humblest craftsman are distinguished by a desire for grace which spreads over them like a reflection from art and beauty, and they helped to carry some knowledge of the brilliant civilization of Egypt to the most distant coasts of the ancient world.

During the earlier ages of antiquity, this civilization exercised upon the nascent art of neighbouring, and even of some distant people, an influence analogous to that which Greece was in later days to wield over the whole basin of the Mediterranean. For many a long century the style of Egypt enjoyed an unchallenged supremacy and offered a forecast of that universal acceptance which was to be the lot of Grecian art, when after two or three thousand years of fertility, of power, and of prestige, the work of Egypt would be done, and the time would arrive for her to fall asleep upon her laurels.

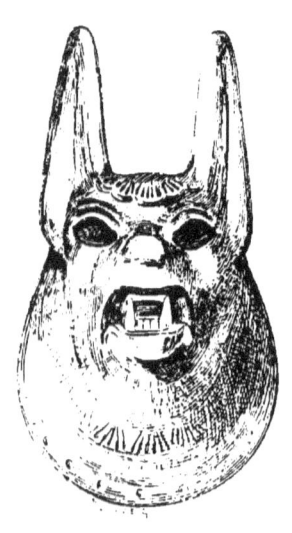

APPENDIX.

APPENDIX.

THE discovery of some thirty-eight royal mummies with their sepulchral furniture, which signalized the accession of Professor Maspero to the Directorship of Egyptian Explorations, was the result, in some degree, of one of those inductive processes of which M. Perrot speaks as characteristic of modern research. For several years previously those who kept account of the additions to public and private collections of Egyptian antiquities had suspected that some inviolate royal tomb had been discovered by the Arabs of Thebes, and that they were gradually dissipating its contents. Early in 1876 General Campbell bought the hieratic ritual of Pinotem I.,—or Her Hor, a priest king, and founder of the twenty-first dynasty—from them; and in 1877 M. de Saulcy showed M. Maspero photographs of a long papyrus which had belonged to Queen Notemit, the mother of Pinotem. About the same time the funerary statuettes of that king appeared in the market, "some of them very fine in workmanship, others rough and coarse."[1] The certainty of a find and of its nature became so great that, in 1879, Maspero was enabled to assert of a tablet belonging to Rogers-Bey, that it came from some sepulchre "belonging to the, as yet, undiscovered tomb of the Her Hor family."[2] The mummy for which this tablet was made has been discovered in the pit at Deir-el-Bahari.

The evidence which gradually accumulated in the hands of M. Maspero, all pointed to two brothers Abd-er-Rasoul, as the possessors of the secret. These men had established their homes in some deserted tombs in the western cliff, at the back of the Ramesseum, and had long combined the overt occupation of guiding European travellers and providing them with donkeys, with the covert and more profitable profession of tomb-breakers and mummy-snatchers.[3] M. Maspero caused the younger of these brothers, Ahmed Abd-er-Rasoul, to be arrested and taken before the Mudir at Keneh. Here every expedient known to Egyptian justice was

[1] MASPERO, *La trouvaille de Deir-el-Bahari*, Cairo, 1882, 4to.   [2] *Ibid*.
[3] See Miss A. B. EDWARDS's account of these gentlemen in *Harper's Magazine* for July, 1882. Her paper is illustrated with woodcuts after some of the more interesting objects found, and a plan of the *locale*.

employed to open his lips, but all in vain. His reiterated examinations only served to prove, if proof had been needed, how thoroughly the Arabs of Thebes sympathized with the conduct of which he was accused. Testimony to his complete honesty and many other virtues poured in from all sides ; his dismal dwelling-place was searched without result, and finally he was released on bail. No sooner had Ahmed returned home, however, than quarrels and recriminations arose between him and his elder brother Mohammed. These quarrels and the offer of a considerable reward by the Egyptian authorities at last induced Mohammed to betray the family secret, in this instance, a material skeleton in the cupboard. He went quietly to Kench and told how Ahmed and himself had found a tomb in one of the wildest bays of the western chain in which some forty coffined mummies, mostly with the golden asp of royalty upon their brows, were heaped one upon another amid the remains of their funerary equipments. This story was taken for what it seemed to be worth, but on being telegraphed to Cairo, it brought Herr Emil Brugsch and another member of the Boulak staff to Thebes in hot haste. They were conducted by Mohammed Abd-er-Rasoul up the narrow valley which lies between the Sheikh-abd-el-Gournah, on the south, and the spur forming the southern boundary of the valley of Dayr-el-Bahari, on the north, to a point some seventy yards above the outer limits of the cultivated land. There, in a corner, bare and desolate even in that desolate region, they were led behind a heap of boulders to the edge of a square hole in the rocky soil, and told that down there was the treasure for which they sought. Ropes were at hand, and Emil Brugsch was lowered into the pit with his companion. The depth was not great, some thirty-six feet, and as soon as their eyes became accustomed to the feeble light of their tapers, they saw that a corridor led away from it to the west. This they followed, and after a few yards found it turn sharply to the right, or north. The funeral canopy of Queen Isi-em-Kheb, which we shall presently describe, was found in the angle thus made. The explorers advanced along this corridor for more than seventy yards, stumbling at every step over the *débris* of mummy cases and funerary furniture, and passing on their right and left, first up piled boxes of statuettes, bronze and terra-cotta jars, alabaster canopic vases, and other small articles, and then some twenty mummies, a few in nests of two or three outer cases, others in but a single coffin, and at least three without other covering than their bandages and shrouds. Finally they arrived at a mortuary chamber about twenty-four feet long and fourteen broad, in which some eighteen more huge mummy cases were piled one upon another, reaching almost to the roof. The distance of this chamber from the outer air was rather more than 280 feet, and its walls, like those of the corridor which led to it, were without decoration of any kind.

The European explorers felt like men in a dream. They had come expecting to find the coffins and mummies of one or two obscure kinglets of the Her-Hor family, and here was the great Sesostris himself, and his father Seti, the conquering Thothmes III., "who drew his frontiers where he pleased," and, like other great soldiers since his day, seems to have been little more than a dwarf in stature, together with several more Pharaohs of the two great Theban dynasties. The coffins of these famous monarchs were in the corridor, some standing upright, others lying down, while the chamber was occupied by the mummies of the twenty-first dynasty, such as those of Queen Notemit, Pinotem I., Pinotem II., Queens Makara and Isi-em-Kheb, and Princess Nasikhonsou. Isi-em-Kheb seemed to have been the last comer to the tomb, as her mummy was accompanied by a complete sepulchral outfit of wigs, toilet bottles and other things of the kind, besides the canopy already mentioned and a complete funerary repast in a hamper.

Preparations were immediately commenced for the removal of the whole "find" to Boulak. Steamers were sent for from Cairo, and several hundred Arabs were employed in clearing the tomb and transporting its contents to Luxor for embarkation. Working with extreme energy, they accomplished their task in five days, and in four days more the steamers had arrived, had taken their remarkable cargo on board, and had started for the capital. And then apparently the native population became alive to the fact that these mummied Pharaohs were their own ancestors, that they had given to their country the only glory it had ever enjoyed, and that they were being carried away from the tombs in which they had rested peacefully, while so many Empires had come and gone, while the world had grown from youth to old age. For many miles down the river the people of the villages turned out and paid the last honours to Thothmes, Seti, Rameses, and the rest of the company. Long lines of men fired their guns upwards as the convoy passed, while dishevelled women ran along the banks and filled the vibrating air with their cries. Thus after more than three thousand years of repose in the bosom of their native earth, the Theban Pharaohs were again brought into the light, to go through a third act in the drama of their existence. This act may perhaps be no longer than the first, as their new home at Boulak has already been in danger of destruction; it is sure to be far shorter than the second, for long before another thirty centuries have passed over their mummied heads, time will have done its work both with them and with the civilization which has degraded them into museum curiosities.

The appearance of this burial place, or *cachette* as Maspero calls it, the nature of the things found in it and of those which should have been found there but were not, prove that its existence had been known to the Arabs and fellaheen of the neighbourhood for many years. Miss Edwards believes that the mummy of Queen Aah-hotep, which was found in the sand behind the temple of Dayr-el-Bahari in 1859, came out of the Her-Hor vault. The contrast between the magnificence of that mummy, the beauty of its jewels, and the care which had evidently been expended upon it on the one hand, and the rough and ready hiding-place in which it was found, on the other,[1] was so great that it was difficult to believe that it had never had a more elaborate tomb; and now the discovery of the outer coffin of the same queen in the pit at Dayr-el-Bahari, goes far to complete the proof that Aah-hotep was disposed of after death like other members of her race, and that the exquisite jewels which were found upon her, were but a part of treasures which had been dispersed over the world by the modern spoilers.[2] The tomb contained about six thousand objects in all, of which but a few have as yet been completely described. Among those few, however, there are one or two which add to our knowledge of Egyptian decoration.

Not the least important are the mummy cases of the Queens Aah-hotep and Nefert-ari. Originally these were identical in design, but one is now considerably more damaged than the other. The general form is similar to that of an Osiride pier, the lower part being terminal and the upper shaped like the bust, arms, and head of a woman. The mask is encircled with a plaited wig, above which appear two tall plumes, indicating that their wearer has been justified before Osiris, while the shoulders and arms are enveloped in a kind of net. The whole case is of *cartonnage*, and the net-like appearance is given by glueing down several layers of linen, which have been so entirely covered with hexagonal perforations as to be reduced to the condition of a net, over the smooth surface beneath. The interior of each hexagon has then been painted blue, so that in the end we have a yellow network over a blue ground. Both colours are of extreme brilliancy. The plaiting of the wig and the separate filaments of the plumes are indicated in the same way as the network. These mummy cases are, so far as we can discover, different from any previously found.

The funerary canopy of Queen Isi-em-Kheb is also a thing by itself. Its purpose was to cover the pavilion or deck-house under which the Queen's body rested in its passage across the Nile. It is a piece of leather patchwork. When laid flat upon the ground it forms a Greek cross, 22 feet 6 inches in one direction, and 19 feet 6 inches in the other. The central panel, which is 9 feet long by 6 wide,[3] covered the roof of the pavilion, while the flaps forming the arms of the cross hung down perpendicularly upon the sides.[4] Many thousand pieces of gazelle hide have been used in the work.

---

[1] See page 29, Vol. I.

[2] For a description of these jewels by Dr. BIRCH, and reproductions of them in their actual colours, see *Facsimiles of the Egyptian Relics Discovered in the Tomb of Queen Aah-hotep*. London: 1863, 4to. See also above, page 380, note 3, of the present volume.

[3] These measurements are taken from *The Funeral Canopy of an Egyptian Queen*, by the Hon. H. VILLIERS STUART; Murray, 1882. 8vo.

[4] Mr. VILLIERS STUART gives a facsimile in colour of the canopy, and a fanciful illustration of it in place, upon a boat copied from one in the *Tombs of the Queens*.

The central panel has an ultramarine ground. It is divided longitudinally into two equal parts, one half being sprinkled with red and yellow stars, and the other covered with alternate bands of vultures, hieroglyphs, and stars. The "fore and aft" flaps of the canopy are entirely covered with a chess-board pattern of alternate red and green squares, while the lateral flaps have each, in addition, six bands of ornament above the squares, the most important band consisting of ovals of Pinotem, supported by uræi and alternating with winged scarabs, papyrus heads, and crouching gazelles. The colours employed are a red or pink, like a pale shade of what is now called Indian red, a golden yellow, a pale yellow not greatly differing from ivory, green, and pale ultramarine. The latter colour is used only for the ground of the central panel, where it may fitly suggest the vault of heaven; the rest are distributed skilfully and harmoniously, but without the observance of any particular rule, over the rest of the decoration. The immediate contrasts are red (or pink) with dark grass-green, bright yellow with buff or ivory colour, and green with yellow. The bad effect of the juxtaposition of buff with red was understood, and that contrast only occurs in the hieroglyphs within the ovals.

The arrangement of the ornamental motives is characterized by that Egyptian hatred for symmetry which is so often noticed by M. Perrot, but the general result is well calculated to have a proper effect under an Egyptian sun. The leather, where uninjured, still retains the softness and lustre of kid.

The Osiride mummy case of Rameses II. is of unpainted wood, and in the style of the twenty-first dynasty. It has been thought that the features resemble those of Her Hor himself,[1] and therefore that it was carved in his reign; they certainly are not those of Rameses, and yet the iconic nature of the head is very strongly marked.

Besides these important objects, the vault contained, as we have said, an immense number of small articles, no description of which has yet been published.

An explanation of the presence of all these mummies and their belongings in a single unpretentious vault, is not far to seek. In the reign of Rameses IX., of the twentieth dynasty, it was discovered that many tombs, including those of the Pharaoh Sevek-em-Saf and his queen Noubkhas had been forced and rifled by robbers, while others had been more or less damaged. An inquiry was held and some at least of the delinquents brought to justice. The "Abbott" and the "Amherst" papyri give accounts of the proceedings in full, together with the confession of one of the criminals.[2] These occurrences and the generally lawless condition of Thebes at the time seem to have led to the institution of

---

[1] Miss A. B. Edwards, *Lying in State in Cairo*, in *Harper's Magazine* for July, 1882.
[2] See Maspero, *Une Enquête Judiciare à Thèbes*, Paris, 1871, 4to.

periodical inspections of the royal tombs, and of the mummies which they contained. Minutes of these inspections, signed by the officer appointed to carry them out and two witnesses besides, are inscribed upon the shrouds and cases of the mummies. At first the inspectors shifted the deceased kings from tomb to tomb, the "house" of Seti I. being the favourite, apparently from its supposed security, but as the power of the monarchy declined, as disorders became more frequent and discipline more difficult to preserve, it appears to have been at last determined to substitute, as the burial-place of the royal line, a single, unornamented, easily concealed and guarded hole for the series of subterranean palaces which had shown themselves so unable to shield their occupants from insult and destruction.

The Her-Hor family therefore were buried in one vault, and such of their great predecessors as had escaped the ghouls of the Western Valley were gathered to their sides.

INDEX.

INDEX.

A

AAH HOTEP, i. 291.
Aa-kheper-ra, *see* Thothmes II.
Abbeville, i. Prehistoric remains near, xxxix.
Abd-al-latif, i. 223, 225; monolithic tabernacle at Memphis called *the green chamber*, 353; obelisk of Ousourtesen, ii. 172.
Abd-el-Gournah, ii. 53.
Abouna, i. 34.
Abou-Roash, i. 165; pyramid of, 204.
Abousir, i. 212; construction of pyramid at, *id.*
Abydos, i. 6. 16; foundation of the great temple at, 28; the early capital in the nome of A., 68; origin there of the worship of Osiris, *id.*; Sculpture more refined than that of Thebes, 76; portrait of Seti at A., 123; entrance to the Egyptian *Hades* near A., 128, 134; situation of the necropolis, 136; *do.* 156; situation of doors and steles in the tombs at A., 157, 241; description of the tombs at A., 243; temple has two hypostyle halls, 385; descriptions of Mariette, 434; ii. fortress at A., 41; necropolis, 241; tomb of Osiris at A., 242; other tombs, 295.
Acacia, *Nilotica*, ii. 54; *Lebbak, id.*
Acacia doors, i. 252.
Achæans, i. 162.
Achoris, ii. 266.
Addeh, speos at, i. 406.
Ægina, i. VII. XI.
Ægis, ii. 382.
Agra, ii. 13.
Ahmes, i. 34. 168.
Alabaster, i. 105, 325.
Alberti, L. B., ii. 82.
Alcamenes, i. VI. XII.
Alexander the Great, i. L. 21, 430.
Alexandria, i. 55.
Almees, ii. 249.
Amasis; his elevation to the throne, i. 33; his deliverance of Egypt, 78, 292; body insulted by Cambyses, 309; his monolithic chapel, 353; dimensions of the monolithic chapel, ii. 75, 97; stele discovered in the Serapeum, 285.
Amada, temple of, ii. 168.
Ambulatory of Thothmes, ii. 135.
Amenemhat III., i. 347; Amenemhats, the, ii. 227, 333.
Amenemheb, i. 279.
Ameneritis, statue of, at Boulak, ii. 263.
Ameni, tomb of, i. 34.
Amenophis III. i. 166; his colossi at Thebes, 267; *do.* 289; builder of Luxor, 371; builder of the great temple at Napata, 385; temple at El-Kab, 400; ii. 66; the colossi at Thebes, 240; portrait head in the British Museum, 242; painted portrait in the Bab-el-Molouk, 332. 337. 347.
Amenophis IV.; his attempt to inaugurate the worship of Aten, the solar disc, i. 69; ruins of his capital, ii. 5; his statues, 244; curious characteristics of his person, *id.*, 289.
Amenophium, i. 268. 289. 376.
Amenoth, i. 159.
Amen-Ra, may be identified with Indra, i. 50, 63; hardly mentioned earlier than the eleventh dynasty, 68, 113; offerings to him as master of Karnak, 155. 268; the chief person of the Theban triad. 333; chapel at Abydos, 389; possibly

symbolized in the obelisks, ii. 170; his statues not colossal, 277.
Ament, the Egyptian Hades, i. 157.
Amoni-Amenemhaït, i. 156.
Amoni, his inscription at Beni-Hassan, i. 39.
Amosis, (see Amasis).
Amulets, i. 159; ii. 371.
Anahit (Anaitis), ii. 262.
Ancyra, expedition to, i. 41.
Animals, sacred, i. 54.
Animals, worship of, i. 54-64; mummified, 314; figures of, ii. 281.
"Answerers," or "respondents," i. 146.
Anta, use of. ii. 141.
Antinoë, ii. 66, 72.
Antiquity, conventional meaning of the word, i. XLV.
Antony, tomb of, i. 161.
Anubis, i. 143, 287.
Apelles, i. XIV. XVI. LI.
Apis, i. 54, 67; the oldest tombs of A. contemporary with 18th dynasty, 295; new rites inaugurated by a son of Rameses II. 305; Serapeum, 306; dwelling for A. constructed by Psemethek, 429.
Aplou, i. 159.
Ap-Môtennou, i. 144.
Apollo Epicurius, i. XII.
Apries, helped to deliver Egypt, i. 78; description given by Herodotus of his tomb, 306; supposed head of, ii. 266.
Arch, the; extreme antiquity of the A. in Egypt, ii. 77; true A. in the necropolis of Abydos, 78; semicircular A. the most frequent, 79; elliptic A. 80; A. in the Ramesseum, 81; inverted A. in foundations, 82; offset A. at Dayr-el-Bahari, 83; *do.* at Abydos, 84.
Architecture; general principle of form, i. 97; *do.* of construction, 103; materials, 103; masonry, 107; vaults, 111; concrete and pisé, 113; assembled construction, 115; restoration of a wooden building, 117; sepulchral A. 126; conditions imposed by the national religion, 134; civil A. ii. 1; must be judged almost entirely from representations on papyri and bas-reliefs, *id.*; the palace, 8; the house, 26; military A. 38; construction examined in detail, 55; motives taken from early work in wood, *id.*; arch, 77; the Egyptian orders, 85; their arrangement, 133; doors and windows, 156; the profession of architect, 176; the supremacy of A. over the other arts in Egypt, 405.
Archæological Survey of India, i. LIII.
Aristophanes, i. XVIII.
Armachis, i. 326.
Aromati, the, i. 434.
Arsaphes, statue in the British Museum, ii. 265.
Artemis, i. 406.
Aryballus, ii. 368.
Ass, the, ii. 217.
Assassif, El, ii. 79.
Assouan, i. 105; Turkish governor of A., his vandalism, 396.
Asychis, i. 347.
Ata, i. 207.
Aten, attempt to inaugurate the supremacy of, i. 69.
Athenê Polias, temple of, i. XIII.
Atta, i. 145.
Avaris, reconquest of, i. 33; ii. 228.

B

Ba, i. 285.
Bab-el-Molouk, i. 255.
Babylon, ii. 13.
Bædeker; guide to Egypt, construction of the Pyramids, i. 201; theory as to the pyramid of Meidoum, 214; edited partly by Dr. Ebers, *id.*; casing of the second pyramid, 233; traces of a door in the tomb of Ti, 290.
Baehr, i., III.
Bahr-Yussef, i. 165.
Bakenkhonsou, ii. 177-8.
Ballu, i. XIII.
Bari, i. 352.
Basalt, statues of, ii. 221, 235.
Bassæ, i. XII.
Battlements, ii. 153.
Beds, ii. 393.
Beggig, obelisk of, ii. 175.
Beit-el-din, ii. 20.
Beit-el-Wali, speos at, i. 407, 418, 421; bas-reliefs at, ii. 246.
Bellefonds, Linant de, site of Lake Mœris, ii. 25.
Belzoni; his discovery of the tomb of Seti I. i. 278, 280; crowded tombs for the lower classes, 314; mummified animals, 315; portico in the temple of the second pyramid, 330.

Benfey, i. 10.
Beni-Hassan, i. 136 ; great inscription, 143, 160, 156-7, 249-252 ; so-called proto-doric columns, ii. 95, 101 ; paintings, 333-344 ; the potter's wheel represented at B. H. 367 ; glass making, *do*. 375 ; the manufacture of gold ornaments, *do*. 380.
Berbers, the, i. 13.
Bercheh, El, ii. 72, 238.
Bernhardy, i. III.
Bernier, i. XIII.
Bes, i. 434 ; ii. 354.
Beschir, ii. 20.
Beulé, i. 305.
Birch, S. ; his translation of the great inscription at Beni-Hassan, i. 143 ; *do*. 159 ; his translation of the inscription upon the London obelisk, ii. 171 ; the *Arsaphes* of the British Museum, 265, 291 ; cylinders in the British Museum. 291 ; *figurines rustiques* of Palissy compared to some works of Egyptian potters, 373 ; thinks iron was known at the commencement of Theban period, 379.
Birds, worship of, i. 65.
Blanc, Charles, i. XIV. ; characteristics of Egyptian landscape and architecture, 98 ; modification of colour under a southern sun, 121 ; ii. 174 ; description of bas-relief of Seti I. at Abydos, 247 ; decadence of art between Seti I. and Rameses IV. 258 ; Sabaco's restorations at Karnak, 263, 294 ; his ideas upon the Egyptian *canon*, 319.
Blant, M. E. Le, i. 159.
Blemmyes. i. 55.
Biouet, i. XIII.
Blow-pipe, the, ii. 378.
Boats found in the tombs, i. 184.
Boeck, i. XXI.
Bœotia, i. XLI. 162.
Boissier, i. XV.
Bonomi, i. 9.
Bossuet, i. 1.
Botta, i. VIII., XXVI.
Brackets in Royal Pavilion at Medinet-Abou, ii. 23.
Bramante, i. 105.
Bricks, manufacture of, ii. 53.
Brongniart, ii. 372.
Bronzes : technical skill shown in casting bronze, ii. 202 ; *Pastophorus* of the Vatican, 265 ; *Arsaphes* in the British Museum, 265 ; bronzes from

the Serapeum, 266 ; figures from the Saite epoch, 271.
Brosses, the President de, i. 57.
Brugsch, Bey, i. 21 ; the Egyptian character, 41 : translation of the great inscription at Beni-Hassan, 143 ; origin of the word *pyramid*, 190 : topographical sketch of ancient Thebes, ii. 29 ; epitaph of Una, 75 ; metal on the capitals of columns, 116. 176 ; social position of Egyptian architects, 177, 178, 197.
Brune ; plans of Karnak, i. 363, 367 ; of Medinet-Abou, 383 : of Dayr-el-Bahari, 419 ; his restoration of Dayr-el-Bahari, 422, 425 ; slight differences from that here given, 425.
Bubastis, i. 18 ; house in, ii. 33.
Bunsen, i. XXIII. 10, 18.
Burnouf, Eugène, i. IX.
Busiris, ii. 30.

C

Caillaud, i. 341, 384, 385.
Cairo, i. 105, 163 : ii. 66.
Cambyses, i. 309, 430.
Camp, Maxime du. ii. 76, 147.
Campania, i. XIII. 162.
Campbell's tomb, i. 311.
Canephorus, ii. 202.
Canon ; had the Egyptians a C. of proportion, ii. 315.
Canopic vases, i. 305.
Capitals, lotiform, ii. 86 ; campaniform. 101 : hathoric, 106 : secondary forms of the bell-shaped capital, 112 : C. plated with copper, 116.
Caricature. confined to small objects. ii. 351 ; battle of cats and rats, 352 : Turin papyrus, *id*; papyrus in the British Museum, 353 ; the God Bes. 354.
Cartonnage, ii. 397.
Caste, i. 31.
Cat, the, ii. 219.
Caviglia. the clearing of the Great Sphinx, i. 321.
Caylus, Comte de. i. XVI.
Cesnola, Palma di, i. V., X.
Chairs, ii. 393.
Chaldæa. i. IV., XXVI., XLIX.
Chanihati. bas-relief on his tomb, ii. 253.
Chamitic race, i. 13.
Champollion. i. VI. VIII. 4. 89 ; first

to appreciate the importance of Beni-Hassan, 249; the valley of the kings, 263; Saite cemeteries discovered by him, 301; his impressions of Karnak, 365; gave its proper name to the Ramesseum, 376; carelessness of Egyptian masonry, ii. 65; his supposed discovery of the origin of the Doric order, 96; distinction made in texts between pylon and propylon, 156; mainly impressed by the grandeur of the Theban remains, 225; his forecast of the important position now held by Egpytian art, 401.

Chardanes, ii. 257.

Charmes, Gabriel, i. 235; ii. 212, 219; his opinion on the bust of Taïa, 242.

Cheops, i. 201; his pyramid, 201; *do.* 227; stele commemorating his restoration of a temple, 319; doubts as to its date, *id.*

Chephren, i. 24, 86; his statues at Boulak, 89; *do.* 139; discovery of statues in the temple of the sphinx, 193, 227, 221; detailed account of the basalt and diorite statues at Boulak, ii. 221-223.

China, i. IV., XLVIII., LIX.

Chinbab, i. 165.

Chisel, ii. 303-328, *passim.*

Chnoumhotep, i. 143.

Choephoræ, i. 130.

Choubra, ii. 20.

Choufou (Cheops), inscribed upon the stones of the Great Pyramid, i. 222.

Chounet-es-Zezib, fortress at Abydos, ii. 41.

Christy, i. XXXVIII.

Cicero, i. 129.

Clemens Alexandrinus, i. 56.

Cloisonné Enamels, unknown to the Egyptians in the proper sense, ii. 384.

Clusium, i. XXXVII.

Cockerell, Prof., i. XI.

Colossi, upon pyramids, i. 226; transport of C., ii. 72; multiplication of C. under the New Empire, 239, 241.

Colours, used by the Egyptian painters, ii. 334, 336, 340.

Columns, ii. 85; metal C., 88; "protodoric" *do.* 96; polygonal *do.* 99; faggot-shaped *do.* 99; at Medinet-Abou, 102; in the Hall at Karnak, *id.*; at Philæ, 104; comparison between Egyptian and Greek C., 121; ordonnance of C., 133; spacing, 137; no rule governing intercolumniation, 143.

Constantinople, ii. 13.

Construction, architectural, ii. 55; imitation in stone of wooden C., 59; huge stones only used where necessary, 65; want of foresight in Egyptian C., 70; carelessness, *id.*; machines used, 72.

Conventions in Egyptian art, ii. 291.

Copper, ii. 378.

Coptic, study of, i. VII.

Copts, i. 13.

Corinth, i. XV.

Corvée, the, i. 25; its influence upon Egyptian architecture, 27, 30.

Coulanges, M. Fustel de, *La cité antique*, i. 130.

Crane, the, in the bas-relief, ii. 219.

Crimæa, i. XV.

Crocodile, the, in the bas-reliefs, ii. 218.

Crocodilopolis, ii. 234.

Crown, the red crown, i. 16; the white *do.*, 16; the pschent, 16.

Cunningham; his descriptions of the remains of Græco Buddhic art, i. LIII.

Curtius, Dr.; history of Greece, i. III. Græco Buddhic art, LIII.

Curtius, Quintus, ii. 33.

"Cutting, the," i. 435.

Cyclopean walls, ii. 64.

Cylinders, earthenware and soft stone, ii. 291.

Cyma, ii. 153; *do. reversa*, ii. 153.

Cyprus, i. X., XXVI.; painted vases, 78, 161.

Cyrus, i. 79.

D

Darius, i. IX.

Darmesteter, James, i. 69.

Dashour, i. 165, 206.

Dayr, i. 407.

Dayr-el-Bahari, i. 265, 268; temple or cenotaph of Hatasu, 421-434.

Dayr-el-Medinet, i. 264.

Delbet, Jules, i. 42.

Delhi, ii. 13.

Denderah, i. 326, 351, 434; ii. 67, 69; pluteus at, 149.

Derri, i. 408.

Desjardins, M. E., i. 302.

Deus Rediculus, temple of the i. 104.

Deveria, his belief that he had found a portrait of a shepherd king, ii. 177.
Diocletian, i. 55.
Diodorus Siculus; his assertion that the first man was born in Egypt, i. 4; Pyramids. 191; height of Great Pyramid, 225; plateau on its summit, 226; Pyramid of the Labyrinth, 227; *Tomb of Osymandias* (Ramesseum), 266, 375; tombs in the Bab-el-Molouk, 279 : πυλών, 341; Mœris (Amenemhat III.), 347; labyrinth, ii. 25; population of Egypt, 26; extent of Thebes, 30; the epithet ἑκατόμπυλος, 40.
Diorite, statue of Chephren in, ii. 221; the influence of such a material upon style, 303-305.
Djezzar Pacha, ii. 20.
Dog, the, in the bas-reliefs, ii. 219.
Doors, ii. 156.
Dordogne, i. XLII., ii. 78.
"Double," the, i. 128, 135.
Doum (palm), ii. 50.
Drah-abou-l'Neggah, i. 217, 253, 291, 315.
Dromos, i. 336.
Duck, the, in the bas-reliefs, ii. 219.

E

EBERS, Georg.; extent of the Memphite necropolis, i. 165; cenotaph in the temple of Abydos, 264; his opinion upon that temple, *id.*; his discovery of a tomb at Thebes, 279; his opinion upon the Ramesseum, 381; the funerary character of the temple at Abydos, 391; his conjectures upon Dayr-el-Bahari, 426; pavilion of Rameses III. not a palace, ii. 16; pyramid of the labyrinth, 25; origin of the quadrangular pier, 90; uses of papyrus, 126; his opinion upon the columns in the Bubastite court, Karnak, 146; propylons of Karnak and Denderah, 157; his belief in the persistence of the Hyksos type, 237.
Edfou, i. 351, 353; peripteral temple, 396; foundations of temple at, ii. 69.
Egger, ii. 126.
Eilithyia, i. 157; ii. 400; temple of Amenophis III. at, *id.*

Elephantiné; peripteral temple at, i. 396 : quarries at, ii. 75, 149.
Empires, classification of the Egyptian, i. 17.
Enamels, ii. 375.
Encaustic painting known to the Egyptians, ii. 336.
Enter, i. 38. 156, 217.
Epochs of Egyptian history, i. 18.
Era, Egypt without one, i. 20.
Erectheum, i. LVII.
Erment, ii. 66.
Esneh, i. 351.
Ethiopia; its civilization an offshoot from that of Egypt, i. 20; its pyramids, 217 : its temples, 404; Ethiopian supremacy in Egypt, ii. 265; Ethiopians in pictures, 348.
Etruria, i. XLII., 131, 162.
Euripides quoted, i. 130.
" Evandale, Lord," i. 136.

F

FAIENCE, i. 146 ; ii. 369.
Fayoum, the pyramids in the, i. 226; statues discovered in the, ii. 233.
Fellowes, Sir Charles, i. X., XXVII.
Feraig, speos of, i. 406.
Fergusson, James, ii. 8.
Festus, i. XXII.
Fetishism, i. 47-9, 56-8.
Ficus Sycomorus, ii. 54.
Figure, the, ii. 341 ; coloured reliefs in the mastabas, 341; Beni-Hassan, 341; Thebes, 344; mandore player at Abd-el-Gournah, 347; harpers in Bruce's tomb, 348; Prisoners. 348 ; winged figure, 349 : different races distinguished, 350.
Flamingo, the, in the bas-reliefs, ii. 219.
Flandrin, i. IX.
" Foundations," for the service of a tomb, i. 144-6.
Fox, the, in the bas-reliefs, ii. 218.
Friedrichs, Carl, i. IV.
Funeral feasts, i. 143.
Funerary figures, i. 145-147.

G

GAILHABAUD, M., ii. 36.
Gartasse, i. 433.
Gau, i. 353, 421.

Gautier, Théophile, i. 136; ii. 174.
Gawasi, ii. 249.
Gazelle, in the bas-reliefs, ii. 218.
Gebel-Ahmar, i. 104.
Gebel-Barkal, i. 218, 407.
Gebel-Silsilis, i. 105, 403; bas-relief at, ii. 246.
Gerhard, i. XV., XVIII.
Gherf-Hossein, hemispeos, i. 407; ii. 138.
Girchch, i. 421.
Glass, its manufacture represented at Beni-Hassan, ii. 375; glass-ena melled statuettes, 376.
Globe, winged, ii. 151, 152.
Goat, in the bas-reliefs, ii. 219.
Gods, age of the Egyptian, i. 321.
Goethe, i. 121, 153.
Goose, in the bas-reliefs, ii. 219.
Gorge, the Egyptian, ii. 149.
Gournah, temple of, i. 267, 268, 391; ii. 140.
Gournet-el-Mourraï, ii. 21.
Græco-Buddhic art, i. LIII.
Græco-Scythians, i. XV.
Granaries, ii. 37.
Granite-chambers, Karnak, ii. 52.
Graphic processes, ii. 1.
Grébaut, M., i. 52.
Group, unknown in its proper sense in Egyptian art, ii. 278.
Guglie, ii. 169.
Guillaume, Edouard, i. 42.

H

HAMILTON, W. J., i. X., XXVII.
Hamy, M., ii. 377.
Hapi-Toufi, i. 144.
Haram-el-Kabbab ("the false pyramid"), i. 215.
Hare, the, in the bas-reliefs, ii. 218.
Harmachis, i. 237, 389.
Harm-Habi, i. 178.
Ha-ro-bes, ii. 289.
Hatasu, Queen, i. 105; her obelisks of Karnak, 122, 265, 268; height of her obelisk, 343; Dayr-el-Bahari, the cenotaph of H., 425; height of her obelisk from more recent measurement, ii. 171; her favourite architect, 178; her bas-reliefs at Dayr-el-Bahari, 245.
Hathor, i. 58, 69.
Hecuba (Euripides), quoted, i. 130.
Hegel, i. XXXIII.

Height of principal buildings in the world. i. 225.
Helbíg, M. W., i. XV.
Heliopolis; its walls, ii. 41; its obelisk, 171.
Hemispeos, i. 253.
Heracleopolis, i. 17.
Hermopolis, i. 15.
Herodotus; Egypt a present from the Nile, i. 2; Amasis, 33; religious observances, 44; Isis and Osiris the only gods whom all the Egyptians worshipped, 68; temples in Delta, 93; Scythians, 145; Pyramids, 191, 202, 219; P. in Lake Mœris, 226, 229; *do.* of the Labyrinth, 227; construction of the Great Pyramid, 233; tomb of Apries, 306; Cambyses' treatment of the body of Amasis, 309; obelisks of Sesostris, 347; Rhampsinite and Asychis, *id.*; propylons and Apis pavilion of Psemethek I., *ib.*; monolithic chapel of Amasis, 428; αὐλὴ built by Psemethek for Apis, 429; Labyrinth, ii. 25; level of towns raised artificially, 27; flat roofs, 36; λευκὸν τεῖχος of Thebes, 40; monolithic chapels in the Delta, 75; *Egyptian beans*, 125.
Hesiod, i. 133.
Heuzey, i. XVII., 130.
Hippopotamus, the, in the bas-reliefs, ii. 218.
Hittorf, i. XIV. 121.
Hobs (a god), ii. 281.
Homer; quoted, i. 129, 130; "Hundred-gated Thebes," ii. 40.
Horeau, his plan of the hemispeos of Gherf-Hossein, i. 408.
Hor-em-khou, i. 321.
Hor-Khom, inscription, i. 157.
Hor-Schesou, i. 196.
Horse, introduced into Egypt about the time of the shepherd invasion, ii. 250; his characteristic features in Egyptian art, *id.*
Horus, i. 63, 69; ii. 273, 383; *do.* a private individual, 270.
Hosi, panels from the tomb of, ii. 189.
Hoskins, his plans of the temple of Soleb, i. 384-5.
House, the Egyptian, ii. 26; its situation, 27; foundation, *id.*; restoration based upon a plan found by Rosellini, 33; models of houses, 34; materials and arrangement, *id.*

Howara, El, i. 217; ii. 25.
Huber, M., i. LVI.
Hyena, the, in the bas-reliefs, ii. 218.
Hyksos, i. 68, 404; ii. 228-38.
"Hypæthra, the Great," at Philæ, i. 33.
Hypogea, general character of, i. 188.
Hypostyle Hall, i. 357; ii. 145-7; of Karnak, i. 365-9; ii. 163; of Luxor, i. 371; of the Ramesseum, 376-7; of Medinet-Abou, 382-3; of Soleb, 385; at Napata, 385; at Abydos, 389; at Gournah, 391; of temple of Khons, ii. 166.

I

IBEX, in the bas-reliefs, ii. 218.
Ibis, in the bas-reliefs, ii. 219.
Ictinus, i. 444.
Illahoun, pyramid of, i. 204.
Illumination; methods of lighting the temples, ii. 162-7; methods of lighting the palaces and private houses, 168.
Incas, the, i. 22.
Indra, i. 50.
Ipsamboul, i. 22; little temple at, 405; great temple at, 407-8.
Isæus, i. 130.
Isis, i. 68, 69, 301, 389, 430.
Ismandes, i. 376.
Ivory, ii. 384.

J

JAPAN, i. IV.
Jewelry, ii. 377; pectorals, 380; ægis, 382; true cloisonné enamels unknown, 384; necklaces, *id.*: materials used, *ib.*; amber unknown, 387.
Jollois, i. 123.
Jomard, i. 152: description of the necropolis of Gizeh, 152, 168, 223: his analysis of the impression produced by the Pyramids, 237; his description of the temple of the third pyramid, 330-4, 397, 400; ii. Egyptian cement, 71.
Josephus, quoted, ii. 26.
Joubert, Leo, i. XXI.
Jour des morts, an Egyptian, i. 239.
Judging the Dead, i. 237.
Justinian, i. 55.

K

Ka, the, i. 128.
Kadesh (or Qadech), goddess, ii. 262.

Kalabcheh, i. 407; ii. 107.
Kalaçoka, i. L.
Karnak, i. 25, 28, 105, 155, 263-70, 362-69; the granite chambers, ii. 52; stele piers, 94, 97; columns, 102; decoration, 104, 130, 132.
Ker-Porter, Sir R., i. IX.
Kha-em-uas, jewelry of, ii. 380.
Khemi, i. 14.
Khetas, i. 266; ii. 327.
Khnumhotep, i. 160.
Khons, i. 54; temple of, 123, 268, 348; ii. 136.
Khoo-foo-ankh, i. 182; sarcophagus of, ii. 59.
Klaft, ii. 222.
Kuyler, i. V.
Kummeh, i. 4; ii. 45.

L

LABYRINTH, the, i. 226; ii. 25.
Lakes, sacred, in the temples, i. 344; ii. 6.
Language, the Egyptian, i. 10-11.
Larcher, his notes to Herodotus, i. 307.
Lartet, i. XXXVIII.
Layard, H. A., i. VIII.
Lenormant, Fr., i. 25, 377.
Leopard, the, in the bas-reliefs, ii. 218.
Lepsius: the Egyptians a proto-semitic race, i. 10; inferiority of Ethiopian to Egyptian art well shown in his *Denkmæler,* 21; Berlin Museum enriched by him, 89; tombs to the number of 130 examined by him in Middle and Lower Egypt, 164; arrangement of the mastabas, 167; portraits of defunct in public hall of tomb, 178; sixty-seven pyramids examined by the Prussian commission, 198; theory of pyramid construction, 201; pyramids at Drah-abou'l-neggah, 217; paintings at Beni-Hassan figured by L., 249; Ramesseum, 376; great temple at Medinet Abou, 382; temple of Soleb, 384; temple of Thothmes III. at Semneh, 400; Ethiopian temples in *Denkmæler,* 401; speos of Silsilis, and hemispeos of Redesieh, 406; Gebel-Barkal, 407; fortress of Semneh, ii. 45; Egyptian methods of preparing for a siege suggested by a plate in *Denkmæler,* 43; building operations figured in *Denkmæler,* 53; supposed discovery of the labyrinth, 66; origin

of quadrangular piers, 90; campaniform capitals in a hypogeum at Gizeh, 101; capitals in the ambulatory of Thothmes at Karnak, 115; old form of winged disc at Beni-Hassan, 152; monuments in Wadi-maghara figured in *Denkmaeler*, 184; thick-set forms discovered in a tomb dating from the fourth dynasty, 190; poverty of invention in Theban art seen by glancing through *Denkmaeler*, 250; works in high-relief from the mastabas figured in *Denkmaeler*, 284.

Leroux, Hector; his sketch of Philæ. i. 433; his opinions on Egyptian painting, ii. 335.

Letronne; his researches, i. 224, 232.

Lion, the, in Egyptian art, ii. 281, 323.

Longperier, de, his opinion on the age of Egyptian bronzes, ii. 197.

Loret, M. Victor, ii. 135.

Lotus, the, ii. 125.

Lycian remains, i. XXVII.

Lucian (pseudo). i. 323.

Lutzow, Carl von, i. IV.

Luxor, temple of, i. 270, 370; ii. 132; obelisk of, 171.

M

Mad, i. 354.

Maghara (Wadi), ii. 95, 184.

Mahsarah, i. 105.

Mammisi, i. 433.

Mandore, ii. 344.

Manetho, i. 18; his account of the shepherd invasion not to be relied on, ii. 239.

Marchandon-de-la-Faye, M., i. 95.

Mariette, Auguste; formation of Egypt, i. 2; accession of Menes, 18; Egyptian chronology, 20; bad workmanship of Egyptian temples, foundations of great temples at Abydos, 28; house in the desert, 41; protest against M. Renan's conception of ancient Egypt, 71; excavations, 86; ancient art chiefly known through his exertions and his contributions to the Louvre and the French Exhibition, 89; M. on the arch, 113; obelisk of Hatasu gilded, 122; sepulchral formula, 135; θυμιατήρια in the tomb of Ti, 143; objects for the support of the *Ka* sometimes modelled "in the round," 145;
position of the stele, 157; tombs constructed during lifetime, 160; his "theory of the mastaba," 164; derivation of the word Sakkarah, 166; boats found in mummy pits, 184; pyramids always in a necropolis, 191; Mastabat-el-Faraoun, 215; pyramids upon Drah-abou'l-neggah, 217; opening of three unexplored pyramids at Sakkarah, 234; tomb of Osiris, supposed site, 243; tombs at Abydos, 244; steles from Abydos, 249; temples of the left bank, Thebes, 264; method of closing tombs in the Bab-el-Molouk, 278; mummy of Queen Aah-hotep, 291; tombs of Apis, 295; the little Serapeum, 302; temple of the Sphinx, 326; Sphinxes at the Serapeum of Memphis, 336; Sphinx avenues ornamental rather than religious, 337; walls of Karnak, 338; extent of the temples at Karnak, 362; sanctuary in the great temple, 384; temple of Dayr-el-Bahari, 425; excavations at Saïs, 433; characteristics of the Egyptian temple, 434; contrast between it and the Greek temple, the Christian church, and the Mahommedan mosque, 435; explanation of its elaborate decoration, *id.*; Royal Pavilion of Medinet-Abou not a palace, ii. 16; building materials, 53; brick-making, *id.*; carelessness of the Egyptian builders, 70; true vaults in the necropolis of Abydos, 77; inverted arches, 81; lotiform capitals in the tomb of Ti, 86; origin of the faggot-shaped column, 99; origin of the campaniform capital, 128; proposal that it should be called *papyriform*, *id.*; discards the notion that the columns in the Babastite court, at Karnak, bore architraves, 145; his assumption that they once enclosed a hypæthral temple, *ib.*; first appearance of the winged disc, 152; obelisks in the Theban necropolis, 170; obelisks of Hatasu gilded, 174; statues in the tomb of Ti, 181; statues of Rahotep and Nefert, from Meidoum, 187; panels from the tomb of Hosi, 188; the Scribe of the Louvre, 192; brought figures from Ancient Empire to Paris in 1878, 211; Nemhotep, 212; picture of geese, 220; statues of Chephren discovered in the temple

of the Sphinx, 213; early Theban works rude and awkward, 226; Menthouthotep, *id.*; groups from Tanis, 228; figure discovered in the Fayoum, 233; definition of the type of these Tanite remains, 237; head of Taia discovered, 242; Amenophis IV. perhaps a eunuch, 243; expedition to Punt, illustrated at Dayr-el-Bahari, 245; belief that Punt was in Africa, 246; detestable style of the remains from the last years of Rameses II., 258; Menephtah, son of Rameses II., statue at Boulak, 260; head of Tahraka at Boulak, 263; opinion as to the character of the statues in Egyptian temples, 276; origin of the Sphinx, 281; tomb of Sabou, sculptures, 285; models for sculptors at Boulak, their probable date, 324.

Mariette, Edouard, ii. 28, 55.

Maspero, G.; our guide to the history of Egypt, i. 8-9; his opinion upon the Egyptian language, 13; periods of Egyptian history, 17-18; Ethiopian kingdom, 21; affiliation of the king to the gods, 22; mildness of rule in Ancient Egypt, 37; prince Entef's stele, 38; Egyptian devotion, 39; *do.* 43; the number of their devotional works of art, *id.*; character of sacred animals, such as the Apis, 66; his theory as to the *ka*, or double, 126, 137-8, 140-6. 148-153, 155-7; translation from Papyrus IV. at Boulak, 161; tomb of Harmhabi, 178; pyramid of Ounas, 194; commentary on the second book of Herodotus, 227; opening of pyramid of Ounas, 235; opinion on the tombs at Abydos, 242; the staircase of Osiris, 243; discovery of remains belonging to royal tombs of the eleventh dynasty at Drah abou'l-neggah, 253; ascription of power of speech and movement to statues, 289; proof that the gods existed in the time of the Ancient Empire, 318; translation of the stele of Piankhi from Gebel-Barkal, 353; Hatasu's expedition to Punt. 426; translations of Egyptian tales, ii. 30; symbolism of papyrus and lotus, 126; translation of stele C. 14. in the Louvre, 176; cause of the Iconic character of Egyptian statutes, 181; materials for wooden statues, 197; his translation of funerary songs, 249; formula by which the right of erecting a statue in a temple was granted to a private individual, 278; on the Palestrina mosaic, 288.

Mastaba, i. 164; in the Memphite necropolis, 165, 189; materials of the, 168; Mastabat-el-Faraoun, 169; Mastabas of Sabou, 171; Haar, *id.*; Ra-en-mar, *id.*; Hapi, 171; general arrangements, 172.

Mastabat-el-Faraoun, i. 169, 214. 326.

Maury, Alfred, i. 286.

Maut, i. 63, 268.

Medinet-Abou, i. 22, 102; the great temple, 260, 267-8, 375; the little temple, 376; ii. 169; the royal pavilion, i. 375; ii. 16; the great temple, method of lighting, 384; brackets in royal pavilion, 23.

Medinet-el-Fayoum, ii. 25.

Medledk, i. 159.

Megasthenes, i. L.

Meh, house of, I. 156.

Meidoum, i. 35, 89. 165; construction of the pyramid of M., i. 200.

"Memnon," statues of, i. 267, 290, 376.

"Memnonium," i. 267; ii. 30.

Memphis, i. 6; discovery of the *Sheik-el-Beled*, 9, 16; political centre of the Ancient Empire, 17, 27; our knowledge of the early period all derived from the necropolis of M., 34; the early Egyptians not oppressed, 37; worship of Ptah at M., 55; significance of apis, 67; situation of necropolis, 136; doors of the tombs turned eastward, 157; mastabas, 165; statue of Rameses II. on the site of M., ii. 240.

Mendes, i. 22.

Menephtah, head of, at Boulak, ii. 258.

Menes, i., X. XLVIII., 15, 17, 22, 38.

Menkaura (Mycerinus), i. 326.

Menthouthotep, a scribe, ii. 226.

Mentou-Ra, ii. 266.

Menzaleh, Lake, fellahs in the neighhood of their race, ii 237.

Merenzi, i. 234.

Mérimée, M., materials employed by Egyptian painters, ii. 334.

Meroë, i. 20, 217.

Merval, du Barry de. ii. 11.

Mesem Bryanthemum Copticum, ii. 375.

Metal-work, ii. 377; blow-pipe known, 378; iron, 379; damascening, 384.

Metopes, ii. 155.
Mexico, i. V.
Michaëlis, i. XIX.
Michelet, i. 64.
Midas, i. XXVII.
Minutoli, i. 213.
Mit-fares, ii. 234.
Mitrahineh, bas-relief at, ii. 271.
Mnevis, i. 54.
Models for sculptors, ii. 322.
Modulus, its absence from Egyptian architecture, i. 102.
Mœris (Pharaoh), i. 347; Lake M. i. 7, 216, 228; ii. 25.
Mokattam, i. 105, 201, 204.
Monolithic columns rare in Egypt, ii. 66.
Mosel i. XVII.
Müller, Ottfried, i. III., V., XXI., XXV., XXXI., LIV.
Mummies, i. 135; m. pits, 181; method of closing m. pit, 183; *do.* of sarcophagus, 182; furniture of m. chambers, 183; decoration of the m. cases, ii. 335.
Mycenæ, i. XLII., 162.
Mycerinus, pyramid of, i. 205, 227, 329; the sarcophagus of his daughter as described by Herodotus, 307; his own sarcophagus, ii. 55-59.
Museums —
Berlin; i. 89; papyrus narrating the dedication of a chapel by an Ousourtesen, 334; funerary obelisk, ii. 170; leg in black granite, 228; enamelled bricks from stepped pyramid, 372.
Boulak; i. 10, 41; the árt of the pyramid builders only to be fully seen at B., 86, 89, 90, 139; papyrus IV., 161; stele with garden about a tomb, 301; statues of gods, 319; sphinxes in courtyard, ii. 337; statue of the architect Nefer, 177; statues in tomb of Ti, 181; Rahotep and Nefert, 183-7; *Sheik-el-beled*, 183, 194; panels from tomb of Hosi, 189; statue of Ra-nefer, 203; *do.* of Ti, 203; wooden statue of a man with long robe, 204; kneeling statues, 204; Nefer-hotep and Tenteta, 207; domestic and agricultural figures, 209; Nemhotep, 212; painting of Nile geese, 219; great statues of Chephren, 221; Tanite remains, 230-5; Thothmes III., 241; Taia, 242; dancing girls, 249; Rameses II., 256; bronze statuettes, 312; models for sculptors, 322; Græco-Roman remains, 274; glass, 376; bronze ornaments and weapons, 379; jewels, 380; ivory-work, 388; wood-work, 395-8.
British; boats found in tombs, i. 185; mummy case of Mycerinus, 234, 319; *Ritual of the Dead*, ii. 287; sceptre of Papi, 198; head of Thothmes III., 241; *do.* of Amenophis III., 242; bronze statuette of *Arsaphes*, 265; comic papyrus, 353; pottery, 368; enamelled faience 371; *aryballus*, 372; enamelled bricks from Stepped Pyramid, 372; enamelled plaques, 374.
Liverpool; boat from tomb, i. 185.
Louvre; i. 38, 89, 122, 127; boats from tombs, 185; tabernacle, 353; models of houses, ii. 33-4; the "Scribe," 183-192; statues from Ancient Empire 181-192; *Canephorus*, 202; Sebekhotep, 226; red granite sphinx, 228; Tanite remains, 235; statues from New Empire, 244-260; works in bronze, 270-281; bas-relief of Amasis from Serapeum, 285; gems, 288; signs of imperfect tools used, 304-5; portraits from Roman epoch, 336; jewelry, 382-387; woodwork, 395-8.
Turin; stele, i. 301; tabernacle, 353; statues of the Theban Pharaohs, ii. 225; Rameses II., 257; satirical papyrus, 351; priapic scene in *do.*, 355; enamel on wood, 375.
Vatican; *Pastophorus*, ii. 265.

N

Naos, i. 353.
Napata, i. 21; pyramids at, 217, 218; great temple at N. 385; speos at N. 404-7.
Naville, E., i. 22; ii. 176.
Nectanebo, i. 17, 77, 86, 353, 430.
Nefer (architect), statue of, ii. 177.
Nefer-hotep, ii. 207.
Nefert Ari, i. 410.
Nefert, statue of, from Meidoum, ii. 187.
Neith, i. 69, 301.

Nekau, i. 24, 78.
Nekheb (goddess), i. 63.
Nem-hotep, ii. 202.
Nepheritis, ii. 266.
Nephthys, i. 54, 301; ii. 350, 361.
Niebuhr, i. XXI.
Nesa, ii. 185.
Nestor L'Hôte, i. 4; ii. 15; his enthusiasm for the art of the early dynasties, 225.
Nile, the creator of Egypt, i. 2, 3; its inundations, 4, 5; homage to the N. as a god, 233.
Nowertiouta, ii. 294.
Num-hotep, i. 35, 251.

O

OBELISKS, the, method of erection, ii. 75; 169; ὀβελός, 170; ὀβελίσκος, id.; O. of Hatasu, 170; do. of Luxor, 171; do. of Ousourtesen, id.; heights of obelisks, id.; O. figured in bas-relief at Sakkarah, 174; ovals of Ousourtesen I. on O. at Beggig, 175.
Offerings, funerary, i. 139-43; ii. 384; tables for offerings, 143-4; ii. 362.
Oliphant, Laurence, ii. 175.
Opisthodomos, i. 354.
"Orders," the Egyptian, ii. 85: asserted derivation from the national flora, 128.
Orientation of the tomb, i. 157.
Ornament, importance of the human figure, ii. 355: vultures, *id*.; origin of ornament, 356; various motives, 357; ceiling decorations, 359; winged globe, 361; mummy cases, *id*.; colour well preserved, 362; use of gold, *id*.; graining, 363.
Osarvaris, i. 159.
"Osymandias, tomb of," or Rameseum, i. 266, 375, 378.
Osorkhon, ii. 362.
Ouaphra, ii. 266.
Oudja, ii. 383.
Ouenephes, or Ata, i. 207.
Ouna, i. 151.
Ounas, Pyramid of, i. 194, 215; mummy chamber of O. 235; the opening of the pyramid, 235.
Oushebti, or *shebti* (answerers or respondents), i. 146.
Ousourtesens, the, ii. 45, 50, 72.
Overbeck, history of sculpture, i. V.

Ovolo (egg moulding), ii. 154.
Ox, faithful treatment of, in Egyptian art, ii. 253.

P

PACCARD, i. XIII.
Painting; Egyptian painting really illumination, ii. 332; how a picture was begun, *id*.; complete absence of shadow, *id*.; tools employed, 333; colours known, 334, their chemical composition, *id*.; good condition of Egyptian painting, 335; procedures, *id*.; treatments of flesh tints, 336: distemper the true Egyptian method, *id*.; portrait of Amasis, 336; easel pictures not unknown, *id*.; colours of the gods, 337; portraits of Queen Taia, *id*.; decorations of tomb of Ptah-hotep, 341.
Palace, the Egyptian, ii. 8.
Palestrina mosaic, the, ii. 288.
Palettes, painters', ii. 333.
Panels, grooved, i. 115: carved *do*., ii. 189.
Papi, i. 235.
Papyrus; the plant, ii. 125; *Papyrus Anastasi III.*, ii. 22; *Papyrus Casati*, i. 159; Papyrus IV., i. 161; Satirical Papyri, ii. 351.
Passalacqua; his descriptions of mummies, i. 136, 143; his discovery of a tomb, 293.
Pastophorus, of the Vatican, ii. 265.
Pat, ii. 185.
Patera, ii. 370.
Pausanias, i. 268.
Pectorals, ii. 380.
Pega, i. 128.
Peiho, i. 172.
Pekh-hesi, on panels in tomb of Hosi, ii. 189.
Penrose, F. C., i. XIV.
Pentaour, a scribe, i. 5: the poet, 266.
Peripteral temples, Elephantiné, i. 396-398; Filithyiâ, Medinet-Abou and Semneh, 402.
Persigny, F. de, his notions about the pyramids, i. 191.
Perring, J. L.; his great work upon the pyramids, i. 195; his perception of the object of the discharging chambers in the Great Pyramid, 221; his drawings of the sarcophagus of Mycerinus, ii. 56.
Perspective, ii. 5.

Petamounoph, tomb of, i. 296, 313.
Petenef-hotep, i. 159.
Petronius, i. 44.
"Phamenoph," i. 268.
Phiale, the Greek, ii. 370.
Philip the Arab, i. 55.
Philæ, the great temple at, i. 351; the island and its ruins, 433; arches at, ii. 82; columns at, 104-112.
Philo, i. 224, 232.
Philostratus, i. 268.
Piankhi, i. 22; married to Ameneritis, ii. 264; father of Shap-en-ap, *id.*
Pier, ii. 85; origin of the quadrangular P. 90; the Hathoric, 91; the Osiride, 92; the stele, 93; the octagonal, 94; the sixteen-sided, 94-8; the polygonal, 95 8; with a flat vertical band, 98; *do.* with mask of Hathor, *id.*
Pierret, Paul, i. 47; his study of the dogma of the resurrection, i. 135, 147, 152, 436; ii. 63, 76, 107, 126, 170, 227, 235, 278; jewelry in the Louvre, 289.
Pietschmann, i. 57, 147.
Pig, in the bas-reliefs, i. 219.
"Pipes" (Theban tombs), i. 255.
Piranesi, i. VII.
Piroli, i. VII.
Pisani, ii. 202.
Pisé, i. 105.
Plans, Egyptian ground-, ii. 6.
Plato, quoted, i. 70, 71, 84.
Pliny, quoted, i. 224, 321; ii. 76.
Plutarch, pseudo-, quoted, i. 242, 327.
Pluteus, ii. 149; at Denderah, *id.*
Polishing statues, the methods of, ii. 307-10.
Polychromatic decoration; of the Greeks, i. XIV.; of the Egyptians, necessary in their sunlight, 126; its influence upon their sculpture, ii. 325.
Pompeii, ii. 89.
Population of Egypt under the Roman Empire, ii. 26.
Porcelain, Egyptian, i. 146.
Porcupine, the, ii. 218.
Portcullis stones, i. 220.
Portraiture, the foundation of Egyptian art, ii. 275.
Posno, collection of M. Gustave, bronzes, ii. 200; enamelled bricks, 374.
Pottery; potter's wheel in use during the Ancient Empire, ii. 367; Dr. Birch's illustrations, 367; *aryballus*, 368; "Egyptian porcelain," 369; should be Egyptian faience, *id.*; colour of designs, 370; doorway in Stepped Pyramid, 372; tiles, *id.*
Priene, i. XIII.
Priests, i. 31.
Prisoners, Figures of, under brackets at Medinet-Abou, ii. 24, 94; upon friezes, 154; in the tomb of Seti I., 348; upon the soles of sandals, 354.
Prisse d'Avennes, his *History*, i. 26; his papers, 95, 249, 356, 408; ii. 54, 66, 80, 94, 146, 155; his ideas upon the so-called canon, ii. 319.
Processions, i. 435.
Profile, its almost exclusive use by painters, and in bas reliefs, ii. 293.
Pronaos, i. 351.
Propylon, i. 341-4; ii. 156.
Proto-doric columns, i. 418; differences between them and doric, ii. 97.
Proto semitic races, i. 10.
Provincial art in Greece, i. XII.
Psemethek I., i. 19, 38, 77, 92, 347, 389, 430; group of, with Hathor, ii. 267; II., ii. 266; Nefer-sam, 271.
Pschent, i. 16.
Psousennes, ii. 233.
Ptah, i. 22, 51, 54, 55, 67, 389, 430.
Ptah-hotep, tomb of, i. 174.
Ptah-Osiris, i. 68; Ptah-Sokar-Osiris, *id.*
Ptolemaic art, ii. 272.
Ptolemy, Philopator, i. 264; Euergetes, ii. 407.
Punt, the land of, i. 260.
Pylon, i. 341-4; ii. 156.
Pyramids, i. 189; derivation of the word, 190; origin of, 195; comparative sizes, 199; mode of constructing, 201; cubic contents of Great Pyramid, 202; Pyramids of Gizeh, 206; of Dashour, *id*; the Stepped P., 207-212; German theory as to the construction of the Pyramids, 208; construction of the Blunt Pyramid, Dashour, 210; Pyramid of Abousir, 212; of Meidoum, 214, of Righa, 216; of Hawara, *id.*; of Illahoun, *id.*; proportions of Nubian pyramids, 218; methods of preventing intrusion, 219; discharging chambers in Great Pyramid, 221; colossi on pyramids, 228; Pyramid of Mycerinus, 329.
Pyramidion, i. 226; ii. 174.

Q

QADECH—see Kadesh.
Quarries, i. 105.
Quintus Curtius—see Curtius.

R

RA, i. 25.
Ra-en-ma (Amenemhat III.), ii. 289.
Ra-hesi, ii. 189.
Ra-hotep, ii. 187.
Rameses I., commences the hypostyle hall at Karnak, i. 378; honoured at Gournah, 392.
Rameses II., i. 19, 22, 27, 76; his tomb, 282; completes Luxor, 370; completes the hypostyle hall at Karnak, 378; builds the Ramesseum, 378-81; the temple of Abydos completed, 386; the temple of Gournah do., 395; causes hypogea to be excavated in Nubia, 405; also in Egypt, 406; his colossi at Ipsamboul, 410-15; his family, ii. 13; his obelisks at Luxor, 171-2; his portrait-statues, 240, 255-8; decadence of art towards the close of his reign, 257.
Rameses III., i. 22, 267; his tomb, 281: his temple at Medinet-Abou, 381-384; his pavilion, ii. 16; bas-reliefs in which he is represented in his gynecæum, 21-22.
Ramesseum, i. 266, 376, 377; ii. 97. 167.
Ra-nefer, ii. 203.
Rannu, i. 64.
Raoul-Rochette, his false idea of Egyptian art, i. 71.
Rayet, ii. 182.
Redesieh, i. 406.
Regnier, Ad, i. 341.
Rekmara, i. 296; ii. 338.
Renan, Ernest, his opinion on the Egyptian language, i. 13; on Egyptian civilization, 19; do. 71.
Resheb, ii. 262.
Revillout, Eug., i. 309; ii. 29.
Rhæcos, ii. 317.
Rhampsinite, i. 347.
Rhind, Henry, his *Thebes*, &c., infiltration in mummy pits, 136; a *Burial place of the poor*, 160; his discovery of a tomb, 166: substitution of a late tenant for an early one, *id.*, extreme length of some of the *pipes*, 296.

Rhone, Arthur, i. 205, 291; his *Égypte à petites journées*, 305; plans lent, 316, 328.
Righa, Pyramid of, i. 216.
Rings, ii. 289.
Ritual of the Dead, i. 39, 146; cap. cxxv., 286.
Rougé, de, his *Mémoire sur l'inscription d'Ahmes*, i. 33: ii. 170; his opinion upon the statues of Sepa and Nesa, 185, 194, 228, 235.
Rosellini, i. 406.

S

SABACO. ii. 27; the great door at Karnak repaired by him. 263.
Sabou, mastaba of, i. 167.
Sais, i. 18, 309; its walls, ii. 41.
Sakkarah, i. 35, 38, 42, 135, 143, 146, 166; stepped pyramid, 204-15; ii. 372; pyramids recently opened at S. i. 234.
Salzmann, i. X.
Sardinians, supposed ancestors of the, ii. 257.
Schasou. ii. 200.
Schenti. ii. 185, 200.
Schliemann, Dr., his discoveries at Mycenæ. i. 162.
Schnaase, Carl, i. III., IV., V.
Scribes, the. i. 30.
Sculpture, ii. 180; the origin of statue-making, 180; S. under the Ancient Empire, 184; process of making a wooden statue, 197; groups in the proper sense unknown, 205; animals in S. 217, 280; extreme fidelity of royal portraiture, 223; S. under the Theban Pharaohs, 226; first appearance of colossi, 239; the "Apollo Belvedere of Egypt," 248; over slightness of proportions characteristic of the Middle and New Empires. 249; the worst of the Saite statues national in style, 272; work under the Roman domination, 273; absence of gods from larger works, 275; religious statues purely votive. 276: statues of Amen and Khons not colossal. 277; the right to erect statues in the temples. 278; busts not unknown, 279; technical methods in the bas-reliefs, 284; tools used in S., 303; their influence and that of materials upon style. 303. 306-314.

Sebek-hotep, ii. 226.
Sebennytos, i. 18.
Secos, the (σηκός, or sanctuary), i. 352, 357, 375, 384, 406.
Sedeinga, i. 402.
Sekhet, i. 54, 58, 354, 406.
Seleucus Nicator, i. L.
Selk, i. 301.
Semneh, ii. 45; cornice of temple at, 153.
Semper, Gottfried, his theories upon the origin of decoration, ii. 356.
Sepa, ii. 184.
Serapeum, i. 305-8; the bronzes discovered in the S. ii. 266.
Serdab, origin of the word, i. 177, 187.
Sesebi, ii. 130.
Sesostris, i. 19, 347 ; ii. 27.
Seti I., i. 29, 123, 278; his tomb, 280, 389; carries on the Hypostyle Hall at Karnak, 378; begins the temple at Abydos, 392 ; *do. Speos-Artemidos* and Redesieh, 406; bas-reliefs at Abydos, ii. 247.
Seti II., ii. 260.
Shap-en-ap, ii. 264.
Sharuten, ii. 257.
Sheik-el-Beled, i. 9; ii. 194.
Sheshonk, i. 19; ii. 262.
Silco, i. 55.
Siout, i. 144, 249; necropolis of, 252.
Siptah, tomb of, i. 281.
Snefrou, ii. 95, 184, 187.
Socharis, i. 166.
Soldi, Émile, ii. 288; his explanation of the influence exercised over Egyptian sculpture by the tools and materials employed, 304.
Soleb, ii. 102, 130, 404.
Solon, observation of a priest of Sais to, i. XXXIII.
Somalis, i. 260.
Soudan, i. 218.
Soutekh or Set, i. 68 ; ii. 93.
Spencer, Herbert, upon the conception of the *double*, i. 128; upon "primitive ideas." 132; upon the hole pierced for the double to pass through, 178.
Speoi and *Hemi-speoi*, i. 402.
Sphinx, types of, i. 58-9; the great S., 237-8, 323; the temple of the S., 323-7; controversy as to its true character, 327-9; avenues of S. 336-7; the S. of the Louvre, 61 ; ii. 228 ; S. from Tanis. 230-3.
Squaring, for transference and enlargement of drawings, ii. 320.

Stark, Carl B., i. XXV., LV.
Stele, i. 155-6.
Stepped Pyramid measurements, i. 197, 207, 212.
Stereobate. ii. 149.
Stern, Ludwig. i. 334.
Steuart, i. XXVII.
Stobæus, i. 307.
Stork, the, in the bas-reliefs, ii. 219.
Strabo pyramids, i. 191 ; passages to mummy chamber, 192 ; pyramid of the Labyrinth, 227 ; *Memnonium* (Amenophium), 267 ; *do.* 279 ; Saite worship of Athené, 307 ; "Barbarous" temple at Heliopolis, 323 ; πρόπυλων, 341; description of the Egyptian type of temple, 347 ; identification of Ismandes and Memnon, 376 ; the *Memnonium* close to the colossi of *Memnon* (Amenophis), *id.* ; labyrinth, ii. 25 ; monolithic supports in labyrinth,66; uses of the lotus,125 ; description of *do. id.*; height of *do. id.*
Style, distinguishing features of Egyptian, ii. 329.
Supports, general types of architectural, ii. 91.
Susa, ii. 13.
Suti and Har, architects at Thebes, i. 436.
Syene, i. 7, 105.

T

TABERNACLE, i. 352-5.
Tahraka, i. 385 ; hypæthral temple of T. ii. 145, 263.
Taia (Queen), bust of, at Boulak, ii. 242 ; painted portrait of, in the tomb of Amenophis III., 337.
Tanagra, terracotta statuettes from, i. XVII., XVIII., 162.
Tanis, i. 18; sculptured remains from T., ii. 230-8; Roman head from T., 274 ; sculptors' models from T., 322.
Ta-ti-bast (Queen), ii. 362.
Tegræa, i. XVIII.
Telecles (sculptor), ii. 317.
Tell-el-Amarna, scene of a new cult under Amenophis IV., i. 69 ; its cemetery on the right bank of the Nile, 157 ; domestic architecture of Egypt may be well studied in the paintings and bas-reliefs at T., ii. 5; the Egyptian house, 28 ; palace, 33, 155 ; painted landscapes at, 287.

Tell-el-Yahoudeh, ii. 373.
Temple, the funerary temples of Thebes, i. 264-275 ; the T. under the Ancient Empire, 318-333 ; under the Middle *do.*, 333-335 ; under the New *do.*, 335-433 ; general characteristics, 434 ; distinction between the T. in Egypt and in Greece, 435-7.
Tenteta, statue at Boulak, ii. 208.
Tet, the, ii. 383.
Teuffel, i. III.
Texier, i. IX., X., XXVII.
Teynard, Felix, ii. 157.
Thebes, i. 6, 16-18, 27, 65-8, 77, 89, 122, 134-6, 151-7 ; its necropolis, 255-317 ; its temples, 333-84 ; the meaning of the epithet ἑκατόμπυλος, ii. 40.
Theodorus (sculptor), ii. 317.
Theophrastus quoted, ii. 125.
Theseum, i. VII.
Thorwaldsen, i. XI.
Thoth, i. 63.
Thothmes II., ii. 381, 400 ; Thothmes III., i. 19, 70, 268 ; Hall of T. at Karnak, 369, 381, 400, 406 : his statues, 241 ; head in the British Museum, *id.* ; his portraits conspicuous for fidelity, *id.* : his porphyry sphinx at Boulak, 242.
Thucydides, ii. 40.
Ti, his tomb, i. LX, 89, 143, 148, 177, 180 ; ii. 86 : his offices of state, 177 : his statue at Boulak, 203.
Tiberias, kiosque, or summer-house of, at Philæ, i. 433.
Tiele, Prof., his manual of the history of religions, i. 57.
Tiryns, ii. 64.
To-deser, i. 135.
Tomb, the, under the Ancient Empire, i. 163-241 ; under the Middle *do.*, 241-254 ; under the New *do.*, 255-317.
Tomb of Osymandias', i. 375.
To-merah, or *To-meh*, i. 15.
To-res, i. 15.
Toum, i. 68.
Tourah, i. 204.
Triglyphs, ii. 155.
Tuaregs, the, i. 13.
Turbehs, tombs of Saite kings compared to, i. 309.
Typhon, ii. 93 : Typhonia, 407, 434.

U

Uggeri, the Abbé, i. 104.
Una, high official under the sixth dynasty, ii. 75.
Uræus, ii. 151, 227.

V

Vases, found in the mastabas, i. 171, 183 ; ii. 367 : domestic V., 367-8 ; ornamented *do.*, 368-372.
Vault, i. 110 ; off-set vaults, 111 : ii. 83 : centred V., i. 112 : V. in pisé, 113 ; theory as to the symbolism of the V. in the hypogea, *id.* ; antiquity of the V. in Egypt, ii. 77 ; (see also *Arch.*)
Vedas, poetry of, i. XLIX., 50.
Verde-antique, i. 224.
Versailles, ii. 11.
Villeroi, Charles, his work upon the columns in Greek temples, i. 96.
Vinet, Ernest, i. XIV., XIX.
Viollet-le-Duc, his theory as to the origin of the Egyptian cornice, ii. 56 : upon the employment of inverted arches in basements, 80-2.
Visconti, E. Q., i. VII.
Vogüé, Melchior de, i. 73 ; his description of the Boulak Museum, 90: ii. 45 his definition of the Egyptian style 327.
Volute, ii. 90.
Vyse, Colonel Howard, his great work upon the Pyramids, i. 195 ; his discoveries in *do.*, 221 ; his discovery of the Sarcophagus of Mycerinus, 234 : his discovery and exploration of Campbell's tomb, 311.

W

Wadi, -Siout, i. 105 : -Seboua, 407-8 : ii. 65 : -Halfah, ii. 42 ; -Maghara, ii. 95, 184.
Walking-sticks, ii. 397.
Wallon, M., i. LX.
Welcker, i. VII., XXV.
Whitehouse, F. Cope, his theory as to the construction of the pyramids, i. 201 : his theory as to Lake Mœris, ii. 25.

Wigs, ii. 203.
Wilkinson, Sir G.; his opinion upon the coating Egyptian works with stucco, i. 122; ii. 33, 38, 72; his theory of the Egyptian *canon*, 319, 366; constituents of Egyptian bronze, 379.
Winckelmann, i. II., V., XV., XX., XXV., LVI.
Witte, de, on the weighing of souls, i. 286.
Wolf, the, in the bas-reliefs, ii. 218.
Woodwork, ii. 390; wooden furniture not scanty, 393; perfume spoons and other small articles, 394.
Worship of the dead, i. 128.

X

Xoïte dynasty, the, i. 17.

Z

Zeus, i. XII. 69, 133.
Zeuxis, i. XIV., XVI.
Zoëga, i. VII.

THE END.

In a Handsome Imperial 8vo Volume, 36s.

RAPHAEL:

HIS LIFE, WORKS, AND TIMES.

From the French of EUGÈNE MUNTZ.

Edited by W. ARMSTRONG.

Illustrated with 155 Wood Engravings and 41 Full-Page Plates.

"We have already noticed at some length the original French edition of the important work of 'Raphael, his Life, Works, and Times,' of M. Muntz, the Librarian of the École des Beaux-Arts, and we are glad now to welcome an English translation. A translation is never quite the same thing as the original, but for those—and they are many—who prefer an English version of a book to a French one, this volume may be recommended as, on the whole, a sound and adequate rendering of M. Muntz's work. The type and paper are excellent, and the volume appears in a substantial Roxburgh binding, suitable to its bulk and in good taste. M. Muntz is a real authority on the history of Art, and is by no means to be ranked among the bookmakers, who abound in that department of literature; and his volume, while intended for popular reading as well as for students, is an advance on anything that has been done before in the biography of Raphael."—*Times*.

"This splendid work deserves a cordial welcome. Its paper, type, and engravings leave little to desire. It was a hazardous undertaking to represent the Madonnas of Raphael by wood engravings; and yet it has proved successful in no ordinary degree. . . . With regard to the literary portion of the work, we can say that it is accurate, catholic in tone, and written with admirable lucidity." - *Daily News*.

"The compendious and profusely illustrated volume forms a valuable addition to the history of art. Passavant's work on the subject, though excellent in its way, cannot be considered exhaustive, many important facts concerning the great master and those who influenced his career having been brought to light since it was written. The present work, accordingly, is not superfluous, and no man, probably, could have accomplished the task more successfully than M. Muntz, who, it should be mentioned, is the Librarian of the École des Beaux-Arts at Paris. Having diligently studied the documentary records of Italian history, and being familiar with the various Italian schools of painting, he is especially qualified for work of the kind. His book presents consequently a complete, and apparently trustworthy record of Raphael's career, from his birth in Urbino in 1483 to his premature death in Rome, thirty-seven years later, and in it may be clearly traced the progress and development of his art and the influences which modified it. The author's remarks moreover, on the works of Raphael and of the other painters he has occasion to mention are thoroughly critical and appreciative, and never dogmatically expressed. The illustrations, of which there are nearly two hundred, form a very important feature of the work; they include, besides engravings from nearly all Raphael's existing pictures, and views of the localities in which he sojourned, a considerable number of faithful copies of his original studies and drawings. These being accurate reproductions of the master's own handiwork, will be regarded with great interest by students of art, the more so that the originals of many of them are in private collections inaccessible to the public." - *Globe.*

"A work of such vast importance and interest as this cannot be adequately treated in the short scope of a notice like the present. It is so perfectly and elaborately carried out that a study of its pages can alone do it any degree of justice. M. Muntz has been enabled to correct in many notable particulars the great work of Passavant, and his biography of Raphael Sanzio is unquestionably the best in existence. The illustrations comprise nearly every work of importance by the master."—*Whitehall Review.*

"Taken altogether the volume is one of great merit, both literary and artistic. . . . Before we pass from it we must pay a tribute to the general excellence of the translation, which has all the spirit and vigour of an original work . . . the vigorous and eloquent language of the original has, as a rule, been rendered with like vigour and eloquence, which make the present beautiful volume as pleasant to read as it is attractive to look at—thus fitting it alike for the library and the drawing-room."—*John Bull.*

CHAPMAN & HALL, Limited.

www.ingramcontent.com/pod-product-compliance
Lightning Source LLC
Chambersburg PA
CBHW022108300426
44117CB00007B/637